Philosophical Approach to the Interculturality of Criminal Law

Dia-Logos

Schriften zu Philosophie und Sozialwissenschaften
Studies in Philosophy and Social Sciences

Herausgegeben von/Edited by
Tadeusz Buksiński and Piotr W. Juchacz

Bd./vol. 12

PETER LANG
Frankfurt am Main · Berlin · Bern · Bruxelles · New York · Oxford · Wien

Bartosz Wojciechowski

Philosophical Approach to the Interculturality of Criminal Law

PETER LANG
Internationaler Verlag der Wissenschaften

Bibliographic Information published by the Deutsche Nationalbibliothek
The Deutsche Nationalbibliothek lists this publication in the Deutsche Nationalbibliografie; detailed bibliographic data is available in the internet at http://dnb.d-nb.de.

Manuscript proofreading:
Małgorzata Kiełtyka

This book has been prepared within the framework of the research project: NN 110 122335 financed by the Polish Ministry of Science

Publication subsidized by the Faculty of Law and Administration, University of Łódź

ISSN 1619-005X
ISBN 978-3-631-60585-1

www.peterlang.de

Contents

Gratitude

This publication was accomplished with the help of many people, for whom I would like to express special words of gratitude. My warmest gratitude is addressed to Professor Marek Zirk-Sadowski, who is a great mentor, inspiring in his scientific inquiries and exuding a truly familial atmosphere around his subordinates, constantly promoting the implementation of emerging ideas. The advice given by Professor Zirk-Sadowski, combined with friendly assessment, is a source of support that is hard for me to overestimate, and many discussions constituted an intriguing intellectual adventure, the significance of which goes far beyond the value of this book.

I am extremely grateful to Dr. Karolina Cern, who has agreed to be the first reader of my dissertation and, as it later turned out, a very careful and critical reader – the best that any author could wish for. Her invaluable comments and guidance undoubtedly increased the value of my work. Similarly, I owe my gratitude to publishing reviewers: Professor Piotr Kardas, Professor Leszek Leszczyński, Professor Marek Smolak, and Professor Jerzy Zajadło who, despite many obligations, have undertaken the review of my book, and whose important observations led me to a deeper reflection on certain issues, considerably enriching the book's argumentation.

I also owe unique appreciation for friendly and disinterested help in achieving my career plans to Professor Andrzej Grabowski and Dr. Michał Królikowski.

This book could not be published without embracing help of my relatives, especially my parents, to whom I express my best gratitude. Above all, I thank my wife Magda, who not only with patience and forbearance bears the costs of my excessive devotion to philosophy of law, but cheerfully supports me in achieving my academic goals.

I am also grateful to Professor Werner Becker of the University of Giessen, Professor Ulfrid Neumann of J.W. Goethe University in Frankfurt, and Professor Maria Kaiafa-Gbandi from the University of Thessaloniki who enabled my research stays in these academic centres and, as a part of consultation, substantively and kindly discussed theses posed in this work with me. I would also like to express my gratitude for Professor Becker and his wife Gabriela for their friendly welcome and hospitality in their home in Bad Homburg.

Introduction

Justification of contemporarily controversial thesis on the intercultural nature of criminal law and legal discourse is a major challenge for modern democratic states.[1] This subject has become very topical in the context of the entitlement of Western civilizations to judge terrorist acts committed by the representatives of Muslim culture, or the problem of so-called crime without frontiers.[2] This issue concerns the definition of universality and proper justification for human rights, the relationship of criminal law and morality in terms of globalization of contemporary social relations, and the interculturality of legal dis-

[1] I would like to note at this point that I use the term "intercultural criminal law" having in mind that it introduces semantic doubts. In this way, however, I refer to the terminology that is already applied in English and German literature. See e.g.: O. Höffe, *Gibt es ein interkulturelles Strafrecht? Ein philosophischer Versuch*, Frankfurt am Main: Suhrkamp Verlag, 1999, p. 67ff.; D. Ivison, "Punishment in Intercultural Context: Whose Norms? Which Values?" in: *Punishment and Legal Theory*, ed. by M. Matravers, Oxford: Hart Publishing, 1999, pp. 98–100; D. Garland, *The Culture of Control. Crime and Social Order in Contemporary Society*, Chicago: The University of Chicago Press, 2001, Chapter 4 ("Social Change and Social Order in Late Modernity"); G. Drosterij, M. Hildebrandt, E.A. Huppes-Cluysenaer, "The Possibility of Intercultural Law," *Nederlands Tijdschrift voor Rechtsfilosofie & Rechtstheorie* 2006, vol. 35, no. 3, pp. 215–221. When applying the term "interculturalism" to criminal law, the latter gains a universal character, embracing in its scope respective norms and their justifications that are acceptable in any culture. I intentionally give up the term "intercultural law" – though this term seems to raise considerably less doubt – because even by means of the very name I want to differentiate between "intercultural criminal law" and "international criminal law." The literature on the subject sometimes uses the term "transnational criminal law," the sphere of which is similar to the scope of "international criminal law." Cf. N. Boister, "Transnational Criminal Law," *European Journal of International Law* 2003, no. 5, pp. 953–976.

[2] Cf. M. Glenny, *McMafia: Crime without Frontiers*, London: Bodley Head, 2008.

course. The arising question is therefore difficult both from a legal perspective and, above all, from a philosophical and ethical one, namely whether Western societies have the power to judge and subject to sanctions – according to their judgment – representatives of other, distant, and different cultures? And if so – what is this authority based on?

The answer to this question would have a significant practical value, since a negative outcome of this discussion calls into question the jurisdiction of international criminal tribunals, which would nowadays seem very disturbing. On the one hand, this issue is particularly important for the crisis of human rights[3] and, on the other hand, for the expansiveness of cultural and moral relativism. One consequence of social and ideological changes is the phenomenon of multiculturalism, which – in the area of Western culture in particular – has resulted in the confrontation of ethnic and cultural minorities as well as marginalized social groups with the dominant tradition established by the canons. The study of this issue takes place in the light of contemporary crises and transformations of philosophical, ethical, and ideological canons in the overall context of Western civilization. The issue of intercultural criminal law relates to universalism – relativism dispute in the area of human rights. This *par excellence* philosophically – legal debate is of a fundamental character, and the manner of its resolution affects not only the understanding of the essence of human rights, but also their practical implementation.

What is therefore particularly interesting is the answer to the question of whether there exists a perfect criminal law, generally applicable regardless of the differences in skin colour, in religion or nationality. It must have as its basis a set of universal human rights grounded in human dignity, and it must meet the requirements of civil society, while providing the victims of human rights violations with confidence in the correctness and effectiveness of the rules gov-

[3] This crisis affects their respect as well as the justification and the development of the theories concerning them. In the latter case we can distinguish two categories of human rights criticism. The first consists in rejecting the idea that human nature has certain rights. The second, on the other hand, amounts to a criticism of the current model (catalogue) of human rights ideology, assuming as natural other entitlements than those which have been officially accepted.

erning the modern world. Law, and human rights in particular, are seen as a leitmotif of human life in social community. The latter seems to be prejudged by the fact that law manifests a certain universe of requirements concerning the basic interpretation patterns that shape mutual understanding and defining of the duties that follow from the latter. The concept of such an approach to criminal law corresponds, in some way, to the subject of "international criminal law" and "criminal law of nations." It is therefore indispensable to undertake an appropriate distinction, to organize the terminology, and to clarify the relations between such differentiated spheres of criminal law.

The fact of accepting such conditions leads to the approval of the claim to the interculturally binding nature of criminal law - a characteristic of global legal order, or rather for the vision of world society.[4] A new cosmopolitan critical theory blurs traditional boundaries between domestic and foreign policy. Such factors as global risks or standards, supranational actors, the quality of life in other parts of the world, and human rights violations in Africa or the Middle East - which have been so far considered as factors of external character - have become "internal variables," which must be reflected in domestic discussion, in national and international politics, and in the activities of NGOs.[5] Cosmopolitan sensibility and ethicality do not automatically result from the unification of the world with the most diverse networks, but from the fact that one's own life and the lives of others can no longer be separated from each other in an appreciable manner. What therefore seems necessary is to develop a global criminal justice system that will prevent the treatment of justice in extremely relativistic ways and making it conditional on national differences of views; on the contrary, it will provide an answer to and support for global processes of developing global civil society. In this

---

[4] S. Benhabib, "On the Philosophical Foundation of Cosmopolitan Norms," in: *Law and Legal Cultures in the 21st Century. Diversity and Unity*, ed. by T. Gizbert-Studnicki, J. Stelmach, Warszawa: Wolters Kluwer, 2007, pp. 61–80; U. Beck, *Macht und Gegenmacht im globalen Zeitalter. Neue weltpolitische Ökonomie*, Frankfurt am Main: Suhrkamp Verlag, 2002, Chapter V.5.

[5] M. Kaldor, *Global Civil Society: An Answer to War*, London: Sage, 2004, p. 38ff.; U. Beck, *Weltrisikogesellschaft. Die globalen Gefährdungen – vom Terror bis Klimawandel*, Frankfurt am Main: Suhrkamp Verlag, 2007, pp. 110–111.

context, Albin Eser aptly notes that the increasing globalization of social life should be understood as a call for a reorientation of criminal law. It should be heading in a human-oriented direction, where a human being should be understood as an individual, a member of the community and a link in a generation chain.[6]

I attempt to prove the need for "intercultural criminal law" by developing the idea of inclusive constructivist community. I derive inspiration in this area from John Rawls' and Jürgen Habermas' conceptions. My project of constructivist community assumes the conception of a rational and reasonable individual as a socialized carrier of a set of social roles, a roles system internalised in the socialisation process, which the individual represents in ongoing interactions. What is of the utmost importance from the perspective of my deliberations is that constructivism takes as its starting point the thesis of pluralism. It therefore takes into account different preferences as to values, views on life, religion, or sexuality. At the same time it justifies the possibility of critical and reflective extraction of some common principles and rules of conduct that constitute the basis of this inclusive community, inclusive community being a result of intersubjectively achieved consensus rather than of the necessities which go beyond human will.

In view of multiculturalism it is crucial to note that constructivist community is of an inclusive character in the sense that its boundaries and participation in it are subject to a negotiated agreement. Inclusive community is not oriented against organic communities (cultural, religious, ethnic, etc., which are rather of exclusive character) and, therefore, it is not constituted by hatred against that what is alien and external in relation to it. What is more, it is by no means closed to others, the strangers. On the contrary, it encourages the adoption of its binding rules and the participation of its active, socially cooperating members. Constructivist community also takes into account the fact that emancipation movements, which occur in a multicultural

---

[6] Albin Eser, "'Menschengerechte' Strafjustiz im Zeitalter von Europäisierung und Globalisierung", in: *Zasady procesu karnego wobec wyzwań współczesności. Księga ku czci profesora Stanisława Waltosia* [Criminal Procedure Rules in the Light of Modern Challenges. A Book in Honour of Professor Stanisław Waltoś], ed. by J. Czapska, A. Gaberle, A. Światłowski, A. Zoll, Warszawa: Wydawnictwo Prawnicze PWN, 2000, p. 169ff.

society, do not form a homogeneous phenomenon. Inclusion, therefore, means that community is open to the involvement of citizens who belong to different traditions, but with no intention to absorb these traditions by means of uniformity to a single national community.[7] The institution of constructivist community allows connecting of different levels, which in my conception serves the justification of punishment. The latter, being a community of communication, is based on the universality of the principles and rules of discourse and, accordingly, on the universality and non-transferability of human rights grounded on human dignity and the need to respect the requirements of democracy. Another factor that justifies the establishment of this community is the assumption of a universal character of the mutual recognition principle, which forces the treatment of all people as equal and free individuals.

The justification of my thesis on interculturalism of criminal law will be carried out by a reference to Fichte's-Hegel's concept of "recognition," updated to current conditions by Axel Honneth, to Mead's-Habermas' concept of "convertibility of attitudes," and to the retributive theory of understanding punishment as a restoration of social imbalance. Only the presentation of these three perspectives allows for a holistic approach of contemporary philosophy of punishment. It should be emphasized that the choice of these very conceptions was dictated by the fact that they all take into account the facts of pluralism, multiculturalism, and the need to respect the rights of Others in the context of intersubjective interactions and discursively shaped law. Moreover, the abovementioned concepts relate to one another by a reference to the principle of mutual recognition, similar to Aristotle's idea of legal friendship. In the field of philosophy of punishment, the abovementioned theories take into consideration the argument of law, which was already emphasised by Immanuel Kant as well as the argument of recognition, especially noted by George W.F. Hegel and by George H. Mead, Peter F. Strawson, and Jürgen Habermas.

---

[7] J. Habermas, "Jürgen Habermas und Gerhard Schröder über die *Einbeziehung des Anderen*. Reihe; Kultur in der Diskussion. Band 5," in: *Philosophie und Politik III*, ed. by J. Nida-Rümelin, W. Thierse, Essen: Klartext, 1998, p. 20.

What is characteristic for such an understanding of punishment is the need to balance liberal and communitarian views. A reference to the concept of recognition implies criticism of the entity that was assumed in liberal conceptions of politics and society[8]. The main object of this criticism is the atomistic nature of liberal conceptions, which assume the conviction that the individual, as a unitary, autonomous and rational being, precedes ontological social relations. At the same time, what is treated as an important argument is the requirement to take into account the presence of the Other who has different views, who prefers different values or lifestyles. Resorting to the concept of recognition is contrasted with such assumptions by the model of discursive communitarian society, in which recognition of social relationships of law itself is held by means of intersubjective communication, which has as its basis a relationship of mutuality of dialogue and consensus with procedures guaranteed by deliberative democracy.

What is therefore of utmost importance is to demarcate the universality of principles and rules of discourse as well as human rights based on the latter. I undertake it by presenting – in my view – the most crucial discourse theories of Karl-Otto Apel, Jürgen Habermas, and Robert Alexy. The selection of these three concepts is not at all accidental. All of them, to a greater or lesser extent, relate to the conception of recognition and, particularly, to substantial discursiveness and intersubjectivity of interpersonal relations, which was most vividly manifested in contemporary times in Axel Honneth's critical social theory. In addition, they complement each other, creating the possibility of complementary and pluralistic justification of punishment at various levels, especially in the normative and sociological dimension, which is methodologically possible by recourse to the concept of the constructivist community. In modern societies there are various types of struggles for recognition or, to put it differently,

[8] Cf. A. Honneth, *Kampf um Anerkennung. Zur moralischen Grammatik sozialer Kämpfe*, Frankfurt am Main: Suhrkamp Verlag, 1994; Ch. Taylor, "The Politics of Recognition," in: *Multiculturalism: Examining the Politics of Recognition*, ed. by A. Gutmann, Princeton, NJ: Princeton University Press, 1994; J. Habermas, *Die Einbeziehung des Anderen. Studien zur politischen Theorie*, Frankfurt am Main: Suhrkamp Verlag, 1999; N. Fraser, A. Honneth, *Umverteilung oder Anerkennung? Eine politisch-philosophische Kontroverse*, Frankfurt am Main: Suhrkamp Verlag, 2003.

moral conflicts, the subject of which is "fair" implementation of the principles of love, equal rights, and fair benefits. The primary objective of these struggles should be the abolition of social asymmetries and exclusions and, therefore, the pursuit of implementing the idea of social justice. In this sense, social equality stands for allowing all members of the community to shape their personal identity.

Recognition is understood as a mutual relationship, whereby the one who undertakes the act of recognition must be recognized himself and, as such, he must be a resident of human society. The act of recognition is inextricably linked with the claim to be recognized. The principle of mutuality implies that each individuality "has itself recognized in the other free man, and is aware of this in so far as it recognizes the other and knows him to be free".[9] From this perspective it is crucial to recall Hegel's finding that a rational criminal – by means of a punishable act – voluntarily deprives himself of the claim to be recognized as a free and equal member of society. This claim undoubtedly constitutes one of the most fundamental elements of intersubjective communication, since it is precisely the relationship of mutuality of dialogue and understanding that underlies human interactions.

What are therefore subject to legal protection are relationships based on mutual recognition and appropriate treatment of rational and free individuals, the justification of which is grounded on the idea of universal human rights, the source of which is inherent human dignity. This dialogic model of law also relies on the assumption of having the force of the rule of law, of relationships between such entities, under which each of them limits their freedom by the concept of freedom of the other, provided that the said other also limits his freedom for the sake of the freedom of others. Subsequently, it will be necessary to show that what should be the aspiration of every democratic state is equal recognition policy, based on the principles of equal treatment of its members. Respecting other people's freedom constitutes the manifestation of the inseparability of recognizing and being recognized, hence it follows that in the social world no individual

[9] G.W.F. Hegel, *Encyclopaedia of the Philosophical Sciences* (1830), transl. by W. Wallace, § 436.

activity can infringe upon others. In other words, modern philosophy of punishment has to refer, and it actually refers, to the problem of the complementary nature of democracy and human rights.

Criminal law and the punishment itself should therefore be the result of a rational consensus arrived at by means of intersubjective discourse: the result of a fair exchange of mutual benefits. In this light, the representatives of the study of criminal law write about "rationalization of punishment," which consists, generally speaking, in determining the goals of punishment or in answering the question of "what the punishment is".[10] Pragmatic rationalization of punishment constitutes a justification of punishment in a general dimension, of a particular type of punishment or particularly imposed sanction. Punishment deeply interferes in the sphere of the individual's fundamental values, such as life, freedom or property, which is why rationalization of punishment is at the same time so necessary and disputable and the principle of simple equivalence of damage and punishment as retribution for the latter is contemporarily considerably oversimplified. Rationalization of punishment justifies which values of a given community or society are so important that their criminal-law protection is justified. What can be therefore observed is a departure from atavistic understanding of punishment as revenge. Coercion of rationality and freedom contained in the latter results in the fact that each individual is consciously and voluntarily bound with the norms of human coexistence which are common, since they derive from discursively reached agreement – recognition. To put it differently, the latter stands for a compulsion to understand and "recognize" that what is "My" for everyone can be realized only by means of that which is valid for all, as "Ours." Punishing a criminal is to allow him to restore recognition of other individuals and to become once again a fully-fledged participant of social interactions, and the means to meet this goal is the loss of recognition and, specifically speaking, the entitlement to claim recognition. Moreover, by applying a punishment, we must have regard to considerations of retributive

---

[10] H.L.A. Hart, *Punishment and Responsibility. Essays in the Philosophy of Law*, Oxford: Clarendon Press, 1968, p. 9ff. Hart presents this problems by means of "general justifying aim" conception and punishment "distribution."

justice that justifies the restoration of the requirement of social balance by means of the application of sanctions.

What is crucial from this perspective is to take into account key antinomies of the cultures of post-modern globalization and locality, particularly in the aspect of distribution of law making and law application competences among national or international bodies. The next aim will therefore be philosophical – legal justification of the appointment of supranational, international courts in order to try crimes against humanity as a result of multicentrality of legal system and transcendentality of mutual recognition of legal entities, despite their cultural, religious, or ideological differences.

What is therefore necessary, as a result of the latter, is to take a new look at law, especially criminal law, taking into account the cultural dimensions of globalization, ethical relativism, or targeted creation of a mosaic society, sanctioned by the state patronage. It is thus highly important to seek answers to the questions of what the limits of intercultural legal discourse are and what the latter consists in, as well as whether an intercultural criminal law can exist. Previous attempts to answer those questions are vague, often undertaken only from a sociological or anthropological perspective. Meanwhile, it seems necessary to carry out an in-depth philosophical and legal analysis, which allows deduction of the conclusions that will be relevant in the process of criminal law making as well as in its application in the conditions of multiculturalism, globalization, and the cross-border nature of crimes.

This book aims at demonstrating that it is possible to talk about intercultural criminal law, searching for its base in the very concept of recognition. The process of struggling for recognition seems to contain a conviction of the drive for emancipation, inherent in the very nature of socialization – the quest for elimination of social asymmetry and exclusion. As a result, struggles over distribution can occur in two forms: as legal struggles, in which demands for the recognition of equal rights (especially economic and social ones) are being formulated, as well as struggles for reinterpretation of the usual ways of evaluating the achievements which regard the recognition of underestimated values or of ignored types of activity. Thereby, interfering with the claim to recognition leads to injustice, and so crime becomes a denial of recognition which, consequently, should meet with disapproval and punishment. The latter, understood as withdrawal of recognition, is closely linked to the restoration of social balance, which involves depriving the offender of benefits unlawfully obtained as a result of the offence committed. This clearly reflects the function of criminal law, involving the protection of an appropriate (fair and equitable) distribution of certain powers in society.[11] The theory of punishment, understood in the aforementioned way, is based on the assumption of complementarity between distributive and commutative justice. What is meant by the latter is the distribution of benefits consisting in negative freedom and burdens, which come down to self-restriction of one's own conduct.

[11] It should be noted that the primary objection against liberalism is that moral conflicts are transformed into entitlements, which is not conducive to an intersubjective way of resolving social conflicts and maintaining social balance. This is due to the fact that the participants of these social interactions are well ensconced in their rights, treating entitlements as guards of their freedoms, such as the right to privacy. This perspective is unacceptable in the context of critical social theory described in my dissertation. This complaint will therefore be subject to a broader analysis.

CHAPTER I

The idea of pluralism and human rights in democratic multicultural societies

The consequence of contemporary social and ideological changes is the phenomenon of multiculturalism, the effect of which in the area of Western culture is the confrontation of ethnic, cultural, and marginalized social groups with the dominant culture of the West, which was established by canons. As a result, it becomes necessary to take a fresh look at law that takes into account cultural dimensions of globalization, multiculturalism, and cosmopolitanism, or the so-called rational pluralism, which implies the assumption that there are many complete forms of life,[1] especially in the discourse on human rights and modern democracy. In this context, it is important to say that among all changes that modern systems of law undergo, the most important ones are the processes of cultural and functional differentiation of social systems.

1. Between the Scylla and Charibdis of cultural relativism

In the study of culture, particularly in cultural anthropology, there is a widely developed thesis of "cultural relativism," aiming to demonstrate that all cultures are equal. But this equality here is understood quite specifically. One of the most outstanding representatives of the cultural relativism doctrine - Melville Herskovits - believed that cul-

[1] J. Raz, *The Morality of Freedom*, Oxford: Clarendon Press, 1986, p. 396.

tures are not comparable, because each of them creates a peculiar and unique frame of reference for individuals living in it.[2] As far as the concept of cultural relativism is concerned, I tend to share this view, according to which people belonging to different cultures represent diverse moral beliefs in relation to one another.[3]

It is pointed out in the literature, however, that there is a necessity of formulating a universal ideal, the fact being borne in mind that people in all cultures are provided with basic instructions for moral life: the ability to love and hate, and experience joy and sorrow, pride and shame, and the differences between these pairs consist only in diverse ways of manifesting these instructions.[4] Every society can be

---

[2] M.J. Herskovits, *Man and his Works. The Science of Cultural Anthropology,* New York: Alfred A. Knopf, 1948, p. 63.

[3] An example of classic legal ethical relativism is Hans Kelsen's standpoint in reference to the concept of justice. Kelsen, taking a sceptical approach towards attempts to find one coherent concept of justice, believed that different conceptions of justice can be seen equally as important and unimportant, and this attitude was referred to by him as "legal and ethical relativism." H. Kelsen, "Das Problem der Gerechtigkeit," in: idem, *Reine Rechtslehre,* Wien: Franz Deuticke Verlag, 1960, pp. 357, 366. The answer to the question of what justice is invariably leads – according to him – to a "relative solution" of the problem of justice. H. Kelsen, *Was ist Gerechtigkeit?,* Wien: Franz Deuticke Verlag, 1975, p. 17: "The absolute in general and absolute values in detail is on the side of the human mind, for which there can only be a certain kind of conditioned and, in this sense, relative solution to the problem of justice as the problem of human behaviour." A similar standpoint was later expressed by Michael Walzer, who noted that justice was not an absolute, but a relative concept, the specific content of which is related to particular goals and ideas. M. Walzer, *Spheres of Justice. A Defense of Pluralism and Equality,* New York: Basic Books, 1983.

[4] I. Lazari-Pawłowska, *Etyka. Pisma wybrane* [Ethics. Selected Works], Wrocław – Warszawa – Kraków: Ossolineum, 1992, p. 116. The author also notes that on the abovementioned basis, universalists talk about essential moral similarity of people in all cultures, whilst relativists talk about rudimentary difference. Jerzy Kmita, in turn, assumes a different methodological approach and concludes that universals interact with relativism; "The task of a humanist (academic scholar) is to report on the way of seeing the world through the culture that he analyses. How, then, could he perform this task, giving up the universals, if he did not analyse a culture of Gellner's 'pre-axial age'? Universals can be presented in parentheses of cultural relativism ... That cultural relativism, which seems to me to deserve acceptance, is partly justified by the rejection of the idea of a narcissistic interpretation. Another part of the latter is justified by the thesis that there are cultures, for which some 'places' of some diverse cultures are non-

characterised by a smaller or greater number of patterns of thinking and lifestyles, i.e. a society of a strictly homogeneous nature is a purely theoretical model. Symbolically and axiologically diverse cultures may have different approaches to such issues as abortion, euthanasia, and soft drugs. It has to be noted, however, that the differences within different moral judgments in differentiated cultural contexts may be only superficial, and the very rules of "moral" conduct can only be similar and express a similar human modality,[5] for which it is desirable to open up at that diversity. After all, primordial,[6] tribal treatment of certain values and beliefs, without the ability to open them up for intercultural dialogue, can only lead to conflict.

In other words, cultural relativism (roughly speaking) uses the argument that all cultures are equally valuable, thus opposing the widely criticised 'western cultural imperialism'. It is therefore appropriate in this context to present the standpoint of multiculturalism, cosmopolitanism, or pluralism. The fact of realising irreducible, all-pervasive disparity of human values, lifestyles, and cultural diversity leads to the conclusion that it is necessary to ensure peaceful coexistence for this modern Tower of Babel.[7]

---

interpreted; in this thesis, the term "some" cannot be replaced by the term 'all' ..." J. Kmita, *Wymykanie się uniwersaliom* [Escaping Universalities], Warszawa: Oficyna Naukowa, 2000, p. 201.

[5] R. Redfield, "The Universally Human and The Culturally Variable," in: *Ethical Relativism*, ed. by J. Ladd, Belmont: Wadsworth Publishing Company, 1973, p. 142ff.

[6] Broadly speaking, primordialism means that group tendencies, or emotions that shape common identity, are based on a bond characteristic for small, intimate communities, in which the core concept is blood relationship or its extended form. In other words, theses of primordialism refer to the concept of community of blood, land, and language, drawing its affective strength from sentiments, which form an element that combines such small, exclusive groups. Cf. A. Appadurai, *Modernity at Large. Cultural Dimensions of Globalization*, Minneapolis: University of Minnesota Press, 1996.

[7] There is, of course, a certain contradiction because if we treated expansive culture as worthy of protection, equally valuable and, therefore, deserving full acceptance, aiming at dominance and the subordination of all others, this argument would fall into a blind alley, constituting a perverse justification for the destruction of other cultures. According to an extreme – or at least controversial – approach, such relativism assumes absolute tolerance towards culturally different values and beliefs, and it assumes a critical attitude only towards its own culture and moral attitudes that result from the latter. What is hidden behind such excessive openness and unjustifiable

A contemporary burning issue of multicultural societies is social integration that would facilitate for respective individuals or groups their sense of participation in the life of the whole community to which they belong or want to belong. Common institutions of liberal democracy aim to provide coherence for the processes of social integration.[8] This, in turn, implies that the costs of multiculturalism will be borne by a dominant culture, which must give up a monopoly for determining standards and must make room for proper and unencumbered functioning of other cultures belonging to ethnic, racial, sexual, or religious minorities.

In *Liberalism, Community, and Culture,* Kymlicka stresses that the policy of multiculturalism should strengthen in individuals their sense of belonging to a particular group and, most importantly, emphasize that the sense of belonging is accepted and even protected by

---

indifference is the danger of implementing the principle of "everything is permissible," realising the idea of society which is indifferent to others. One can therefore come to the undesirable conclusion that since everything is of equal value, it is actually just ourselves that count – our own forms of existence and patterns of behaviour – and that what others do does not interest us and, therefore, leads us to extreme moral indifference. (A. Bloom, *Closing of the American Mind,* New York: Simon & Schuster, 1987).

Bloom writes, among other things, that relativism uprooted the true purpose of education, which is to seek a decent life, that there is now a completely new language of good and evil, born of the attempts to go "beyond good and bad"; this language does not allow for a convincing differentiation between good and evil. This new language is a language of relativism of values. That is why Allan Bloom identifies contemporary American liberal democracy with egalitarianism and relativism without limits, without being able to identify good and evil. Criticism of moral relativism was presented in an interesting way by Peter Singer, who shows that if morality is always relative to society, then everyone has his own moral standards. In the situation when I criticize your moral principles, I express the ethics of my community. Vice versa, when you condemn me for criticizing moral standards of your community, you explicate moral standards of your social group. Consequently, the latter stand for the impossibility of going beyond the morality of one's own society, and thus the inability to express supracultural or objective moral judgment. Ironically, it leads to an undermining of the idea of respect for cultures of other people, because in the culture promoting the subordination of others and suppression of other cultures, such is our morality, and a relativist cannot provide any coherent argument against it. (P. Singer, *One Word. The Ethics of Globalization*, New Haven: Yale University Press, 2004).

[8] W. Kymlicka, *Multicultural Citizenship: a Liberal Theory of Minority Rights*, Oxford: Oxford University Press, 1995, p. 26, 138.

the remaining, larger part of society as something precious. This protection will take different forms from the policy of equal opportunities which gives priority to minorities (*affirmative action*), through a guarantee of representation in the government, protecting and nurturing history, language, literature and culture of a particular community, preventing racist behaviour and practices aiming at exclusion, and by means of an educational system addressed both to minorities (e.g. learning support) and the majority of the population by, for example, showing the beauty and value of other cultures.[9]

In this context, Jacob T. Levy points to claims of a legal nature that are culturally conditioned:

(a) exemption from laws which criminalize certain cultural practices (such as the consent of the Sikhs not to wear helmets or official cover of their heads, or the consent to chew peyote by South American Indians);

(b) assistance in activities which the majority can perform without assistance (such as the consent to non-official languages whilst voting);

(c) self-governments (one example of this is a consent to federal political system);

(d) the introduction of legal rules that restrict the freedom of strangers in order to protect the rights of its members (such as Quebec legislation);

(e) introducing internal legal rules – binding in the community – which restrict the rights of its members (one example is a ban on marriages with strangers);

(f) recognizing the traditional code of rights of a particular community (one example is recognition of Aborigines' collective right to land);

(g) ensuring the presence of minorities in governing bodies (for example by means of special election clauses for minorities);

(h) public recognition of cultural values and symbols of certain minorities (such as granting the rights to celebrate one's own public holidays).[10]

---

[9] Cf. W. Kymlicka, *Finding our Way. Rethinking Ethnocultural Relations in Canada*, Oxford: Oxford University Press, 1998, p. 42.

[10] J.T. Levy, *The Multiculturalism of Fear*, Oxford: Oxford University Press, 2000, p. 127.

Essential doubts concerning the abovementioned vision were expressed by John Gray, who believes that this is only one of the possible means of organizing a multi-ethnic society, and it is not the one that prevails in an obvious way as the most effective one.[11] In his view, no policy has a monopoly on rationality, even more so, there is no such policy that would be acceptable by all reasonable people. Multiculturalism does not only perpetuate existing borders, hostility, and misunderstanding, but it is actually developing and strengthening ideologies based on cultural fundamentalism, separatism, or racism. Therefore, it should be noted that the consent to the multiplicity of cultures does not automatically mean tolerance for diversity, approval, or attempts to understand. Amartya Sen observes that the world has always experienced a plurality of cross-interactions between cultures, and the protection of one's own culture and traditions must not prevent us from understanding other people and cultures and appreciating their work.[12] Kant's words, therefore, come as crucial ones in this perspective; namely, that it is difficult on a spherical planet to depart from each other and, even more so, to do it at a safe distance.

In other words, criticism of multiculturalism implies a concern that its message, at least in the strong version, will serve to justify social segregation, since communities which are based on the same identity and which cultivate the latter divide society into two parts: we and others. If there is no common denominator (common beliefs) even of procedural character, it is not possible to establish a dialogue. If there is no universality, we encounter a division, various social groups or communities are relying on their identity and individuality, and they are trying to present their arguments or even impose the latter not by means of discursive agreement, but by force, insult, and discrediting of one another. It seems, therefore, that there is the need to find alternatives to such an extreme multicultural social theory that allows the extraction of common features of humanity as one species, thus enabling discursive consensus on essential issues for the sake of the society functioning as a whole.

[11] J. Gray, *Two Faces of Liberalism*, Cambridge: Polity Press, 2000.

[12] A. Sen, *Development as Freedom*, Oxford: Oxford University Press, 2001, pp. 246–248.

2. Cosmopolitanism: The philosophy of world citizenship

The diversity in which we live is filled with a peculiar cosmopolitan spirit with no Huntington's *clash of civilizations*. In other words, a network of international connections resulted in the fact that we are – or, in a more moderate version, we are becoming – members of the "world society" or "world civilization." In this context, Roland Robertson notes that globalization is a "combination of processes which render the world common."[13] The essence of cosmopolitanism seems to orbit around the struggle for coexistence in a polyethnic world of contradictions that mutually exclude one another or clash with one another, namely in a world of a permanent struggle to recognize the other, the stranger, despite his cultural diversity.[14] In a cosmopolitan ideology an individual is simultaneously: a specific person, a member of the family and tribe, a member of various (sometimes territorially mutually exclusive) communities of different professions, competition, or political sympathies. Meanwhile, multiculturalism is characterized by collective categories that relate to more or less homogeneous groups conceived as equal or different, but separated, and in this demarcation embracing individuals who belong to the latter. In this sense, multiculturalism is opposed to individualism because for the one who believes in this ideology there are no particular individuals, since they are only epiphenomena of culture, community, and society. A relevant approach to cosmopolitanism was presented by Thomas Pogge, namely the individually-centric approach, which assumes the existence of universal moral rights (moral equality of all human beings which, in turn, implies universal moral claims) and their universal applicability (which is expressed in a widely respected equality and the existence of binding moral obligations).[15] Global society is thus not only a global network of interac-

---

[13] R. Robertson, *Globalization: Social Theory and Global Culture*, London: Sage, 1992, p. 396.

[14] U. Beck, *Weltrisikogesellschaft. Die globalen Gefährdungen – vom Terror bis Klimawandel*, Frankfurt am Main: Suhrkamp Verlag, 2007, pp. 110–111.

[15] Th. Pogge, *World Poverty and Human Rights. Cosmopolitan Responsibilities and Reforms*, Cambridge: Polity Press, 2005, p. 169.

tions linking all human communities, but what is first and foremost meant by it is a sense of common interest and common values which can constitute grounds for common institutions.[16]

The cosmopolitan perspective allows the giving up of the division "We and Others" because a cosmopolitan lives in a double homeland, being both a citizen of the world as well as citizen of a *polis* (i.e. city and state). In this context, we all live in a "cosmopolis," understood as a political unity extended to all nationalities, cultures, religions, classes, whilst being still residents (citizens) of one's own city (state). A special place in the space is occupied by metropolises that combine the global scope of their influence with a constellation of cultural enclaves. The city, called cosmopolis, is not some isolated place - a cultural island and mainstay - but rather an archipelago of discontinuous, fragmented cultures.[17] Such cosmopolitanism is therefore of a special character because despite all the freedoms offered by the latter, all people remain locally rooted, that is to say - as Ulrich Beck writes - they have both "wings and roots." A cosmopolitan finds a place for himself in the spaces between the local and national, national and global, and local and global dimensions of social life.

This concept of a cosmopolitan brings the latter to Rawls' citizen, who affirms both a comprehensive doctrine and a political conception that is located on a smaller area; however, the two are in some way linked. It is important and comforting that a cosmopolitan is not a man without his own history, tradition, or values, but he is a person open to otherness, able to find himself in the world where different perspectives coexist, and different worldviews and ideas about the future shape of our reality collide. Ultimately, it is the place of Gadamer's (pre)-trials (*Vorurteile*),[18] which are specific to every local

---

[16] B. Buzan, *From International to World Society?*, Cambridge: Cambridge University Press, 2004, p. 37.

[17] E. Isin, "Metropolis Unbound: Legislators and Interpreters of Urban Form," in: *City Lives and City Forms: Critical Urban Research and Canadian Urbanism*, ed. by J. Caufield, L. Peake, Toronto: University of Toronto Press, 1996, p. 123.

[18] H.-G. Gadamer, *Wahrheit und Methode, Grundzüge einer philosophischen. Hermeneutik*, Tübingen: J.C.B. Mohr (Paul Siebeck), 1960. For Gadamer, these "(pre)-trials" are an integral part of humanistic experience, which by its nature is shaped by historical context in which experience of understanding and interpretation take place. He

culture, understood as beliefs and convictions involved in intercultural dialogue that goes beyond the locality of their universe. In other words, such dialogue - despite the diversity of these beliefs or even their axiological antinomies - must take into account the expectations and values of all its participants, thereby setting a common ground for a variety of relationships, arrangements, and mutual concessions. A cosmopolitan respects and cherishes his own locally-rooted culture, and hopes that it will be respected and seen as valuable by others. Such a claim requires from him respect for other cultures which he encounters, including the emerging 'cosmopolitan culture', provided these cultures are not only a source of violence, poverty or humiliation. It should be noted that today - unlike in the ancient world which is, after all, the cradle of cosmopolitanism - cosmopolitan sensitivity and ethicality do not automatically result from uniting the world with the most diverse networks, but from the fact that their own lives and the lives of others can no longer be separated from each other in an appreciable way. Contrary to what opponents suggest, cosmopolitanism - unlike globalization - does not seek to arrive at a timeless alliance or elimination of all differences, but its aim is discovery and acceptance of Others in five dimensions: otherness of other cultures, otherness of the future, otherness of nature, otherness of the object, and otherness of different rationalities.[19]

Global threats, starting from terrorism, through to global inequality and climate change are contemporary problems of all people. It is not only about ordinary human sympathy expressed for the victims of September 11, the tsunami, or famine in Somalia, but about protecting our own lives, the lives of our children, and those of our relatives. Fear of global consequences of common decisions enforces universal global consciousness and the need for political cooperation between foreign national bodies, the manifestation of which is the creation of supranational government and judicial organizations, and interna-

---

believes that no researcher (interpreter) can completely free himself from his "(pre)-trials," but sometimes he should do the latter in order to become open to "(pre)-judgments" of others, and thus assume the attitude of an independent observer, liberated from his historical context.

[19] U. Beck, *Macht und Gegenmacht im globalen Zeitalter. Neue weltpolitische Ökonomie*, Frankfurt am Main: Suhrkamp Verlag, 2002.

tional NGOs. U. Beck believes that such new cosmopolitan critical theory blurs traditional boundaries between domestic and foreign policy. Factors which have been so far considered as external, such as forms of global risk, supranational actors, the quality of life in other parts of the world, and human rights violations in Africa or the Middle East have contemporarily become the "internal variables" that must be reflected in intranational discussion, in national and international politics, and in the activities of NGOs. In other words, when assuming a cosmopolitan attitude, that which is national is hard to be clearly distinguished from what is international. There is a new perspective of space and time, new coordinates of what is social and what is political. Consequently, even regional armed conflicts and political and cultural crises start to be global.

Martin Shaw, similarly to U. Beck, notes that it is common to experience fundamental problems and the need to give a common response to the latter that shape global society and the existence of global crises allows the identification of global society.[20] Beck's views seem accurate in this context since he writes that the path to cosmopolitanism has been taken wherever democracy and human rights are placed higher than authoritarianism and nationalism, i.e. where the decision-making process allows effective opinion of culturally different Others so that they can affect consequences that are harmful for them, and where there are attempts to redefine and to link the rights of minorities and majorities, and individual and universal rights.[21]

The basic requirement for recognizing another entity, particularly one that is characterized by "otherness," is giving up contempt for the "speech of the Other." Kwame Anthony Appiah aptly notes that such a negative attitude is mostly presented by people who live in the cen-

---

[20] M. Shaw, *Global Society and International Relations*, Cambridge: Polity Press, 1994, p. 3, 20–21. The cosmopolitan approach stands for the responsibility vis-à-vis the whole world, thus global problems of other, culturally different individuals, groups or societies must be present in world politics. In the world called the global village, the poverty of others becomes our own problem, manifested in: limited markets, illegal immigration, environmental pollution, infectious diseases, insecurity, fanaticism, and terrorism.

[21] U. Beck, *Macht und Gegenmacht im globalen Zeitalter...*, op. cit., p. 138.

tre of civilization, which is still the West. One should therefore take into account, at least partially, frequent malevolent opinions expressed by inhabitants of other cultural centres about the West.[22] Appiah is one of the leading American philosophers who combine praise for diversity with criticism of multiculturalism ideology. Treating the assumptions of liberal democracy as the basis of his theory, in *The Ethics of Identity*, he defends the cosmopolitan approach, which assumes a balance between the attachment to universal values and respect for particularisms. In his view, global civil society is based on the fact of common occurrence and professing common ideas, values, institutions, organizations, networks of interactions beyond the borders of national societies, countries, and economies.[23] The foundation of such a society should be the dimension of consciousness, the basis of which is global memory of the Holocaust tragedy or the nuclear attacks on Hiroshima and Nagasaki.[24]

The challenges of globalization and transculturalism are characteristically handled by Arjun Appadurai, the author of *Modernity at Large*, who perceives dialectical movement taking place in the globalization process; it is a continuous production and, at the same time, decay of locality caused by this process, consisting of many cultural dimensions resulting from various configurations of media factors and the phenomenon of migration. Contemporary endless flow of cultural-economic landscapes creates a tension between cultural homogeneity and cultural heterogeneity. According to this anthropologist, a crucial feature of contemporary social processes is deterritorialisation, which conditions and characterizes globalization. Deterritorialisation stands for diffusion of technical, financial, ideological, media, and ethnic determinants of modernity, which is thus free from inhibiting factors such as boundaries, topography, and state institutions. In other words, deterritorialisation means thinking about a global world, specifically as a culture without space, "deterritorial-

[22] K.A. Appiah, *Der Kosmopolit. Philosophie des Weltbürgertums*, München: C.H. Beck Verlag, 2007, p. 196ff.

[23] M. Kaldor, *Global Civil Society: An Answer to War*, London: Sage, 2004, p. 38ff.

[24] H. Arendt, *Elemente und Ursprünge totaler Herrschaft. Antisemitismus, Imperialismus, totale Herrschaft*, München – Zürich: Piper, 1986; M. Kaldor, *Global Civil Society...*, op. cit., p. 39.

ised," which refers to the culture of "here and now."[25] The idea of deterritorialisation does not stand for homogeneity of cultures and uniformity of life, but for "weighing the anchor" of cultural experience from its past, traditional, and local ports. According to A. Appadurai, it is deterritorialisation of various ethnic groups (such as Hindus, Sikhs, and the Palestinians) which is the core of a variety of fundamentalism. He emphasizes that an essential feature of global culture is the policy of mutual "devour of identity and difference" which, on the one hand, leads to the triumph of universalism and, on the other hand, to stubborn particularism. In the opinion of this anthropologist, mutual cannibalism constitutes a negative side of such a process, it reveals its hideous face in the riots, streams of refugees, torture used by the state, and ethnocide. A positive side, on the other hand, is perceived in the broadening individual horizons, improving the quality of life in poor countries, and increasing the impact of global opinion on political, social, and economic matters.

As a result, the lofty idea of a cosmopolitan global citizenship seems to be a beautiful, though not completely fulfilled, desire. According to cosmopolitan principles, life is given to few individuals, open to the world, and the otherness of other people and the diversity of their views. Hence, despite the validity of a critical look at the ideology of multiculturalism, the latter seems to be a more realistic approach to social and political practices, especially in Honneth's "soft" version. A characteristic feature of both cosmopolitan ideology and so-called soft multiculturalism is a focusing on understanding "the other" and, in particular, on his cultural diversity. Soft multiculturalism encourages the individual to explore his own cultural identity, and it approves ethnic and cultural differences. Such a moderate version of multiculturalism aims to demand respect for foreign cultures, otherness and difference, but it does not seek to achieve its goals through antagonizing the society, or opposing different cul-

[25] It should be noted that Appadurai treats culture as a set of differences that constitute common aspects of human discourse, which uses differences for manufacturing various concepts of group identity, around which individual communities are focused. The advantage of such an understanding of culture is heuristic usefulness, which emphasises similarities and differences. A. Appadurai, *Modernity at Large…*, op. cit., p. 24.

tures, communities or groups motivated by different values or lifestyles by setting up a new hierarchy. Soft multiculturalism respects the primacy of individual rights over group rights and the inviolability of fundamental principles of liberal democracy, thus requiring some sacrifice of one's own beliefs on the part of religious communities or ethnic groups. As indicated by Axel Honneth, a soft version of multiculturalism is one way of achieving our democratic rights. Of course, there remains a controversial question of how to agree on what constitutes the essence of human rights, while maintaining respect for cultural, religious, and ideological differences.[26]

The abovementioned statement corresponds to the view expressed by Appiah, who advocates reflecting on whether a crude assessment of our Western morality by the representatives of other cultures does not contain a grain of truth. Above all, however, we should get rid of contempt for the diversity or simply for the otherness of people who we do not know much about.[27] Both multiculturalism (especially in its soft version) and cosmopolitanism can function only within an open society governed by democratic principles. Thomas McCarthy also emphasizes that it is clear that in a multicultural or even cosmopolitan political and legal discourse the rule is rather the common act of acquiring binding and agreed upon rights and principles than the claim to universal validity or imposing them by force (authority) and authoritarian impact on others which is, in turn, characterized by monocentric, imperialist discourse.[28] Multiculturalism and cosmopolitanism do not, obviously, stand for the same ideologies, but move significantly closer to one another when they call for openness and freedom in the process of argumentation, treating ideas and values protected by human rights and democracy as the basis of their assumptions and deliberations.

---

[26] A. Honneth, "Universalismus als moralische Falle? Bedingungen und Grenzen einer Politik der Menschenrechte," in: idem, *Das Andere der Gerechtigkeit. Aufsätze zur praktischen Philosophie*, Frankfurt am Main: Suhrkamp Verlag, 2000, p. 268ff.

[27] K.A. Appiah, *Der Kosmopolit…*, op. cit., p. 208.

[28] Th. McCarthy, "Dialogical Freedom and Democratic Deliberation," in: *Multiculturalism and Law: a Critical Debate*, ed. by O.A. Payrow Shabani, Cardiff: University of Wales Press, 2007, p. 51.

3. Ronald Dworkin's right of equal treatment as the basis of liberal pluralistic society

While cosmopolitanism is more focused on the individual, who it wants to understand as a simultaneous member of many different communities, pluralism is oriented on the group, and it is inclined to identify the individual on account of a single, basic community. In contrast to these two ideologies, multiculturalism is based on the assumption that the world is a multiplicity of cultures, but members of these different cultures are in a sense the prisoners of their cultural conventions, even by the fact that they had to be inculturated in a certain society which constitutes a separate and self-sufficient entity. David Hollinger also points out that cosmopolitanism seems to be more sceptical than pluralism in relation to the potential of conformist pressures within communities, acclaimed by the pluralists, while pluralism is more suspicious than cosmopolitanism in the area of volatility and lack of structure in the wide world, which is appreciated by cosmopolitanism.[29]

Ronald Dworkin tries to balance both these approaches when presenting his concept of a liberal democratic society. He argues that there must be no agreement for depriving anyone of the freedom of choice of values that designate individual goals in life, even if those imposed values coincided with the ones that he himself would choose.[30] As a result, Dworkin states that the existence of many cultural factors that determine our life choices does not mean that we must submit ourselves to a political authority that deliberately and forcibly manipulates our political choices.[31] In Dworkin's opinion, state authority is not entitled to restrict freedom only because those who rule perceive a particular conception of the good life as nobler to another.[32]

---

[29] D.A. Hollinger, *Postethnic America*, New York: Basic Books, 2000, p. 182.

[30] R. Dworkin, *Is Democracy Possible Here?: Principles for a New Political Debate*, Princeton: Princeton University Press, 2006, p. 76.

[31] Ibidem, p. 85.

[32] R. Dworkin, *Taking Rights Seriously*, London: Duckworth, 1977, p. 273. Dworkin subsequently goes on to write that "constraints cannot be defended, for example,

As a result, he has no doubt that people of a "genuinely democratic community" should consider moral and ethical judgments as their own issue and not as the issue of the collective. The advantage of democracy boils down primarily to the fact that no democratic authority can impose on its citizens a certain way of thinking in political, moral and ethical issues. On the contrary, it should encourage citizens to formulate their own opinions and reinforce their individual beliefs. It should be noted that Dworkin draws a distinction between what is ethical, namely concerning personal responsibility for the search, selection, and implementation of values in one's own, individual way of life, and what is moral, and thus related to the responsibilities and obligations vis-à-vis others.[33] Ethical responsibility is of a subjective and relative character because it is a consequence of choosing the values that a particular individual considers as desirable from the perspective of his concept of the good life. It may, of course, turn out that specific values will also be objectively seen as worthy of desire and the opposition to them will raise some responsibility, but it need not be so. By contrast, commitment and ethical responsibility will be based on some partly objectivised assumptions, which are reduced by Dworkin to two principles of respecting dignity of other people. The first rule requires allowing other people the freedom to search and choose the values that they consider appropriate for their own concept of the good life, and the second requires equal treatment of all human beings as equally valuable. The second principle stresses the

---

directly on the ground that they contribute to a culturally sophisticated community, whether the community wants the sophistication or not, because that argument would violate the canon of the liberal conception of equality that prohibits a government from relying on the claim that certain forms of life are inherently more valuable than others" (ibidem, p. 274). Dworkin therefore assumes that society is pluralistic in its views on the rules of distribution of goods and burdens, of the access to political decisions, or the principles of fair trial.

[33] R. Dworkin, *Is democracy possible here?...*, op. cit., pp. 21–22. It should be also noted that for Dworkin political community, differently than in Aristotle and his followers, is not based on virtue, but on rights. It is therefore why political rights can be taken away or restricted solely for the violation of law, and not morality. Idem, *Sovereign Virtue: The Theory and Practice of Equality*, Cambridge, Mass.: Harvard University Press, 2000, p. 201.

importance of the principle of equality, which plays a crucial role in Dworkin's philosophy of law and policy.

Dworkin distinguishes four basic ideals that should be implemented within political community: the first three of which are fair political structure, equitable distribution of resources and opportunities, and equitable procedure for applying the rules, which ensures achievement of the two previous values.[34] However, what is of crucial importance for us is the fourth core value – moral integrity of moral law, which is a specifically legal ideal. That integrity is expressed, inter alia, in the assumption that the state authority (the government) should act in a consistent manner vis-à-vis all citizens and to extend on citizens these principles of justice and equality, which are applied only to some. This ideal is of particular importance when people differ as to the understanding of justice as a general social distributive ideal.[35] In other words, political community should treat its members (citizens) impartially, with equal concern and respect (Dworkin refers to this principle as an "abstract egalitarian principle"). What is crucial for us is treating people as equal in such a way as to provide every person with everything that is indispensable for him or her to realize their own purposes, while protecting them from incurring excessive costs that may arise for him due to choices made by others.[36]

The author of *Law's Empire* differentiates the right to equal treatment, i.e. to equal distribution of opportunities, resources, and burdens, and the right to treatment as an equal, namely the right to be given such respect that is granted to others.[37] He therefore indicates that the realization of the right to treatment as an equal is associated with the formation of certain social inequalities in terms of the uneven distribution of resources, opportunities, and burdens. As a result of this, the fundamental right is the right to be treated as an equal in the form of a right to equal concern and respect.[38] Therefore, it should be

---

[34] R. Dworkin, *Law's Empire*, London: Fontana Press, 1986, p. 164.

[35] Ibidem, p. 16; 165.

[36] A. Ripstein, *Equality, Responsibility, and the Law*, Cambridge: Cambridge University Press, 2001, p. 267.

[37] R. Dworkin, *Taking Rights Seriously*, op. cit., p. 227.

[38] Similarly: J. Finnis, *Natural Law and Natural Rights*, Oxford: Clarendon Press 1992, pp. 221–223.

noted that discrimination against any person or their exclusion only due to the fact that other people do not want to treat them as equal constitutes a violation of basic, fundamental moral norms, and such attitude in a modern state of liberal democracy cannot be accepted, irrespective of the grounds of such observation (e.g. opposition to terrorist acts carried out by the representatives of Muslim culture). This issue was similarly presented by Marek Piechowiak, for whom equality (expressed in three components: equality vis-à-vis law, equal legal protection, and equality in law) is a fundamental element in democratic society.[39] The author of *Philosophy of Human Rights* argues that violation of this rudimentary equality does not occur when there are any differences in the treatment of people by law, but only when these differences lack appropriate reasons. As a result, the requirement of law integrity, based primarily on an equal legal protection, corresponds to some genuine needs of collective life, because it provides a consistent and relatively stable set of rules, which are applied consistently rather than merely on an *ad hoc* basis.

Dworkin rightly observes that we deal with the rejection or misunderstanding of the right to equal treatment in a situation when the restriction of liberty is justified by moral preferences of the majority of society in determining how others should live.[40] In other words, according to the ideal of equality, the state cannot restrict individual freedom justifying it with the requirements of moral preferences of the majority of the society who perceive the values recognized by the minority as inferior and, as such, deserving condemnation. The principle of equality, therefore, constitutes protection of the individual's autonomy, of the choices made by them; a protection against unjustified "tyranny of more valuable ideals of the majority of the society." The protection of moral pluralism thus becomes one of the most important objectives of political community, founded on the accepted concept of justice, equity, and due trial in the course of decision-making process of political, legislative, or judicial character. Dworkin

[39] M. Piechowiak, *Filozofia praw człowieka. Prawa człowieka w świetle ich międzynarodowej ochrony* [Philosophy of Human Rights. Human Rights in the Light of their International Protection], Lublin: Towarzystwo Naukowe KUL, 1999, p. 130.

[40] R. Dworkin, "Rights as Trumps," in: *Theories of Rights*, ed. by J. Waldron, Cambridge: Harvard University Press, 1998, p. 161.

even thinks that it is the equal importance of every human life understood as the principle of the intrinsic value of a human life that constitutes – apart from every human being's personal responsibility for the selection and implementation of other values in their lives – the basis for human dignity, thus creating an axiological foundation of democracy.[41] Therefore, he urges a person's self-realisation, using the possibilities offered by human life. Leszek Kołakowski also stresses that it is precisely the ability to make life choices and not the way in which it is implemented that makes all human beings worthy.[42]

In conclusion, the value of pluralism is not only evident in the fact that the multiplicity, diversity, and uniqueness of experience is stressed, but also in that it contains criticism of dogmatism and fanaticism, that it exposes as compromising a prerequisite for social life, in which there are no goods and values indifferent to values and goods diverse from ours. William A. Galston's and George Crowder's interpretations constitute a kind of specific summary of the idea of pluralism. The former characterizes pluralism of values by means of the following five theses:

(a) Pluralism of values is not identical with relativism. The distinction between good and evil is objective and it is possible to defend by means of rational argumentation.
(b) It is impossible to fully sort out objective goods. There is no common measure for qualitatively heterogeneous goods. There is also no *summum bonum,* which would be the highest good for all individuals.
(c) Some goods are of basic nature, in the sense that they are part of any – worthy of choosing – concept of human life.
(d) In addition to this 'sparse' list of basic goods, there is a wide range of legitimate diversity – individual concepts of the good life, social, cultural, and public purposes.

---

41 R. Dworkin, *Is democracy possible here?...*, op. cit., p. 9ff. He drew attention to this issue already in his earlier works. See e.g. idem, *Sovereign Virtue...*, op. cit., Chapter 7; as well as his response to Samuel Scheffler's allegations; idem, "Equality, Luck and Hierarchy," *Philosophy and Public Affairs* 2003, vol. 31, no. 2, p. 194ff.

42 L. Kołakowski, *Mini-wykłady o maxi-sprawach* [Mini-Lectures on Maxi-Issues], Kraków: Znak, 2004, p. 25.

(e) Pluralism of values must be distinguished from various forms of monism. Theory of value is of a monistic character if it reduces goods to a common measure or creates a complete hierarchy or order of goods.[43]

In Crowder's conception, in turn, we can distinguish four main features which characterise the idea of pluralism of values:

(a) Firstly, pluralists argue that there are some fundamental, objective, *universal values*, deriving from, which constitutes a contribution to human "flourishing."

(b) Secondly, both the universal and local values are *varied* and numerous, and also internally complex.

(c) The third component of pluralism is the most distinctive. It comes down to the statement that values are not only manifold, but they can also be radically varied, that is *incommensurate* with each other. For a pluralist there is no fundamental value that would be inherently more important or more dominant than any other; there is no value that would cover or contain in itself all other values.

(d) Fourthly, these multiple and disproportionate values may in specific cases come into *conflict* with each other. This means that may be impossible to reconcile or they can be mutually exclusive in the sense that one of them can be accomplished only at the expense of the other or by means of sacrificing or restricting the other.[44]

Herbert Schnädelbach writes that the fact that the right of existence is also vested in other cultures which are governed by rules different than ours and, therefore, require an approach which rejects the valuation, that is, they may not be immediately assessed or condemned in the light of our notions of value, is not only a result of scientific understanding of culture, but is also the result of liberal beliefs of our culture that other cultures do not share.[45] It is in this sense

---

[43] W.A. Galston, *Liberal Pluralism: The Implications of Value Pluralism for Political Theory and Practice*, Cambridge: Cambridge University Press, 2002, pp. 5–6.

[44] G. Crowder, *Liberalism and Value Pluralism*, London – New York: Continuum, 2002, pp. 2–3.

[45] H. Schnädelbach, "Kultura" [Culture], in: *Filozofia. Podstawowe pytania* [Philosophy. Fundamental Questions], ed. by E. Martens, H. Schnädelbach, transl. by K. Krzemieniowa, Warszawa: Wiedza Powszechna, 1995, p. 550.

that the assumption of a non-valuating concept of culture should be made. This liberalism and tolerance are the result of unfortunate historical experiences, or totalitarian or monistic conception of culture. The latter can be undoubtedly perceived as a cultural achievement. At the same time, I believe – like Andrzej Szahaj – that if we are doomed to a certain form of benevolent, weakened axiological and political ethnocentrism, we should reject the strong version of multiculturalism and limit ourselves to a tolerance typical for Western culture.[46] Szahaj concludes that, unfortunately, not all communities will feel comfortable in the circle of political culture and axiological practices of the West, or the latter can be even a source of discomfort. What thus becomes important is to find a common denominator, which will allow for substantive and peaceful discussion between different nations, ethnic groups, nomads, and diasporas. It is not easy to find common ground for mutual agreement and understanding, examples of which are recent events on the Balkans, in Afghanistan, or in Darfur. In the subsequent chapters I shall try to demonstrate that there are – despite the undoubted argument from ethical pluralism – universal values, principles, and rules that must be respected in every culture and which can be legitimately presented in the form of positive and universally binding rights.

4. Human rights as the nature of intercultural consensus

The most frequently asked questions with regard to human rights are as follows: Are human rights truly a Western concept? Are there any religions and cultures that are not in any way associated with modern human rights? Is it really so that the arguments justifying the existence of these rights may be just as well used to indicate the existence of unicorns and witches?[47]

---

[46] A. Szahaj, "Kilka uwag o idei wspólnotowości oraz ideologii wielokulturowości" [Few Comments on the Idea of Community and the Idea of Multiculturalism], in: *Pytania współczesnej filozofii polityki* [Questions of Contemporary Philosophy of Politics], ed. by D. Pietrzyk-Reeves, Kraków: Wydawnictwo Uniwersytetu Jagiellońskiego, 2007, p. 71.

[47] I refer here to a well-known allegation made by Alasdair MacIntyre. Cf. idem, *After Virtue: A Study in Moral Theory*, Notre Dame, Indiana: University of Notre Dame Press, 2007.

In contemporary public discourse the answer to these questions would have to cover many topics. The latter will range from historical, cultural, ideological and, ultimately, to legal perspectives. What is already problematic is the mere understanding of those rights that are defined in very different ways. A convincing definition is applied in international public law, according to which human rights are defined as those freedoms, security measures, and benefits, the respect and recognition of which - as rights in accordance with contemporarily accepted freedoms - can be demanded by all people from the society in which they live.[48] In this sense, they are inalienable moral rights of a fundamental and universal character. It should be noted that the controversy over the universality of human rights does not only take place in intercultural dialogue between the representatives of Western culture and Muslim, African, or Asian cultures, but also within the same seemingly homogeneous ideological formation of the West. Determination of the nature of human rights has dominated a large number of contemporary intellectual disputes: in political philosophy between liberalism and communitarianism, in philosophy of law between positivism and non-positivism, in the theory of international relations between pluralism and solidarism, and in ethics between universalism and relativism.[49]

4.1. Human rights - the creation of "Western" imperialism?

The idea of human rights was not created naturally as *creatio ex nihilo*, and in the European culture it is combined with both classical phi-

---

[48] *Encyclopaedia of Public International Law*, vol. 8: *Human Rights and the Individual In International Law: Internationals Economic Relations*, North-Holland, Amsterdam, New York, Oxford: North Holland Publishing Company, 1985.

[49] J. Zajadło, "Uniwersalizm praw człowieka w konstytucji - bezpieczne i niebezpieczne relatywizacje" [Universalism of Human Rights in Constitution - Safe and Dangerous Relativization], *Przegląd Sejmowy* 2007, no. 4, p. 93. Jürgen Habermas points out in this context that this intellectual debate is not only of an intercivilisational character, but it also constitutes a crucial dispute of "the West with itself." J. Habermas, "Zur Legitimation durch Menschenrechte," in: *Das Recht der Republik*, ed. by H. Brunkhorst, P. Niesen, Frankfurt am Main: Suhrkamp Verlag, 1999, p. 386.

losophy and Christianity.[50] It cannot be denied that the "Western" legal tradition has played an important role in communicating some deeply-rooted indigenous values, i.e. those that affect the perception and interpretation of interests in different historical periods.[51] The latter does not obviously mean that the idea of human rights was not and is not generally valid also in other world religions or philosophies.[52] One can safely state that it is associated with nearly all major world religions and philosophies. However, the most common modern allegation against the idea of human rights is that they articulate typical Western values, which stand in opposition to the so-called Asian values. In other words, according to this view, moral validity of human rights depends on ethics that are binding in a certain community, which challenges the very universality of those rights.[53] This claim is false since the idea of human rights is not dependent on a particular conception of a human being, which the abovementioned

---

[50] K. Bayertz, "Die Idee der Menschenwürde. Probleme und Paradoxien," *Archiv für Rechts- und Sozialphilosophie* 1995, vol. 81, no. 4, p. 465; W. Becker, *Das Dilemma der menschlichen Existenz. Die Evolution der Individualität und das Wissen um den Tod*, Stuttgart: W. Kohlhammer Verlag, 2000, p. 233ff.; H. Bielefeldt, "Ideengeschichte(n) der Menschenrechte," in: *Menschenrechte – Globale Dimensionen eines universellen Anspruchs*, ed. by N. Janz, Th. Risse, Baden-Baden: Nomos Verlag, 2007, p. 177. This author particularly points at the Stoics, Seneca, Epictetus, and Marcus Aurelius. In Christian culture, by contrast, he indicates the biblical Psalms (especially Psalm 8).

[51] M. Krygier, "Legal Traditions and Their Virtue," in: *Prawo w zmieniającym się społeczeństwie* [Law in Changing Society], ed. by G. Skąpska et al., Kraków: Uniwersytet Jagielloński – Wydawnictwo Adam Marszałek, 1992, p. 251. J. Merryman notes that legal tradition is a set of deeply rooted, historically conditioned beliefs about the nature of law and its role in society. J.H. Merryman, *The Civil Law Tradition*, Stanford: Stanford University Press, 1985, p. 2.

[52] On this issue see e.g.: G. Krämer, "Islam, Menschenrechte und Demokratie: Anmerkungen zu einem schwierigen Verhältnis," in: *Menschenrechte – Globale Dimensionen...*, op. cit., pp. 39–54; J. Zhang, "Ist das Menschenrechtsbild in China konfuzianisch oder universal? Fortschritte und Probleme in Theorie und Praxis der Menschenrechte," in: *Menschenrechte – Globale Dimensionen...*, op. cit., pp. 101–111; J.A. Dohrmann, "Ursprung und Entwicklung der Menschenrechte in Indien," in: *Menschenrechte – Globale Dimensionen...*, op. cit., pp. 113–143; L. Leszczyński, "Prawo japońskie" [Japan Law], in: *Główne kultury prawne współczesnego świata* [Main Legal Cultures of Contemporary World], ed. by H. Rot, Warszawa: PWN, 1995, p. 161ff.

[53] A. Sen, *Development as Freedom*, op. cit., p. 227.

standpoint seemed to suggest. On the contrary, philosophical and ideological conceptions of a human being and of society are contemporarily on the basis of Western legal traditions something external to law, and even provide competitive and incompatible interpretations of the basic idea of a human being. This destroys the paradox that the idea of human rights, indicating the universality of certain values, cannot in itself make claims to universality. There is no contradiction between the aspiration to material universalism of some idea and its local, culturally and historically particular character. As a result, particularism of the origin of human rights cannot constitute a serious argument denying their universality.

One who wants to maintain that human rights are an expression of the hegemony of the West falls into a different paradox, because human rights protect a man irrespective of the prevailing political, economic, and social system. The manifestation of their impact on public awareness were and are many emancipatory movements born in the West, and oriented against authority or social inequalities, to name only the abolitionist movement at the turn of the eighteenth and in the nineteenth century, modernist feminist movements, and contemporary movements fighting for the rights of indigenous peoples. The fact that the recognition of human rights had to be won is indeed a common element in all cultures, particularly Western, Islamic, Asian, or African. They do not constitute a primary element in a particular cultural or religious tradition, but arise in the course of public political discussion.[54]

The second most frequent complaint against the universality of human rights is based on the belief that they are an expression of the Western culture of individualism. Support for this view appears to be Kant's heritage. It was aptly put by J. Gray, who noted that being an autonomous entity does not mean being the timeless essence of humanity.[55] In his view, autonomous bodies are artefacts whose exis-

---

[54] H. Bielefeldt, *Menschenrechte in der Einwanderungsgesellschaft. Plädoyer für einen aufgeklärten Multikulturalismus*, Bielefeld: Transcript, 2007, p. 28ff.; L. Leszczyński, "Importance and Topicality of the Problems of Human Rights," in: *Protection of Human Rights in Poland and European Communities*, ed. by L. Leszczyński, Lublin: Wydawnictwo UMCS, 1995, pp. 11-16.

[55] J. Gray, *Two Faces of Liberalism*, op. cit., p. 197.

tence has been made possible by the authority of a modern state. The argument of the individualism of human rights appears to be ineffective, in particular in a reference to a reformulation of modern thinking about human rights as a result of discussions between communitarians and liberals. Today, even Western liberal countries try to articulate and protect individual rights, as well as highlight the responsibilities of each individual to community and society. One can pre-present the rights that only apparently have individual character, such as freedom of expression and freedom of religion, since they largely concern communities (e.g. political parties or religious communities) and thus collective identity.[56]

Amartya Sen further distinguishes two allegations against human rights, which he called criticism of legitimacy and coherence.[57] The former is based on the assumption that the importance attached to human rights undermines the status of a legal system, since it refers to prelegal norms without indicating their sources and methods of their enforcement. In this context, Jeremy Bentham stated that "natural laws" are "nonsense upon stilts," "utter nonsense," "phantom," or "sounds without substance."[58] The allegation of lack of legitimacy of human rights now appears to be incorrect, given the prevalence of references to the concept of human dignity as the source of those rights. Their excuse, therefore, does not require their necessary manifestation in a "positivist" form supported by the authority of the state, but they can be extracted from general principles and requirements of morality, given the fact that the law–state relation has ceased to have the character of the *state-dependent* paradigm.

Criticism of coherency points out, in turn, the exclusively verbal character of these rights because they stipulate what everyone is entitled to but do not specify who is obliged to realize this law in the case that it is articulated. Kant's thinking constitutes the basis of contemporary doubt about these rights because in his times people did not even dream of social rights (such as the right to food and social

[56] Cf. J. Raz, *The Morality of Freedom*, op. cit., pp. 251–253.

[57] A. Sen, *Development as Freedom*, op. cit., pp. 227–230.

[58] J. Bentham, *A Comment of the Commentaries; a Criticism of William Blackstone's on the Laws of England*, Oxford: Clarendon Press, 1928, p. 14, 20.

care).[59] There was neither any clarification of who was supposed to provide this food or care and, therefore, there were inconsistencies between the entitlements on the part of one entity and the obligations on the part of another specified entity. This allegation appears to be at least anachronistic, not to say completely ineffective. What seems to be most crucial in the area of human rights is the potentiality, the ability to articulate one's own needs. They create opportunities that should be followed by structural institutional transformations of society. Human rights, in their universality, contain the prerogatives enjoyed by all, and even though sometimes there is no specific person who must meet the latter, it is possible to turn with particular requirements arising from these entitlements to certain entities, bodies which - by virtue of their social function or role - allow the requirements to be met, or at least assist in obtaining them. Most of these rights are obviously addressed to the state or international community, as in the case of famines in Africa. As a result, they are obliged to assist in obtaining them.

From a positively - legal perspective, universality of human rights can be evidenced by the fact of their manifestation in international instruments, which have finally been ratified by almost all countries of the world. Thus, we can speak of a cultural legislative consensus, consisting in the widespread recognition of the most fundamental human rights.[60] Robert Alexy notes in this context that human and citizen's rights are the result of the historical development of mankind, a far-reaching consensus on basic rights.[61]

---

[59] I. Kant, *The Philosophy of Law: An Exposition of the Fundamental Principles of Jurisprudence as the Science of Right*, transl. by W. Hastie, Edinburgh: Clark, 1887, p. 235.

[60] Th. Risse, "Menschenrechte als Grundlage der Weltvergemeinschaftung? Die Diskrepanz zwischen Normanerkennung und Normeinhaltung," in: *Menschenrechte – Globale Dimensionen…*, op. cit., p. 19.

[61] R. Alexy, *Begriff und Geltung des Rechts*, Freiburg - München: Verlag Karl Alber, 1992, p. 94ff. Similar views were also expressed by Otfried Höffe (idem, *Vernunft und Diskurs. Bausteine zu einem interkulturellen Rechtsdiskurs*, Frankfurt am Main: Suhrkamp Verlag, 1998, p. 55ff. Critical opinion, on the other hand, was voiced by Armin Engländer (idem, *Diskurs als Rechtsquelle? Zur Kritik der Diskurstheorie des Rechts*, Tübingen: Mohr Siebeck Verlag, 2002, pp. 94–95). Firstly, he notes that even in Western societies there are strong fundamentalist movements, particularist and discriminatory in morality, law, religion, and politics, which constitutes empirical counterargument

Another issue is the effective observance of ratified human rights and fundamental rights. It may be noted that contemporarily we encounter a disturbing tendency that violations of these rights are less and less frequently due to national governments, but increasingly due to non-state actors such as terrorist groups, separatists, or organized crime, who commit acts of genocide, ethnic cleansing, or fundamentalist or terrorist actions. This follows from the consciousness of modern authorities; namely, if the latter want to remain "civilized" i.e. generally recognized members of the international community, they must respect the universal validity of international human rights. In turn, these political and state systems which practice genocide, torture, religious persecution or discrimination against particular ethnic or national communities or social groups do not deserve recognition of being legitimate and worthy of protection. One could even attempt to bring about an idealising assertion that most modern states treat the Kantian idea of perpetual peace seriously. Democratic rule of law is, therefore, concerned with preventing the threats of war and the destructive use of force and tending to the real policy of security and prosperity.[62] The fact that most countries have a policy of human rights in the name of the universal binding nature of legal norms of international relations means that, contemporarily, we have to deal with a global offensive of the system of world citizenship oriented at human rights. In this sense, human rights receive priority over the laws of nations, which in case of a conflict situation enables humanitarian intervention to protect the rights of world citizens (human rights), which clearly violates the sovereignty of the nation-state.[63]

---

against the thesis of historical consensus in relation to human rights. Moreover, he points out that historical development does not permit the drawing of any normative implications. This argument, however, is ineffective to the extent that it is not a matter of normative justification for the universality of human rights by showing their universality and the fact of historical consent. The latter should rather represent a certain tendency, which empirically justifies such universality. On the other hand, particularist and fundamentalist tendencies should be treated as an exception to what has been widely recognized, worthy of criticism and disapproval.

[62] See: D. Senghaas, "Internationale Gerechtigkeit. Überlegungen im Lichte des zivilisatorischen Hexagons," in: *Probleme der Internationalen Gerechtigkeit*, ed. by K.G. Ballestrem, B. Sutor, München: Otto-von-Freising Vorlesungen der Katholischen Universität Eichstätt, 1993, p. 48ff.

[63] U. Beck, *Macht und Gegenmacht im globalen Zeitalter*, op. cit., pp. 104–107.

That reasoning is not sufficient in terms of individual communities, ethnic groups, and, ultimately, the individuals comprising citizens of a given state. Justification and sanctioning of such universality has to be deeper, referring to generally applicable arguments. Universalism is understood here as a belief about the existence and universal applicability of elementary legal norms expressed in binding legal norms. It is contemporarily believed that human rights are the source of cosmopolitan authority, namely that it is over the sovereignty of national state, as it entitles a specific state to humanitarian military intervention. In this context, the term 'cosmopolitan' stands for "the set of fundamental values indicating standards and boundaries that no one - irrespective of whether it is a representative of the government, the state or civilian association - can violate."[64] The determination of these values common to all is difficult, but as far as not everyone grants equal value to human rights as such, human dignity is believed in everywhere.

4.2. Human dignity as the basis of human rights

Contemporarily it is quite common to encounter views maintaining that the "human being is extinct." The activities of public institutions, the task of which is to reinforce democratic structures, imply that the concept of "humanism" is often regarded as a relic of an era that has come to an end. Such radical statements raise obvious objections, or at least distractions, but they primarily provoke the reflection on the contemporary state of the "conditio humana," and they lead to the promotion of activities that show the practical meaning of occasional declarations on human dignity. The depreciation of human dignity is the result of the dominance of hedonistic attitudes and lifestyle, overwhelming power of money, hypertrophy of law, its fluidity and politicization, or, ultimately, the divergence of moral norms.

In order to prevent practices that undermine human dignity and broadly understood humanitarianism, it is necessary to find a com-

[64] D. Held, "Die Rückkehr der Politik," in: *Was wird aus der Demokratie?*, ed. by T. Assheuer, W.A. Perger, Opladen: Westdeutscher Verlag, 2000, p. 5.

mon denominator – the essence of humanity, that is what Fukuyama called "factor X," and that which is worth a minimum of respect.[65] Factor X is understood as the most fundamental sense of being a human being, and if all human beings are endowed with equal dignity, then factor X must be their common and universal characteristic. The consequence of having factor X is to grant not only human rights (legal entity), but also, if you are an adult, political rights (broadly understood as the capacity to perform acts in law). Presumably the most famous attempt to establish a philosophical basis for human dignity was made by Kant, who claimed that the "factor" of dignity is derived from the human capacity of making moral choices.[66] Kant defines personality as "freedom and independence on the mechanism of nature, yet, regarded also as a faculty of a being which is subject to special laws, namely, pure practical laws given by its own reason."[67] Man as a free and rational being, deserves the name of a person and a person should be treated as an objective in itself rather than merely as a means:

> By virtue of the autonomy of his freedom he is the subject of the moral law ... Just for this reason, every will, even every person's own individual will, in relation to itself, is restricted to the condition of agreement with the autonomy of the rational being, that is to say, that it is not to be subject to any purpose which cannot accord with a law which might arise from the will of the passive subject himself; the latter is, therefore, never to be employed merely as means, but as itself also, concurrently, an end.[68]

These arguments convince that dignity is the quintessence of the human person, which means that it is inextricably linked with every

[65] F. Fukuyama, *Our Posthuman Future: Consequences of the Biotechnology Revolution*, New York: Picador, 2003, p. 149.

[66] The concept of dignity has been highlighted by Kant, particularly in his early works, later becoming consistent with the assumptions of a democratic society. Accordingly, the essence of dignity, due to which a man is to be treated as an objective and not merely a means, is interpreted by Kant as the ability to be a universal legislator. I. Kant, *Grundlegung zur Metaphysik der Sitten*, Leipzig: Ph. Reclain, 1797, Abschnitt Zwei.

[67] I. Kant, *The Critique of Practical Reason*, 1788, transl. by Th. Kingsmill Abbott, Book I, Chapter I.

[68] Ibidem.

man, regardless of who he is, or how and where he lives. Dignity is thus rooted in entelechy of ideal humanity. Human dignity constitutes an ontological quality and a constitutive feature of selfhood. Therefore, this semantically open dignity is called the "sanctity of the human person"[69] and it constitutes a value that is confirmed rather than stipulated by positive law. Human dignity is inherent, and therefore constitutes an intrinsic, fundamental, and universal value. "Humanity as such" is the source of the latter.[70] Inherence of dignity means its non-transferability. It follows further that it is the prerequisite of every person, regardless of individual characteristics, i.e. irrespective of race, religion, nationality, height, obesity, talents, or origin, etc., and therefore it has a non-gradable and inalienable character because if someone is a man, it is to the same extent as any other man. You can deduce a conclusion that is not widely accepted in the contemporary world: that human dignity is independent not only of social affiliation, ethnicity or gender, but also moral or physical qualities of the individual. The preamble to The Universal Declaration of Human Rights of 1948 thus reads: "... recognition of inherent dignity ... of all members of the human family" and in the International Covenant on Civil and Political Rights of 1966 we find that "these rights derive from inherent human dignity." The preamble to the Polish Constitution also makes a reference to this value: "taking care to preserve inherent human dignity." Article 1 of the Charter of Fundamental Rights of the European Union of 2000, in turn, provides that all human beings are born free and equal in dignity and rights. They are endowed with reason and conscience and should act towards one another in a spirit of brotherhood. It should be noted that the fact of treating dignity as the first value is an achievement only of modern times.

A universalistic and egalitarian concept of dignity assumes that all people deserve to be treated with respect. In other words, the notion

---

[69] It is worth mentioning that it is precisely in this context that St. Paul preached the identical status of all people, regardless of gender, social or ethnic affiliation. R. Dworkin also believes that "every human life is sacred" but he adds that "the idea of sanctity, apart from religious interpretations, has also secular interpretations."

[70] I. Kant, *The Philosophy of Law*, op. cit., p. 50. It is worth noting that such an understanding of dignity is also presented in the Koran in Sura 17.70.

of dignity has assumed the form of claims to recognize the equal status of entire cultures and eliminate inequality of gender, origin, or race. This is based on the fundamental belief that as human beings we are persons, and in this respect we are all equal, even if we are different in all other respects.[71] Dignity is thus a criterion for establishing whether a specific law is fair, simply because fair law protects dignity, and a violation of such law is contrary to the innate dignity. It is, therefore, relevant to say that one should not treat anybody as morally inferior on the basis of diverse physical or racial characteristics, since these are the features that nobody has influence on.

It is noteworthy that the idea of treating people as free and equal is affirmed and raised to the rank of a general (universal) law in various conceptions. After all, the ability to profess and promote different concepts of good and of various philosophical or religious doctrines is founded on precisely the same rights and freedoms, and the same universal measures like income and wealth (views expressed particularly by A. Sen); and all that should be based on respect for oneself. Universality of human rights means that they are granted to all men, precisely because they are human beings. In this context, it is worth recalling the provisions of the Vienna Declaration of 1991 (I.5.), according to which:

> All human rights are universal, indivisible and interdependent, and interrelated. The international community must treat human rights globally in a fair and equal manner, on the same footing, and with the same emphasis. While the significance of national and regional particularities and various historical, cultural, and religious backgrounds must be borne in mind, it is the duty of States, regardless of their political, economic, and cultural systems, to promote and protect all human rights and fundamental freedoms.[72]

The declaration also provides that the universal nature of these rights is not subject to discussion. Such a radical formulation is opposed to attempts to challenge human rights in the name of cultural relativism. Thesis of relativism in relation to those rights impair the

[71] Cf. J. Finnis, "The Priority of Persons," in: *Oxford Essays in Jurisprudence: Fourth Series*, ed. by J. Horder, Oxford: Oxford University Press, 2001, p. 1.

[72] Adopted by the World Conference on Human Rights in Vienna on 25 June 1993.

very dignity which constitutes their source. Meanwhile, the idea of dignity can be encountered everywhere, that is in every culture, irrespective of assumed moral, religious or legal system, regardless of features or abilities of particular human beings, and regardless of their individual beliefs. The possibility of invoking freedom and equality by means of referring to human dignity opens the way for a better argument, and in particular, it enables a recognition of differentiated perspectives in addressing complex, global problems. This, in turn, corresponds to the trend to rely on those rights also in connection with the globalization of law. The idea of human dignity is a constitutional principle, and it constitutes the notion of reference, and thus it specifically directs fundamental rights of freedom and equality. This direction allows their better implementation and compliance.[73]

Human rights are the basis for the formation of a pluralistic society due to the fact that they assume subjective responsibility of a human being, which is expressed through respect for his dignity - and it manifests itself in a multiplicity of forms of life, beliefs, and perceptions about the world - as a normative point, which binds and leads to libertarian and egalitarian legal consensus.[74] Human rights are in this sense a manifestation of respect for the dignity of man recognized as an equal and free entity capable of unencumbered self-determination. Understanding of a man as an entity fully capable of personal responsibility connects human rights with numerous philosophical and ideological standpoints, influential in the past and present.

Belief that in modern, pluralistic societies there is no common set of values that could serve as a source of social solidarity requires

---

[73] S. Baer, "Menschenwürde zwischen Recht, Prinzip und Referenz. Die Bedeutung von Enttabuisierungen", *Deutsche Zeitschrift für Philosophie* 2005, no. 4, p. 588. It does not mean, of course, that the concept of "dignity" should be associated with the notion of "omnicompetence," so that it should be always and everywhere relied upon, because not every decision against the welfare of a human being stands for a decision against his dignity. This may lead to a devaluation of this concept and result in a counterproductive effect. Broadly on this issue see: E. Picker, *Menschenwürde und Menschenleben. Das Auseinanderdriften zweier fundamentaler Werte als Ausdruck der wachsenden Relativierung des Menschen*, Stuttgart: Klett-Gotta, 2002, Teil C.I.2 and 3.

[74] H. Bielefeldt, *Menschenrechte in der Einwanderungsgesellschaft...*, op. cit., p. 49.

a search for something that will enable the survival of such societies. And it is law itself that must – by means of channelling and resolving conflicts – contribute to the emergence of what Durkheim referred to as "organic solidarity." In other words, law becomes moral practice treated as a substitute for common values and beliefs. Law is responsible for coordinating and structuralising various moral environments in a social whole.[75] Obviously, law that aims at integrating all these diverse interests and preferences in a coherent system must develop new ways of communication between participants of social interactions, rather than subjectively imposing common systems of values or preferences. The latter aptly reflects the role of human rights, which form a common ground in a multicultural, pluralistic, and cosmopolitan world.

It is noteworthy that "global ethics" – commonly sought after these days – refers to the universalist tradition of human rights. Being granted human rights means that humanity has something in common, namely a certain minimum of shared values and moral standards, which express the sense and essence of human solidarity: a holistic understanding of the world, and global responsibility for the world and future generations. In this sense, human rights are of an inclusive rather than discriminatory, or even worse, exclusive character. Human rights cannot be therefore treated as part of Western imperialism, a tool of conquest in subduing the rest of the world. The controversy related to the universality of human rights was borne in mind by the creators of the Declaration of Vienna, writing that "when formulating opinions, one must realize the importance of national and regional differences and a diverse historical and religious past." Universalism – as Michael Freeman writes – can accept diversity in two ways.[76] Firstly, by requiring that certain moral principles were applied in all cultures, despite their diversity. Secondly, by explaining how and to what extent universal principles might need different interpretations and applications in different social contexts.

---

[75] Broadly on this issue see: R. Cotterrell, *The Sociology of Law*, London: Butterworths, 1984, p. 100ff.

[76] M. Freeman, *Human Rights. An Interdisciplinary Approach*, Cambridge: Polity Press, 2004, p. 103.

Universality is also confirmed by the procedure of legislating norms on human rights which are not created arbitrarily, but their enactment is preceded by a public and democratic debate which does not aim at defending gained dominance, but supports and develops internal (domestic), intercultural, and international dialogue. It is only during communication with others in which we try to grasp what is our own in that which is different and diverse, that conditions the possibility of extracting and determining the substance of human rights. Yet human rights are a part of the culture which exists, which is formed and develops in a dialectic of familiarity and strangeness, whilst looking through the eyes of "an alien" (the other) at what is our own, which can exceed a precise differentiation of "our own" and "the other," and as such the claims to those rights are raised in a variety of religious or cultural symbols. Application and interpretation of human rights cannot be therefore detached from local, particular cultures and the contribution that they make to the protection of human dignity. Without the recognition of the latter, human rights cannot be traced and observed in an appropriate way, because they will not reflect the diversity of lifestyles. Emancipatory orientation of human rights implies an unencumbered comparison of the multiplicity of human lifestyles, preferences, values, and perceptions. As I have already noted, the ability to make free life choices constitutes the basis of human dignity. At the same time, maintaining dignity requires ensuring equal rights of all citizens to participate in political community.[77] One can have a reasonable doubt over whether a culture of people who live in fear of accidental or unwarranted arrest or women who are excluded from public life is represented by the political community. Freeman draws the conclusion that it is respect for cultural diversity - often pointed to as a threat to the universality of human rights - that may paradoxically require a determined implemen-

[77] M. Środa, *Idea godności w kulturze i etyce* [The Idea of Dignity in Culture and Ethics], Warszawa: Multiprint, 1993, pp. 48–49. The author writes as follows: Civic dignity - embedded in law and in privileges laid down by law - constitutes one of a set of democratic values. Civic dignity is inextricably linked with equality and freedom and rule of law, which ensure protection of these values. Relevance of this matter can be proved by the fact that most social groups or individuals who demand "recognition of dignity" de facto demand recognition of the rights and guarantees which is sufficient and necessary to avoid an illusory character of dignity."

tation of these rights.[78] Human rights are universal and essential since they ensure respect for dignity and the equality of minority and weaker groups with the strong majority.

5. Democracy in the globalization age

5.1. Democracy in the 21st century

Contemporarily, there is no better system of law than that of the democratic state, which either as a *modus vivendi* or as a well-ordered society based, for example, on *overlapping consensus,* would fully realize the idea of human dignity, and would respect human rights. A characteristic feature of modern states is to refer to norms of democracy in their activities. This appears somewhat difficult, given the fact that globalization to some extent stands for de-democratisation of binding collective decisions.[79] It does not mean that democracy has become something unnecessary. On the contrary, without democracy, a modern, cosmopolitan world cannot exist, but it is necessary to express it in other forms, corresponding to modern changes, due to which everyone will be able to affect a new formation of a global policy, to express opposition against the violation of human rights, and to counter global threats. Democracy, like human rights, has become common and desirable by the fact that the circumstances that created it, namely, capitalism and the nation-state, have been globalized.[80] However, it is justified to express the view under which cross-cultural diversity is important from the standpoint of democracy. Such a view refers to the views of Samuel P. Huntington and Robert Putnam, who argue that cultural traditions are extremely durable and they shape political and economic behaviour of societies.[81] It follows that differ-

---

[78] M. Freeman, *Human Rights,* op. cit., p. 109.

[79] U. Beck, *Macht und Gegenmacht im globalen Zeitalter…,* op. cit., p. 308.

[80] J. Donnelly, *Universal Human Rights in Theory and Practice,* Ithaca – London: Cornell University Press, 2003, p. 129ff.; C.C. Gould, *Globalizing Democracy and Human Rights,* Cambridge: Cambridge University Press, 2004, p. 159ff.

[81] S.P. Huntington, *Clash of Civilizations and the Remaking of World Order,* New York: Simon and Schuster, 1996; R. Putnam, *Making Democracy Work: Civic Traditions in Modern Italy,* Princeton: Princeton University Press, 1993.

ent societies vary in relation to the "values conducive to survival" and "values conducive to free expression." It follows, then, that societies in which values conductive to free expression are preferred are better and more likely to adapt to conditions of democracy rather than societies in which the predominant values are those conducive to survival.[82]

Democracy allows the realization of important social values. Amy Gutmann notes that democracies are not neutral political systems in the sense that they institutionalise in politics more ethical treatment of individuals than their political alternatives, in particular, autocracy or oligarchy.[83] Accordingly, democracy - in a better way than other political systems - guarantees freedom and equality of all people. The latter obviously stands for a community in which the rulers are obliged to treat the ruled "with concern, that is, as human beings who are capable of suffering and frustration, and with respect, that is, as human beings who are capable of forming and acting on intelligent conceptions of how their lives should be lived."[84]

In modern times, community identity is less defined by a common territory, language, or tradition but, above all, by active membership (citizenship), which assumes mutual respect of people. A. Szahaj, therefore, aptly defines community as follows:

> ... they are loyal to each other, what binds them is their fraternity resulting from deliberate approval and adoption of certain unifying values, mutual responsibility for their fate, and from experiencing a certain kinship in perceiving the world.[85]

---

[82] R.F. Inglehart, "Culture and Democracy," in: *Culture Matters. How Values Shape Human Progress*, ed. by L.E. Harrison, S.P. Huntington, New York: Basic Books, 2000, pp. 88–97.

[83] A. Gutmann, *Identity in Democracy*, Princeton: Princeton University Press, 2004, p. 27. This statement corresponds to prophetic message of Hannah Arendt, that some people enjoy human rights since they belong to a community that is ready to defend them. Arendt therefore writes: "It is not a loss of certain rights, but the loss of community, ready and able to guarantee any rights that constituted a misfortune which a growing number of people encountered" (H. Arendt, *The Origins of Totalitarianism*, Part 2, New York: Harvest Book, 1973).

[84] R. Dworkin, *Taking Rights Seriously*, op. cit., p. 272.

[85] A. Szahaj, *Jednostka czy wspólnota? Spór liberałów z komunitarystami a „sprawa polska"* [An Individual or Community? Dispute between Communitarians and 'Polish Issue'], Warszawa: Aletheia, 2000, p. 131.

In turn, J. Gray – by means of accepting the thesis of plurality of values and even perceiving the latter as a *modus vivendi* of contemporary liberalism – treats democratic authority not as an "embodiment of [a] universal right to national self-determination," but as a means of enabling different communities to take joint decisions and to change the authorities without violence.[86] Democracy successfully functions both in culturally homogeneous and heterogeneous societies, which are geographically and culturally distant from the places in which it originated. A democratic system does not implement pre-determined axiological goals, but gives equal rights to every pursuit of axiological goals, and possible joint purposes are determined by means of democratic institutions and procedures. In other words, democracy is not specific to any particular culture, on the contrary, supporters of democracy, as well as democracy itself, are located within very different cultures, to name only a few: German, Eskimo, Navajo Indian, Hindi, Chinese, Muslim, Flemish, New Zealander, or American.[87] As a result, the intention of every culture is to make democracy their part, and in the case of a multicultural society, all cultures and society as a whole. Furthermore, in multicultural and pluralistic societies democracy is especially needed, because it is due to these democratic procedures that diversity can be manifested, thus enriching the social mind and reviving the state. The essence of democracy is in fact a clash of different views, values, and interests. Democracy, therefore, requires constant intellectual activity and, accordingly, continuously renewed intellectual underpinning. Otherwise, the level of misunderstanding and positive distrust to ever-changing democratic procedures may lead to a radical opposition to its new rules, and such a populist rejection of democratic procedures is by no means the intention here.

What is especially interesting today is how contemporary theory of democracy should explain the readiness of every citizen to actively participate in social and political processes of collective creation of ideas and will. The active role of ordinary citizens in the political process is contemporarily understood – particularly in theories of

---

[86] J. Gray, *Two Faces of Liberalism*, op. cit., p. 105ff.

[87] A. Gutmann, *Identity in Democracy*, op. cit., p. 80.

deliberative democracy – as a normative assumption of legitimized exercise of authority. This conviction is important in the context of the abovementioned and continually growing pluralism of values. Currently, various citizens admit their preferences of a different hierarchy of values, and democratic participation largely determines the level of pre-political compatibility.[88] The escape from the stagnation of democratic participation is mainly indicated by the theories of deliberative democracy, and re-popularised John Dewey's theory of democracy, understood as a reflective form of cooperation or as R. Dworkin's partnership view of democracy.[89]

Broadly speaking, according to the representatives of deliberative trends, politics (democracy) is defined as the transformation of citizens' preferences through rational discussion, and thus it takes the form of an open and public activity, which aims to formulate the idea of the common good.[90] Jürgen Habermas[91] is the most typical repre-

---

[88] Ch.F. Zurn, "Anerkennung, Umverteilung und Demokratie. Dilemmata in Honneths Kritischer Theorie der Gesellschaft," *Deutsche Zeitschrift für Philosophie* 2005, vol. 53, no. 3, p. 439.

[89] On the issue of partnership view of democracy see: R. Dworkin, *Is democracy possible here?...*, op. cit., p. 131ff.

[90] P.W. Juchacz, *Demokracja – deliberacja – partycypacja. Szkice z teorii demokracji ateńskiej i współczesnej* [Democracy – Deliberation – Participation. Essays on the Theory of Athenian and Contemporary Democracy], Poznań: Wydawnictwo Naukowe Instytutu Filozofii UAM, 2006, p. 11. It is noteworthy that the literature on the subject uses various interchangeable terms: deliberative, discursive, communicative, or dialogue democracy, which – as can be clearly seen – are embedded in different philosophical conceptions and do not necessarily stand for the same notion. Representative distinction between liberal and constitutional deliberative democracy and discursive democracy was made by John Dryzek, who stated that what was typical for the model of deliberative democracy was the fact of narrowing public debate to the contents of political culture of liberal democracies, while the discursive model, in contrast, focuses on an inclusive, multicultural and pluralistic public sphere open to all, including new and alien participants, in shaping public opinion and will, especially on the views formulated by the latter. J. Dryzek, *Deliberative Democracy and Beyond: Liberals, Critics, Contestations*, Oxford: Oxford University Press, 2002.

[91] Habermas' views on democratic proceduralism will be discussed in the next chapter. It can be only pointed out that according to this German philosopher (similarly to the representative of republicanism – Hannah Arendt), the idea of democratic creation of will and views may only take place in the public sphere of linguistic agreement, and it is only in this way that the individuals can pursue communicative

sentative of this theory, but the latter is also represented by the supporters of participative democracy, such as John Stuart Mill and Carole Paterman.[92] James Bohman notes that different concepts of deliberative democracy have something in common, namely a strong emphasis on mutual interrelation of normative, descriptive, and practical issues. The theory of deliberative democracy must be adequate at all three levels if it is to be a guide for political practice and reforms.[93] Bohman believes that normativeness consists in negating the act of bringing politics and decision-making processes only to instrumental and strategic rationality. It is therefore the case that in deliberative processes, taking a particular political decision is preceded by its consideration and by the presentation of all the arguments in a public forum. This allows for a virtually unlimited argumentative discretion but, more importantly, requires the citizens who participate in this process to include in the decision-making process common interests or arguments that could be accepted by all participants.[94] Deliberative democracy, however, accepts only such arguments, presented by respective citizens, which treat other citizens as equals.

The answer to the abovementioned question about the cause (source) of every citizen's readiness to participate in the democratic process of taking public decisions can be found in the conception presented by Joshua Cohen, for whom deliberative democracy means a relation in which citizens are obliged to coordinate their activity, using appropriate institutions which enable deliberation, using the norms which they have agreed on in the course of joint discussions.[95]

---

freedom. Cf. J. Habermas, *Between Facts and Norms. Contributions to a Discourse Theory of Law and Democracy*, Cambridge, Mass.: The MIT Press, 1998, Chapter 3 and *Popular Sovereignty*, [idem, "Human Rights and Popular Sovereignty: The Liberal and Republican Versions," *Ratio Juris* 1994, vol. 7, no. 1,] pp. 463–490.

[92] Broadly on this issue see: J. Elster, "The Market and the Forum," in: *Deliberative Democracy. Essays on Reason and Politics*, ed. by J. Bohman, W. Rehg, Cambridge: The MIT Press, 1997, pp. 3–33.

[93] J. Bohman, *Public Deliberation. Pluralism, Complexity, and Democracy*, Cambridge: The MIT Press, 1996, p. 4.

[94] Ibidem, p. 5.

[95] J. Cohen, "Deliberation and Democratic Legitimacy," in: *The Good Polity. Normative Analysis of the State*, ed. by A. Hamlin, Ph. Pettit, Oxford: Polity Press, 1989, p. 21: "The notion of a deliberative democracy is rooted in the intuitive ideal of a democratic

Consequently, it can be concluded that it was the unencumbered debate of equal citizens, namely equal members of the established association, which constitutes the basis for the legitimization of public and state institutions. Deliberative democracy supports rational discussion and consensus, thus contributing to the elimination of intolerance, inequality, and violence from public life. Such a conception of democracy implies that public decisions are the result of free and rational deliberation between entities regarded as morally and politically equal.[96] Deliberation is significant in the face of the assumption that the essential characteristic of democratic states is the fact of the multiplicity of conflicting religious, philosophical, and moral reasonable doctrines. Rawls notes that "the ultimate idea of deliberating democracy is reflection," and the latter assumes that in the course of political debate, citizens exchange views and their opinions are not immutable, but may be revised in the course of the discussion.[97] In other words, democracy requires contractual establishment - being the result of deliberations - of procedural rules of agonistic confrontation and rivalry, which constitutes the forum in which all free human entities can participate on an equal footing. These human entities are endowed with dignity, which neither political rivalry, nor a defeat in the latter, can deprive them of.

Contemporary literature on the subject devotes much attention to the updating of Dewey's model of democracy,[98] according to which

---

association in which the justification of the terms and conditions of association proceeds through public argument and reasoning among equal citizens."

96 S. Benhabib, "Toward a Deliberative Model of Democratic Legitimacy," in: *Democracy and Difference. Contesting the Boundaries of the Political*, ed. by S. Benhabib, Princeton: Princeton University Press, 1996, p. 68ff. Thomas McCarthy writes in this context that all participants of the discourse of global modernity basically operate on the same discursive level, and that this discursive symmetry makes all epistemic and evaluative assumptions essentially disputable (objectionable). Th. McCarthy, "Dialogical Freedom and Democratic Deliberation," in: *Multiculturalism and Law: A Critical Debate*, ed. by O.A. Payrow Shabani, Cardiff: University of Wales Press, 2007, p. 51.

97 J. Rawls, *The Law of Peoples*, Cambridge: Harvard University Press, 1999, p. 135.

98 I briefly present this theory not only in order to outline its relevance and importance, especially for Honneth's recognition conception, which is of key importance in my deliberations, but also so as not to lose the main issue of the dissertation in question. I would also like to indicate an alternative form of justification of human rights presented in American pragmatism.

social cooperation is possible only if individual, socially shared problems, are taken in defence. Only then will the citizens, as co-operating actors, engage themselves in deliberation processes as a part of which they will estimate competing measures to achieve envisaged goals, assign specific tasks according to abilities and interests, and reflectively justify these processes in the light of experience.[99] Law is the very medium which allows such co-operation. In particular, what is meant by "Laws" is intersubjectively shared human rights, particularly rights of freedom, the right to political participation, and so-called social rights.[100] John Dewey understands democracy as a reflective form of community co-operation. He maintains that democracy provides a political form of organization in which human intelligence reaches full development, because only where methods of public discourse on individual beliefs assumed institutional shape does there exists a possibility of generating – as a part of social life – a rational solution of a communicative character.[101]

Honneth considers that, for Dewey, the political sphere constitutes a cognitive medium, with the help of which society is trying to explore their own problems in the coordination of social activity and then to assess them and find a resolution. As a result, it has to be stated that political self-steering of society must be carried out democratically, and the more actively the interconnected audience reacts to social problems, the more rational is the process by which the state may develop such resolutions of social problems that merit widespread approval.[102] Honneth notes that social cooperation allows for arriving at more intelligent solutions to emerging problems, since by means of the latter all participants exchange information in an unconstrained and equally legitimised way and they offer different solutions that are subject to subsequent discussion. In this way, participants learn both individually and

[99] Ch.F. Zurn, *Anerkennung, Umverteilung und Demokratie…*, op. cit., p. 440.

[100] A. Honneth, "Universalismus als moralische Falle? Bedingungen und Grenzen einer Politik der Menschenrechte," in: idem, *Das Andere der Gerechtigkeit. Aufsätze zur praktischen Philosophie*, Frankfurt am Main: Suhrkamp Verlag, 2000, p. 271.

[101] J. Dewey, *Die Öffentlichkeit und ihre Probleme*, Bodenheim: Philo, 1996, p. 175.

[102] A. Honneth, "Demokratie als reflexive Kooperation: John Dewey und die Demokratietheorie der Gegenwart," in: idem, *Das Andere der Gerechtigkeit. Aufsätze zur praktischen Philosophie*, Frankfurt am Main: Suhrkamp Verlag, 2000, p. 302.

collectively how social cooperation functions at its best.[103] The experience of the collective resolution of problems and conflict creates contexts in which individuals may be recognized for their own specific contribution and performance. In other words, these contexts create the basis for a proper self-respect and for one's own assessment. A positive assessment will encourage the individual to a further participation in the process of socio-political problem-solving, finding in the latter social respect and personal benefits.[104]

The significance of social cooperation was also emphasized by Rawls, who understood it as an action aiming at mutual benefit. In other words, fair terms of cooperation are such "which each participant may reasonably be expected to accept, provided that everyone else likewise accepts them."[105] As a result, fair terms of cooperation express the idea of reciprocity and mutuality. We can cooperate only as equal individuals and on the basis of mutual respect. In this sense, Rawls' "overlapping consensus" assumes such an agreement that allows the existence of society as a fair system of cooperation between intelligent, rational, free, and equal persons. This is particularly important, given the fact that people differ among one another not only in their perceptions and preferences, but also in their skills and abilities. Therefore, such social cooperation constitutes a ground for externalizing one's own expectations, and thereby fosters the plurality of values and social diversity of views, but it also gives every individual – as equally valuable – the chance to contribute to the common good by participating fully in a specific social association. In other words, Dewey's paradigm of social cooperation and fair social distribution of work provides a reliable epistemic justification for democratic process of resolving social conflicts, and it constitutes a convincing explanation of motivationally shaping sources of democratic participation.[106]

---

[103] Relations between a democratic form of community life, distribution of work, and educational value of cooperative activities are broadly discussed by Dewey in his work published under the title *Democracy and Education. An Introduction to the Philosophy of Education*, New York: Free Press, 1966, particularly in Chapter VII: "The Democratic Conception in Education".

[104] Ch.F. Zurn, *Anerkennung, Umverteilung und Demokratie…*, op. cit., p. 440.

[105] J. Rawls, *Political Liberalism*, op. cit., p. 300.

[106] Ch.F. Zurn, *Anerkennung, Umverteilung und Demokratie…*, op. cit., p. 441.

Dewey's conception of radical democracy becomes particularly attractive and current, taking into account the constantly growing pluralization and heterogeneity of various lifestyles. Paradoxically, the plurality of diverse lifestyles, and thus different distribution of work, does not destructively impact the society, but can effectively realize social goals, forcing social consensus, for example, in the form of specific rights. The formation of specific patterns of behaviour that function within institutionalized forms of social life and the formation of some ethical systems do not take place as an individual process in a human being's consciousness, but they occur as a part of commonly accepted category of the awareness of political community. Herbert L.A. Hart also treats political community as a cooperative community, and thus a one in which voluntary cooperation among members of the community creates moral duties and rights for the realization of common goal.[107]

5.2. Are democracy and human rights compatible?

Beth J. Singer, in reference to Dewey's and George H. Mead's views, makes an interesting concept of human rights, treating the latter as a relation that has developed between cooperating members of community.[108] In her view, participation in the rights is a consequence of participation in relation with others. Mead noted that:

> One participates in the same process the other person is carrying out and controls his action with reference to that participation. It is that which constitutes the meaning of an object, namely, the common response in one's self as well as in the other person, which becomes, in turn, a stimulus to one's self.[109]

---

[107] H.L.A. Hart, "Social Solidarity and the Enforcement of Morality," in: idem, *Essays in Jurisprudence and Philosophy of Law*, Oxford: Oxford University Press, 1968, pp. 252–253; idem, "Are There Any Natural Rights?" in: *Theories of Rights*, ed. by J. Waldron, Oxford: Oxford University Press, 1984, p. 77ff.

[108] B.J. Singer, *Pragmatism, Rights and Democracy*, New York: Fordham University Press, 1999, p. 16.

[109] G.H. Mead, *Mind, Self, and Society*, Chicago – London: The University of Chicago Press, 1967, pp. 73–74.

In this context, Mead's social interactionism (conscious and actual participation in social reality) is possible due to the fact that the individual is able to transcend its own perspective and assume the role of others, especially the role of the so-called "generalized other," namely an organized community or social group. As a result, Mead notes that "we cannot be ourselves unless we are also members in whom there is a community of attitudes which control the attitudes of all. We cannot have rights unless we have common attitudes."[110] This means that the individual identifies itself in the process of socialization with members of the group by taking over the roles of others, which leads to the act of coordinating the activities of this individual with the activities of others treated as a group, community, and thus as a certain whole.

Moreover, it follows that rights are not independent of the community in which they operate, and in the areas where they operate they must be observed and respected. Rights are not, therefore, justified in our nature, but are rather perceived as a learned attitude, the assumption of which is in our interest.[111] In this context, rights have the structure of a double obligation, since when claiming that "I have the right," an individual entity is able to recognize such a right in another person and assume the obligation to comply with this right, whilst the same obligation is imposed on other individuals remaining in interaction. B.J. Singer draws the conclusion, therefore, that rights do not have the character of claims, since by saying "I have a right," I state that "I have the same right as you," and "the rights which we recognize in others, may be recognized by others as ours."[112] Conse-

[110] Ibidem, pp. 163–164. It should be noted that Mead's conception corresponds with social communication and, to a lesser extent, with intercultural communication. This issue is more closely analyzed in section IV.5.

[111] B.J. Singer, *Pragmatism, Rights and Democracy*, op. cit., p. 34: "Thus, it seems to me that the institution of rights is grounded in, and rights are justified by, the requirements of social interaction. All social norms evolve out of the need of individuals to organize and coordinate their behavior, which requires them to know what to expect of others and what others expect of them as well as to have common purposes and goals and a shared understanding of these. In this process, among the norms that evolve are standards and values."

[112] Ibidem, p. 129.

quently, Singer derives the existence of rights referring again to Mead, since all members of a given community recognize these rights as a common good, the good of everybody, and everyone highly values this good.[113]

What is, therefore, so crucial in the process of recognizing these rights is to treat democracy as a form of societal organization. This becomes particularly important in the view of the abovementioned pluralism of values, as well as cultural, ideological, and religious pluralism. As pointed out by Gray, ethical pluralism results in emphasising the differences of a particular community or even of an individual guided by its own lifestyle, which can sometimes lead to its exclusion from social life. It is therefore essential to create inclusive community, the bases of which will be acceptable to all, thus ensuring peaceful coexistence of different lifestyles and values. In the opinion of B.J. Singer, universal normative community – emerging in this way – should be based on two fundamental rights: the right to be recognized as a moral authority and the right to autonomy.[114] Adam Chmielewski notes that the latter constitutes the expression of epistemological egalitarianism, which was the basis for human rights and liberal Western culture.[115] B.J. Singer's conception points out that, on the one hand, it is possible to maintain neither liberal theses of self-justification of rights, of their absolute, objective and universal character nor, on the other hand, the theses of communitarists that human rights distort a sense of belonging to a community and cause a crisis of the individual's identity. According to the author of *Pragmatism, Rights and Democracy*, rights based on reciprocity are an integral and supportive element, which institutionalises democratic society in which individuals may assume their interlocutor's perspective, and

---

113 Ibidem, p. 131.

114 Ibidem, p. 29. The author writes: "I call these the *fundamental generic rights*: fundamental in that they are necessary conditions for the continuing existence and stability of any normative community, and generic in the sense that they ought to be made universally operative" (ibidem, pp. 30–31).

115 A. Chmielewski, *Społeczeństwo otwarte czy wspólnota?* [An Open Society or a Community?], Wrocław: Wydawnictwo Uniwersytetu Wrocławskiego, 2001, p. 139. It can be noted that Singer, at the same time, approaches Richard Rorty's inclusive ethnocentrism.

thus better understand and, ultimately, agree on solutions to social problems.

It is noteworthy that we contemporarily observe a widening scope of the international sphere of social and political participation in which individuals, groups of citizens, and social movements are engaged in dialogue, debate, and negotiations among themselves, and with various national and international, governmental, nongovernmental, and local actors. This means that human rights are also the result of interactions taking place on these communicatively differentiated levels. Therefore, what can be still noticed is an increasing tendency towards negotiating lawmaking. This is most visible in the so-called responsive model, where communication and discourse have the leading role in normative systems.

As a result, it can be safely concluded that human rights and democracy are interdependent and they mutually reinforce each other, which has been particularly expressed in the quoted Vienna Declaration of 1991 (adopted in 1993) in the following words:

> Considering the major changes taking place on the international scene and the aspirations of all the peoples for an international order based on the principles enshrined in the Charter of the United Nations, including promoting and encouraging respect for human rights and fundamental freedoms for all and respect for the principle of equal rights and self-determination of peoples, peace, democracy, justice, equality, rule of law, pluralism, development, better standards of living and solidarity.

It can be aptly stated that similar values, including, in particular, respect for the individual's dignity, form the basis for both human rights and democracy. Despite many obvious objections, the latter seems to be the best form of authority for protecting human rights.[116]

---

[116] J. Donnelly, *Universal Human Rights...*, op. cit., p. 191ff.; M. Freeman, *Human Rights*, op. cit., p. 72.

CHAPTER II

Discursive – ethical justification of human rights and democracy

1. The Ethics of Discourse in Karl-Otto Apel's Transcendental-Pragmatic Philosophy

The effect of globalization processes was that cosmopolitan, or just multicultural, society formed the basis of new ethics, which entail the need of justifying our behaviour not only within national frames, but also in the face of the whole world. Such new ethics do not only have universalistic aspirations but, most of all, supranational and trans- and inter-cultural ones, because its aim, above other things, is to match broadly understood interests (of good and well-being) of all human beings worldwide.[1] In my opinion, worldwide transformation in the sphere of communication activities points at the problem of global ethics. It is therefore the reason why, when referring to already characterised basic ethical categories, I would like to emphasise an increasing role of ethical and social conceptions – deriving from the Frankfurt school – which contain the seed of this globalization. They all refer to universality of rules and principles of discourse which form communicative community based on the existence of certain common ethical requirements and, in particular, on the universality of human rights. It is crucial to quote Jürgen Habermas' words:

> The universalist position does not have to deny the pluralism and the incompatibility of historical versions of "civilized humanity;" but it regards

[1] Broadly on this issue see: C. Kessler, "Globalization: Another False Universalism?," *Third World Quarterly* 2000, no. 21, pp. 931–942.

> this multiplicity of forms of life as limited to *cultural contents*, and it asserts that every culture must share certain *formal properties* of the modern understanding of the world, if it is at all to attain a certain degree of "conscious awareness" or "sublimation."[2]

The ethics of discourse is the ethics oriented at duties which regulate interpersonal cooperation. It is the kind of ethics which calls for mutual restriction of freedom and which indicates the interests and aims which should be commonly denoted, as well as the basis of their mutually accepted realization. This ethics, then, refers to such a pattern of norm and duties justification which, in case of collision between particular moral and religious beliefs or standpoints, can constitute a fundamental and common area of possible agreement.[3]

1.1. The basis of discourse ethics

Special attention should be paid to discourse ethics, developed by Karl-Otto Apel as a part of transcendental pragmatics. In the approach of this philosopher, ethical issues were interwoven in communication relations. Discourse consists of creating binding solutions for all imaginable problems which can appear in lifeworld. At the same time, discourse is not a self-sufficient game, but rather a possibility of solving conflicts without the use of violence. Transcendental pragmatics is based on "transcendental unity of interpretation," which is deeply rooted in community of communication. The idea of communication community is perceived by Apel as theoretically connected with Kant's idea of "the state of aims," which – as he writes – constitutes "metaphysical *a priori* prefiguration of an ideal community of communication," which can be, in this perspective, recognized as a regulative idea of human communication.[4] In other words, Apel

[2] J. Habermas, *The Theory of Communicative Action*, vol. 1, Boston: Beacon Press, 1984, p. 180.

[3] A.M. Kaniowski, *Supererogacja. Zagubiony wymiar etyki* [Supererogation. Lost Dimension of Ethics], Warszawa: Oficyna Naukowa, 1999, p. 418.

[4] K.-O. Apel, "Diskursethik als Verantwortungsethik – eine postmetaphysische Transformation der Ethik Kants," in: *Ethik und Befreiung*, ed. by R. Fornet-Betancourt, Aachen: Augustinus-Buchhandlung, 1990, pp. 10–40; idem, "Discourse Ethics as

modifies Kant's thought in such way that he reallocates transcendental conditions of possibilities of knowledge from the sphere of the individual mind to the sphere of intersubjectivity. These conditions are understood as validity claims which were recognized by Apel as universal.[5] For the existence and binding nature of ethical content "the institution of linguistic communication" rather than a given historical language or a form of specialist language seems indispensable. "The institution of linguistic communication" is at the same time irremovable; that is, it is always realized in every respective language, though it can never be associated with the latter. In this context, Apel regarded it as the "transcendental meta-institution of all other linguistic institutions." Therefore, it can be seen that the latter is a source of conditions legitimizing other institutions, particularly moral norms and social institutions established on the basis of moral norms. In

---

a Response to the Novel Challenges of Today's Reality to Coresponsibility," *The Journal of Religion* 1993, vol. 73, no. 4, pp. 496–513.

[5] Similarly to Habermas, Apel mentions the following validity claims: (1) the claim to understand intersubjectively valid meaning together with other participants of the discourse; (2) the claim to the truth as a postulate of aiming at a truly universal consensus; (3) the claim to truthfulness or honesty of linguistic acts which express the intentions of the participants of communication; (4) the claim to adequate correctness of linguistic acts as communicative acts, broadly oriented at all possible partners of communication. K.-O. Apel, "Die Vernunftfunktion der kommunikativen Rationalität. Zum Verhältnis von konsensualkommunikativer Rationalität, strategischer Rationalität und Systemrationalität," in: *Die eine Vernunft und die vielen Rationalitäten*, ed. by K.-O. Apel, M. Kettner, Frankfurt am Main: Suhrkamp Verlag, 1996, pp. 21ff.; idem, "Diskursethik als Ethik der Mit-Verantwortung für kollektive Aktivitäten," in: *Rehabilitierung des Subjektiven. Festschrift für Hermann Schmitz*, ed. by M. Grossheim, H.-J. Waschkies, Bonn: Bouvier, 1993, pp. 191–207; idem, "Diskursethik als Ethik der Mit-Verantwortung vor den Sachzwängen der Politik, des Rechts und der Marktwirtschaft," in: *Prinzip Mitverantwortung. Grundlage für Ethik und Pädagogik*, ed. by K.-O. Apel, H. Burckhart, Würzburg: Königshausen & Neumann, 2001, pp. 69–96. The abovementioned claims correspond to Habermas' following validity claims: (1) the claim to comprehensibility, (2) the claim to truthfulness or sincerity, which assumes that the speaker is sincere, (3) the claim to propositional truth: the speaker communicates true statements so that his listener can regard his statement as certain, (4) the claim to correctness: the statement is correct in that the participants of communicative activities accept the speaker's statement in a certain assumed axiological system. J. Habermas, *The Theory of Communicative Action*, op. cit., p. 38.

other words, the meta-institution of communication permanently provides normative conditions of the possibilities of criticism and reasonable legitimization of social institutions.

Such an approach to "community of communication" and to "the idea of linguistic communication" - as presented by Apel - implies the necessity of working out communicative ethics, which he later calls discourse ethics.[6] One of the most fundamental theses of discourse ethics assumes that the conditions which enable an argumentative process are ethically-normative by their nature and, consequently, they form the grounds for the procedures of justifying ethics. The latter allows the relation of discourse ethics to serious universal claims, and the perception of it as the project of universal ethics. It is how the idea of ultimate justification of norms has found its fundamental place in the philosophy of transcendental pragmatics. I will now present its fundamental assumptions, crucial for the argumentation that is to follow.

"Universally-pragmatic" justification of particular rules of the discourse consists in proving that such rules must be binding because they constitute a condition which justifies and enables interpersonal communication. In other words, they ultimately justify the principles which constitute communication.[7] Human nature indicates that contradicting this idea and, at the same time, negating the argumentation process would lead to schizophrenia and self-destruction.[8]

Similar views are held by Habermas, according to whom the binding nature of certain rules is constitutive in order to enable the performance of specific speech acts. Disregarding these speech acts would imply discarding such forms of behaviour that are perceived as typically human.[9] Apel presents his conception of transcendental argument in the following way:

---

[6] K.-O. Apel, "Diskursethik als Verantwortungsethik...," op. cit., p. 12ff.

[7] K.-O. Apel, *Transformation der Philosophie*, Band 2. *Das Apriori der Kommunikationsgemeinschaft*, Frankfurt am Main: Suhrkamp Verlag, 1973, p. 222: "In einer modernen Transzendentalphilosophie geht es m. E. primär um die Reflexion auf den Sinn ... des Argumentierens überhaupt. Dies allerdings ist für den, der argumentiert ... offenbar das *Letzte, Nichthintergehbare*."

[8] Ibidem, p. 414.

[9] J. Habermas, *Vorstudien und Ergänzungen zur Theorie des kommunikativen Handelns*, Frankfurt am Main: Suhrkamp Verlag, 1984, p. 353ff.

> He who argues admits in an implicit way all possible claims of all participants of a community of communication which can be justified by reasonable arguments ... and assumes the obligation to justify all his claims vis-à-vis others by means of presenting his arguments.[10]

Discourse rules are of a two-stage character, namely the ones that refer to the ultimate formally–procedural and to consensually–communicative justifications of norms. The first stage norms would be those rules of discourse which refer to formally–procedural norms (acknowledged in freedom), which are implicitly contained in ethics, and as second-stage norms they are differentiated from substantive ones (that is ones referring to a particular situation) provided only by practical discourses.[11]

Theoretical process, which serves the idea of ultimate justification of norms, was realized in the conception of universal pragmatics on four levels: first of all, in the course of detailed critical analyses of philosophical constructions that question the theoretical or practical value of normative theses and the possibility of philosophical procedures of justification; secondly, by means of the construction of transcendental, or, more specifically, purely reflective, arguments of ultimate justification; thirdly, on the level of a general theory of communicative rationality and; fourthly, in the area of discourse ethics conception, which was supplemented in time with the conception of the so-called ethics B (elements of B ethics) or, from another perspective, in the area of discourse ethics, gradually supplemented with the construction of ethics of responsibility. At this moment I will focus on the last level, in which Apel's project of universal ethics of co-responsibility, namely of every person's responsibility for the consequences of joint acts and undertakings, is most comprehensively manifested. Apel considers such co-responsibility in the aspect of peaceful coexistence of different cultures as well as in the aspect of the binding nature of human rights in all cultures.

It should be noted that Apel was also influenced and inspired by critical assessment of John Rawls' justice theory. Apel noticed that Rawls did not provide a universally valid basis for global ethics of

---

[10] K.-O. Apel, *Transformation der Philosophie*, op. cit., p. 424.

[11] K.-O. Apel, *Diskurs und Verantwortung. Das Problem des Übergangs zur postkonventionellen Moral*, Frankfurt am Main: Suhrkamp Verlag, 1997, p. 122.

responsibility, and that this was the case due to at least two reasons.[12] Rawls did not manage to provide a rational basis of universal validity of the principle of justice as fairness since the author of *Theory of Justice* himself emphasised in his later works that a primordial situation did not provide a primordial basis for his theory, concluding that such grounds were rather provided by the fairness principle developed when preserving reflective balance based between his reasonable intuition and the intuition of his listeners or participants of voting in the primordial situation. Rawls did not claim later – as accurately pointed by Apel – that common sense intuition, which served as a point of departure for reflective balance, has universal validity.

Apel – inspired by Rawls (and communitarists who criticised Rawls) – wonders, then, whether it is possible to create a common, universally valid ethics of solidarity, justice, and co-responsibility. Ultimately, he answers positively to this puzzling question and calls such transcendental universalism of a Kantian character "ethics of transcendental-pragmatic discourse."[13]

1.2. Universalistic ethics of co-responsibility

In Apel's approach, universal validity of discourse ethics is based on the transcendental–reflective and communicative type of rationality.[14]

---

[12] K.-O. Apel, *Diskurs und Verantwortung…*, op. cit., pp. 174–175; idem, "Diskursethik vor der Problematik von Recht und Politik: Können die Rationalitätsdifferenzen zwischen Moralität, Recht und Politik selbst noch durch die Diskursethik normativ-rational gerechtfertigt werden?" in: *Zur Anwendung der Diskursethik in Politik, Recht und Wissenschaft*, ed. by K.-O. Apel and M. Kettner, Frankfurt am Main: Suhrkamp Verlag, 1992, pp. 29–61. In one of the latest texts, in turn, Apel analyses Rawls' *The Law of Peoples*. Cf. K.-O. Apel, "Discourse Ethics, Democracy, and International Law. Toward a Globalization of Practical Reason," in: *The Challenges of Globalization. Rethinking Nature, Culture, and Freedom*, ed. by S.V. Hicks, D.E. Shannon, Oxford: Blackwell Publishing, 2007, pp. 60–66.

[13] K.-O. Apel, "Diskursethik als Ethik der Mit-Verantwortung vor den Sachzwängen der Politik…," op. cit., p. 75.

[14] Broadly on this issue see: K.-O. Apel, "Das Problem der philosophischen Letztbegründung im Lichte einer transzendentalen Sprachpragmatik. Versuch einer Metakritik des »kritischen Rationalismus«," in: idem, *Auseinandersetzungen in Erprobung des transzendentalpragmatischen Ansatzes*, ed. by K.-O. Apel, Frankfurt am Main: Suhrkamp Verlag, 1998, pp. 33–80.

Discourse ethics, understood in this way, provides a basis both for the ethics of global justice and solidarity, and for co-responsibility, namely for every person's responsibility assumed as a part of social cooperation on the level of such discourses of community of communication, which functions as the meta-institution of all human institutions and social sub-systems.[15] For Apel, the latter constitutes the third task of discourse ethics, which consists of providing a regulative principle for acting or taking decisions in situations in which we have to mediate between ethical and strategic rationality, since in our particular historical situation there are no (or there are yet no) conditions to apply a pure discourse ethics.[16]

The basic theoretical as well as practical assumption of discourse ethics, its "primordial situation," is an "argumentative situation," which allows every individual to be aware of the fact that they are members of a real community of communication. It is manifested in assuming the principle of action (distinguished in part A[17]), which is understood as a formally determined principle of universalization:

> Act only upon the maxim, according to which – on the basis of real agreement with the interested parties (*Betroffenen*) or, alternatively, their plenipotentiaries or – vicariously – on the basis of a corresponding mental experiment – you can assume that the consequences and side effects which result from their universal application in order to satisfy the interests of every single potentially interested party in some real discourse can be, without coercion, approved by everyone who is concerned by the latter (by all interested parties).[18]

It leads to another conclusion, namely that the norm is binding only when its activity (consequences) could be approved, without coercion, by all interested parties in every discourse.

---

[15] K.-O. Apel, "Diskursethik als Ethik der Mit-Verantwortung vor den Sachzwängen der Politik...," op. cit., p. 76.

[16] Ibidem, p. 76.

[17] Part A concerns the "justification of an ideal procedural principle of solving all morally – normative problems in the sense of discursive (that is purely argumentative and non-strategic, though constraint-free) creation of consensus". K.-O. Apel, "Diskursethik vor der Problematik von Recht und Politik...," op. cit., p. 60ff.

[18] K.-O. Apel, *Diskurs und Verantwortung...*, op. cit., p. 123.

Apel ultimately formulates a maxim, corresponding to Kant's categorical imperative, which is as follows: "Always act as if you were a member of an ideal community of communication."[19] In other words, every participant of a discourse must be aware of the fact that he is a member of a real community of communication, or even of a counter-factually assumed ideal community of communication. The assumption of an ideal community of communication is transcendentally significant, since the solutions arrived at within the latter constitute a condition of interpersonal communication. As a consequence, we realize that we are actually the members of a real community of communication. It is therefore true that "the institution of linguistic communication" is irremovable, and that it is realized in every language in every community. Obviously, when we speak about an ideal community of communication, which the principle of universalization of discourse ethics counter-factually concerns, there are merely attempts to accomplish it.[20] I am the participant of a real community of communication as an empirical human being who uses a particular language and who is a part of a given community, whilst when using an argumentation which has claims to universal validity, I exceed the borders of my community and I anticipate the judgment of an unspecified audience because only the latter are able to fully understand and assess my claim to universal validity.[21] In *Transformation der Philosophie,* Apel accurately points out that such a dual structure of community connects argumentation characteristic for a particular community and for a historical context with the necessity of referring to "preplanned assumptions of a post-enlightenment meta-institution of discourse."[22] Due to the possibility of referring to this meta-institution of discourse and looking from its perspective, we can question every accidental historical tradition conditioned by the world of

---

[19] K.-O. Apel, "Diskursethik vor der Problematik von Recht und Politik...," op. cit., p. 36.

[20] Ibidem, p. 36ff.

[21] K.-O. Apel, „Diskursethik als Ethik der Mit-Verantwortung den Sachzwängen der Politik...," op. cit., p. 79. This thought to a large extent refers to the notions of particular and universal audience differentiated by the representatives of rhetorical – topical school (Chaim Perelman or Theodor Viehweg).

[22] K.-O. Apel, *Diskurs und Verantwortung...*, op. cit., p. 154ff.

daily life. It also allows the solution of the conflicts of interests which occur in daily life as a part of non-coercion discourse. In order to illustrate the latter, Apel gives an example of international politics, specifically, disarmament negotiations which lack any legal sanction that would lead to conflict resolution, and where the solution of such a problem is only made possible by means of discourse rules supplemented with responsibility ethics. Apel is aware of the fact that relying on morality and justice of negotiating politicians does not suffice to resolve a particular conflict. This is precisely why this principle of supplementing discourse rules with ethics of responsibility is so highly valued. The latter supports the project of creating communication frames – a requirement which is never satisfied, but rather progressive by its very nature.[23] Apel presents the principle of supplementing the ethics of responsibility in the following way:

> Primarily, all patterns of behaviour should aim at ensuring the survival of the human race; secondly, an ideal community of communication should be realized in a real one. The former goal is a sine qua non condition of the latter, and the latter goal enhances the meaning of the former, the meaning which is already anticipated with every argument.[24]

The supplementation principle allows discourse ethics to fulfil the function of political ethics of responsibility since it reveals why it is necessary – also from the perspective of universalization principle – to strategically manage one's own political goals. Consequently, the supplementation principle requires ethically responsible politics.[25]

An ideal ethics of communication implies that all potential participants of a discourse have equal rights and bear equal co-responsibility for all possible problems of community of communication caused by everyday life, as well as for solving the latter exclu-

---

[23] K.-O. Apel, "Diskursethik vor der Problematik von Recht und Politik...," op. cit., p. 37.

[24] K.-O. Apel, *Transformation der Philosophie*, op. cit., p. 431. Apel calls it here "the second regulative principle which constitutes the basis of long-term moral strategy of every man's activity". See also: idem, *Diskurs und Verantwortung...*, op. cit., p. 145ff. This touches upon the supplementation principle (*Ergänzungsprinzip*).

[25] K.-O. Apel, "Diskursethik vor der Problematik von Recht und Politik...," op. cit., p. 61.

sively by means of arguments. Apel points out, at the same time, that the fact of acknowledging fundamental norms of an ideal community of communication means that particular solutions of moral problems, conditioned by a given situation, should not be anticipated on the level of transcendental–pragmatic grounds.[26] He accurately emphasises that particular solutions of moral problems should be the issue of practical discourses carried out by people entangled in a given situation. As I believe, legal discourse is a part of such practical discourses. It is obviously problematic whether a non-coercive discourse allows state coercion. Apel allows the justification of legal norms, referring to argumentation similar to that which accompanies politics.[27] Apel points out, however, that the supplementation principle distinguishes between real conditions and an ideal community of communication, which allows the possibility "of using counter-strategy of power administration against anti-authority strategies."[28] The abovementioned universalization principle obliges all participants of the discourse to arrive at a non-strategic consensus, namely, one that is free from authority and control. Realistically speaking, however, this requirement cannot be met and, as a consequence, means of coercion can be exceptionally applied in order to stop discursively distorting authority. According to Apel, the situation in which discourse ethics will be recalled in order to justify the coercion of acknowledging the validity of the binding nature of legal norms is only seemingly paradoxical since what the latter involves is "arriving at a consensus with a strategically counter-strategic coercion."[29] The monopoly of the authority of a certain state under the rule of law would, to a great extent, allow individuals to be driven by moral considerations and act morally without risk.

On account of the latter, Apel concludes that discourse ethics is a formal and procedural one, though its principles are not entirely

[26] K.-O. Apel, "Diskursethik als Ethik der Mit-Verantwortung vor den Sachzwängen der Politik…," op. cit., p. 78.

[27] Broadly on this issue see: K.-O. Apel, "Diskursethik vor der Problematik von Recht und Politik…," op. cit., p. 40ff.

[28] Ibidem, p. 57: "*Strategiekonterstrategien* bzw. *Anti – Gewalt – Gewaltausübung* zu praktizieren."

[29] Ibidem, p. 57ff.

devoid of substantive content. Principles are of a regulative character, and they determine the procedures of norm institutionalisation as well as the ways of carrying out discourses devoted to them. It is, therefore, why discourse ethics ensures discursive transfer of fundamental issues, indispensable in the process of creating substantive norms. In other words, due to the principles of discourse ethics we know what limitations were placed on differentiated patterns and forms of life, namely that they should provide all concerned parties with the ability to arrive at the consensus in all important problems, also the ones implied in the future.[30] What Apel means by the latter are conditioning (regulative) restrictions which, by their very nature, enable the consensus on all important issues to all those to whom they relate or may relate to, because that is the meaning of regulative idea. In turn, the ability to achieve consensus constitutes the principle of discourse ethics (practical discourse).

It should be pointed out that Apel himself stresses that "the fundamental norms of discourse ethics do not prescribe any particular form of self-realization or the good life," on the contrary, they require tolerance and protection of the multiplicity of existing forms of life. The only thing required by discourse ethics is that all individuals and cultural as well as social forms of life subject their moral decisions and judgements to the discourses and assessments that acknowledge the priority of universally valid norms of justice and co-responsibility for problems common to humanity. Apel believes that every individual - already when reading the morning newspaper - should think about how it might - as far as it is possible - participate in the organization of collective responsibility.[31] Such an organization of collective responsibility consists of the participation of virtually all of the individuals participating in practically significant discourses that take place at the level of various institutions, starting - as Apel writes - from the level of legislation and ending with furnishing a kindergarten.

---

[30] K.-O. Apel, *Diskurs und Verantwortung…*, op. cit., p. 210: "Die philosophische Begründung der Diskursethik liefert nur - allerdings - ein *formales* (*prozedurales*) *Argumentationsprinzip* für praktische Diskurse überhaupt: nämlich ein Prinzip im Sinne der von mir skizzierten *Forderung der Konsensfähigkeit der gültigen Problemlösungen für alle Betroffenen* - auch für die voraussichtlich in der Zukunft Betroffenen."

[31] K.-O. Apel, *Diskurs und Verantwortung…*, op. cit., p. 206.

Each individual on the level of argumentative discourse, being a member of the community of communication, acknowledges a kind of co-responsibility which connects humanity *a priori*, by creating a certain primordial solidarity with all possible members of the argumentative community". According to Apel, this does not allow the shirking of responsibility by escapism or parasitism. It should be also added that cultural, religious, or worldview diversities do not allow the abandonment of responsibility since they do not lead to exclusion from this community of communication. Apel then postulates the generating and nurturing of our co-responsibility, differentiated in the aforementioned manner, by increasing the global scale of "formal and informal dialogues and conferences, committees and teams working at all levels of national politics, and especially international politics, including of course the policy in the sphere of economy, culture and education."[32] This standpoint presented by Apel is similar to Dewey's conception of cooperative society. The cooperation would consist here in an endless discourse that enables the resolution of all conflicts and solution of all problems. Of course, in the real world this task is much more difficult, but not impossible. Assumptions of a democratic state of law should encourage citizens to create better chances of meeting social and political conditions that allow discursive organization of collective responsibility for joint action at national and international levels.[33] The fundamental requirement of ethical discourse consisting of creating discursively organized solidarity of responsibility of mankind for its collective actions entails the demand of the necessity to relate the imperative of maintaining human life and dignity to the social and emancipation imperatives of humanitarianism.[34]

From this perspective, a man is treated as a self-interpreting individual whose primary responsibility is the selection and hierarchization of values and behaviour. He is such an individual who has his own identity, free will, but who is subject to a team of discursive rela-

---

[32] K.-O. Apel, "Diskursethik als Ethik der Mit-Verantwortung vor den Sachzwängen der Politik...," op. cit., p. 80ff.

[33] K.-O. Apel, *Diskurs und Verantwortung...*, op. cit., pp. 205–206.

[34] Ibidem, p. 213.

tions. Everyone is treated as a full participant of social interactions who, in the struggle for his recognition in every sphere, may make different demands that must be considered and evaluated by others within the framework of intersubjective communication. Each member of the discursive community does not only have freedom of arguing, but also of assessing the arguments presented by other participants of the discourse and counter argumentation. Apel introduces an idealising assumption in which argumentation is associated with reason. He highly values victory of consensual rationality, but that might only take place under an ideal community of communication. In a discursively ordered legal order, legitimisation of moral and legal norms and the expression of approval for social institutions corresponding with the latter takes place through rational dialogue. This is especially problematic when argumentation fails in contacts with others who belong socially or culturally disadvantaged or marginalized groups and, therefore, are unable to issue the representatives who would be able to participate in discourse with the representatives of dominant culture. The lesson here is that a genuine discussion, namely, one in which the parties really care to clarify and settle the matter, is based on the rationality of domination. Every reasonable human being involved in the argumentation process is, therefore, a "citizen of two worlds" because, on the one hand, he acknowledges his membership in the perfect community of communication and, on the other hand, his participation in a certain real community. In this context, tension between these two realms is of a dialectical character, creating in effect a standard, which is intended to overcome the difference between the anticipated state of ideal communication and the actual state.[35]

The most controversial element of discourse ethics is a belief in the existence of a "final justification" – fundamental for the transcendentally-pragmatic project. According to Apel, challenging this philosophical construction would deprive the ethics of responsibility the possibility of recognising any rules as absolutely binding and, consequently, would deprive it of the opportunity to make and defend its claims to intersubjective validity. Hans Albert, when using the notion

---

[35] K.-O. Apel, *Diskurs und Verantwortung...*, op. cit., pp. 259–260.

of the so-called Münchhausen Trilemma, refers to a theoretical situation in which every justification attempt must appear.[36] The final justification is exposed to three negative outcomes: an infinite recourse of justification (*regressus in infinitum*); the vicious circle of logic (*petitio principii*); or termination of justification procedure by means of a reference to dogma.[37] Broadly speaking, Apel refutes Albert's allegation, claiming that no one can say without performative self-contradiction: "I do not refer any claim to normative correctness [accuracy - note B.W.]."[38]

It should be noted that Apel's discourse ethics aims to achieve the golden mean between the imperative of practical reason, which commands absolute respect for human dignity, and the imperative of systemic rationality. Jan Hudzik accurately notes that the aim of systemic rationality is to achieve such social justice, the ideals of which will not create any social utopias, on the contrary, they will be agreed with the existing political, economic, or cultural realities.[39] Everyone

---

[36] H. Albert, *Traktat über kritische Vernunft*, Tübingen: Mohr Siebeck Verlag, 1968. Reconstruction of the Münchhausen Trilemma is based on the following basic assumptions: (1) the current expression can be achieved only through reasoning; (2) justification is understood as a reference to external reason vis-à-vis things which are subject to justification; and (3) one can demand justification for everything, even for reasons themselves.

[37] Modest frames of this study do not allow for a thorough analysis of this issue, and therefore it has been only briefly outlined. The issue which is still disputable in the process of transcendental argumentation is whether each step of argumentation and all claims can be infinitely undermined. It should be emphasized that one cannot reasonably question the existence of proper reasoning rules (without falling into contradictions), or justify them forever (without falling into *petitio principii*), as well as resolve against such rules, assuming their existence even implicitly. The very act of questioning must be based on accepted rules of practical discourse. In this approach, the situation of the one who sensibly argues is impassable because these are the rules of discourse that cannot be questioned or challenged. Sierocka - referring to the views of Kuhlmann and Hintikki - concludes that the principle of avoiding performative contradiction leads to an irrefutable observation that "the validity of argumentation rules cannot be meaningfully challenged."

[38] K.-O. Apel, "Grenzen der Diskursethik? Versuch einer Zwischenbilanz," *Zeitschrift für philosophische Forschung* 1986, no. 40, pp. 3–31.

[39] What is crucial in this context is the reservation that only competent people, with preparation in rhetoric and theory, and knowledge in the fields of law, econom-

is responsible not only for adherence to moral norms, but also for all the consequences of their actions, including those that relate to the implementation of moral standards (for example, the requirement of authenticity and sincerity of expression), which can be in certain circumstances fatal in their effects. In this context, it is crucial to recall Apel's words, that

> ... on the one hand – on account of the responsibility for individual or collective members of real community of communication – one must combine the willingness to consensually-discursive conflict resolution according to the assessment of the situation with readiness for strategic action. For example, when confronted with the criminal world or an organization such as the Gestapo, they (people) cannot give up lies, deception, and even violence, but must try to act strategically, namely according to the rule that the maxim of their actions could be considered as being a norm subject to arrangement, if not in real, at least in a fictional, ideal discourse of all voluntary stakeholders.[40]

On the other hand, if there is a violation of moral norms in the name of accountability requirements, it imposes a duty to appoint a

> ... commitment to cooperate in a long-term, approximate abolition of the differences between the historically conditioned situation of the real community of communication and the counter-factually anticipated ideal situation, in which the conditions of discourse would be satisfied. It is a principle of the duty of tireless involvement on the part of moral progress.[41]

We should, therefore, seek to trigger changes that will enable a practical application of the principles of discourse ethics and which will introduce the ideal of community of communication as a part of

---

ics, politics, philosophy and history, can be the beneficiaries of that justice. In other words, a participant of an argumentation process, being a full member of society, must have certain preparation in order to fully enjoy the benefits guaranteed by his communication community.

[40] K.-O. Apel, "Zasada samoufundowania swoich podstaw w hermeneutycznej rekonstrukcji historii" [The Principle of Self-Founding One's Own Basis in Hermeneutic Reconstruction of History], in: *Rozumność i racjonalność* [Reason and Rationality], ed. by T. Buksiński, Poznań: Wydawnictwo Naukowe IF UAM, 1997, p. 35.

[41] Ibidem, p. 36.

real society. Indeed, discourse ethics unites all people, while leaving room for freedom of choice among the multiplicity of possible forms of life. The principle of universalization covers basically formal realm of interpersonal relations, without destroying, but even endorsing the otherness and diversity of particular individuals involved in social interaction. It is, therefore, necessary to create such conditions for real communities of communication and practical discourses, to allow for the minimum extent of disrupting the rules and principles of argumentation, and especially to eliminate exclusion from the process of reasoning carried out by individuals or groups differing in the sense of culture, religion, or world-view. It should be once more emphasised that Apel's discourse ethics is founded on "the institution of linguistic communication" and on communicative rationality. Such a universalistic assumption allows the application of this meta-institution to all language processes, deriving from diverse cultures and other human social institutions. It is worth noting that the classical and transcendental conditions of experience have been redefined in Apel's philosophy in such a way that they take into account historical and social changeability and diversity, as well as fluidity of the discourse at the level of its content, despite the fact that he opts for a strong basis and takes a stance against relativism.[42] Discourse ethics is based on two principles: consensual justification of norms, and historically-pragmatic setting of standards. Participating in a rational process of argumentation and complying with the rules of discourse allows the achievement of a consensus with other individuals; in other words, it enables participants to seek the best solution of real conflicts arising from differences or even conflicts of practical interest. As a result, Apel believes that argumentative rationality, and a core ethical principle underlying it, constitutes a reference to intersubjective relationships which were not actually covered by Kant's moral law, and the regulation of which should constitute a real sense of law.[43] Referring to the ongoing discussion in the previous delibera-

---

[42] This redefinition is caused by taking into consideration social, cultural and linguistic conditioning of the individual and acknowledging that the structure of "pure subject" is secondary (artificial) in comparison with intersubjective subject.

[43] K.-O. Apel, "Diskursethik als Verantwortungsethik – eine postmetaphysische Transformation…," op. cit., p. 10.

tions, it is worth noting that, according to Apel, political orientation on human rights (treated as fundamental rights in democratic countries) in international law can explain the transcendentally pragmatic basis for the universal application of law with the ethics of an ideal community of communication.[44] Our conduct in an ideal and non-ideal situation of international relations must ultimately be the subject of a discursive ethics of co-responsibility. In other words, our actions, communication, and cooperation on international policy must be acceptable to all alleged members of a potential community.

2. Jürgen Habermas' theory of discursive reconstruction of law

The search for Rawls' *overlapping consensus* may take different forms, one of which is "a method of avoidance," coming down to the question: What should be the minimum that must be adopted, and if it must be accepted, what should be its minimum contentious form?[45] As pointed out by Kenneth Baynes, this interpretation comes close to the model of "conversational constraints" proposed by Bruce Ackerman, and Charles Larmore's model of discursive legitimacy.[46] Ackerman proposes that in the event of a dispute as to a specified value, one should neither refer to some common values, nor attempt to explain this moral disagreement on the basis of potentially neutral conditions, but rather to solve the problem by introducing premises which everyone agrees to. The author of *Social Justice in the Liberal State* noted in his famous article "Why Dialogue" that fundamental rights are defined in the dialogue – understood as *modus vivendi*. In

---

[44] K.-O. Apel, "Discourse Ethics, Democracy, and International Law...," op. cit., p. 57, p. 66.

[45] J. Rawls, *Political Liberalism*, New York: Columbia University Press, 1996, p. 143. The "method of avoidance" consists in the fact that one cannot agree on the conception of good, but only on the principles of justice, rejecting all that one cannot reasonably agree on beyond the realm of politics and, hence, outside the public sphere.

[46] K. Baynes, "Discourse Ethics and Civil Society," in: *Universalism vs. Communitarianism: Contemporary Debates in Ethics*, ed. by D. Rasmussen, Cambridge Mass: The MIT Press, 1990, p. 74.

pursuing this dialogue, supported by actual premises, the individuals work out ways in which the differences or even social conflicts focused around the concept of good can be eliminated[47]. The theory of Ackerman's argumentation is, therefore, situated in opposition to German theory of discourse, which does not recognize virtually any limits of dialogue[48] and thus it is explicitly oriented to the search for consensus rather than, as in this case, the elimination of communicatively-interpretative distortions.

Larmore, in turn, introduces the institution of the "universal norm of rational dialogue," whereby in the event of a dispute over the specific issue, the interlocutors wishing to solve the problem through a dialogue should disregard the convictions rejected by their interlocutor: "1) in order to construct an argument based on his/her other beliefs or 2) in order to move to another aspect of the problem, where the possibility of agreement seems to be higher."[49] Both of them propose, therefore, removing from the argumentative process some personal points of view that cannot be agreed on, but neither Rawls' method of avoidance, nor Ackerman's or Larmore's "limited dialogue," allow for *a priori* exclusion of any circumstances that the participants of the discourse might disagree on. In addition, the obtained consensus is not immutable, but the arrangements achieved in the public debate are open for future discursive claims.

2.1. The role of procedural communicative rationality in justification of law

John Rawls' conception was – in a particularly interesting way – critically developed in the philosophy of law by the author of *The Theory of Communication*. At this point, I would like to demonstrate the fea-

---

[47] B. Ackerman, *Social Justice in the Liberal State*, New Haven: Yale University Press, 1980, p. 9; idem, "Why Dialogue," *Journal of Philosophy* 1989, vol. 86, no. 1, p. 16.

[48] Critically, on the issue of *conversational restraints* see: J. Habermas, *Between Facts and Norms. Contributions to a Discourse Theory of Law and Democracy*, Cambridge, Mass.: The MIT Press, 1998, pp. 308–311.

[49] Ch. Larmore, *Patterns of Moral Complexity*, Cambridge: Cambridge University Press, 1986, p. 53.

tures that guide Rawls' constructivist approach in the direction of Jürgen Habermas' discursive ethics, particularly the one referring to the idea of deliberative democracy. The theory of discourse is in fact directly applicable to the theory of democracy. The assumption that every participant of the discourse has the opportunity to present every argument means that the interpretation of individual preferences cannot be arbitrarily excluded. What is problematic is the existence of legitimate arguments in favour of excluding some preferences or conceptions of good from the impact on the choice of principles of justice, which could not be rejected by any participant of the discourse.[50] Such an approach to social justification of political principles corresponds to the rudimentary idea of discourse ethics, which assumes that the norm is justified only if all participants of the actual discourse can agree on it, and in the situation where the force of argument prevails over the argument of violence.[51] In addition, undertaking a discourse creates the obligation to abide by certain claims to validity (rationality, truth, honesty, and fairness of what is said). Of course, the discourse on rights is subject to certain limitations arising precisely from the existing legal order.[52] What seems most crucial in the context of the latter are the limitations arising from democracy, which, paradoxically enough, are also subject to discursive justification.

It is important to distinguish different types of discourses, depending on the assumed limitations, which allows the statement that a legal discourse differs from a moral one, as well as both of them differing in their limitations from political discourse.[53] Consequently,

---

[50] K. Baynes, "Discourse Ethics and Civil Society," op. cit., p. 76.

[51] J. Habermas, "Moralität und Sittlichkeit. Treffen Hegels Einwände gegen Kant auch auf die Diskursethik zu?" in: *Das Problem Hegels und die Diskursethik,* ed. by W. Kuhlmann, Frankfurt am Main: Suhrkamp Verlag, 1986.

[52] R. Alexy, *Theorie der juristischen Argumentation,* Frankfurt am Main: Suhrkamp Verlag, 1978, p. 62ff.

[53] Broadly on this issue see: J. Habermas, "Towards a Communication-Concept of Rational Collective Will-Formation. A Thought-Experiment," *Ratio Juris* 1989, vol. 2, no. 2, p. 147ff. This issue is connected with a controversial and widely debated thesis that legal discourse constitutes a special case of practical discourse. Habermas, in *Between Facts and Norms* (op. cit.), writes that these two discourses overlap. The rational discourse presupposed by the discourse principle accordingly branches out, on one

the model of discursive ethics neither implies nor requires that unanimous consent be the effect of every actual discourse. It is only in actual discourse that the requirements of individual autonomy may be explained and justified. Kenneth Baynes aptly notes that discourse ethics required that the compromises which are being achieved, or which have been actually achieved, should be fairly considered in the sense that the principles, rules, and arguments that order such discourses are open to public discussion, and, as a rule, they can be agreed on a deeper level of justification.[54] However, the debates taking place at this deeper level and concerning the issues of fundamental constitutional rights or a preferred model of political and legal institutions are less suitable subjects for a fair compromise or a majority rule, because it was only in the context of these laws and institutions that decision-making rules are considered reliable. Baynes further notes that changes in constitutional matters and in the basic legal institutions require a broader agreement, and even unanimity, which, as we know, is virtually impossible. Is also insufficient to solve this problem by merely introducing the so-called "stimulated discussions"[55] because even they do not provide for participation of all citizens in the same way in this public debate, and thus they cannot lead to the unanimous agreement of all. Hence, the calls to refer to the complementary theory of social institutions, in which it would be contemplated to create such institutions that are necessary to broaden the opportunities and the diversity of actual discourses in the public sphere at all levels, namely, both on the level of civil society, as well as on the political–state (constitutional) level, and, finally, on the plane of the counterfactual ideal of unaffected moral-practical discourse, understood as the ultimate justification for various forms of institutionalised debate.[56]

---

side into moral argumentation, on the other into political and legal discourses that are institutionalized in legal form and include moral questions only in regard to legal norms" (ibidem, pp. 232–233).

[54] K. Baynes, "Discourse Ethics and Civil Society," op. cit., pp. 79–79. A deeper level of justification of rights and political ideals require a recognition and consideration of the conditions and presupposition of how justification itself operates.

[55] Cf. J. Rawls, *A Theory of Justice*, Oxford: Oxford University Press, 1999, p. 313ff.

[56] K. Baynes, "Discourse Ethics and Civil Society," op. cit., p. 79.

Reconstruction of law from the discursively-theoretical point of view stands for the application of procedural rationality with the support of social order and system of laws. Habermas understands by the latter the rights that citizens must give to each other if they want to organize their coexistence with the norms of positive law.[57] In *The Theory of Communication Action,* Habermas approaches from the belief that the source of communicative rationality is a certain unifying power of discourse, which establishes – without any coercion – consensus among the participants. By communicative rationality, therefore, he understands speech based on arguments by means of which diverse participants of the discourse overcome their initially subjective beliefs, and, due to the fact that they commonly share reasonably justified assumptions, they come to the unity of the objective world and to the intersubjectivity of their life-relation.[58] In this way, the participants of the discourse (citizens) not only determine the truth of propositions and efficacy of teleological actions (theoretical discourse – cognitive – instrumental rationality), correctness (rightness) of norms of actions (practical discourse – moral – practical rationality) or comprehensibility or well–formedness of symbolic constructs (explicative discourse),[59] but also rightness of legal norms (legal discourse). Law is, therefore, understood as the expression of "the reasonable regulation of interaction in an intersubjectively shared form of life."[60] In other words, communicative reason is confirmed in the binding force of intersubjective agreement and mutual recognition, but it also provides a common universe of life forms. Communication action is of an emancipation character, since it confirms the desire to overcome the discord by means of argumentation and it manifests systematic interest of reason in ensuring material conditions that enable its fullest development. Habermas writes in this context that the communication action is renewed with every act of unfettered understanding, with every moment of life in solidarity, with successful personaliza-

---

[57] J. Habermas, *Between Facts and Norms…*, op. cit., p. 82. See also: K. Tuori, "Discourse Ethics and the Legitimacy of Law," *Ratio Juris* 1989, vol. 2, no. 2, pp. 125–142.

[58] J. Habermas, *The Theory of Communication Action*, op. cit., p. 10.

[59] Ibidem p. 23.

[60] J. Habermas, *Between Facts and Norms…*, op. cit., p. 155.

tion, and redemptive emancipation. Communicative reason is present in history as the soothing power.

Everyone who joins the discourse assumes the ability of all its participants to participate in rational argumentation, to renounce violence as a means which imposes the adoption of specific reasons, and also agrees to accept the conclusions which constitute the effect of a well justified, unconstrained dialogue. To put it differently, rational argumentation conditions the truth and effectiveness of a particular communication action; it is an element that allows the assessment of judgments and activities. As a result, rationality is manifested in the fact that when the participant of an argumentative process makes a claim to validity, this act implies the existence of rules and processes that are indispensable in order to recognize a judgment as genuine or activities as effective. Furthermore, what is meant by the argumentative process is to clarify: the claims to appropriateness or comprehensibility (wellformedness); claims to truthfulness – it implies that the speaker speaks frankly; the claim to truth – the speaker communicates true sentences in such a way that the listener considers his statements to be reliable; claims to normative rightness, correctness – the statement is correct in the sense that the participants of communication action accept statements in their assumed axiological system.[61] Rationality is, thus, – as Habermas believes – of a procedural nature, and a measure of the rationality of the discourse participants is the ability to reasonably justify their views in all circumstances. This means that the concept of communicative rationality is a part of a cognitive stream of ethics, as the rules of universal, normative, and irreducible character constitute the assumption of every argumentative discourse and they allow for a consensual agreement. Habermas also assumes that the knowledge of formally-pragmatic speech acts is implicitly included in communicative activities and it has intercultural validity. The consequence of such a belief is the assumption that "the communicatively acting individuals must commit themselves to pragmatic presuppositions of a counterfactual sort."[62] In other words, the latter

[61] J. Habermas, *The Theory of Communicative Action*, op. cit., p. 39. Habermas rightly argues that it is not possible to achieve mutual understanding and consensus in the situation (reality) which is dominated by lies, deception, and manipulation.

[62] J. Habermas, *Between Facts and Norms…*, op. cit., p. 4.

must carry out the idealization consisting in the necessity of realizing the abovementioned claims to validity.

From this perspective, the rules, principles, and standards recognized in the discourse as irreducible are used for a rational designation and settlement of social expectations and, consequently, for a reduction of social tensions. It is worth noting that even in regard to law (in particular, the process of law application) the basic criterion of acceptability of the reasoning process should be sought in the universal rules of discourse.[63] It is, therefore, crucial to recall the principle which holds that:

> Any final (binding) norm must meet the condition that the effects and side effects, presumably stemming from the universal respect for the latter in order to satisfy the interests of each individual, could be accepted without coercion by all stakeholders.[64]

This principle is of a universalistic character, but it rejects Apel's ultimate transcendentally-pragmatic justification, which, according to Habermas, is neither possible nor necessary.[65] At the same time, it is the assumption of every practical discourse, being an irreducible principle.[66]

---

[63] Cf. M. Zirk-Sadowski, "Pozytywizm prawniczy a filozoficzna opozycja podmiotu i przedmiotu poznania" [Legal Positivism and Philosophical Opposition of the Subject and the Object of Cognition], in: *Studia z filozofii prawa* [Studies in the Philosophy of Law], vol. 1, ed. by J. Stelmach, Kraków: Wydawnictwo Uniwersytetu Jagiellońskiego, 2001, p. 83.

[64] J. Habermas, "Über Moralität und Sittlichkeit – Was macht eine Lebensform 'rational'?" in: *Rationalität. Philosophische Beiträge*, ed. by H. Schnädelbach, Frankfurt am Main: Suhrkamp Verlag, 1984, p. 219.

[65] Habermas' following words can be recalled as a proof of the differences in justifying validity claims: "The validity we claim for our utterances and for practices of justification differs from the *social validity or acceptance (soziale Geltung)* of actually established standards and expectations whose stability is based merely on settled custom or the threat of sanctions. The ideal moment of unconditionality is deeply ingrained in factual processes of communication, because validity claims are Janus-faced: as claims, they overshoot every context; at the same time, they must be both raised and accepted here and now … The universalistic meaning of the claimed validity exceeds all contexts, but only the local, binding act of acceptance enables validity claims to bear the burden of social integration for a context-bound everyday practice". J. Habermas, *Between Facts and Norms…*, op. cit., pp. 20–21.

[66] R. Alexy, *Theorie der juristischen Argumentation*, op. cit., p. 74. Alexy notes that this rule applies – subject to a change of human life forms and conventions of language – to any linguistically active individuals, i.e. to contemporary people.

Habermas transfers the assumptions concerning discourse ethics to deliberations concerning law, while at the same time transferring the principle of discourse to the level of law, which, despite its moral content, is neutral in relation to law and morality: "Just those action norms are valid on which all possibly affected persons could agree as participants in rational discourses."[67] Following this application, Habermas aims to find a system of rights which conforms to this discourse principle, namely such in which "it becomes clear why private and public autonomy, human rights, and popular sovereignty mutually presuppose one another."[68] The intention of the latter is the justification of the rule of law and democracy by means of the discourse principle. In this sense, rights (mostly subjective rights) are understood as elements of the legal order, which assumes co-operation of people who recognize each other as equal and free actors of law. The discourse principle implies that the conclusive, namely, binding norms (and reasons underlying them), need to be approved virtually by all members of the same political community; they "must be acceptable to all members sharing 'our' traditions and strong evaluations."[69] Of course, in the event of conflicts of interest there must be a reasonable balance between conflicting attitudes toward values and arrangements of interests, leading to a compromise. Such a compromise should occur under conditions of fair negotiations, and it also needs to be approved by virtually all parties, regardless of whether the same reasons gave rise to this agreement. Law regulates interpersonal relationships between actors who recognize one another as equal and free members of the community created only by legal norms.[70] Belonging to such a community requires that everyone must be able to expect from everyone else the compliance to binding norms. It should be noted that the "private autonomy extends as far as the legal subject does *not* have to give others an account or give publicly acceptable reasons for her action plans."[71] Therefore, it be-

---

[67] J. Habermas, *Between Facts and Norms…*, op. cit., p. 107.

[68] Ibidem, p. 84.

[69] Ibidem, p. 108.

[70] Ibidem, p. 112.

[71] Ibidem, p. 120.

comes so crucial to distinguish the public sphere, which would be, unlike the private sphere, subject to significant changes in the state and supranational structures.

Application of the discourse principle in relation to law allowed Habermas to formulate five groups of basic rights which can be defined as the principles of justice manifested in legal form:

"(1) Basic rights that result from the politically autonomous elaboration of the *right to the greatest possible measure of equal individuals' liberties;*

(2) Basic rights that result from the politically autonomous elaboration of the *status of a member* in a voluntary association of consociates under law;

(3) Basic rights that result immediately from the *actionability* of rights and from the politically autonomous elaboration of individual *legal protection;*

(4) Basic rights to equal opportunities to participate in processes of opinion (and will)formation in which citizens exercise their *political autonomy,* and through which they generate legitimate law;

(5) Basic rights to the provision of living conditions that are socially, technologically, and ecologically safeguarded, insofar as the current circumstances make this necessary if citizens are to have equal opportunities to utilize the civil rights listed in (1) through (4)."[72]

Habermas recognizes modern law as a system operating in the medium of basic rights, which not only constitute a part of the structure, but also directly determine the function of law. Distinguished fundamental rights are not hierarchical, but they are designed to functionally combine private and public spheres (or rather political sphere by means of public one) of human autonomy. The categories of rights presented by Habermas are given, therefore, as specific thematic areas. The above distinction and understanding of these rights in the theory of discourse is, according to Habermas, to explain the inherent relation between human rights and sovereignty of the people, and

[72] Ibidem, pp. 122–123.

also to solve the paradox of deriving legitimacy of law from legality. Habermas, in *The Theory of Communication Action,* ultimately comes to the conclusion that the procedural nature of the reconstruction of law is manifested in the fact that it is only the discourse principle and not pre-positive (natural or moral) law that limits the generation of new rights. The discourse principle requires, in particular, the establishment of rights (2), which govern the membership of a particular association of common law and, thereby, protect the membership of that community. Moreover, it should be noted that Habermas argues that:

> ... the classic liberal rights – to personal dignity, to life, liberty, and bodily integrity; to freedom of movement, freedom in the choice of one's vocation, property, the inviolability of one's home, and so on – are interpretations of, and ways of working out, what we might call a "general right to individual liberties," however these may be specified.[73]

In other words, legitimated law does not require anything other than the mobilization of citizens' communication competence. Habermas' theory of discourse is based on the belief that human reason is so strong that it can halt the progressive atomization and fragmentation of a social environment, which pose a threat to traditional values integrating social life, such as equality, solidarity and mutual assistance. Habermas' "human reason – public reason" is able to create normative conditions and institutions that restrain this process of breakdown and instability. The medium, which is to prevent the latter, is a discursively justified law. Law is one of the manifestations of lifeworld (*Lebenswelt*),[74] and its primary function is a constitutive one. Law should care for a man, but this concern is manifested mainly in imposing and reinforcing the idea of justice and equality, namely in the application of the concept of lifeworld in the world of the systemic society which we face today.

---

[73] Ibidem, pp. 125–126.

[74] The concept of "lifeworld" refers to Edmund Husserl's ideas and it concerns pre-interpretive and pre-reflective background of everyday life. It includes a set of axiomatically treated social activities, while at the same time referring to the tradition and established ways of thinking and acting.

2.2. Communicative reinforcement of democracy – deliberative policy

According to Habermas, law must be used if the discourse principle is to be realized – by means of equal rights in terms of communication and participation – as a principle of democracy in legislative procedure. Law, as a part of social order, should be involved in procedural rationality of discourse ethics. In this sense, law requires continuing legitimization. The burden of the legitimization of law will be borne by its democratic origins.[75] In other words, positive law does not borrow its legitimacy from superior moral law, but from the procedures of reasonable creation of opinions and will. When focusing on the sphere of law and politics, the main emphasis is placed on prudent action, cultivating Aristotle's *phronēsis* as practical wisdom, which is used by Habermas in a redefined sense.[76] What, therefore, constitutes the underlying basis of the legitimacy of law is the belief that people/citizens know best what should or should not constitute the text of law, and the discourse becomes here a tool by means of which they can actively participate in its creation. Communication theory restores the lost link between ethics and politics, stressing that the public should be guided primarily by principles deriving from practical rationality rather than instrumental ones. It should again be noted that practical rationality consists in argumentative agreement that was approved by all participants of the discourse and not only by those who were interested in achieving benefits. In addition, discursively produced and intersubjectively shared beliefs have, at the same time, a motivating force, and they imply a tacit acceptance of obligations, expressing the very communication power of common beliefs.[77] Ethical-political discourses should at the same time meet those conditions of communication that are necessary for hermeneutic self-communi-

---

[75] J. Habermas, *Between Facts and Norms…*, op. cit., p. 428. Habermas writes: "With the growth and qualitative transformation of governmental tasks, the need for legitimation changes; the more the law is enlisted as a means of political steering and social planning, the greater is the burden of legitimation that must be borne by the *democratic genesis* of law."

[76] Ibidem, p. 9.

[77] Ibidem, p. 147.

cation of the community and for genuine self-understanding, which, consequently, should enable a resolution in favour of a certain form of life. Ethical-political discourses entail a belief that practical will is a manifestation of a shared form of life, or rather "the reasonable regulation of interaction in an intersubjectively shared form of life."[78] This is possible only through undistorted communication, which protects members against attacks and reprisals from those who prefer a different lifestyle, while it does not tear them from their own traditions, culture, or "genuine contexts of experience and interests."[79] Such an approach points out a convergence of Habermas' views with those of republicanism. Politics constitutes here the reflective form of ethical life; it is understood as the means by which members of the political community become citizens who are aware of their rights, without sacrificing inter-community relationships, or who even support the latter.[80]

Discursive theory of law conceives the democratic state of law as an institutionalization of procedures and communicative objectives for discursive creation of opinions and will - based on legitimated law (which protects private autonomy) - which then enables the legitimised law making (using political autonomy).[81] In order to justify this legitimization, Habermas introduces the concept of "deliberative policy," referring to Joshua Cohen's concept of "deliberative democracy."[82] Cohen argues that the decisive criterion for the democratic

---

[78] Ibidem, p. 155.

[79] Ibidem, p. 182. Habermas accurately points out that: "Discourses for achieving self-understanding require that the cultural traditions formative of one's own identity be dealt with in a manner at once anxiety-free, reflexive, and open to learning. In the present context, it is especially important that there be no nonparticipants in processes of self-reassurance; in principle, the taking of a yes/no position cannot be delegated to others."

[80] J. Habermas, "Human Rights and Popular Sovereignty: The Liberal and Republican Versions," *Ratio Juris* 1994, vol. 7, no. 1, p. 7; idem, "Drei normative Modelle der Demokratie," in: idem, *Die Einbeziehung des Anderen. Studien zur politischen Theorie*, Frankfurt am Main: Suhrkamp Verlag, 1999, pp. 279–280.

[81] J. Habermas, *Between Facts and Norms...*, op. cit., p. 437.

[82] J. Cohen, "Deliberation and Democratic Legitimacy," in: *The Good Polity. Normative Analysis of the State*, ed. by A. Hamlin, Ph. Pettit, Oxford: Blackwell, 1989, pp. 17–34. The issue of deliberative democracy is broadly discussed in Chapter I, Section 5.1. of this dissertation.

ideal is the assumption that the conditions of social order were directed by means of a rational public argumentation among equal citizens. Citizens must be naturally confident that their institutions assume legitimated framework conditions for the unencumbered search for a resolution by means of a public argumentation.[83] Habermas is, nevertheless, critical of Cohen's conception, noting that the latter lacks "the relation between decision-oriented deliberations, which are regulated by *democratic procedures*, and the informal processes of opinion-formation in the public sphere."[84]

The theory of discourse proposed by Habermas is a combination of liberal and republican approaches to the democratic process, integrating them – as he says – "in the concept of an ideal procedure for deliberation and decision making."[85] The said democratic procedure puts emphasis on the rules of discourse and forms of argumentation, the content of which is based on significant grounds aimed at agreement – on the structure of linguistic communication. Habermas, relating to Mead's views, aptly notes that "to the extent that normative validity claims become dependent on confirmation through communicatively achieved consensus, principles of democratic will-formation and universalistic principles of law are established in the modern state."[86] Referring to the republican model, discursive theory of democracy emphasizes the role of public process focused on shaping opinions, and will that can be institutionalized within the specific procedures and communicative assumptions, and which are ultimately manifested in the rule of law. Such procedural approach to the state of law allows the reaching of different compromises between diverse interests, which constitutes a distinguishing feature of the liberal model. Habermas argues that the discursive theory, namely, the procedure and communicative assumptions of democratic opinion-forming processes, not only legitimizes (liberal model) or constitutes (a republican model), but also rationalises the decisions of state authority.[87] As a result of this rationalisation, deliberative policy ob-

[83] J. Cohen, "Deliberation and Democratic Legitimacy," op. cit., pp. 21–22.

[84] J. Habermas, *Between Facts and Norms…*, op. cit., p. 307.

[85] Ibidem, p. 296.

[86] J. Habermas, *The Theory of Communicative Action*, vol. 2, op. cit., p. 96.

[87] J. Habermas, *Between Facts and Norms…*, op. cit., p. 300.

tains for itself legitimizing power in communicative power created by means of discursive structures of forming opinions and wills, which, besides money and administration, has a socially integrative function due to the assumption of rationality of the ensuing consequences. This solution enables the taking of public and political decisions despite the polarization of multicultural societies or ethical, cultural, ideological or religious pluralism. Discursive decision-making procedure and the process of arriving at agreements on important public issues in fact constitutes "the sole source of solidarity among strangers – strangers who renounce violence and, in the cooperative regulation of their common life, also concede one another the right to *remain* strangers."[88] Only such an approach to democracy provides the possibility of concluding agreements that constitute the core of contemporary public and political interpersonal relationships.

Political leaders must therefore assume neutrality of the procedure, namely of the rules of discourse and forms of argumentation, taking care only of a discursively correct choice of arguments, which would allow them to convince their citizens of the rightness of the quoted reasons. Habermas cites here B. Ackerman's words:

> No reason is a good reason if it requires the power holder to assert: (a) that his conception of the good is better than that asserted by any of his fellow citizens, or (b) that, regardless of his conception of the good, he is intrinsically superior to one or more of his fellow citizens.[89]

The author of *The Theory of Communication Action* at the same time tries to avoid dangerous effects of formulating ethical issues in political discourse, introducing a distinction between ethics as a field that permits competing conceptions of the good life and morality as an area in which it would be allowed to develop and apply some universal binding normative principles. Transition "from ethical disagreement to a higher level of abstraction, characteristic for a discourse

---

[88] Ibidem, p. 308. According to Habermas, "in a pluralistic society, the theory of justice can expect to be accepted by citizens only if it limits itself to a conception that is postmetaphysical in the strict sense, that is, only if it avoids taking sides in the contest of competing forms of life and worldviews" (ibidem, p. 60).

[89] B. Ackerman, *Social Justice in the Liberal State*, New Haven: Yale University Press, 1980, p. 11.

about justice" is therefore treated by him as a special case of the general argumentation rule. Habermas, therefore, advocates pluralism of values (systems of values). In public discourse, a consensus among groups which represent competing values is only possible by complying with universal rules of discourse. Discourse ethics has a universal dimension, which goes beyond cultural relativism of ethical content and, as such, it must have a cognitive, universalistic, and formal character. From this point of view, Habermas writes about "the nation of citizens," which finds its identity not in ethnic and cultural commonalities, but in the practice of citizens who actively exercise their rights to participation and communication.[90] Thus, he refers to Karl Jaspers' words, for whom a common ground for a plurality of faith and, in our approach, for the multiplicity of lifestyles, is only clear thinking, truthfulness, and the same basic knowledge. It is only after the fulfilment of these three assumptions that an unlimited communication is possible.[91] Such communication should be the base of mutual agreement between the foreign traditions and lifestyles.[92] As a result, Habermas notes that the subject and the task of political discourse (deliberative policy) is not a determination of what constitutes the idea of the good life, but the establishment of legitimate rules of procedure and rules of procedural fairness that should constitute the basis of social cooperation rather than of a defined vision of good.

When analyzing Jaspers, Habermas notes that the veracity of conscious life serves as an ethical criterion by which on can judge existential capacity of propounded views (in Jaspers' understanding – faith).

---

[90] J. Habermas, *Between Facts and Norms…*, op. cit., p. 494. He notes subsequently that: "In a pluralistic society, the constitution expresses a formal consensus. The citizens want to regulate their living together according to principles that are in the equal interest of each and thus can meet with the justified assent of all. Such an association is structured by relations of mutual recognition in which each person can expect to be respected by all as free and equal. Each and every person should receive a three-fold recognition: they should receive equal protection and equal respect in their integrity as irreplaceable individuals, as members of ethnic or cultural groups, and as citizens, that is, as members of the political community" (ibidem, p. 496).

[91] K. Jaspers, *Die philosophische Glaube angesichts der Offenbarung*, München: R. Piper Verlag, 1984, p. 7.

[92] J. Habermas, *Vom sinnlichen Eindruck zum symbolischen Ausdruck*, Frankfurt am Main: Suhrkamp Verlag, 1997, Chapter II.

For this purpose, we assume equal respect for every person, regardless of what lifestyle they prefer and what traditions underlie their decisions in life. According to Habermas, a legitimate articulation of identity of such a coloured society-nation should be a "constitutional patriotism," in which loyalty to the constitution is expressed in the consistent participation of all citizens in social and political life. This is a loyalty to universal laws, which are treated by Habermas as a prerequisite for the coexistence of people, especially in a multicultural and pluralistic society. In this context, the discourse principle – formulated by Habermas – should be understood so as to exclude as invalid such norms that cannot obtain the qualified consent of all concerned parties. It follows further that the moral principle cannot be determined theoretically, but its confirmation must be the result of an intersubjective process of reaching a reflective consent (discursive verification of its claim to universality).

It is controversial, however, whether in fact the power of these rules is so strong that they can create a political community and, further, whether procedural communicative rationality may be a sufficient bonding layer between different cultural, religious, or ethnic communities. The practice of modern states, based on the principle of the democratic rule of law, seems to confirm this thesis and acts of opposition against power – legitimated in the latter way – reflected, for example, in the form of terrorist attacks of its own citizens, constitute only disruptions in communication and may not be a criterion for denying the acceptance of such a procedure. The procedure resulting from the theory of discourse would, therefore, encompass not only legislative procedures or other legitimated activities of state authority (forms of direct or indirect democracy), but also the activities of NGOs and even some acts of civil disobedience. In this sense, democracy, and hence deliberative policy, constitutes rather a more basic means of conflict resolution and of collective activity than a process that has a specific, institutional location.[93] I want to say by the latter that deliberative democracy (deliberative policy) consists of the proc-

---

[93] M.E. Warren, "The self in discursive democracy," in: *The Cambridge Companion to Habermas*, ed. by S.K. White, Cambridge – New York: Cambridge University Press, 1995, p. 169.

esses of discourse institutionalization, which aims at reaching agreement on political, economic, and social matters. Therefore, one cannot clearly point at such an institutionalised location.

This means that the boundary between the state and civil society is blurred, because the issues of economic regulations, monetary and fiscal policies, industrial development and technology, civil rights, education, etc. should be based on discursive, namely, real moral, commitment of the citizens. This conditions the process of widening the public sphere and the accumulation of the importance of public law. In this sense, civil society must be understood as *consisting of citoyen* without *bourgeois*, that is, a society which is not considered in the context of – strangely enough, necessary – economic relations. At the same time, Habermas speaks of the ethical content of "constitutional patriotism," which enhances the understanding of the multiplicity and integrity of various forms of life coexisting in a multicultural society.[94] He notes, naturally, that while such diverse forms of life can function (coexist) on an equal footing in a democratic state of law, they should at least touch on the common area of political culture. In this respect, a kind of litmus test of legitimacy of each state (and therefore legal system) is its effectiveness in the field of mediation between conflicting values. This becomes inevitable, given the fact that today's societies necessarily reflect the pluralistic and hybrid character of common identities. In my opinion, it is a greater responsiveness and negotiating power that determines the advantage of a discursive democracy over an antagonistic one.

Habermas at the same time distinguishes procedural constraints on public discourses from constraints or limitations on the range of topics open to public discourse.[95] This means that the process of shaping opinions and will – governed by the procedure of discourse – should be able to relate to the ethical issues of the good life or collective identity. It cannot be the case, for example, that considering the "ritual of circumcision" of girls and "forced marriages" in Muslim culture will be excluded from public discourse, since it belongs to

---

[94] J. Habermas, *Die Einbeziehung des Anderen. Studien zur politischen Theorie*, Frankfurt am Main: Suhrkamp Verlag, 1999, p. 263.

[95] J. Habermas, *Between Facts and Norms…*, op. cit., p. 313.

a private discourse. Thus, Habermas makes a distinction between public and private affairs in two areas, namely in terms of availability and subject matter, and in terms of regulating the powers and responsibilities. A standpoint that criticises the engagement of authority, community or society in issues such as domestic violence, and based only on the argument that they belong to the intimate sphere should be evaluated negatively. It is not the case that for this reason family members, mostly children and women, are not worth protecting and the handling of their situation in terms of gender equality and protection from violence during public hearing. Concealment of these matters behind a cloak of religiosity or privacy is an escape from responsibility and constitutes a distortion of discourse procedures. Of course, matters within the intimate sphere should be protected from criticism or insistence on the part of strangers. However, the task of deliberative policy is to extract - by means of communicative activities - controversial issues concerning lifeworld, so that after having been determined and subjected to express public discourse, these issues could be once more illuminated and brought into agreement, and so integrated with the world.

The task of law is to establish procedures and assumptions of communication (e.g. via electoral rights, freedom of speech and the media, and restrictions on the authority), which enables discursive and public development of standpoints and will. Deliberative politics - by means of civil society and the political public sphere (in Dewey's sense) - creates substantive content of this procedural paradigm of law, and thus the material power to communicate.[96] Law is, thus, not only a guarantor of freedom (which is a liberal paradigm) or the tool of substantive comparison (social paradigm), but it is the guarantor for the creation and maintenance of conditions due to which there can be spontaneous public communication, and due to which legal order can be continuously legitimated.[97] It is also important to determine

[96] Ibidem, p. 445. Emphasising the idea of self-legislation and recognizing that law is legitimized by implicit consent of the universal audience, argue in favour of placing Habermas in the mainstream of jurisprudence, which advocates a non-instrumental understanding of law as a product of culture, largely autonomous in relation to the activities of political and economic systems.

[97] A. Tschentscher, *Prozedurale Theorien der Gerechtigkeit. Rationales Entscheiden, Diskursethik und prozedurales Recht*, Baden-Baden: Nomos Verlag, 2000, p. 246.

that every citizen becomes an "author" of such a legal order, not as a participant of the discourse, but rather as a "legal subject."[98] From this point of view, rights are not merely subjective claims arising from objective rules of discourse, but universal human rights. And so we have the right to freely express our views or standpoints not because such right must be assumed for free and equal participants of the discourse, but because everyone has such a right as a legal subject.[99]

---

[98] J. Habermas, *Between Facts and Norms…*, op. cit., p. 122ff.

[99] A. Tschentscher, *Prozedurale Theorien der Gerechtigkeit…*, op. cit., p. 296. Habermas puts it as follows: "To arrive at the system of rights, then, we need the concept of the 'legal forms,' which stabilizes behavioural expectations in the manner already discussed, and the 'discourse principle,' in light of which the legitimacy of legal norms can be tested. With these we have what we need to introduce the three categories of rights *in abstracto* that generate the legal code itself by defining the status of legal persons ...". J. Habermas, *Between Facts and Norms...*, op. cit, p. 122. A. Tschentscher indicates that this statement could be interpreted in three ways: "1. Rights are justified because they are assumed already by the very 'concept of legal form'; 2. Rights are justified because the discourse principle defines their binding nature as a result of verifying the norms of activity; or 3. Rights are justified because when applying the discourse principle, it must be stated that legally formed norms of activity have always assumed those rights." (A. Tschentscher, op. cit., p. 297). See also: J. Habermas, *Towards a Communication-Concept...*, op. cit., p. 153ff. It seems that Tschentscher's standpoint is not fully justified in Habermas' views. In this context it is crucial to quote the following words of Habermas: "According to this principle, just those regulations are legitimate that satisfy the requirement that the rights of each be compatible with equal rights for all." Idem, *Between Facts and Norms...*, op. cit., p. 123. In this sense, the right to freely express one's views or standpoint constitutes a manifestation or the effect of imbuing legally formed political autonomy, or, in other words, the possibility of discursive implementation of political autonomy. This possibility is our right, because it is legally guaranteed, namely an institutionalized condition of the possibility to participate in the discourse of lawmaking. Shaping the possibilities in the medium of law is also understood as shaping its framework and limits. Legal code is intended to express only that which stabilizes mutual opportunities and expectations in relation to common (and not community) actions. Therefore, the latter is intended to ensure: moral autonomy (private rights) and our sovereignty (political rights). It constitutes a novelty to discourse ethics, namely the minimum conditions of discourse are stabilized (institutionalized) in such a way that a particular community can decide what is in the moral sphere (private space of autonomous decisions), and what is not. As a result, it can also decide what should be regulated as belonging to the public sphere by means of political rights. What Habermas means is to combine these spheres and rights rather than to alternatively enumerate them as Tschentscher did. Such institutionalized combination legitimizes itself, creating

In other words, a legal subject achieves such a degree of autonomy that he himself becomes a legislator of his conduct, and therefore he does not treat existing social norms as obvious, but is rather interested in the procedures of their justification.

As a result, the process of legitimization of law is based on democratic assumptions, namely on the public confirmation of the binding nature of certain rights. The universality of human rights originates from the assumption of the universal validity of convictions. Habermas assumes that a specific standpoint remains valid on the basis of rational arguments until better arguments are presented. This is important for all participants of the discourse, because they are under the influence of mutually formulated assessments and judgments, in which the dynamics of communication activity is expressed. In my opinion, the defence of "universalism" in Habermas' conception is based on the belief about the possibility of presenting a rational justification of individual beliefs and, more importantly, to achieve universal consensus on a specific ethical or legal issue. Such an assumption allows the claim that in some cases – like in Rawls' *overlapping consensus* – the achieved consensus is of permanent and rational character, and it does not only come down to changeable, coincidental covenants or utilitarian agreements.[100] Only such a consensus may constitute the source of communitarian and social solidarity, set legal certainty, and security because it does not refer to pre-political values or to subjective feelings of compassion, but relies on the universality of human rights.

Unfortunately, the transition from philosophical assumptions of Habermas' theory of discourse to universal human rights is not justified in a complete manner. Firstly, it is difficult to derive the content of the first three fundamental rights, as described by Habermas, from the very "form of law."[101] By contrast, when the starting point is the discourse principle, the criterion of the correctness of norms should

---

a peculiar *perpetuum mobile*. Ms Karolina Cern drew my attention to these issues, for which I once again expresses my gratitude.

[100] G. Borradori, "Reconstructing Terrorism. Habermas," in: idem, *Philosophy in a Time of Terror. Dialogues with Jürgen Habermas and Jacques Derrida*, Chicago: The University of Chicago Press, 2003, p. 62.

[101] J. Habermas, *Between Facts and Norms…*, op. cit., pp. 122–123.

be the ability to arrive at the consent in a rational discourse. It should also be noted that Habermas does not refer in any way to real discourses, providing justification of accuracy and fairness of norms. On the contrary, in his view, such correctness can be definitely justified in ideal discourses.[102] Such an interpretation of fundamental rights draws Habermas' conception closer to the Kantian concept of transcendental justification. It does not necessarily mean, after all, that these discourses necessarily imply universal human rights. Only a supplementation of this concept with the argument of freedom that is binding in real discourses, as suggested by Robert Alexy, which will be discussed in a moment, enables acknowledgement of their universality. The need for such an argument in real discourses, however, has not been clearly assumed in Habermas' concept.[103] Such an argument can be only indirectly interpreted from the conditions of

---

[102] The following fragment is being represented here: "This system should contain precisely the rights citizens must confer on one another if they want to legitimately regulate their interactions and life contexts by means of positive law" (ibidem, p. 122). Habermas proves that such rights can be legitimated only if they are definitely justified by ideal discourses. Cf. A. Tschentscher, *Prozedurale Theorien der Gerechtigkeit...*, op. cit., p. 298. Legal code (1)–(5) must only give the necessary conditions, namely the possibilities for this coexistence to be actually implemented.

[103] Similarly, in: E. Arens, "Der Beitrag der Diskursethik zur universalen Begründung der Menschenrechte," in: *Begründung von Menschenrechten aus der Sicht unterschiedlicher Kulturen*, ed. by J. Hoffmann, Frankfurt am Main: Verlag für Interkulturelle Kommunikation, 1991, p. 69ff. He writes: "At the same time there arises the question whether certain structurally embedded human right does not underlie these discursively justified rights. Such human right would not be the content of practical discourses but rather an assumption allowing its realization and fulfilment and thus it would belong to presupposition and procedures of the discourse. This is the right to participate in the discourses. It is possible for this right to be discursively-ethically understood as a fundamental human right." In this respect we can speak of the innate human dignity, understood as "being worthy" to speak in the discourse, and thus to become a full participant in the discourse. Dignity – construed in this way – which implies the most primordial recognition of me as a participant of (institutionalised) discourse, is also the first act which socialises me. This, in turn, leads to the conclusion that, under such understood dignity, vested in me, I must always be the subject (member) of any actual politically-legal community, because the possibility of being such an entity constitutes the necessity of belonging to any community of participants who carry out institutionalised discussions.

deliberative democracy. The discourse principle assumes here a legal form, and is transformed into a principle of democracy. However, the justification for universality and reality of human rights cannot be interpreted from the fact that democracy is the "correct" form of governance. Indeed, it is impossible to forget that real discourses (including in particular political discourses) are not free from interference and do not allow for proper extraction of relevant and fully respected fundamental rights. This is a problematic issue: how to move from ideal discourse to positive law that fully respects the principle of discourse. In other words, it makes the transition from abstract approach to law to its concretization-actuality more problematic. It is not feasible to give a simple answer, even on account of different approaches to the concept of democracy itself, as exemplified by the disputes between the representatives of concepts being the part of the so-called antagonist democracy, and the representatives of deliberative or discursive democracy as well as radical or liberal ones. This issue is further complicated by the need to dispose of the legal code, which is determined by the duty to "the creation of the status of possible legal persons, that is, of persons who belong to a voluntary association of bearers of actionable individual rights."[104]

A weak point in his conception is also the notion of the subject of law. According to Habermas, a man does not become the subject of law, but this trait constitutes his natural characteristic feature. Naturalness is combined with the ability to be a participant in discourse. To put it another way, a man assumes the natural role of subject of law only when it comes to the justification (validation) of rights. What is meant by Habermas – as I mentioned earlier – is the institutionalisation of abstract private autonomy by means of law. This represents *ratio essendi* (and even *cognescendi*) of subjective rights. It follows that without private autonomy there is no such thing as positive law. This personal autonomy is warranted by human rights (especially the classic right to liberty, life, or property) whilst political autonomy of state citizens is anchored in the principle of sovereignty of the people and, ultimately, it takes the form of "democratic *self-legislation*."[105] Subse-

[104] J. Habermas, *Between Facts and Norms...*, op. cit., p. 455.
[105] Ibidem, p. 454.

quently, by means of the democracy principle, democratic self-legislation creates the conditions of discursively pursued political autonomy, or the legitimization of the public lawmaking process. This leads to the conclusion that without the classic laws which ensure freedom, namely personal autonomy of legal entities, it is not possible to constitute the medium of legal institutionalisation of conditions under which citizens can exercise their public autonomy. Such a solution of legal entity is incomprehensible and inadequate either from dogmatic legal perspective (especially the conception of subjective rights presented in the study of civil law) or for the practice of law. Another point of controversy is the lack of a clear determination by Habermas of when an act of will is a legal obligation. Thus, for example, for Hans Kelsen a natural person (legal entity) is a personified unity of legal norms that oblige it to a specific action, but which also constitute a source of authority to create new legal relations. In such a sense, legal entities adopt and unconditionally abide by legal normativeness. It should be noted that, according to Kelsen, a legal norm obtains its manifestation in the sanction itself, which distinguishes it from social norms.[106] There is a lack of such external pressure in the form of sanctions in Habermas' conception, and that is its defect in the context of its practical application and compliance. Of course, this is due to some idealising assumption of the discourse principle that is manifested in the medium of law. The latter, however, does not prejudge its innocence, but it requires further positive supplementation.

The theory of communication action is based on the assumption that it is impossible to combine an abstract level concerning the validity of moral norms with a specific dimension of experience. The validity of moral norms must be then justified by means of a rational argumentation so they can have a certain purely cognitive claim to validity. In respect to relations between law and morality, however, Habermas advocates the so-called complementation thesis (*Ergänzungsthese*). Habermas writes in this context as follows:

> Rather than subordinate positive law to natural law or morality, I start with the assumption that at the postmetaphysical level of justification,

---

[106] H. Kelsen, *Reine Rechtslehre*, Wien: Franz Deuticke, 1960, p. 52ff.

> legal and moral rules are *simultaneously* differentiated from traditional ethical life and appear *side by side* as two different but mutually complementary kinds of action norms.[107]

Legal norms indeed make a claim to be consistent with moral norms and, accordingly, not to contravene the latter. This issue constitutes the so-called axiological validity. The validity of legal norms, therefore, requires compliance with procedural requirements under the rules of discourse, thus meeting the claim to impartiality. Positive law is, therefore, associated with morality through legitimating components of law (what is meant by the latter is also tetic validity). Reference to moral law enables full realization of its tasks, aiming at social integration of society. As a result, Habermas argues that positive law must be morally justifiable. Habermas, however, does not present any convincing arguments that would allow one to consider that legal norms actually raise a claim to moral correctness (*Richtigkeit*). The thesis of necessary connection between law and morality is in fact exposed to all these allegations, which are formulated against cognitivism, particularly the belief that "the world of duties" cannot be the object of cognition.[108]

3. Main assumptions of Robert Alexy's legal argumentation

Robert Alexy, in his theory of legal argumentation, treats legal discourse as a special case of general and practical argumentation. In

[107] J. Habermas, *Between Facts and Norms...*, op. cit., p. 105.

[108] Apel, among others, expresses critical views in this regard, noting that law (and as much democratic politics) should naturally be discursively-theoretically justified, in the sense of certain primordial differentiation, equal to that of morality, from a normatively-procedural discourse principle. However, this principle of all justifications should be morally neutral. As an example of this, Apel indicates the NATO intervention in Kosovo, which took place without the UN mandate, only by means of invoking human rights. It provides an instructional example for him that the problem of *Teil B* discourse ethics, as he refers to it, cannot be resolved by politically operating legal order in the contemporary world. Cf. K.-O. Apel, "On the Relationship between Ethics, International Law and Politico-military Strategy In our Time: a Philosophical Retrospective on the Kosowo Conflict," *European Journal of Social Theory* 2001, no. 1, pp. 29–40.

other words, the theory of practical discourse forms the basis for the construction of legal discourse, whilst the need to identify legal discourse is due to the shortcomings of the rules and forms of legal discourse[109]. Imperfections of the procedures and forms of practical discourse result from the fact that, first of all, rules of this discourse do not specify any normative premises as a starting point of discourse. Secondly, not all steps of justification are designated by the rules of discourse, and some rules may be satisfied only approximately. Legal discourse should serve, similarly to a practical one, compliance with the claim to correctness (equity (*Richtigkeitsanspruch*)), but with the limitation arising from the need to reflect existing law. Reasonableness of normative statements in legal discourse is thus determined by legislation, case law, and dogma, and thus is highly relative to the legislator's reason. The correctness and rationality of legal reasoning are determined by its compatibility with the procedure contained in a certain system. Alexy builds a theory of procedural legal argumentation based on the fundamental thesis: "Normative statement 'N' is right (correct) only if it could be the result of procedure 'P'."[110]

Alexy, expounding his procedural theory of discourse, enriches it with elements of liberal conception, the so-called liberal ideas of autonomy and universality, which contain moral content. The latter can be consolidated in the following few rules:

"1) Everyone who can speak may take part in discourse.
2) (a) Everyone may question any assertion.
(b) Everyone may introduce any assertion into the discourse.
(c) Everyone may express his or her attitudes, wishes, and needs.
3) No speaker may be prevented from exercising the rights laid down in (1) and (2) by any kind of coercion, internal or external to the discourse."[111]

---

[109] R. Alexy, *Theorie der juristischen…*, op. cit., C I. It should be stressed once again that the problem of *Sonderfallthese* constitutes a key element of criticism against discursive justification of human rights.

[110] R. Alexy, *Recht, Vernunft, Diskurs. Studien zur Rechtsphilosophie*, Frankfurt am Main: Suhrkamp Verlag, 1995, p. 96.

[111] R. Alexy, *Theorie der juristischen…*, op. cit., p. 240; idem, *Recht, Vernunft, Diskurs…*, op. cit., p. 130 (idem, "Discourse Theory and Human Rights," in: *Challenges to*

As a result, Alexy determines the validity of each norm according to whether it is the effect of a specified and binding procedure, namely some rational discourse. It follows, therefore, that law is not a mere set of positive rules, but it must take into account discursive reasons and justifications, which imposes the need to combine law with practical and moral discourse. The issue of legal argumentation plays a considerable role in contemporary discussions on law. The fundamental principle of a democratic state is the right to present arguments, but also to obtain arguments from a person who occupies a specific position. You can even attempt the assertion that, according to representatives of discursive theory, the possibility of being a man equals the possibility of making arguments. The theory of legal discourse treats law not only as professional (specialised) speech, but also as a discursive unity and harmony, and legal sentence is not only the text of norm or formalised act of speech but also a discursive statement. It conceptualises legal notions not only as primarily and textually associated with the norm, but also as discursive concepts.

3.1. The theory of discourse and human rights in Alexy's philosophy of law

In order to justify human rights, in *Theorie der juristischen Argumentation,* Alexy raises two basic questions. Firstly, one has to justify the rules of practical discourse, and then proceed to the justification of human rights, namely, defined rules of activity, including recognition of autonomy in action. Rules of operation, in order to develop fully, need support in the form of legal regulation, and, moreover, correct, reliable, and effective justification of rules of discourse.

The point of departure in Alexy's deliberations on the issue of combining the theory of discourse with human rights is Kant's concept of human rights, which emphasises a respect for private and public autonomy and the implementation of the principle of univer-

---

Law and the End of the 20th Century (*17th IVR World Congress Bologna,* 17–21 June 1995, vol. II: Plenary and Parallel Sessions), Bologna: Cooperativa Libraria Universitaria Editrice Bologna, 1995, p. 22).

sality. Alexy treats these conditions as necessary presuppositions of arguments, and by means of them he creates a theory of "analytical liberalism."[112] The main requirements of this theory include the principles of universality, freedom, and autonomy. The principle of universality implies that all people have certain rights. Autonomy, on the other hand, is divided, similarly as in the work of Habermas, into private and public. Private autonomy ensures individual choice and implementation of individual concepts of good. Public autonomy, by contrast, involves the selection and implementation of political concepts of justice and good. The principle of autonomy can "achieve" full development only in a democratic, constitutional state, in which human rights and fundamental rights are guaranteed and respected. In a democratic state of law, "autonomous" human rights, particularly those expressed in the universal theory of liberal policy, play the most significant role.

In order to justify human rights, Robert Alexy formulates three types of theses.[113] Firstly, he refers to a transcendentally-pragmatic version of justifying the rules of discourse. He touches upon the universal validity of discourse principles because the justification of human rights can be – according to him – achieved only by a strict and accurate compliance with discourse procedures. It is necessary to respect proper, justified, reliable norms, which reject unilaterally imposed arguments. A discursively established norm, and therefore one consistent with the argumentation of liberty and equality, obtains the consent (approval) when the consequences of compliance with such norm are also generally accepted. Freedom and equality are normatively introduced as discourse principles, whereas general consensus is understood as an argument for the correctness and validity of the norm. Alexy's argumentation lacks explication of the meaning of accuracy and validity notions. Alexy only generally describes correctness (*Richtigkeit*) as the criterion of an ideal discourse. Moreover, justification of the practical discourse rules – as the rules of speech – constitutes the necessary presupposition of justifying human rights, namely rules or norms of action. The introduction of correctness ar-

[112] R. Alexy, *Recht, Vernunft, Diskurs...*, op. cit., p. 10.

[113] Ibidem, pp. 127–164 (Chapter: "Diskurstheorie und Menschenrechte").

gument is a consequence of the thesis about necessary relation (*Verbindungsthese*), according to which Alexy points at a necessary conceptual link between law and morality.[114] A claim to correctness is, on the one hand, a necessary element of positive law; on the other hand, it can and should be fulfilled in a practical and moral discourse. A claim to correctness of law is an instance of a normative claim of general theory of discourse. In this context, the accuracy and equity of law depend on the justifiable character of claims, theses, rules, and arguments of the theory of discourse. It also follows that a non-positivist conception of law must be based on at least rudimentary non-relativistic ethics.[115] For this purpose, law must be morally falsified, and criteria for evaluating whether a given legal norm is morally correct are the rules and principles of discourse ethics. Thus, Alexy takes the view that moral correctness of any norm is cognitively justifiable.

The author of *Theorie der juristischen Argumentation* builds an abstract principle of Habermas' discourse and argues that "a norm can only find universal agreement in a discourse if the consequences of its general observance for the satisfaction of everyone's interest can be accepted by all."[116] Justification of "universally – pragmatic" rules of discourse is to demonstrate that the validity of certain rules is a condition of interpersonal communication. Validity of certain rules is constitutive to enable certain speech acts. Resignation of these speech acts is not possible without a denial of forms of behaviour considered to be typically human. What constitutes a key issue and a problem, however, is the justification of the liberal conception of theory of discourse. Alexy, unlike Habermas, justifies universal validity of discourse principles by using a three-part argument. The first part covers transcendental argument, which consists of two premises and a conclusion. It has the form of *modus ponens*:

1) Premise: affirmative act of speech is always required;

---

[114] Broadly on his issue see: R. Alexy, "On Necessary Relations Between Law and Morality," *Ratio Juris* 1989, vol. 2, no. 2, pp. 167–183; idem, *Begriff und Geltung des Rechts*, Freiburg – München: Karl Alber Verlag, 1992, p. 41ff.

[115] R. Alexy, *Begriff und Geltung des Rechts*, op. cit., p. 93.

[116] R. Alexy, *Recht, Vernunft, Diskurs…*, op. cit., p. 131 (idem, "Discourse Theory and Human Rights," op. cit., p. 23).

2) Premise: There is a list of specific rules, which are conditions of the correctness of expressing affirmative act of speech. These rules read:
   a) by saying something, one takes into account the claims to truthfulness and correctness (and other discourse premises),
   b) the claims to truthfulness and correctness, in consequence, require compliance with the claim to justifiability,
   c) a claim to justifiability implies *prima facie* obligation to justify an assertion on demand,
   d) the justification should take into account the claims to equality, non-compulsion, and universality.

Conclusion: All categories and principles that are binding in discourse are required in argumentation and must be respected.[117]

Therefore, transcendental argument can be reformulated in the following formal sentence:

Premise 1: x is necessary (dialogue and argumentation are necessary),

Premise 2: y is necessary, and thus x is possible,

Conclusion: y is necessary (all categories and discourse principles are needed, and thus it is required to comply with the so-called necessary presuppositions, such as freedom and equality of argumentation).

Transcendental argument may indicate the hypothetical importance of specific discourse principles, which must be necessarily taken into account by everyone who has an interest in the correctness in assertive speech acts. Indeed, they manifest liberal ideas of autonomy and universality. According to Alexy, "he who all his life did not make any statement (in the meaning defined by (a-c) and did not give any justification (in the meaning defined by (d)), is not involved in a universal form of life."[118] In other words, co-existence is impossible, apart from extreme exceptions, without problematizing statements and asking questions (making assertive speech acts).

---

[117] Ibidem, p. 133ff. Cf. also: P. Grill, "Alexys Version einer transzendental-pragmatischen Begründung der Diskursregeln im Unterschied zu Habermas," *Archiv für Rechts- und Sozialphilosophie* 1997, vol. 83, p. 207ff.

[118] R. Alexy, *Recht, Vernunft, Diskurs…*, op. cit., p. 139.

Every act of speech is inherently combined with argumentation. In turn, communication actions, by their very nature, are argumentative actions where the situation of the one who is sensibly arguing cannot be exceeded from the standpoint of the transcendental-pragmatic approach. Consequently, it can be concluded that the rules of discourse do not define a particular form of life, but reveal the potential of reason - existing in the human being - so characteristic of human community. The theory of discourse is, in this sense, preoccupied with the explanation of human nature and, therefore, it has its place in the tradition of natural law.[119]

Other elements of justification of universal discourse principles include the supplement of transcendental argument with an individual maximization of profits (rationality model deriving from Hobbes) and empirical interest of correctness. Alexy's basic thesis says that everyone, especially a particular elite - if their actions are long-term - benefits if these actions are legitimized whilst discourse principles are at least externally complied with. Moreover, legitimization of certain decisions and actions is also made possible by means of a reference to the interest of correctness. Such domination, even in a model of purposive rationality is more stable than the one based only on authority. One might obviously conclude that it is not necessarily the one who maximizes his profits, as a result of a long-term calculation of costs/profits, who must adopt Alexy's concept of equity (correctness) to protect their own benefit.

In his second and third part of justification of human rights, Alexy assumes that even Machiavellian methods of the pursuit of profit are also taken into consideration in free and equal argumentations because they constitute a strategic assumption of every human action. Unfortunately, in the abovementioned version of transzendentally-pragmatic argument, Alexy does not avoid the Münchhausen Trilemma.[120] Apart from the objection of failure to resist the Trilemma, Alexy does not sufficiently justify why he who has no interest in accuracy, and who is oriented at profit maximisation, must

[119] Ibidem, p. 140.

[120] P. Grill, "Alexys Version einer transzendental-pragmatischen Begründung...," op. cit., p. 215ff.

accept the binding nature of discourse rules. Alexy only *a priori* claims that even the one who participates in argumentation process as the egotistical profit-maximiser assumes already indicated presuppositions of argumentation, and he demands the recognition of human rights. In Alexy's opinion, justification and recognition of discourse rules constitute an essential basis for the justification of human rights.

3.2. Direct and indirect patterns of discursive justification of human rights

When discussing the discursively-theoretical conception of justifying human rights, one has to reflect on how far they are guaranteed by positive law. Human rights can be transformed in positive law e.g. through their establishment in the form of a catalogue of fundamental rights in the constitution. There arises the issue of necessity of law, which addresses three issues: cognition, insistence, and organization. The problems of cognition and insistence highlighted by Alexy correspond to Kant's argument about the transition from the state of nature to the civic state. Discourse theory does not propose any particular course of action, which may lead to a large number of possible decisions and operations. There arises the problem of cognition of due behaviour, which can be prevented by a legally regulated model of action.[121] In turn, the problem of insistence involves the need to establish law for the application of the rules of correctness and legitimacy of norm, and not only for their understanding. The problem of organization derives from the fact that not all demands and social objectives, even if they are reasonable and necessary, may be implemented by individual and spontaneous activity. The need for legal regulation and the essence of law is to consist in providing necessary institutions and establishing measures designed to meet legitimate social objectives.

Justification of human rights is therefore not only a justification of a mere form of rights, but the system of rights of a specific content and structure.

---

[121] R. Alexy, *Recht, Vernunft, Diskurs...*, op. cit., p. 145.

Alexy distinguishes between two types of justification of human rights: direct and indirect:

- "A direct" justification takes place if it can be shown that certain rights are valid independently of actually carrying through real discourses, solely on the basis of discourse theory.
- "An indirect" justification takes place if the decision about human rights is delegated to a factual political process which, however, has to meet certain discourse-theoretically founded demands.[122]

What seems interesting from the perspective of Alexy's theory is the direct justification of human rights. Undoubtedly, discourse principles are rules of speech, and, therefore, the interlocutor should be treated as an equivalent partner. However, linguistic-pragmatic recognition does not entail moral and legal recognition. To move from discourse principles to rules of activity, additional premises should be introduced. These premises belong to discourse theory when it comes to direct discursively-theoretical justification, which leads to discursive necessity in a narrow sense.

Alexy distinguishes three types of direct discursive-theoretical justification of human rights: the arguments for autonomy, consensus, and democracy.[123] The argument for autonomy stipulates that anyone who seriously participates in the discourse assumes full autonomy of their interlocutor in conversation, and excludes the possibility of negating certain human rights. In order to justify the principle of autonomy it is necessary to define the phrase "genuine participant in discourse." In the first sense, one who is seriously involved in discourse

---

[122] R. Alexy, "Discourse Theory and Human Rights," op. cit., p. 23ff. On the concept of discursive necessity, possibility, and inability see: R. Alexy, *Theorie der juristischen...*, op. cit., p. 256; "Some judgments, values and commitments, as well as rules will be persuasively required, or, alternatively, excluded, by discourse principles. Discursive necessity and possibility in the narrow sense, which relate directly to discursively-theoretical justification, are differentiated from discursive necessity and possibility in a wider sense, which is attributed to indirect justification, and which is carried out in relation to a variety of people and time points." See: R. Alexy, "Die Idee einer prozeduralen Theorie der juristischen Argumentation, Probleme der Diskurstheorie," in: idem, *Recht, Vernunft, Diskurs...*, op. cit.

[123] R. Alexy, *Recht, Vernunft, Diskurs...*, op. cit., p. 147.

is a person interested only in ensuring moral truth and correctness. In this context, in order to persuade the interlocutor, it is possible to refer to the authority and to abandon discursive equality and freedom, and thus the autonomy principle. In another approach, one who "is seriously involved" in moral discourse, is such a person who wants to solve social conflicts through discursively achieved and controlled means in order to arrive at the consensus.[124] In order to resolve social conflict, the participant of discourse accepts his interlocutor's right to talk and to free and unfettered argumentation, and seeks to achieve a just and true decision. From this perspective, it is possible to obtain permanent discursive verifiability of all autonomy-based norms of operating. One who has the interest of correctness and truth is also equipped with autonomy interest. In addition, anyone who participates in discourse with a very well-formed interest of moral equity may be defined as "a true, honest discourse participant."[125] What underlies his action is a duty of complying with the autonomy principle, discursive autonomy, and freedom.

Alexy also demonstrates that for those who do not have an interest in correctness and do not comply with the autonomy principle (in a subjective or motivational sense), objective or institutional validity of this principle can be justified. The argumentation here is similar to the case of proving that one who is interested only in maximizing profits should recognize objective validity of discourse principles; "one who, by means of discourse, wants to achieve legitimization for his actions, must in such a discourse at least act as if he accepted his partner's autonomy."[126] Otherwise, his actions may not address any effects, or at least desired effects. In other words, to be able to contradict the position of the second participant and to legitimize one's own actions, one should at least simulate a major participation in the discourse.

The autonomy principle can be justified in two ways. First of all, anyone who genuinely, sincerely, and seriously participates in the discourse, should assume this principle. Even one who has no interest

---

[124] Ibidem, p. 149.

[125] Ibidem, p. 151.

[126] Ibidem, p. 152.

in genuine participation in the discourse should proceed at least as if they accepted the principle in question if they want to maximize their profits in the long term. Hence, the approval of the autonomy principle constitutes a presupposition of rational participation in practical and legal discourse.

However, the autonomy principle must be limited in a legal system if its use would violate the freedom of others or when it interferes with the collective interests.[127] Of course, it is desirable to ensure the greatest possible autonomy for each individual. It is, therefore, necessary to justify all these rights that protect both the private as well as public rights of autonomy. To achieve this, first of all it is necessary to create a catalogue of fundamental rights and of human rights that will provide protection for the right of autonomy. Basic rights will constitute the element of directly legitimate rights, the existence of which is necessary when taking into account the criterion of legality and equity for the constitution of human freedom and human rights, and ensuring at the same time the right to minimum subsistence.[128]

The autonomy argument is based on the contention that it is necessary to presuppose true, genuine, and sincere participation in the discourse. However, in order to justify human rights, the latter must be enforced by the argument of consensus, which creates a central element of Habermas' justification of legal system.[129] Legitimacy of law will, therefore, be associated with the universal consent of all participants in rational discourse. The essence of discourse, according to German philosopher, is a consensus based on the intersubjective process of arriving at an agreement in the course of meeting structural and rational characteristics of argumentation. Universal agreement in connection with the acceptance of the democracy principle and legal system creates a "logical genesis of law," which constitutes the basis for a system of fundamental rights that protect private and public autonomy.[130]

---

[127] R. Alexy, *Theorie der Grundrechte*, Baden-Baden: Nomos Verlag, 1985, p. 75; idem, *Recht, Vernunft, Diskurs…*, op. cit., p. 232ff.

[128] R. Alexy, *Theorie der Grundrechte*, op. cit., p. 454; idem, *Recht, Vernunft, Diskurs…*, op. cit., p. 155.

[129] J. Habermas, *Between Facts and Norms…*, op. cit., pp. 83–84.

[130] R. Alexy, *Recht, Vernunft, Diskurs…*, op. cit., p. 138.

According to Alexy, the argument of consensus thus leads to necessary supplementation of the autonomy argument by introducing elements of equality and impartiality as discursively-theoretical criteria of law justification.[131] Equality of human rights is binding in any discourse conducted under ideal conditions. Impartiality and equality of rights, justified by the argument of consensus, may be rebutted by various complaints, particularly the one that no mortal has ever taken or will ever take part in an ideal discourse. However, this cannot be an argument for unequal distribution of rights or for legitimization of control of a certain elite. The act of waiving the equality of rights to the reign of a particular group gives rise to a number of hazards and it poses a considerable risk.

The aim of the consensus argument is only to reinforce the argument of autonomy in order to justify human rights. The autonomy argument implies that everyone, as a genuine partner in a discourse, participates in the latter and accepts the autonomy of all interlocutors, even if he wants to maximize his profits in the long term. By contrast, the aim of the consensus argument is to ensure equal distribution of a justified interest of autonomy, particularly a political one. It should be noted that whoever positively assesses political autonomy has to negatively assess unequal distribution of political rights.[132] Consensus argument, which presupposes the equality of human rights, ultimately leads to the realization of a liberal principle of universality. For those who are interested in moral correctness, the latter justifies the subjective or motivational binding force of discourse principles, human rights, and the principle of universality; whilst for those who have no such interest – their objective or institutional validity.[133]

The third argument that serves the purpose of the discursively-theoretical justification of human rights, is the democracy argument. It assumes that the discourse principle can be approximately achieved only by legal institutionalization of democratic procedures aimed at shaping thoughts and will. Only democracy provides an approximation of correctness of legitimacy of the settlement, where fundamental

---

[131] Ibidem, p. 157.

[132] Ibidem, p. 162.

[133] Ibidem, p. 163.

rights and human rights are binding and carried out, both in the political and apolitical dimensions (right to life, subsistence minimum, or freedom of speech). Therefore the following principle applies:

> One who is interested in correctness and legitimacy must also be interested in democracy, and one who is interested in democracy, must also be interested in observance of fundamental rights and human rights.[134]

The concept of discourse can thus be realized in a democratic state of law and, due to the latter, fundamental rights and human rights are justified and observed. Discourse theory is not only a basis to justify law, but it also constitutes a basic theory for creating a democratic constitutional state.[135] From this perspective, a democratic state of law succeeds in meeting Habermas' objectives of an ideal – though systematically distorted – speech act, and in ensuring recognition of criticised validity claims.[136] Conditions of rational discourse can be implemented under institutionally existing law. It will be a way to reduce the uncertainty of obtaining consent as well as the number of possible rational solutions as a part of a practical discourse. "Discursive ability" may be limited by the rules prevailing in a parliamentary democracy, such as the representation principle and the principle of majority.

Alexy's theory of justifying human rights, based on transcendentally-pragmatic justification of discourse principles, does not achieve the intended purpose effectively. Alexy does not entirely avoid the criticism against the Münchhausen Trilemma, which consists in the fact that the ultimate justification of normative expressions is excluded by non-normative expressions. This argument depends on other deep-reaching norms, and therefore there is the danger of infinite regress in the participant. Moreover, Alexy does not convincingly explain the necessary binding nature of discourse principles for those people who are not equipped with the interests of procedural correctness, nor do they seek to maximize their profits. Validity of universal discourse principles and, accordingly, of human rights is not based

---

[134] Ibidem.

[135] Ibidem, p. 164.

[136] J. Habermas, *Vorstudien und Ergänzungen…*, op. cit., p. 355.

solely, as in Habermas, on the concept of communicative reason and consensus-oriented human activities in non-strategic social interactions. According to Alexy, discourse principles, similarly to Habermas' view, constitute a linguistic conceptualization of traditional ideas of liberty, equality, and justice. However, he introduces additional assumptions, such as empirical interest of correctness, individual maximization of profit, and the arguments of autonomy, consensus, and democracy, which are to be the manifestation of "analytical liberalism." Despite this consideration, they do not constitute sufficient grounds for justification and acceptance of human rights within an ideal discourse, and even more so in the real discourse (Alexy does not avoid many allegations, such as the performative contradiction of normativeness of discourse principles).[137] Indeed, not every participant – even the most reasonable one – of an argumentation process must positively assess the calculation of losses and profits, having regard to the criterion of correctness and truth, universality, and autonomy, even on account of the weaknesses of transcendental justification of procedural theory of discourse.

The most controversial argument pursued by Alexy is that mere simulation of serious participation in discourse is sufficient. It cannot be stated that the participant of a discourse respects the freedom of others, when he admits to himself that it was not his intention when taking into account the arguments and will of others. Alexy says that:

> ... it is not attractive to pursue discourses on justice with someone whose invitation to a dialogue takes the following form: "Before I force you to live according to my beliefs, I want to see whether I cannot achieve this goal by simpler means, namely by persuasion (conviction)."[138]

It is difficult to recognize such an interlocutor as sincere and truthful, since he presupposes the possibility of using violence against his interlocutor in order to attain his goal. His discourse is not, in fact, of a communicative nature, but rather of strategic one. What underlies such discourse is also the urge to achieve consensus, which does not

[137] S. Wesche, "Robert Alexys diskurstheoretische Menschenrechtsbegründung," *Rechtstheorie* 1999, no. 30, p. 83ff.

[138] R. Alexy, *Recht, Vernunft, Diskurs...*, op. cit., p. 152.

have to be a condition of a simulated serious participation in a discourse.

In my opinion, however, simulating the discourse will lead in the future to its serious distortions; even consensus achieved in a simulated discourse will be the same as what would be achieved in a real discourse. Alexy, having regard to the possibility of simulating a serious participation in the discourse, avoids the allegation of having utopian conceptions, which is often made against the ideal situation of speech. We will never be sure of the true intentions of our dialogue partner (opponent), and a lack of trust will lead to a lack of recognition of the interlocutor. As far as this element of Alexy's argumentation is concerned, the criticism of his concept is, therefore, based on the assumption that multilateral obedience to discourse principles does not constitute a precondition for the existence of discourses. Axel Honneth expresses his view on this issue in the following words:

> ... only such society can be ultimately effective – in terms of ethical discourse – as a fair one, when in its operative infrastructure it keeps requirements for domination-free dialogue in readiness and when it, above all, ensures all its members' opportunity of voluntary and legitimated bargaining of conflicting norms.[139]

As a result of this consideration, real "opportunity of discourse" and real "obedience to discourse" do not recognise the necessity of the assumptions of human communication.[140] This implies a positive and optimistic conclusion that willingness to participate in the discourse and the existence of discourse is realistic already when there is a chance of influencing the activity, and thus it pays to maintain readiness to participate in the discourse in the future. Even if, in fact, the spirit of cooperative discourse is not always observed, it does not mean that the discourse is impossible. As a result, simulating the ini-

---

[139] A. Honneth, "Diskursethik und implizites Gerechtigkeitskonzept. Eine Diskussionsbemerkung," in: *Moralität und Sittlichkeit. Das Problem Hegels und die Diskursethik*, ed. by W. Kuhlmann, Frankfurt am Main: Suhrkamp Verlag, 1986, pp. 268–274; J. Habermas, "Moralität und Sittlichkeit. Treffen Hegels Einwände gegen Kant auch auf die Diskursethik zu?" in: *Moralität und Sittlichkeit. Das Problem Hegels...*, op. cit., p. 188.

[140] A. Tschentscher, *Prozedurale Theorien der Gerechtigkeit...*, op. cit., p. 304.

tial participation in the discourse should not be considered as an indispensable discursively-theoretical condition.

Another controversial element in discursively-ethical justification of human rights is the cognitive nature of the claim to correctness of legal norms. Due to the subject matter of this dissertation, I will not consider this issue in details. It should only be noted that Habermas perceives the sense of "correctness" in "perfectly fair acceptability."[141] Habermas naturally emphasizes that moral cognition is of a fundamentally different character than empirical cognition, and as such it should be considered in the light of appreciating the recognition of any standard or action. According to Habermas and Alexy, the importance (dignity of recognition) of norms or actions is reinforced by ideal conditions of communication, resulting in universal, discursively and theoretically legitimated human rights. Armin Engländer challenges such considerations, noting that the adoption of rules and principles of discourse leads to an *a priori* model of justification, and thus leads their conclusions to cognitively-theoretical deadlock.[142] In his view, the latter condemns morally-philosophical and cognitive justifications of law to failure because it is not possible to identify an objective measure for assessing moral correctness of a particular norm. As a result, he criticizes Alexy's thesis on supplementation based on the claim to correctness that positive law has. Engländer concludes that, as long as it is impossible to provide an objective criterion for evaluation, it is pointless to present semantic criteria of correctness as a definitional element of law. As far as the issue in question is concerned, Lech Morawski was also sceptical about the views of Habermas and Alexy, doubting the possibility of creating a universal ethical system, understood as a system of substantive rules, which would, on the one hand, take into account and integrate culturally, religiously, or ethnically diverse societies, whilst, on the other hand, would not destroy diversity of lifestyles.[143]

---

[141] J. Habermas, "Richtigkeit versus Wahrheit. Zum Sinn der Sollgeltung moralischer Urteile und Normen," in: idem, *Wahrheit und Rechtfertigung. Philosophische Aufsätze*, Frankfurt am Main: Suhrkamp Verlag, 2004, p. 284.

[142] A. Engländer, *Diskurs als Rechtsquelle? Zur Kritik der Diskurstheorie des Rechts*, Tübingen: Mohr Verlag, 2002, p. 93.

[143] L. Morawski, *Główne problemy współczesnej filozofii prawa. Prawo w toku przemian* [Main Problems of Modern Philosophy of Law. Law in the Course of Transforma-

The discursive approach to law, however, allows the connection of law with unencumbered interpersonal communication that is regulated by ethical norms. Application of the abovementioned rules does not provide a complete agreement, rationality, or ultimately reached consensus, but it serves the purpose of approximating such a state and legitimating argumentative practices. Discursively-theoretical justification of human rights indicates the need for effectiveness of and obedience to these rights in democratic processes, whilst taking into account universal rules of discourse. In this context, Alexy's theory opposes non-liberal and non-personal concepts of human rights. It constitutes an idealistic demand of a constraint of a better argument, a request for a general consent, aiming at consensus, correctness, and achievement of universal discourse ethics.

4. Critical character of discourse theory

It is, therefore, argued in literature that discourse ethics requires a supplement or even the support of critical social theory, which considers the types of institutions required to develop its model.[144] Indeed, it is alleged that ethics discourse remains uncritical towards existing social relations as a result of its formal character. It seems that Axel Honneth's critical social theory, based on the principle of mutual recognition may be such a theory. Representatives of critical social theory postulate that discourse ethics was not only ethical conduct, but that the intersubjectively justified norms included in the latter were also of an enriching and substantive power. In other words, the aim of the latter is to refer procedural discourse ethics to a particular and real society of life, to make formal and material elements complementary ones. Such a request is important since the recognition of

---

tions], Warszawa: LexisNexis, 2003, p. 120ff. The author notes that while he does not believe in the idea of a common code of ethics, he believes that even for the most different cultures and traditions it is possible to create a common ethics of communication and conflict resolution.

[144] M. Becka, *Anerkennung im Kontext interkultureller Philosophie*, Frankfurt am Main – London: Verlag für Interkulturelle Kommunikation, 2005, p. 158ff. The author refers here to Enrique Dussels' views.

"the other" takes place in the very discourse. If someone is then excluded from the discourse, he should be seen as a victim. Consequently, it should be stated that the recognition of "the other" constitutes the basic claim to validity, a sine qua non of every correct argumentation.[145]

I would like to emphasise at this point that both the abovementioned opinions as well as further deliberations on the issue of discourse theory do not allow agreement with the standpoint that discourse ethics is devoid of a critical element. It is particularly with regard to Habermas' views that we can state that he continues the tradition of "critical theory" when he speaks of the ills of modern society, problems of democracy, "a supranational constellation," terrorism, fundamentalism, and intellectual discourse.[146] Giovanni Borradori also indicates that, both for Habermas and Apel, the purpose of criticism is to ensure rationality of communication and its potential for self-reflection and self-control. The critical dimension of their theory is expressed mainly in order to extend the consensus based on free and undistorted communication between participants of discourse. In other words, the criticism becomes the examination of conceptual and practical procedures that allow the creation of a rational consensus. Presenting criticism as a procedure consists in emphasizing the unity of theoretical and practical elements, and thus the unity of theoretical identification of distortions in social communication and their practical elimination. In other words, Habermas' critical theory formulates a programme to overcome the situation of subjective treatment and treatment of ethical base as the grounds for social life by means of an awareness-raising process, which draws attention to reification of social relations. The next chapter will try to show that the theory of discourse is not only of a critical nature, but also that it is complementary in a multicultural democratic society for Axel Honneth's critical social theory, which is particularly applicable in case of disrupting communication by means of human rights violations and criminal activities.

---

[145] Ibidem, p. 160.

[146] Broadly, on this issue see: R. Coles, "Identity and Difference in the Ethical Positions of Adorno and Habermas," in: *The Cambridge Companion to Habermas*, op. cit., pp. 19–45.

CHAPTER III

The principle of mutual recognition as a condition of intercultural legal discourse

1. Philosophical roots of the theory of recognition

The theory of recognition[1] constitutes, contemporarily, one of the basic paradigms of researches on the issue of society, mostly from a sociological perspective but also from a philosophical, political, and legal one. The state of being concerned about social recognition overlaps with concern over one's own identity. This concern often changes into a fight because this peculiar "social recognition" is very often challenged. Fight for recognition becomes, then, the subject of a conflict, sometimes transforming into fierce, sometimes very brutal and violent, dispute. It was Seneca who wrote "... Iniuriam nemo immota mente accipit, sed ad sensum eius perturbatur, caret autem perturbatione vir ereptus erroribus, moderator sui, altae quietis et placidae."[2]

1.1. Interpersonal character of human relations in Fichte's idea of law

The sources of the conception of recognition can be traced back mainly to German idealism and, most of all, to the works of Fichte

[1] German literature uses the term of *Anerkennung*, Anglo-Saxon literature – the term *recognition* and French one – the term *la reconnaissance*.

[2] "... Nobody accepts a wrong with imperturbable calmness of mind, but after experiencing it he is seized with anger." Seneca, *Myśli* [Thoughts], Kraków: Wydawnictwo Literackie, 1989, pp. 60–61.

and Hegel. It was Kant who first noted that mutual recognition consists in a certain existential simultaneity, intersubjective relation.[3] In his theory of morality he assumed that all individuals should be treated with equal respect and their interests ought to be equally taken into consideration. In other words, Kant represented universalistic "morality," which demands equal respect for all individuals as "goals as such" or as independent subjects. Fichte, referring to Kant's concept of categorical imperative, modified this moral principle in the following way: "Always act according to your belief in the rightness of one's own duty, namely, act in accordance with your conscience."[4] It does not mean, however, that a rational and independent individual is alienated, or even separated, from other individuals – just the opposite – Fichte points out that the awareness of oneself as an independent and free individual can be obtained only in the course of interactions with other equally free people. A rational person is not isolated, but arrives at a full and complete knowledge of himself only by means of a conscious contact with another individual. Fichte proved that a real and independent ego is conditioned by the freedom of another ego.[5] Treating an individual as "a tool of moral law" forces him or her to respect formal freedom of the Other, and allows the possibility of influencing him purely by means of persuasion.

From the point of view of the deliberations at issue, it is crucial to recall Fichte's statement that as far as every individual aims at realizing his own ideal of a human being and wants other individuals to approach this ideal, in trying to familiarise them with this ideal, the urge to take control over them or to treat other individuals as irrational things is unacceptable. Fichte stated in this context that the one who perceives himself as a master of others remains a slave himself.[6]

---

[3] I. Kant, *The Critique of Pure Reason*, Cambridge: Cambridge University Press, 1999, p. 378.

[4] J.G. Fichte, *Das System der Sittenlehre nach den Prinzipien der Wissenschaftslehre*, Hamburg: Felix Meiner Verlag, 1995, p. 153.

[5] Ibidem, p. 215ff.

[6] J.G. Fichte, "Einige Vorlesungen über die Bestimmung des Gelehrten," in: *Johann Gottlieb Fichte – Gesamtausgabe der Bayerischen Akademie der Wissenschaft*, ed. by R. Lauth, H. Jacob, Stuttgart – Bad Cannstatt: Frommann Verlag, 1964, Serie I, vol. 3, p. 39. From the historical perspective this thought has already appeared in J.J. Rous-

In this context, the words *hominem te memento* become very significant and characteristic. In other words, the individual who tries to realize his own goals by means of others, whilst treating them as things, turns out to be on a very low level of development of interpersonal relations that approve slavery, and thus remains in contrast with rational interpersonality. Social drive urges a human being to search for other rational beings who exist outside him, and it urges him to create a community with them. The science of interpersonality (*Interpersonalitätslehre*) is treated as one of the most fundamental elements of Fichte's social philosophy.[7] According to Fichte's principal point of view, the moral world consists of people who live together as a part of determined social relations.

Fichte perceives the nature of mutual reactions among rational beings in mutual giving and taking. The result of such interactive processes will be the elimination of social inequality. Primeval law (*Urrecht*) consists in the fact that "everyone restricts one's own freedom and the scope of one's own activities by means of assuming the other's freedom". What is meant by the latter is such law that "should be absolutely granted to every person as such."[8] This law should be consequently treated as a legal principle that ought to be binding in every legal system, and according to which "everyone should restrict the use of one's own freedom on account of the rights of other people." When taking into consideration the formal structure of interpersonality, the individuals share a complete and absolute area of freedom, leaving only the margin for the scope of its realisation. In other words, by means of recognition I "grant" to the Other the scope of activity. Respecting the freedom of the Other constitutes the manifestation of the inability to distinguish between recognising and being recognised, which can be observed in external activity.

---

seau's conception of the social contract, and it is also present in I. Kant's principle of autonomy understood as a goal in itself, namely, autonomous legislative authority.

7 Cf. M.J. Siemek, "Dwa modele intersubiektywnosci" [Two Models of Intersubjectivity], in: idem, *Hegel i filozofia* [Hegel and Philosophy], Warszawa: Oficyna Naukowa, 1998, p. 174ff.

8 J.G. Fichte, *Grundlage des Naturrechts nach Prinzipien der Wissenschaftslehre*, Hamburg: Felix Meiner Verlag, 1960, p. 111.

One's own formal freedom deserves defence, however, only when taking into account the freedom of another individual. In the situation when somebody wants to take away one's life - namely the first and fundamental condition of formal freedom - then it is one's privilege, or even one's duty, to try to protect it, however, not necessarily at the expense of the offender's life. In this context, Fichte expresses his opinion that "the whole physical strength should be subordinate to reason." Rationality of justifying the freedom of every human being has been accurately presented by this philosopher in the following fragment: "*everybody* is free due to the fact that they live their lives as human beings, everyone represents a form of reason placed in time *in the same way*, that is why everyone has the same right to freedoms and - *beyond* this - they have nothing. Everyone, therefore, is *equal*, they do not constitute two states, but one."[9] As I believe, the interpretation of Fichte's views, according to which freedom and equality constitute inseparable and complementary elements of law, does not raise any doubts since freedom is founded on equality of all people. Their stable relation is manifested in the ethical-social sphere by means of recognising every individual as a fountain of freedom and rationality.

The individual's rationality and his moral good that he is willing to serve require that the individual to be driven by the assumption of "formal freedom of all rational beings" in relations with other people. Fichte then wants everybody - without any exceptions - to be formally free and to make them use this freedom for the purpose of accomplishing material freedom, namely to become obedient to the law of autonomy. External freedom constitutes a result of common agreement of individuals to a certain legal relation, which respects and protects this relation by means of recognising it. Fichte treats earthly life as a fight for freedom. Maintaining this constitutes a fundamental goal of human freedom because everybody is free in their own parts, and therefore everyone has to protect his own freedom in his own part. The most crucial task for a rational individual is to interpret whether the behaviour of others constitutes a manifestation of

---

[9] J.G. Fichte, "Die Staatslehre, oder über das Verhältnis des Urstaates zum Vernunftreiche," in: *Fichtes Werke*, Bd. IV: *Zur Rechts- und Sittenlehre II*, Berlin: Walter de Gruyer & Co., 1971, p. 410.

rational freedom or not. Therefore, what becomes significant from the perspective of equitable law is the following principle:

> A complete rational being cannot accept other rational beings - besides himself - without establishing himself as an individual who remains in a certain relation, that is, a legal relation (*Rechtsverhältnis*) with other individuals.[10]

Respecting another person's freedom constitutes a manifestation of the inseparability of recognising and being recognised; that is, no individual activity can collide with others in the social world. It is treated as a development of the principle of recognising "myself as a synthetic unity on the basis of my own awareness and the awareness of somebody who recognises the other." According to this principle "I can demand from a given rational being to be treated as a rational being only when I treat myself in the same way."[11]

1.2. Mutual recognition in Hegel's philosophy of law

The principle of mutual recognition is also fundamental in Hegel's vision of social relations. It is emphasised in contemporary interpretations of Hegel's works that "ontologically" constitutive notion of intersubjectivity[12] - fundamental for humanity - which is related to the institution of mutual recognition - plays a crucial role for this philosopher. Hegel took his conception of recognition from Hobbes' and Fichte's philosophy. It was particularly the latter who shaped Hegel's views.

The following fragment seems indispensable when aiming at understanding Hegel's conception of mutual recognition:

> Self-consciousness has before it another self-consciousness; it has come outside itself. This has a double significance. First it has lost its own self,

---

[10] J.G. Fichte, *Grundlage des Naturrechts...*, op. cit., p. 40.

[11] Ibidem, p. 44.

[12] See: L. Siep, *Anerkennung als Prinzip der praktischen Philosophie*, Freiburg - München: Karl Alber, 1979; M.J. Siemek, "Przedmowa. Nowa obecność Hegla" [Preface. Hegel's New Presence], in: idem, *Hegel i filozofia* [Hegel and Philosophy], op. cit., p. 4.

> since it finds itself as another being; secondly, it has thereby sublated that other, for it does not regard the other as essentially real, but sees its own self in the other.[13]

What is characteristic is that recognition, namely perceiving oneself in that which is different, should be present in all manifestations of social coexistence. The latter is based on Hegel's belief that human beings come into existence only by means of a fight for recognition. It is a fierce fight for prestige or, ultimately, for social approval which is manifested in law, and without which there would be no human beings in the world. Hegel perceives mutual recognition of human beings, on the one hand, as something that should take place and, on the other hand, as constituting the subject (a goal) of frequent fight. What is significant is that the relation of mutual recognition is a dynamic process because the development of the knowledge about our identity is simultaneous with changes in our social and ethical life. The gesture of recognition, which constitutes the basis of ethical relations among individuals, is then perceived as a chain of multiple interchangeable stages of reconciliation and fight.[14]

This fight for recognition is apparently manifested in law. Law is therefore understood by Hegel as a multilateral relation of mutual recognition of free and equal individuals. What can be inferred from this - and what has been already emphasised - is that law is discovered only when we live in a community. The most fundamental and constitutive element of "legal recognition" is granting every individual the ability to rationally determine - within the scope of individual autonomy - moral issues. This entitlement concerns all individuals treated as subjects of law, who should be able to determine - in the course of social agreement - binding legal order.[15]

In Hegel's philosophy a (human) being is the source and subject of law, at the same time remaining the source of modernity:

---

[13] G.W.F. Hegel, *Phenomenology of Mind*, transl. by J.B. Baillie (1910), § 179.

[14] A. Honneth, "Moralischer Entwicklung und sozialer Kampf. Sozialphilosophische Lehren aus dem Frühwerk Hegels," in: *Zwischenbetrachtungen. Im Prozeß der Aufklärung*, ed. by A. Honneth, Th. McCarthy, C. Offe, Frankfurt am Main: Suhrkamp Verlag, 1989, p. 549.

[15] Cf. A. Honneth, *Kampf um Anerkennung. Zur moralischen Grammatik sozialer Kämpfe*, Frankfurt am Main: Suhrkamp Verlag, 1994, pp. 184–187.

> Personality implies, in general, a capacity to possess rights, and constitutes the conception and abstract basis of abstract right. This right, being abstract, must be formal also.[16]

Hegel derives from this his "categorical imperative" of a purely formal character: "*...Be a person and respect others as persons.*"[17] However, it mainly constitutes the source of a ban on infringing on another person's rights because the law that is based on this principle is to determine exclusively the limits of will. Hegel strongly presents his thesis about human dignity, taking into consideration the issue of equality of all human beings which is treated as the fundamental element of modernity (the world of "culture"):

> It is the essence of education and of thought, which is the consciousness of the individual in universal form, that "the" I should be apprehended as a universal person, in whom all are identical. Man must be accounted a universal being, not because he is Jew, Catholic, Protestant, German, or Italian, but because he is a man. This thinking or reflective consciousness is of infinite importance.[18]

As it has been accurately pointed out by M.J. Siemek, this is where universality of human rights takes its origins.

Hegel also emphasises that moral law consists in an independent determination of what is good and in bearing responsibility for one's own choices. Moral law, which is perceived as the law of the individual, is the place where a moral subject reveals his tendency to good as such. It is a call of the individual for a real freedom, that is, "being on one's own in that which is different." The principle of mutuality (*Gegenseitigkeit*) assumes that every individuality "knows itself recognized in the other free man, and is aware of this in so far as it recognizes the other and knows him to be free."[19] This claim constitutes one of the most fundamental elements of intersubjective communica-

---

[16] G.W.F. Hegel, *Philosophy of Right*, Kitchener: Batoche Books, 2001, § 36.

[17] Ibidem, § 36.

[18] Ibidem, § 209.

[19] G.W.F. Hegel, *Encyclopaedia of the Philosophical Sciences* (1830), transl. by W. Wallace, § 436.

tion because it is the relation of the mutuality of dialogue and agreement that is considered the basis of abstract law.[20]

Hegel assumes that human reality can be created and maintained exclusively as a recognised reality. Reactions which take place among free individuals are symmetrical and transitive because one cannot effectively act without attributing to oneself unencumbered activity, and this is not feasible without granting it also to other individuals. When presenting the "ethical" order of society, Hegel distinguishes three institutional spheres in which an individual functions, namely, family, bourgeois society, and the state, differentiating – at the same time – among three spheres of recognition (love, law, and solidarity). Life on these three levels, and using all these three spheres of recognition, allows the individual to fully use individual freedom. Respecting these three spheres of recognition enables the presence of *Sittlichkeit* – namely, total ethicality, which constitutes the proper substance of the objective spirit. The notion of "ethicality" can be, therefore, treated as a substitute for Hobbes' notion of artificiality. Distinguishing these three spheres of recognition constitutes the manifestation of historical compromise between the requirements of speculation and empirical experience.[21]

We become the subjects of law – free individuals – not as a result of some virtues or our position, but we are endowed with this from the moment we are born and we cannot be devoid of it. This principle constitutes a development of the fundamental assumption of the legislation of practical reason, according to which human freedom is treated as the highest value, manifested in the sphere of intersubjective references to other – equal – subjects. The main categories of these intersubjective references are "property" and "agreement," which are based on the complete system of equivalent exchange of mutual recognition.

When assuming a theoretically–legal point of view, two aspects of Hegel's conception of recognition seem of utmost importance: a positive and negative one. The positive aspect is understood as subjective

---

[20] G.W.F. Hegel, *Philosophy of Right*, op. cit., Comment to § 71.

[21] P. Ricoeur, *The Course of Recognition*, Cambridge: Harvard University Press, 2005, p. 172.

belief in the fact that I am regarded as a legitimate participant of legal relations. The negative aspect, on the other hand, is interpreted as the consequences of infringing binding norms (for example, due to committing a crime) manifested by the loss of recognition (*Anerkennungsverlust*).[22]

The theory of recognition - being also a moral theory - is closely connected with neo-Aristotelian views and, in particular, with the philosophy of political friendship - contemporarily discovered anew by Jacques Derrida.[23] There are undoubtedly numerous parallels between Aristotle's notion of "legal friendship" and the conception of recognition. Aristotle writes about friendship (*filia*) primarily in book VIII of *Nicomachean Ethics*. According to Aristotle, friendship can be perceived in political terms, as a political category, being "something vital for life; since without friends nobody would want to live, even if he had all other goods."[24] Aristotle then writes:

> ... the nature of bonds between the states is friendship, and the belief that legislators care more for the latter than for justice ... People who live in friendship do not yearn for justice, but those who are just need friendship nevertheless, and the most proper form of justice is, as it seems, friendly attitude.[25]

Friendship is based on the most advantageous conditions of mutual recognition and - as such - it comes closer to justice.

A special place in Aristotle's political (or even legal) philosophy is taken by the interpretation of the notion of *synallagma,* which, generally speaking, constitutes the source of obligation in private law. The latter also refers to the exchange in economic sense in relation to complementary justice as referring to the exchange of goods among the inhabitants of a *polis*.[26] What becomes crucial from the perspective of the theory of recognition is understanding *synallagma* as a kind of

---

22 This aspect of Hegel's conception of recognition is broadly discussed in subsection IV.2. of this dissertation.

23 J. Derrida, *Politik der Freundschaft,* Frankfurt am Main: Suhrkamp Verlag, 2000.

24 Aristotle, *Nicomachean Ethics,* transl. by M. Ostwald (1962), 1155a (hereinafter quoted as *NE*).

25 *NE* 1155a20–25.

26 Cf. *NE* 1130b. Broadly, on the issue of *synallagma.*

legal friendship, referred to by Aristotle as a relation based on advantage and regulated by law.[27] Legal friendship is based on equality of individuals, and it derives from an agreement.[28] It is based on the advantage of both parties and it constitutes the fundamental element of a political system and a guarantee of the existence of political community (*polis*) which, as a rule, relates to legal friendship. A characteristic feature of a community based on legal (civic) friendship is a friendly trust in respect to everyone who wants to belong to our community. At the same time, legal friendship constitutes the outcome of concluding an agreement, which, however, – as it seems – should be broadly understood since it does not refer to a particular institution of law in Greece or Athens, but rather to the most fundamental political institution.[29]

Hegel also perceived agreement and property as the most fundamental notions of philosophy of law since in civic society the private interest of every individual can be forced through only by means of the interests of other individuals. Economic and legal freedom of every single person is based on unconditional equality of all in the eyes of law. On the other hand, one who is driven by the urge to accomplish his own private interest must keep in mind that this is possible only upon voluntary agreement of others, in other words, he must abide by the binding rules of social life. Primitive fight is here supplanted with the intersubjective logics and ethics of common game models. Private interests are subject to a peculiar compulsion of

---

[27] Cf. Aristotle, *The Eudemian Ethics,* Oxford: Oxford University Press, 2005, 1243a (hereinafter quoted as *EE*), *NE* 1162b.

[28] See: *EE* 1242b.

[29] In *Rhetoric* (*Rhetoric,* New York: The Modern Library, 1954), Aristotle expresses the view that the whole law which is made is to some extent an agreement (*Rhetoric* 1376b): "We may argue that a contract is a law, though of a special and limited kind; and that, while contracts do not of course make the law binding, the law does make any lawful contract binding, and that the law itself as a whole is a contract, so that any one who disregards or repudiates any contract is repudiating the law itself." This statement corresponds with his views on the forms of political systems as presented in *The Eudemian Ethics,* where he points at a similar kind of *politeia* and legal friendship (*EE* 1241a). A characteristic feature of both these political institutions is equality of all individuals, which is manifested in the assumption that none of them is subordinate to another.

agreement, which comes into existence as a result of a clash of numerous basically legitimate particularistic interests. Coming to terms with the question of whether to respect such interests is a necessity that develops a dialogue-based manner of thinking and acting, and an agreement-based manner of settling conflicts.[30] These principles of intersubjective game – which have been arrived at in the process of compromise – have to be obeyed even by new participants, because in case of a collision of their claims with the claims of others, it is the only situation in which they can count on approval. In other words, recognition requires that every individual should be recognised in his drive for prosperity.

It can be seen from the above that the basic categories of private law, such as the subject of law, property, and agreement embody an irremovable basis of interpersonal space in public social life. Property and agreement universalise, then, external freedom and equality of people who previously acted as individuals and were driven exclusively by their own individual interests, because abiding by the conditions of an agreement serves the purpose of accomplishing one's own claims and preserving one's own property. The requirement of mutuality, in turn, forces the participants of social interactions to take care not only of their own, but also of others' freedom because their egoism, paradoxically, does not allow egoistic behaviour to be manifested in unjust activity since it can turn against them. As a consequence, social and legal order is based on intersubjective agreement, the procedure of fair exchange, and mutuality of consideration and expectations. Recognition of the subjects of law, members of a family, owners, parties to a contract, producers, and consumers is then mutual and horizontal.

Rudolf von Ihering also made a significant contribution to the theory of recognition, the description of which was presented in his famous work *Der Zweck im Recht*.[31] He discusses a crucial relation between "legal recognition" and "respect towards another person."

---

[30] M.J. Siemek, "Prawo etyczności i etyczność prawa" [Law of Ethics and Ethics of Law], in: idem, *Hegel i filozofia* [Hegel and Philosophy], op. cit., p. 101.

[31] Particularly the second part of the work: R. von Ihering, *Der Zweck im Recht*, Leipzig 1905.

Ihering states that legal recognition means that every human being, irrespective of their personal qualities, constitutes "a goal in itself," whilst "social respect" emphasises "the value" of a particular individual from the point of view of intersubjectively measured social significance.[32] Legal recognition assumes universalistic respect for the individual's "freedom of will," and respect is of a gradable character since it is related to the extent to which the individual's achievements and activities are significant for the society.

The urge for being recognised constitutes then the basic element of human life, which starts from self-identification and self-recognition and ends in dialectics, which expresses the mutual relation of the need for a permanent fight for recognition and its institutionalisation. Fear of refusal sometimes amounts to the fear of death; therefore, the intention of obtaining recognition or protecting against its loss becomes a driving force of every human being in a society, the main incentive for his activities on every level of his existence.

2. General assumptions of the modern theory of recognition

The problem of recognition is of an ethical character because it is closely connected with the issue of justice as procedural, commutative, and distributive. The theory of recognition manifests Kant's proceduralism, which guarantees universality of normative claims, and which consists in drawing universally-anthropological and structural bonds between different forms of intersubjective life and between individual development and self-realisation. Contemporary theory of recognition resigns from empty formalism, emphasising the importance and the worth of individual rights and democracy.[33] We can even risk the statement that it seeks a certain code of rules and principles that could serve as a point of reference for all people, and in this way it accepts – to a considerable extent – the universality of human rights.

---

[32] Ibidem, p. 389ff.

[33] Ch.F. Zurn, "Schwerpunkt: Anerkennung," *Deutsche Zeitschrift für Philosophie* 2005, vol. 53, no. 3, p. 380.

The theory of recognition constitutes not only a developed moral conception, but it also serves the purpose of a critical theory, which analyses social and political relations that can be encountered in modern societies. The latter, in particular, points at external connection between individual experience of a lack of recognition or its loss, and numerous social fights for greater and more appropriate recognition from different social groups. In other words, the theory of recognition critically analyses the causes of social conflicts, presenting them as a fight for developing human rights, and applying them in relation to all individuals, a fight for ensuring a certain sphere of private life that would be immune from state authority and, ultimately, for ensuring a social environment which – in spite of being culturally diversified – would be free from humiliation and discrimination.[34] The conception of recognition is not purely of a descriptive or theoretical character but – what is significant – it includes a strong normative accent. From such a perspective, this conception is of an interdisciplinary character since it is not only a critical social theory but also a developed reflective moral, philosophical, political, and legal conception.

Generally speaking, the theory in question focuses on granting equal and mutual recognition in interpersonal relations to different individuals who are representatives of national, racial, or ethnic minorities, practising different religions, placed lower in the social hierarchy due to their material status. By fair and equitable relations of mutual recognition we mean such that would enable one to regard every individual – in interpersonal relations – as an equal and free interlocutor as well as prevent humiliation and discrimination and in the area of economic relations, leading to redistribution. The moment which precedes recognition and, at the same time, is included in the latter is the feeling of one's own worth, manifested in preserving one's own authentic identity.[35] The process of building one's own identity is accompanied by discovering the difference between one's own and the Other's. What is meant by this is the taking into consid-

[34] Ibidem, p. 383.

[35] Ch. Taylor, "The Politics of Recognition," in: *Multiculturalism: Examining the Politics of Recognition*, ed. by A. Gutmann, Princeton, NJ: Princeton University Press, 1994, pp. 28–44; also P. Ricoeur, *The Course of Recognition*, op. cit., pp. 69–149.

eration both the negative character of the Other as well as his internalisation in the process of self-determination. In other words, the source of identity is in the Other, namely in internalised difference from the Other and difference of the Other. The sum of differences, that is adding that what differentiates me from the Other and that which differs the Other from me, constitutes the knowledge of oneself. It can be stated that mutual recognition stands for combining self-reflection and orientation at the Other, conditioning the attitude to oneself and intersubjectivity.

The characteristic feature of the recognition at issue is mutuality, whilst we do not mean here reciprocal mutuality, rather as a participant of a merely binary relation.[36] Mutuality is most vividly manifested in the relation I to the Other, as described by Lévinas, and mutuality of my obligation becomes my obligation when I become the Other for the Second Party or the Third Party. In other words, if I take care of another individual (the Second Party), I also require such care and attention for the Second Party from other individuals (the Third Party), and if such care and attention is to be full and omnipresent then *I* also require it from the Other (the Second and the Third Party) in relation to the Other from their viewpoint (Me). What intermingles here is a moral order of the obligation of I towards the Other, and the duty of the Other towards the Other (including Me). In other words, we pass from self-identification to dialectic relation, which can be observed on an existential level and which leads to mutuality or reciprocity. Mutual recognition stands for a certain intellectual simultaneity, intersubjective communion, or becoming one[37]. Ricoeur writes that dialectics of recognition starts from "something" in general, going then through "someone" and "oneself," in order to ultimately arrive at some symbol of identity obtained in mutuality (Greeks

[36] Zygmunt Bauman writes about such mutuality, taking into consideration the difference between an agreement and morality. This difference consists in the fact, as noted by this recognised sociologist, that meeting the obligation which results from an agreement depends on meeting the obligation by the partner, and in the case of morality such conditional mutuality is excluded. See: Z. Bauman, *Etyka ponowoczesna*, Warszawa: Wydawnictwo Naukowe PWN, 1996 (*Postmodern Ethics*, Cambridge: Basil Blackwell, 1993), pp. 76–82.

[37] P. Ricoeur, *The Course of Recognition*, op. cit., p. 151ff.

allēlōn – "one another;" "each other").[38] The principle of mutuality has the character of a universal norm that is binding irrespective of cultural differences. In this context we can talk about *homo reciprocus*.

Mutuality plays a crucial role in well-ordered society understood as a system of social cooperation, though as a universal principle it functions in all societies, even those "badly-ordered." In a well-ordered society it has the most complete manifestation because the citizens are treated here as rational only when they perceive one another as free and equal.[39] The criterion of mutuality means that the conditions of ordering society are considered reasonable by all those who can accept them as free and equal citizens rather than as dominated and manipulated people who are placed lower in the social hierarchy. From Kant's perspective, the principle of mutuality is manifested in the following belief:

> … Equality belonging to every man, which consists in his Right to be independent of being bound by others to anything more than that to which he may also reciprocally bind them. It is, consequently, the inborn quality to every man in virtue of which he ought to be *his own master by Right* (*sui juris*).[40]

There arises a fundamental question, namely, "Do we accept the otherness (strangeness) of another person, whilst still preserving the feeling of his equal dignity, his authentic identity? What needs emphasizing is that the notion of recognition refers both to recognition of diversity and recognition of the equality of all members of society in relation to one another." Hans Krämer writes in this context about diversifying and identifying recognition.[41] He assigns diversifying recognition to tolerance, so he postulates that the strangeness of the other should be accepted and preserved. On the other hand, what seems of greater importance is moral recognition that meets another individual half way, recognising his existence and his needs, and respecting his equality. To put it differently, moral recognition stands for formal recognition,

---

[38] Ibidem, p. 250.

[39] J. Rawls, *Political Liberalism*, New York: Columbia University Press, 1996, p. 15ff.

[40] I. Kant, *The Philosophy of Law: An Exposition of the Fundamental Principles of Jurisprudence as the Science of Right*, transl. by W. Hastie, Edinburgh: Clark, 1887, p. 56.

[41] H. Krämer, *Integrative Ethik*, Frankfurt am Main: Suhrkamp Verlag, 1995, p. 73.

whilst the call for tolerance concerns the approval of a particular individual in his otherness. Krämer points out that diversifying recognition helps to prevent the instrumentalization of another individual and constitutes an assumption for formulating obligations (*Sollen*), which – in communion with the other – perceive his otherness.[42]

3. Patterns of intersubjective recognition: Axel Honneth's moral grammar of social conflicts

These forms will be shaped in different ways and to different extents in respective spheres of recognition – typified by Hegel (love, law, and solidarity). Max Scheler differentiates in this context between: "community of life" (*Lebensgemeinschaft*), "society" (*Gesellschaft*), and "community of people" based on solidarity (*Personengemeinschaft*).[43] Helmuth Plessner, in turn, defines them respectively as "primeval relations" (*Primärbindungen*), "social relations" (*der gesellschaftliche Verkehr*), and "professional community" (*Sachgemeinschaft*).[44] Charles Taylor, on the other hand, writes about two levels of recognition, the first of which constitutes an intimate sphere, where we get to know our identity and we discover ourselves in contacts with others, whilst the second refers to the public sphere, where the most crucial role is played by the politics of equal recognition.[45] In other words, three normative principles of recognition, namely, particular love, equal respect for everybody, and judging individual activities, are considered in relation to one another on three relatively distinct levels of social activity, that is, in family, civic society, and in the state of law.

3.1. Love and the fight for recognition

Axel Honneth somehow modifies the spheres differentiated by Hegel, referring them to modern social relations. He presents the spheres of

---

[42] Ibidem, p. 330.

[43] M. Scheler, "Der Formalismus in der Ethik und die materiale Wertethik," in: idem, *Gesammelte Werke*, Bern: Francke Verlag, 1966, Bd. 2, p. 509ff.

[44] H. Plessner, "Die Grenzen der Gemeinschaft," in: idem, *Gesammelte Schriften*, Frankfurt am Main: Suhrkamp Verlag, 1981, Bd. V, p. 7ff.

[45] Ch. Taylor, "The Politics of Recognition," op. cit., p. 37.

recognition in such a manner the allows the bringing out of internal conflict over legitimate application of a proper principle of recognition. The first level consists of intimate relations, which serve – when referring to mutual love – as the basis for formulating new needs or such that have not yet been recognised in order to gain greater or simply different support. The first sphere of recognition – referred to as love – comprises the whole spectrum of erotic, friendly, or family relations, so "it implies strong emotional bonds among a small amount of people."[46] What arises here is pre-legal mutual recognition, in which individuals arrive at mutual approval in their specific needs. It is obvious that in practice recognition will be different in respective relations between parents and children, or children and parents, because in some conditions recognition can be of an asymmetric character and recognition for children can be differently defined from that of parents. The source of recognition will primarily be an affectively-emotional relation of love, which cannot be forced on anyone. When taking into consideration this sphere of recognition, the individual develops trust to oneself in primary, family relations. The principle of mutual recognition is expressed here by means of love, regarding this feeling as the strongest cement of interpersonal relations based on autotelic bonds. Love respects free will, since nobody can be forced to share free will. It also stands for the urge to be responsible towards another beloved person, and also to be responsible for him or her. Mutual love shapes strong bonds, which can be characterised by respect and approval for the personality of another person – often so distinct from ours.

Sigmund Freud states, in turn, that the commandment according to which "you shall love your neighbour as you love yourself" constitutes one of the most fundamental principles of civilised life. He points out, at the same time, that this commandment stands in contradiction to other principles promoted by civilisation, like being driven by one's own interests and aiming at happiness.[47] However, it is problematic as to why we shall love everyone, since people should deserve love. This message is apparently applied in the religious community which we are members of; in other words, it becomes

---

[46] A. Honneth, *Kampf um Anerkennung…*, op. cit., p. 153.

[47] S. Freud, *Civilization and Its Discontents*, New York: W.W. Norton & Company, 1989, p. 92ff.

reasonable only when we succumb to religious admonition *credere quia absurdum*.[48] We can ponder over the question of whether love can be oriented at "humanity" as such. In my opinion, love constitutes rather a feeling which is oriented at real people with whom we can experience real bonds. Hegel and Honneth write in this context about love only in the family sphere, so there is no dilemma over why I should love a stranger. We love members of our families even only due to the fact that they are our family or friends, or that we are mutually loved (marriage, friendship).[49] Love constitutes, then, totality of existence, whilst love to numerous groups (humanity) bears no relation to anyone. As I have already noted, interpretation of family can be broader, but if this is the case, there appear different dilemmas, and this relation ceases to be intimate and starts to bear some features of sympathy (religious community, colleagues, workmates, or countrymen can be referred to as family). Such relation of recognition comprises – to a certain extent – different levels of recognition.

3.2. The fight for recognition in the sphere of modern law

When taking into consideration the sphere of modern law, conflict comes down to defining – by means of a reference to the principle of equality – whether some social groups which have been previously devoid of recognition, deserve to be granted it, and this leads to the question of whether there is a need for specifying legal principles,

---

[48] Z. Bauman, *Szanse etyki w zglobalizowanym świecie* [Chances of Ethics in a Global World], Kraków: Znak, 2007, p. 7.

[49] The relation of mutuality among family or friends is somewhat differently presented by R. Dworkin, who writes: "I have special responsibilities to my brother in virtue of our brotherhood, but these are sensitive to the degree to which he accepts such responsibilities toward me; my responsibilities to those who claim that we are friends or lovers or neighbors or colleagues or countrymen are equally contingent on reciprocity." R. Dworkin, *Law's Empire*, London: Fontana Press, 1986, p. 198. What is meant by this is recognition, which in Hegel's and Honneth's model is placed in two respective spheres, namely, modern law and solidarity. Mutual recognition between beloved people, based exclusively on deep feeling, is referred to by him as altruism (ibidem, p. 215).

taking into account the discarded state of facts.[50] What emerges as most the significant feature is the cognitively-formal relation of recognition in law (or more precisely in civic society). Legal recognition means that we hold certain rights and - as such - we have a claim to realize them, however, only on the condition that we are aware of normative obligations that we have to keep in respect to another individual.[51] When assuming such an interpretation, recognition has a double reference, that is, a norm, namely, binding legal order, and another person, which forces everyone to identify another individual as a free and equal being. Legal recognition stands for combining the universal significance of a norm and the uniqueness of every human being.

Honneth notes that legal recognition - as understood by Hegel and Mead - means equal recognition for ideas professed by respective subjects of law.[52] Consequently, the latter constitutes an approval for pluralism of values. It has to be distinguished, however, from the extent of social assessment of values. In other words, we have to differentiate two forms of respect, that is, legal recognition and social assessment, as was already pointed out by Rudolph von Ihering. It was also Stephen L. Darwall[53] who perceived the necessity of differ-

---

[50] See: J. Habermas, *Between Facts and Norms. Contributions to a Discourse Theory of Law and Democracy*, Cambridge, Mass.: The MIT Press, 1998, pp. 414–418; idem, *Die Einbeziehung des Anderen*, Frankfurt am Main: Suhrkamp Verlag, 1999, pp. 237–276; I.M. Young, *Justice and the Politics of Difference*, Princeton: Princeton University Press, 1990, pp. 25–39.

[51] A. Honneth, *Kampf um Anerkennung*, op. cit., p. 174.

[52] Ibidem, p. 179.

[53] S.L. Darwall, "Two Kinds of Respects," *Ethics* 1977/1978, no. 88, p. 36ff. The significance of his conception was particularly appreciated by Axel Honneth (*Kampf um Anerkennung*, op. cit., p. 181ff.). It is worth noting that the notion of respect was highly valued already in Kant's philosophy. For Kant, respect stood for stimulus by means of which practical reason directly marks emotionality. For Kant, respect and dignity constituted correlative notions. He writes that man is obliged, therefore, that on the basis of his actions he should recognize [anzuerkennen] dignity, or otherwise: the humanity of every human being. Therefore, this obligation requires the respect due to every human being. I. Kant, *The Metaphysics of Morals*, Cambridge: Cambridge University Press, 1996, p. 211. In other words, respecting somebody means regarding him as the subject of moral laws.

entiating two forms of respect. Respect of a human being as a person leads Darwall to *"recognition respect"*, which stands for universalistic, cognitive recognition of a human being. What remains problematic, however, is the question of how we are to discover legal obligations imposed on us in relation to autonomous individuals. In order to do this we need to refer to cognition and experience, at least for the purpose of determining the state of things of a given individual. Recognition of a human person as such should be differentiated from gradable assessment (social judging) of the particular properties and activities of a given individual. Despite certain differences between these two forms of respect, both in case of legal recognition (general properties of a human being as such) and an evaluative system of assessment (particular properties of specific people); every individual would aim at respect in both these aspects.

It would then be controversial to determine criteria and scales of justice of social assessment of particular properties. John Rawls also emphasised the importance of mutual respect as a part of social cooperation. He noted that fair conditions of social cooperation are such on which we - being free and equal individuals - want to cooperate in good faith with other members of society all our lives. Such proper and fair cooperation is possible only in the situation where it can be recognized by everyone without anger or humiliation (or guilty conscience). Such conditions are met when the individuals (citizens) perceive themselves and one another as having moral abilities which constitute the basis of equal citizenship,[54] and - as I truly believe - equal humanity. Respect for oneself is manifested in equality of the most fundamental freedoms,[55] authentic value of political freedom (like real possibility of holding public office), and, what is most sig-

---

[54] J. Rawls, *A Theory of Justice*, Oxford: Oxford University Press, 1999, pp. 386–391; idem, *Political Liberalism*, op. cit., p. 306ff.

[55] Broadly on this issue see: J. Rawls, *A Theory of Justice*, op. cit., p. 205ff. American philosopher points out that participation in public life, where every participant is taken into consideration, creates the basis of friendly relations among citizens and shapes the political ethos. Consequently, it fosters the feeling that every participant of public life has about his own authentic value, and it generates self-confidence that other participants count on his cooperation in shaping society and take his or her standpoint into consideration.

nificant, this respect is also supported by the principle of difference.[56] Equal respect for every human being reinforces respect for oneself, and this, in turn, enables and requires the responsible assumption of one's own, individual and irreplaceable, attitude in life; it forces the situation in which one has to come to terms with oneself, in the situations when self-cognition and existential decisions overlap. As Habermas notes, "the intrusion of reflection into the life-historical process generates a new kind of tension between the consciousness of contingency, self-reflection, and liability for one's own existence."[57] Such intrusion of reflection into biographies and cultural traditions increases the individual character of life projects as well as the pluralism of collective forms of life.

Respect for oneself causes us to feel, as valuable cooperative members of society, able to be driven by the principles of a particular, individual conception of good that is worth all endeavours. By means of public confirmation of the most basic freedoms, citizens of a well-ordered society express their mutual respect for one another as reasonable and trustworthy individuals, and they give their voice to recognition of the importance that all citizens attach to their own lifestyles. Therefore, it is important for a human being to live in a manner that enables him to preserve his inborn self-dignity, determined by a certain minimum resulting from the fact of being a human being.[58] The measure of this value is our respect for ourselves, our respect for others, and respect that others have for us. There is no denying the fact that without self-respect it is hard to expect respect from others,

---

[56] See J. Rawls, *Political Liberalism*, op. cit., p. 182ff.

[57] J. Habermas, *Between Facts and Norms…*, op. cit., p. 96.

[58] This is why Honneth – in his subsequent works – focuses much attention on the problem of redistribution, the aim of which is to guarantee recognition. See: a discussion between Axel Honneth and Nancy Fraser on this issue: N. Fraser, A. Honneth, *Umverteilung oder Anerkennung? Eine politisch-philosophische Kontroverse*, Frankfurt am Main: Suhrkamp Verlag, 2003; also: S. Thompson, "Is Redistribution a Form of Recognition? Comments on the Fraser – Honneth Debate," *Critical Review of International Social and Political Philosophy* 2005, vol. 8, no. 1, pp. 85–102. It merits noting that § 25 of the Vienna Declaration and Programme of Action (similarly art. 34 section 3 of the Charter of Fundamental Rights of the European Union) confirmed, among other things, that utter poverty and rejection from society constitute infringement of human dignity, and such a state of things shall be prevented.

or have respect for other individuals. It is then crucial to recognise and nurture one's own personal dignity, however, this – due to economic, social, or political situations – can come as a great difficulty or can sometimes be unfeasible. Protection of one's own dignity means that we expect its recognition from other people, but having in mind one's own dignity one should respect the dignity of other people.

In other words, it can be stated that the human condition is preoccupied with two issues: identity and recognition. Whilst the former concentrates on self-discovery, the latter constitutes the result of social activity based on democratic principles, requiring at the same time respect for otherness, and differentiation in terms of culture, outlook on life, and religion. Charles Taylor points out in this context that identity does not stand for isolation, but it constitutes the effect of negotiations "by means of half-open and half-closed dialogue with others," "it depends on the ability to preserve dialogue with others" and, consequently, it depends on the society itself, constituting a peculiar "social derivate." Recognition, on the other hand, derives from social identity due to the fact that it was based on social categories, assumed by everyone as natural.[59] Taylor's views correspond in this scope with Karl Jaspers' standpoint, according to which "being oneself and being in communication are inseparable." Jaspers believes that it is communication with another individual (another "being oneself") that constitutes the source of our willingness to be ourselves.[60] Habermas shares a similar view and states that the knowledge of who we are is acquired by us as autonomic individuals on the basis of our relations with others, and the basic relation is the act of communication.[61]

Taylor points out that our identity is being shaped as a result of a dialogue (and sometimes a fight in case of lack of recognition or failure to get good reception from other people) with others and, consequently, it constitutes the effect of self-creation by means of interaction with our social and cultural environment. Democratic

---

[59] Ch. Taylor, "The Politics of Recognition," op. cit., pp. 34–35.

[60] K. Jaspers, *Von der Wahrheit*, München: Piper Verlag, 1991, p. 546.

[61] J. Habermas, *The Theory of Communicative Action*, vol. 1: *Reason and the Rationalization of Society*, Boston: Beacon Press, 1984, pp. 75–76.

order introduced the politics of equal recognition, which has so far assumed different forms, and has contemporarily returned in the form of a claim for an equal status of cultures and genders. Taylor perceives two contradictory political discourses, namely of equal dignity and human rights and the politics of difference, emphasising diversity of individuals and groups.[62] In other words, he juxtaposes "politics of difference" with politics based on the principle of universal equality. At the same time, he criticises abstract universalism, alleging that in the name of liberal neutrality it remains "blind to differences." What is meant here is also equality in an internal sense because people differ from one another due to their self-development and autonomous self-determination. Human rights assume, therefore, that every human being can aspire to his individual goals – to self-realization – on account of being an individual internally entitled to "creative self-development." Taylor's politics of difference – by means of approval of otherness – emphasises every person's dignity, which is sometimes hidden behind the hedge of diversity. Politics of difference by no means constitutes the basis for discrimination or humiliation, just the opposite – paradoxical as it may seem – it uncovers hidden taboo, fears, and prejudice. It seems to me that Taylor's goal – which is not entirely met, as noted by some critics – is to show that the beauty of another person can be seen in otherness towards ourselves. Experiencing legal recognition enables, as a result, the perception oneself as a person (subject of law) who can enter with others into discursive relations of shaping one's will. The point of departure is dialogue recognition of the other in his dignity, his own subjectivity, and – in the effect of the latter – universal dignity is enriched with confirmation of individual identity. Attaching importance to differences, namely, to otherness, does not automatically lead to unequal treatment.

When assuming the perspective of positive law, we could state that legal recognition consists primarily in mutual recognition as individuals because such a duty arises from binding legal norms. Such recognition is no longer of an emotional character, but rather a rational one. It consists in realising one's own worth, confirmed by

[62] Ch. Taylor, "The Politics of Recognition," op. cit., p. 38.

norms of the democratic legal order. Recognition enables participation in interactions that take place among equal individuals who are granted individual rights, without which creating self-respect would hardly be possible.[63] In other words, the result of recognition – in the sphere of recognition that was differentiated as the second one – is self-respect from the perspective of public legal relations, conditioned by confirmation of one's own dignity. Habermas accurately noted that rights are not properties that individuals naturally possess, but they are, rather, relations based on mutual recognition which is, at the same time, a form of social cooperation.[64]

In the abovementioned sense, juridical recognition stands for "the connection between the enlarging of the sphere of rights recognized as belonging to persons and the enriching of the capacities that these subjects recognize in themselves."[65] Honneth and Ricoeur accurately point out that the act of widening the normative sphere of entitlements corresponds with the act of enlarging the spectrum of abilities granted to subjects of law; so, on the one hand it means presenting (enumerating) the catalogue of such subjective rights (entitlements) and, on the other hand, it stands for allocating these rights to new categories of individuals or groups.[66] In other words, legal recogni-

---

[63] A. Honneth, *Kampf um Anerkennung*, op. cit., p. 194.

[64] Similarly: J. Habermas, *Between Facts and Norms...*, op. cit., pp. 88–89. Habermas writes here as follows: "*At a conceptual level*, rights do not immediately refer to atomistic and estranged individuals who are possessively set against one another. On the contrary, as elements of the legal order they presuppose collaboration among subjects who recognize one another, in their reciprocally related rights and duties, as free and equal citizens. This mutual recognition is constitutive for a legal order, from which actionable rights are derived. In this sense 'subjective' rights emerge co-originally with 'objective' law."

[65] P. Ricoeur, *The Course of Recognition*, op. cit., p. 198.

[66] A. Honneth, *Kampf um Anerkennung*, op. cit., p. 186; P. Ricoeur, *The Course of Recognition*, op. cit., p. 199. By presenting such a catalogue and justifying such individual rights, both these authors refer to Robert Alexy's conception of fundamental rights presented in his famous work *Theorie der Grundrechte* (Baden-Baden: Nomos Verlag, 1986). Honneth classifies them in the following way: "... the first category includes negative rights, which protect a person's freedom, life or property against illegitimate usurpation of the state; the second category consists of positive rights, which are granted to a person on account of his or her participation in the process of shaping public will and, ultimately, the third category is understood as such positive

tion stands for protection of the individual's sphere of freedom and legally ensured participation in public process of creating will, which is hardly possible without ensuring a certain measure of social standard of life. Being awarded with individual rights means that a given individual can have socially accepted claims, that is, carry out legitimate social activity, whilst being self-assured that all other members of society have to treat him or her with respect. Rights, therefore, serve the purpose of creating self-respect since they equip the individual with a symbolic means of expression that enables this individual to show his or her social activities and leads to the situation in which he or she is universally recognised (also in a moral sense) as a valuable and talented person.[67]

The duty of mutual respect reinforces the picture of us as irreproachable individuals, but it also assumes unity and particularity of human race. Lack of respect harms human dignity, resulting in well-known atrocities like slavery, rape, ethnocide etc. What follows lack of respect is designation of people between more and less human, namely those who are worthy of living and those who do not deserve it. In this context, respecting human rights stands for respecting certain requirements that are indispensable for respecting human beings. Respect means that what we think, do, or plan to do counts for others; that we are relatively important people. As a consequence, the fact that we are alive "is of importance for others" and we deserve others' care. In this meaning, the abovementioned commandment "you shall love your neighbour as yourself" would lead to a situation in which one's neighbours would feel the urge to notice, recognize, and confirm that they themselves represent something exceptional, irreplaceable, and permanent. In other words, "equal love for one's neighbours and for oneself would stand for mutual recognition of one's own uniqueness - mutual respect for the differences between us."[68] Morality - which can have a claim to fulfil the idea of a good person who is a cooperation partner in interpersonal relations - is

---

rights that enable fair participation in the distribution of fundamental goods" (ibidem, p. 186).

[67] A. Honneth, *Kampf um Anerkennung*, op. cit., p. 194.

[68] Z. Bauman, *Szanse etyki…*, op. cit., p. 12.

regarded as morality of universal and equal respect. To put it differently, a true and accurate moral attitude consists in regarding every stranger (Other) as a subject of equal rights and, consequently, this means that the duties that are imposed on us in respect to others correspond with the rights of the Other.[69] The task of modern law is to protect the relations of intersubjective recognition by means of sanctions, at the same time leading to the least severe infringement of the integrity of a single subject of law.

Infringement of mutual relation of recognition, namely, of our obligations towards the Other, harms his identity. This obligation has to be mutual, that is – as it has already been noted – the responsibility for and towards the Other must assume a complete and equal responsibility of the Other. It is unacceptable to release him from the duty of respecting the rights of the other people on account of his weaker position or his strangeness. Depriving him of the right to be responsible disqualifies his moral decisions and makes him an inadequate participant of social interactions and, at the same time, inequality becomes an element of the relation of mutual recognition. Such inequality of obligations and lack of balance in the sphere of obligation entail the danger of a patronising and top-down mode of granting privileges, which results from the belief in the superiority of one's own knowledge and morality and which, consequently, leads to lack of respect for and humiliation of the Other. It can be, therefore, seen that the Other has to be fully responsible for his own acts which disturb the relation of recognition and, what merits emphasising – the Other can be subject to a punishment – despite his otherness and strangeness.[70] Responsibility should be then recognised both by the society and by its respective members who participate in rational creation of will, and these are primarily members of society as individuals who are granted the ability to express themselves rationally and independently on moral issues.[71]

---

[69] E. Tugendhat, *Vorlesungen über Ethik*, Frankfurt am Main: Suhrkamp Verlag, 2001, p. 360.

[70] This issue will be broadly discussed in the subsequent chapters of this dissertation.

[71] A. Honneth, *Kampf um Anerkennung*, op. cit., p. 185.

3.3. The role of social respect in shaping mutual recognition

In the third sphere, conflict is based on the criterion of achievements. Individuals or social groups appeal for attaching significance to activities or abilities that have been so far ignored and, consequently, they aim at ensuring greater social respect and share in the distribution of resources. What we encounter here is an intellectually visualised or emotionally enlightened relation of the state recognition (solidarity).[72] Every individual is a member of a community, which allows him to live an authentic, real life of his own as a part of a common coexistence with others. It was Rousseau who first pointed out that in the structure of the state the fact of being dependent on others neither stands for being dependent on political authority nor entails other dependencies that condition survival or accomplishment of a certain goal, but stands rather for the urge to gain respect.[73] The notion of respect contains the moment of approval, or even social and psychosocial affirmation. It can be, therefore, seen that we approve (affirm) our contribution in creating the world (universalistic moment), in such way as we want to see it (individualistic moment). It is then of utmost importance what we do and who we are, or rather who we could be and what we could do. It has to be noted, at the same time, that equal legal status does not directly mean that we are seen and perceived (respected) by others. In the cacophony of numerous sounds coming from – at least formally – equal individuals – our voice can be completely lost and remain inaudible, which can constitute the source of our fears and feelings of injustice. Emancipation, therefore, aims at protecting uniqueness in society and this, in turn, means that the goal of the public sphere is to enhance and protect the private sphere.

In this third model of recognition (solidarity), we are recognised – in the sense of social recognition – on the basis of our particular, indi-

---

[72] See: Axel Honneth's interpretation of Hegel's "*System der Sittlichkeit*". A. Honneth, *Kampf um Anerkennung*, op. cit., pp. 43–46 and idem, *Leiden an Unbestimmtheit. Eine Reaktualisierung der Hegelschen Rechtsphilosophie*, Stuttgart: Reclam, 2001, p. 93.

[73] J.J. Rousseau, *Discourse on the Origin of Inequality*, Indianapolis: Hackett Publishing Company, 1992.

vidual properties and qualities. In this sphere, that is in the sphere of the relations on state level, what comes as the most crucial task is a proper determination of a cooperative model, democratic distribution of work, and social respect.[74] A possible conflict that can arise is based on the criterion of accomplishments. Individual or social groups make a claim of attaching significance to such activities and abilities that have been so far ignored and, as a consequence, they aim to ensure greater social respect and their fair share in the distribution of resources. It can be stated from this point of view that every individual is treated as valuable for society, which, in turn, allows for every individual's positive self-appraisal as a part of particular community.[75] Rawls writes "that not only are citizens normal and fully cooperating members of society, but further they want to be, and to be recognized as such."[76]

Restricting or even preventing a proper self-appraisal by means of despising or discriminating against individuals due to their race, ethnicity, nationality, gender, or lower social status must be viewed critically. In contrast to legal recognition, social recognition concerns particular properties which allow the characterization of people in accordance with their personal differences and their distinctive features. Law, on the other hand, constitutes a medium of recognition which causes general human qualities to be differently manifested. Social recognition requires, then, a different, symbolic, and intersubjectively articulated medium, which develops the common nature of cultural self-understanding of the society.[77] Honneth then notes that cultural self-understanding provides criteria that constitute the aim of social respect of some people because, due to cultural self-understanding, their abilities and activities can be intersubjectively assessed in the context of culturally defined, common values which play a significant role in the life of the society and in the realization of the goals assumed by the latter. The significance and recognition of these val-

---

[74] Honneth refers here to Mead's and Dewey's views.

[75] M. Becka, *Anerkennung im Kontext interkultureller Philosophie*, Frankfurt am Main – London: Verlag für Interkulturelle Kommunikation, 2005, p. 152.

[76] J. Rawls, *Political Liberalism*, op. cit., p. 84.

[77] A. Honneth, *Kampf um Anerkennung*, op. cit., p. 197ff.

ues and goals becomes particularly important in case of their multiplicity, diversity, and relative significance. This will come as a considerable challenge in a pluralistic society.

What is crucial, then, is to determine that the forms of social recognition (valuation) change, depending on epoch, historical contexts, and symbolic constitutions. When assuming such a perspective, society is formed by itself, constituting a set of values and aims which are continually activated. Consequently, the notion "estimable person" depends on the type of mediation, and on social media which contribute to the determination of the horizon of common values.[78] It can be, therefore, assumed that the notion of social respect is also of a contextual and diverse character due to pluralism of values. Such an assumption is undeniable when examining it in the context of historical and anthropological researches, namely both diachronically and synchronically. What can be seen already at first glance are the differences resulting from cultural differences between social respect in African, Asian, and European culture. In my opinion, however, this consideration does not contradict the assumption about universality of subjective rights in a modern, pluralistic society. The source of this universality is the notion of "human dignity," which has universal significance, ensuring all people equal legal protection of their social respect[79] together with their claim to equality of rights (Dworkin's respect and equal treatment of others), and the reinterpretation of well-established ways of judging achievements, which consist in recognizing undervalued properties or ignored forms of activity. Such

---

[78] P. Ricoeur, *The Course of Recognition*, op. cit., p. 202. In order to justify his standpoint, Ricoeur refers to (p. 203) Jean-Marc Ferry's interpretation, quoting the following words: "The question bears centrally on the conditions under which personal identities can be produced and maintained in a social context where the recognition of persons is highly mediated by systemic 'regulators,' such as monetary considerations and legal rules, and what in general constitutes the 'system' in its different-technical, monetary, fiscal, bureaucratic, legal, democratic, publicity, pedagogical, and scientific-aspects, along with all the 'signs' that correspond to them, which are all indicators of behavior meant to coordinate individual actions within collective undertakings on a large scale." J.-M. Ferry, *Les Puissances de l'expérience*, Paris: Editions du Cerf, 1991, p. 9.

[79] A. Honneth, *Kampf um Anerkennung*, op. cit., p. 202ff.; idem, *Das Andere der Gerechtigkeit. Aufsätze zur praktischen Philosophie*, Frankfurt am Main: Suhrkamp Verlag, 2000, p. 158ff.

an assumption allows for a certain hierarchization of values and, consequently, creates sufficiently symmetrical social relations and strong interpersonal bonds. A lack of such universal significance of human dignity can lead to a situation in which the subjective limit of respect and ideological social respect result in treating some groups of people as *Untermenschen* (sub-human) or even as animals and, consequently, in racism, ethnic cleansing, totalitarianism, and eugenism.

As it has been previously pointed out, social respect is also inseparably connected with the economic situation of the members of a given community and their share in distribution of goods.[80] We do not mean here a standard situation of aiming at financial benefits, but the intersubjective need that the other person should recognize our social position.[81] What arouses controversy in reference to fair distribution is division of goods according to achievements. It seems, however, that referring to an individualistic principle of achievements can merely constitute the justification of real social inequality, so characteristic of capitalistic societies. This principle contains a normative claim to take into consideration – in an honest and adequate form of mutual recognition – individual achievements of all members of society. The third sphere of the fight for recognition, based on "the principle of achievements" has been contemporarily enriched with the principle of "social minimum," which should protect human dignity irrespective of real services. It constitutes – to a certain extent – a realization of the idea of justice that assumes a search for balance between the individual's rights and common claims of the society. A similar approach is applied in case of affirmative activities that aim at compensating for inequalities that result from different race, gender, or ethnic grounds. It should be noted that ignoring real services of a particular group is met with a reaction of questioning already developed patterns of assessments and with a fight for recognizing their social contribution that aims at economic redistribution. It is obvious that every individual's urge is for the appreciation of their intellectual involvement, input of work, and devoted time. An individual or

---

[80] It has to be noted that social goods are – by definition – limited.

[81] F. Fukuyama, *Our Posthuman Future: Consequences of the Biotechnology Revolution*, New York: Picador, 2003.

a social group wants to be perceived and appreciated, and they aim at participation in fair distribution. It has to be noted, at the same time, that different arbitrary circumstances shape the demands which are formulated, which in the case of poor people often means that their preferences are muffled – restricted by their living conditions and lack of perspectives. There arises the problem of adaptive and endogenous conditions. Improvement of living conditions and help provided to the victims of oppressions increases their trust in the community or society that they are members of.

The reaction to the refusal of recognition is not only negation of existing, harmful social relations but also the fight for changing such an unfair system. In other words, referring to civil disobedience can result from a moral belief that a given, commonly applied principle of recognition is bad or insufficiently applied in relation to a particular group or in particular conditions. Referring to Aristotle's views, it can be stated that the principle of achievements demands treating particular individuals commensurately with the differences among them (e.g. in respect of the input of their work, abilities, or needs). In order to achieve this, the differences have to be expressed in common units and allocated goods have to be shared.

The third sphere of recognition means that every individual perceives his or her activities in terms of cultural standards but, at the same time, preserves respect for his or her self. In other words, even in a pluralistic or changing society, the experience of social respect should ensure that – within certain patterns – the individual's activities and abilities resulting from the necessity of respecting human dignity – are recognized by other members of society as "valuable." In the conditions of a modern society which has as its basis the assumption of social relations of symmetric judging among individual and autonomous individuals, solidarity stands for treating one another in the light of values which allow the revealing of the abilities and qualities of every individual, diverse and different from ourselves, and the perceiving of this individual not only as valuable but also as crucial and indispensable for the process of creating a common social and political practice.[82] Honneth refers to such relations as "relations

[82] A. Honneth, *Kampf um Anerkennung*, op. cit., p. 209ff.

of solidarity" because they lead not only to "passive tolerance" but they create the possibility of active and cooperative participation of other people – who differ in terms of their culture, outlook on life, or religion – in the public creation of common will. It can be, therefore, seen that common social goals can be realized only if I take care of the development of such properties which are strange to me. A symmetric pattern of relations means that every individual, without collective grading, is given a chance to experience themselves in their own activities and abilities as valuable members of a society.[83]

3.4. The principle of mutual recognition and the rules of discourse as constitutive elements for political and legal constructivist community

According to Axel Honneth's theory of recognition, the conception of human mental development is connected with the conception of social participation and with the change the human being undergoes. The point of departure is then a determination of one's own identity as an intersubjective process of justifying the claim of mutual recognition of the subjects of social interactions. Francis Fukuyama, when referring to Plato, noted that *thymos* as "a proud side of human personality" requires from others recognition of our value and dignity.[84] Lack of recognition on any of the abovementioned three spheres, assuming the form of disrespect or contempt, arouses the feeling of shame or anger and this, in turn, can lead to the social fight for recognition. What is most severely felt and experienced is the contempt caused by the refusal to grant civic rights, frustration resulting from inability to participate in the process of shaping public will, and, ultimately, the feeling of exclusion caused by poverty and, in the effect, a lack of access to basic and fundamental material goods. To sum up, refusal or loss of recognition is every time manifested in a different form and emotional modality.

---

[83] Ibidem, p. 210. Also: R. Dworkin, *Law's Empire*, op. cit., p. 206ff. Dworkin perceived relations of solidarity as constitutive element of society understood as the community of principles.

[84] F. Fukuyama, *Our Posthuman…*, op. cit., p. 42.

The above is the manifestation of the normative quality of Honneth's conception since permanent deliberations of the relations of recognition anticipate a hypothetical state of a formal conception of a good life – ethicality (*Sittlichkeit*). Ethicality is manifested not only the ethos of a particular lifeworld, but it is also manifested as a community of intersubjective conditions, which constitute the assumption of individual self-realisation.[85] In other words, different patterns of recognition present intersubjective conditions that we have to enhance in order to describe the structures of desirable life, whilst the anticipated state is already included in the community of values, which is ensured by relations of solidarity, as a part of which social judging takes place.

Those common values are universal human values justified by human dignity. Those values ensure peaceful coexistence of different lifestyles. What we mean here is law that lays the grounds for a commonly accepted community of values, which are indispensable at the state level (relations of solidarity). There arises a problem – already pointed out in the first chapter of this dissertation – of whether this common horizon of values in an intercultural context is always given or assumed. This problem entails disturbances in intercultural dialogue, which aims at recognising the diversity of every human being in his particularity of values. What has to be, therefore, assumed is a certain intransgressible canon of values presented in the form of universal and sacred human rights. It has to be noted that the issue of intercultural dialogue touches upon the belief in the minimum of common values despite cultural diversity,[86] like the ethos of freedom and equality. What seems indispensable is a minimum "ethical consensus."[87] Without the latter, no meaningful intercultural dialogue

---

[85] A. Honneth, *Kampf um Anerkennung*, op. cit., p. 275ff.

[86] M. Becka, *Anerkennung im Kontext…*, op. cit., p. 154.

[87] This minimum consensus often comes down to the so-called golden rule formulated by Confucius "What you do not want done to yourself, do not do to the others." This principle can be also found in Judaism: "That which is hateful to you, do not do to your fellow," in Christianity: "Do to no one what you yourself dislike" or "And as you would that men should do to you, do you also to them likewise" (Lucas, 3: 31), in wisdom of Africa: "Just as pain is not agreeable to you, it is so with others." This principle is related to Kant's categorical imperative, according to which "I should not act

that aims at discursive consent makes sense. On the other hand, heterogeneity of certain values makes recognition true and complete. It is, thus, crucial to recognise the Other, irrespective of the diversity of his lifestyle, beliefs, and values. In other words, recognition of the Other consists also in exceeding and widening one's own horizon of values, which can be observed in the example of Christian societies being open for the values of Muslim culture. It should be noted that being open for the Other and exceeding limits determined by origin, gender, religion, race, or ethnicity is vividly emphasised in the society based on the idea of dignity of human beings in which recognition – in reference with the cooperative character of this society – depends exclusively on the individual's activity. In this sense, the fight for recognition is manifested in the omnipresent language of identity, referred to by Taylor.

From the perspective of intercultural dialogue it is indispensable not only to recognize the values professed by the Other, but also a specific situation in which the Other lives. The difficulties with agreement and understanding require "a merger of horizons," as noted by Gadamer. This is possible to accomplish only by means of assuming the role of "the speaker" or "the listener."[88] A change of dialogue perspective means engagement in symmetry, which constitutes the basis of every act of speech. What constitutes a point of departure is the conception of a generalised Other, which allows us to treat each individual as a rational being and as an addressee of such rights and duties as correspond with ours. "A generalised Other" is "an important Other," namely, the point of reference for our activities. Mutuality of perspectives allows the creation of a common horizon of the most fundamental values, which are intersubjectively shared. The latter originates from granting all subjects equal and inborn dignity and, at the same time, recognising equal rights. Such an abstract and formal conception does not always constitute a guarantee of fair treatment of a particular other because it can lead to a dan-

---

differently than *to aim at my maxim becoming a universal law.*" I. Kant, *Metaphysics of Morals*, op. cit., p. 190.

[88] J. Habermas in: G. Borradori, *Philosophy in a Time of Terror. Dialogues with Jürgen Habermas and Jacques Derrida*, Illinois: The University of Chicago Press, 2003.

ger of improper unification of differences or diversities that occur among various individuals.[89] Such danger has been pointed at by American law philosopher, Seyla Benhabib, who is contemporarily the finest exponent of communitaristic criticism of liberalism and feministic criticism of normative ethics.

Benhabib postulates the complementing of ethical theories with the conception of "a particular Other", which would enable us to introduce fair activities to a greater extent than when applying merely the notion of "a generalised Other." What is meant by this is to treat every rational being as an individual with a specific history, identity, and affectively-emotional structure. In *Another Cosmopolitanism,* Benhabib notes that such a perspective allows for a better understanding of the needs of the other, his motives, aims, or wishes.[90] Benhabib criticises here the abstract nature of Rawls' "veil of ignorance," assuming that a fair behaviour towards the other can take place only when we are aware of his needs and wishes as well as of his own history. It is primarily a dialogue that serves as a source of such cognition.[91] A Similar view was expressed by Otfried Höffe, who accurately writes that what is crucial in intercultural discourse about human rights is knowledge of history, culture, language, and values of the different communities that are the participants of this argumentative process. Due to this consideration, one can anticipate the anthropological and – to a certain extent – also communitaristic goal that every human being is placed and deeply rooted in a specific culture or in a cultural "mixture" and is conditioned by the latter.[92]

Benhabib supplements obligation (*Sollen*) with the postulate of care, and formal justice with the claim for compassion for the Other (*ethics of care*).[93] It is not her aim, as she writes, "to attribute a con-

---

[89] M. Becka, *Anerkennung im Kontext…*, op. cit., p. 155.

[90] S. Benhabib, *Selbst im Kontext,* Frankfurt am Main: Suhrkamp Verlag, 1995, p. 176.

[91] Ibidem, p. 180.

[92] O. Höffe, *Vernunft und Recht. Bausteine zu einem interkulturellen Rechtsdiskurs,* Frankfurt am Main: Suhrkamp Verlag, 1996, p. 60ff.

[93] Such view of hers encountered a justified criticism of A. Honneth, who alleged that in her conception moral discourse begins in the place where abstract claims are made in favour of a specific Other. Idem, *Das Andere der Gerechtigkeit…*, op. cit., p. 151.

formist, moral, or political theory to the standpoint of a specific Other." Benhabib would be more wiling to develop a universalistic theory of morality that perceives a moral point of view in the light of reversibility of perspectives and, at the same time, aims at widening one's own pattern of thinking by means of encompassing other types of thinking.[94] Such reversal (change) of perspectives does not serve a prescriptive, but rather a critical function. The conception of a particular other determines ideological limits of universalistic discourse, in other words, it manifests limits that originate from lack of attention on any other than universal ways of constructing morality. She wants moral discourse applied equally to "full-blooded human beings."

Such a conception refers to George H. Mead's or Peter F. Strawson's conception of "exchangeability of perspectives," which is – according to Alfred Schütz – assumed by the natural attitude.[95] When assuming a natural attitude, we remain with others in such a relation that everything that we experience, namely sensual perception of objects, the ability to interact with them, and motives, seem to be fully reciprocated and, at the same time, we deal with mutual understanding. It can be, therefore, seen that mutual understanding is a natural state, whilst misunderstanding is something unnatural. When assuming the latter attitude, it is possible to act in accordance with the abovementioned golden principle that "I should not act towards others in a way that makes them feel as if I infringed their rights and freedoms, because if I were them I would not wish to have my rights and freedoms violated."

Infringement of the relations of mutual recognition stands for violating human dignity; life is then made harder or even impossible. By means of refusing recognition, we exclude human beings from interpersonal discourse because the latter constitutes its sine qua non. Due to this consideration, the relation of recognition – which is anticipated in the discourse – supplements the discourse with existential and material conditions. It also crystallises the discourse by means of referring it to a particular Other, who has his own beliefs, values, history,

---

[94] S. Benhabib, *Selbst im Kontext*, op. cit., p. 183.

[95] A. Schütz, T. Luckmann, *The Structures of the Life-World*, London: Gordon and Breach Science Publishers, 1974, p. 4ff.

and properties. When taking a cosmopolitan perspective it can be stated that the process of enlarging the discourse requires opening it for diversities resulting from its intercultural character, leading it beyond geographical borders of the previous colonial world.

A Pluralistic, let alone a cosmopolitan perspective, means that when there is a coexistence and combination of different cultures, nationalities, and loyalties - as a part of one single sphere - it is crucial that one's right to cultural self-determination was connected with granting the same right to diverse, or even utterly strange cultures. The latter constitutes the grounds of recognition for every human being, also the one who has different beliefs, not always comprehensible in our set of notions, assumptions, and convictions. Fukuyama infers that recognition - as expectation or claim for respect for oneself - means that one can also demand approval for one's gods, sacrum, nation, or legitimate aim. Demand for respect stands exclusively for the right of being free in practising and professing one's own beliefs and convictions. However, according to the principle of mutuality, the latter cannot turn into domination or imposing one's beliefs on others. It has to be also kept in mind that, despite ostensible, external differences there is a community of deeply hidden beliefs, alluding to universal humanity as such, namely, to a common value of human dignity and discursive claims to significance. As a consequence, the claim to mutual recognition arrives at its institutional dimension in fundamental rights, which allow for free and unencumbered self-determination, that is, such rights as grant freedom and equality, and thus constitute human rights.[96] It is crucial to refer to Joel Feinberg's statement that "human dignity is defined as a recognised ability to claim one's rights."[97] The idea of dignity - as I have already pointed out - assumes that every individual as a human being is endowed with awareness and responsibility and the latter entails moral unity of the human race and its exceptional nature in relation to the animal

---

[96] H. Bielefeldt, *Menschenrechte in der Einwanderungsgesellschaft. Plädoyer für einen aufgeklärten Multikulturalismus*, Bielefeld: Transcript, 2007, p. 20.

[97] J. Feinberg, "The Nature and Value of Rights," in: idem, *Rights, Justice, and the Bounds of Liberty. Essays in Social Philosophy*, Princeton, NJ: Princeton University Press, 1980, p. 151.

world. Bearing responsibility is also justified by Kant's assumption that every human being has reason and conscience, so all people should treat one another in accordance with reason and conscience, namely, according to the principle of respecting inborn dignity. It has to be noted, at the same time, that such respect, tolerance, and recognition are not unlimited. One can differentiate types of behaviour, hidden behind the veil of cultural equality ("modification of race" by Arawakan, or ritual murder of unfaithful women in Muslim culture) which do not deserve recognition or respect. Amy Gutmann accurately points out that:

> Mutual respect requires a widespread willingness and ability to articulate our disagreements, to defend them before people with whom we disagree, to discern the difference between respectable and disrespectable disagreement, and to be open to changing our own minds when faced with well-reasoned criticism. The moral promise of multiculturalism depends on the exercise of these deliberative virtues.[98]

Intercultural dialogue is understood as a real situation of speech which has as its basis universal values and claims. From this point of view, one demands not only the protection of a generalized Other as a representative of the human race, but most of all the protection of a particular Other whom I cooperate with (even unconsciously) in social existence. Individual experience of another human being is crucial for me because it allows me to learn, perceive, respect, and understand this particular other to overcome existing stereotypes. The experience of the other – as it has already been stated – allows me to find my own identity. The ability to look at the world from the perspective of the Other and Otherness minimizes the danger of increased anger aroused by feelings of rejection, disrespect, or contempt. The attitude of recognizing the otherness of the Other in a divided political world constitutes political *common sense,*[99] which enables safe life in a world which is diversified in terms of culture, outlook on life, or

---

[98] A. Gutmann, "Introduction," in: *Multiculturalism: Examining the Politics of Recognition*, ed. by A. Gutman, Princeton, NJ: Princeton University Press, 1994, p. 24.

[99] U. Beck, *Macht und Gegenmacht im globalen Zeitalter. Neue weltpolitische Ökonomie*, Frankfurt am Main: Suhrkamp Verlag, 2002, p. 13.

religion; it also makes it possible to overcome some ostensible borders between races, classes or even genders. This recognition of the dignity and significance of the Other constitutes the basis, a type of language which allows for a common, peaceful coexistence and, ultimately, for creating a pluralistic society. Social respect and regard become a bridge which enables communication among differentiated individuals and groups. What is crucial then is to preserve family love, friendship, respect in law and for law, as well as social solidarity, regard, and tolerance. These relations should be mutual in such a way that their violation would stand for infringement of the principle of mutual recognition, would have all the hallmarks of intolerance, and therefore it would constitute a violation of rights and freedoms (irrespective of whether it were caused by a dominant group or by a minority). What constitutes the basis of Rawls' partial consensus, perceived as a realization of the idea of human rights, is mutual rather than unilateral respect.

What merits noting at this point is the ethics of authenticity, which allows the combination of my own lifestyle, namely, my individual and communitarian identity, with every person's right to freedom as a complementary aspect of the modern "fight for recognition."[100] The modern fight for recognition stands for connecting the difference and equality of relatively historically-cultural particularity with normative universalism. What is equally important, both determination of one's own authenticity, and identity as well as the fight for recognition are of a dialogue, or even of a discursive character. At the same time, procedural requirements of a discourse are complemented with substantive content inferred from human dignity and from a claim for mutual recognition among people as equal and free human beings. Honneth's conception of recognition is based on the belief that the individual should be treated in the experience of legal and state recognition as a being who shares all his properties with other members of the community and they, in turn, allow him to participate in discursive creation of public will.[101] This allows the crea-

---

[100] Ch. Taylor, *The Ethics of Authenticity*, Cambridge: Harvard University Press, 1991.

[101] A. Honneth, *Kampf um Anerkennung*, op. cit., p. 195.

tion of a political community understood as "a set of democratic institutions determining a goal that a particular legal order in the state should serve" and the feature that distinguishes such a community from other social groups is the possibility of shaping the vision of the individual in a society.[102]

In this context, it is worth recalling James Tully's statement that we are currently present in the third phase of antiauthoritarian politics: the first one was a fight for democratic citizenship, the second one a fight against global imperialism, and the third one the "politics of cultural recognition." This author distinguishes two fields of the fight for recognition. The first one is a fight for legal and political recognition of various types of differences and equalities such as: endogenous, ethnic, national, supranational, religious, cultural, civilization and language ones; whilst the second constitutes a practical answer to the first in the form of numerous practices of law making.[103] Tully thinks that contemporary constitutions should take into account cultural differentiations, in other words, they should be based on intercultural dialogue.[104] Only if this is the case it is guaranteed that the view of every individual will be appropriately taken into account. In his opinion, intercultural dialogue - constituted in the abovementioned way - based on cooperative, deliberative democracy and on common discourse ensures fair cultural recognition, at the same time rejecting unfair claims to recognition.

What becomes necessary is the act of combining the ethics of discourse with the conception of mutual recognition. In order to undertake the latter, Habermas - when referring to Émil Durkheim, Max Weber, and Talcott Parsons - tries to combine the normative dimen-

---

[102] In this context, John Finnis notes that the community (or rather communitarianism and affiliation) should be presented as evolving states of things, common life, activity and community of interests, affiliation, and joining groups. In other words, community is understood as a relation connecting human beings, rather than as a social group or association. J. Finnis, *Natural Law and Natural Rights*, Oxford: Clarendon Press, 1992, p. 136, 154–156.

[103] J. Tully, "The Practice of Law-Making and the Problem of Difference: An Introduction to the Field," in: *Multiculturalism and Law: a Critical Debate*, ed. by O.A. Payrow Shabani, Cardiff: University of Wales Press, 2007, p. 19.

[104] Ibidem, p. 27ff.

sion in law with critical theory as well as the philosophical perspective with the sociological one. It is law that constitutes institutional level allowing the combination of those diverse perspectives. Habermas writes as follows:

> The philosophical discourse of justice misses the institutional dimension, towards which the sociological discourse on law is directed from the outset. Without the view of law as an empirical action system, philosophical concepts remain empty. However, insofar as the sociology of law insists on an objectivating view from the outside, remaining insensitive to the symbolic dimension whose meaning is only internally accessible, sociological perception falls into the opposite danger of remaining blind.[105]

Such understanding of law corresponds with Neil MacCormick's and Ota Weinberger's, for whom law is an institutional fact. Law is perceived as an institutionalised system of norms, which gives meaning to specific types of behaviour, events, or states of facts.[106]

The theory of discourse searches for something rational, namely communicative reason, in that which is empirical, that is in intersubjective practice of communicative activities. To put it differently, empirical processes of institutionalisation are juxtaposed with symbolical processes of legitimising communication. The theory of discourse, being a justification of normative and axiological elements included in a critical attitude, constitutes an attempt of removing ontological dualism that occurs between that which is factual (the fact of being binding), namely the practice of communicative activities, and that which is normative, namely an ethically justified ideal of communication undisturbed by violence (communicatively justified binding nature). Factuality is understood in this context as a legality, the legitimacy of

---

[105] J. Habermas, *Between Facts and Norms...*, op. cit., p. 66. It is accurately pointed out by M. Rosenfeld that law – justified by procedurally reconstructed communicative rationality, i.e. presented as a part of the theory of discourse – aims at bridging the gap between the rights of the individual and democracy. M. Rosenfeld, "Law as Discourse: Bridging the Gap between Democracy and Rights," *Harvard Law Review* 1995, vol. 108, pp. 1163–1189.

[106] N. MacCormick, O. Weinberger, *An Institutional Theory of Law. New Approaches to Legal Positivism*, Dordrecht – Boston – Lancaster – Tokyo: Kluwer Verlag, 1986, pp. 49–76.

which we question. Such dialectics can be also observed in Habermas' approach to the notion of law. Law is, on the one hand, a social fact - factuality (*Faktizität*) and, on the other hand, it is of a normative character (*Geltung*). From such a perspective, that which is normative is based on that which is factual.

Habermas - in the theory of discourse in question - does not refer us to moral recognition in order to justify recognition of equality and equal rights of citizens. He treats the equality of all people–citizens as a fundamental condition of a discursive situation. This is why he treats integration of the members of different cultural, religious communities, or ethnic or sexual minorities, as a basic condition of social integration of multicultural and pluralistic democratic society. Members of these groups must be granted the status of free and equal participants in cooperating society (state) in order to be granted full and unencumbered participation in discursive democracy. From this point of view, the right of being the Other must be treated as the fundamental right. Diversity cannot be the source of restrictions or discrimination - just the opposite - the procedure of discourse, discursively reconstructed law, and deliberative politics have to guarantee obeying "the rights of others" and recognising their equality in their otherness. The structure of "the system of law" - as presented by Habermas - encompasses respective forms of "a fight for recognition," in other words, it already contains and recognises the achievements of particular forms of this fight. As I have already noted, the state - by means of law - should enable the process of cultural reproduction of life worlds; it should not guarantee, on the other hand, preservation of a specific culture.[107] From the perspective of the theory of law, multiculturalism imposes ethical neutrality of legal and political order[108]. In this context, what comes as a basic task of the

---

107 J. Habermas, "Kampf um Anerkennung im demokratischen Rechtstaat," in: idem, *Die Einbeziehung des Anderen. Studien zur politischen Theorie,* Frankfurt am Main: Suhrkamp Verlag, 1999, p. 259; S. Benhabib, *Kulturelle Vielfalt und demokratische Gleichheit. Politische Partizipation im Zeitalter der Globalisierung,* Frankfurt am Main: Suhrkamp Verlag, 1999, p. 68.

108 J. Habermas, "Kampf um Anerkennung im demokratischen Rechtstaat," op. cit., p. 252. Habermas understands the notion "ethical" as "all issues which concern a good or accurate life. Ethical issues do not allow for their assessment from 'a moral

authority, based on discursive democracy, is enabling citizens a free choice of lifestyle, values, or culture, and ensuring an equal access to political system to all citizens, irrespective of the form of life chosen by them. At the same time, moral self-realisation of political community should be manifested in the possibility of abiding by the principle of democracy, thereby enabling a real will of the whole community to be voiced in public sphere.

Habermas shows that the system of laws differentiated by him by means of assuming a discursive and, at the same time, rational communication, should guarantee and protect different moments of life-world. This conception critically complements Taylor's view, pointing out that the state ceases then to be "blind to colours" when the individuals who are subjects of laws are granted intersubjectively understood identity.[109] As a result of this, the problems of multiculturalism and pluralism, that is, the issue of recognising equality and dignity of the most distant options of life – in terms of culture and outlook on life – should be discursively settled. It has to be noted that the subjects of law will be individualised only by means of socialising. This is why the theory of law demands the politics of recognition, which supports integrity of individuals also in its relations of life that are developed in terms of identity. As a result of this, private autonomy of a citizen who is granted equal rights can be ensured only in case of activating his civic and state autonomy. The Defective nature of the "liberal" variant of the legal system consists in the fact that it ignores this relation, which prevents perception of universalism of basic rights as an abstract unification of differences.[110] In other words, the "liberal" variant of the legal system makes it hard to undertake a proper politics of recognition. The modern democratic pattern of legal systems

---

point of view,' whether something is equally good for everyone; impartial judgment of these issues would be rather undertaken on the basis of strong evaluation, by means of self-understanding and perspective concept of life of particular groups, namely on account of what is 'good for us' when assuming a general attitude. What is an ethical issue is the reference to the first person together with grammatically inherent reference to group (individual) identity."

[109] J. Habermas, "Kampf um Anerkennung im demokratischen Rechtstaat," op. cit., p. 243.

[110] Ibidem, p. 245.

also encompasses collective goals, which are manifested in fights for recognition.

It has to be noted that the universalising principle of discourse allows the recognition of not only ontological obligation and its justification, but also the recognition one's own moral idea, namely the idea of a community in which one is placed. In other words, the principle of discourse enables us to check whether ontological obligation is really something which can be regarded as a legitimate challenge in respect to others, and to check whether principles (norms, customs, and ideas) of my community allow identification of this challenge as morally justified, or that I should rather abandon the moral convictions of my community, do away with its particularism, and assume the vision of a wider community. By this wider community, I can understand a certain constructivist communicative community, which allows me to assume the responsibility towards "a generalised Other." Such a community constitutes the effect of a particular project rather than necessities that exceed human will. Constructivist community is of an exclusive character in the sense that its limits and participation in it are subject to agreement; they depend on a consent arrived at in the process of negotiation.[111] Constructivism accepts the fact of pluralism and rationality of the thesis about inadequacy of values and lifestyles. The idea of constructiveness treats the argument of pluralism as a point of departure for reflective and critical deliberation on the basis of society, both from the perspective of particularistic as well as communitaristic and multicommunitaristic thought.[112] At the same time, constructivism makes it possible to enhance the elements that constitute the basis of objective significance of certain principles and values. Referring to the idea of communicative community allows t the combination of the conception of obligation as an external compulsion, according to which moral demand requires support and social external reinforcement (morality will be then perceived as a socionomic, heteronomic, and external creation in respect

[111] Such a constructivist community allows the preservation of everything that is valuable in the idea of community and, at the same time, what is significant in the idea of uniqueness, diversity, autonomy, multiplicity, and individuality.

[112] P. Roberts, *Political Constructivism*, London – New York: Routledge, 2007, p. 4, 10ff.

to a given person[113]) with Kant's conception, which treats moral obligation as "self-compulsion and self-obligation."

Communicative community and the principle of discourse – which constitutes the basis of the latter – allow verification of the legitimacy of compulsion arising from society (this peculiar constructivist community), and they ensure an accurate identification of ontological obligations, which can then be subject to a discursive test. This means that correct and fair principles, according to which a society functions, can be presented as a result of a given procedure of construction that is primarily based on practical reason.[114] In the effect, the consent concerning values is obtained only in the course of a procedurally ensured consensus, which is established on the basis of communicative ethics.[115] Fair conditions of social cooperation are then determined by the principles of justice, which are agreed on by the representatives of free and equal citizens, in the situation when these principles are fairly authorised and when they abide by the principles of discourse in the process of making choices.[116] Rawls accurately indicates that this leads to the ideal of democratic citizens who arrive at order with fundamental differences that divide them, in accordance with the idea of public reason.

Such inclusive community is not oriented against other communities, it is not constituted due to hatred towards something strange or external, and it is not closed to others, to strangers; just the opposite, it encourages individuals to assume the principles that are binding in it and to become its members. Such a community takes into consideration the fact that emancipation movements that occur in multicul-

---

113 H. Krämer, *Integrative Ethik*, op. cit., p. 42f. Krämer questions the possibility of self-compulsion and self-obligation.

114 J. Rawls, *Political Liberalism*, op. cit., p. 91.

115 J. Habermas, *The Theory of Communicative Action*, vol. 2: Lifeworld and System: A Critique of Functionalist Reason, Boston: Beacon Press, 1987, p. 108. Habermas even claims that: "Cultural values that have not been abstracted into basic formal values (such as equality, freedom, human dignity, and the like) surrender their authority and stand at the disposition of processes of mutual understanding which are prejudged."

116 J. Rawls, *Political Liberalism*, op. cit., p. 97. Rawls makes such a conclusion assuming that in the conditions of reasonable pluralism "citizens cannot agree on any moral authority, whether a sacred text, or institution. Nor do they agree about the order of moral values, or the dictates of what some regard as natural law."

tural society do not constitute a homogenous phenomenon. Inclusion, then, means that community is open for including citizens who are representatives of different traditions, without the intent of absorbing these traditions by means of unifying a homogenous national community.[117] We could follow Habermas' thought and point out that the basic cement of such a community is communicative practices, which allow us to understand one another. Due to these, the members of such a community agree on certain principles (a set of grammar principles and cultural rules) which shape the community or society. These principles constitute the basis given by the beliefs deriving from common source, obvious cultural truths, and mutual expectations, which, in turn, allows symmetrical conditions to be met, enabling a mutual assumption of perspectives.[118] Norms, the values of

---

[117] J. Habermas in: "Jürgen Habermas und Gerhard Schröder über die *Einbeziehung des Anderen*. Reihe; Kultur in der Diskussion. Band 5," in: *Philosophie und Politik III*, ed. by J. Nida-Rümelin, W. Thierse, Essen: Klartext, 1998, p. 20. Habermas persuades that the possibility of creating such a community (common political culture) is ensured by democratic process, due to its civic legitimization. He obviously points out that in order to undertake the legitimization, the culture of majority – which has claims to national culture – would have to release itself from this merger with political culture so as to allow all citizens representing also the cultures of minorities identification with the culture of their country. Habermas points out, at the same time, that national identity, which is not primarily based on republican self-understanding and constitutional patriotism, undeniably collides with universalistic principles of mutual coexistence of human beings. J. Habermas, "Yet Again: German Identity – A Unified Nation of Angry DM – Burghers," in: *When the Wall Came Down: Reactions to German Unification*, ed. by H. James and M. Stone, London: Routledge, 1992, pp. 86–102.

[118] It is worth noting at this point that Honneth is critical about the mechanism – approved both by Habermas and Mead – of participation in ethical discourse, which is understood as "assuming the role of the Other." Honneth indicates that there are various interpretations of this thesis, and that what is particularly problematic is determination of whether such "change of perspectives" is of an exclusively cognitive character or an affective one. According to Honneth, "as far as the first alternative vividly enhanced argumentative character that moral discourses should have since universality of norms ought to be rationally verified in them, the second alternative would – on the contrary – emphasise that such an intersubjective verifying approach cannot be successful without a certain extent of readiness to mutual feeling (empathy)." A. Honneth, "Das Andere der Gerechtigkeit. Habermas und die Herausforderung der poststrukturalistischen Ethik," in: idem, *Das Andere der Gerechtigkeit...*, op. cit., p. 150.

which we appreciated in a reflective manner, appeal more strongly to us. Constructivist community and its values have greater chances to be preserved, and there is a greater likelihood of abiding by legal rules represented by the latter because it refers to the political value of public life undertaken in such conditions as can be approved and accepted by all people being co-originators and co-operators.[119]

When using Durkheim's terminology, we could state that such a community constitutes a new form of solidarity. It is then a development of Durkheim's thought about social progress from mechanic solidarity, which consists in sharing common beliefs and standards, to organic solidarity, which depends on the differences occurring among people and on their mutual needs of complementing within different relations and communities. What comes as the most crucial issue in this development is the unification of law and morality, connected with breaking a spell on law so far established in *sacrum*. As a consequence, the rules of law and morality were "linked at first to local circumstances, to particularities, ethnic, climatic, etc., they free themselves little by little, and with the same stroke become more general. What makes this increase of generality obvious is the uninterrupted decline of formalism."[120] On the other hand, solidarity shaped within our constructivist community requires that the consensus over the values was arrived at by means of cooperation of all its members. In other words, social integration takes place in such a community due to cooperation, and its aim is a greater rationality. Inclusive community is then also understood as cooperative community. Durkheim wrote that "we shall see that what characterizes the morality of organized societies, compared to that of segmental societies, is that there is something more human, therefore more rational, about them. ... We know only too well what a laborious work it is to erect this society in which each individual will have the place he merits, will be rewarded as he deserves, where everybody, accordingly, will spontaneously work for the good of all and each."[121]

---

[119] J. Rawls, *Political Liberalism*, op. cit., p. 97ff.

[120] É. Durkheim, *The Division of Labor in Society*, New York: The Free Press, 1997, p. 289.

[121] Ibidem, pp. 407–408.

The community of a constructivist character is driven by the principle of mutuality and by reliable, fair procedures, being based on the equality of its members and their cooperative participation. It is worth noting that active participation in political discourse creates reality and importance of politics and provides justification for creating such a political community. Such a community is ultimately based on the symmetry of relations. The assumption of the symmetric nature of relations enables intercultural agreement among different organic communities[122] that function within this constructivist community, including the agreement on numerous conceptions of successful life. Social integration is then accomplished by means of intersubjective recognition of valuable claims expressed in the course of the act of speech. Agreement is possible because the members of this constructivist community assume that they learn from one another and they exchange perspectives - which bridges the gap between diverse horizons. The source of agreement can be found in the principle of discourse, namely in the universalistic potential of reason manifested in language. The principle of communication organizes such community. This principle assumes the participation of everyone, including the Other who belongs to a diverse organic community, so it also assumes intercultural communication, which aims at common understanding.[123] When assuming a broader perspective, the aim of such understanding would be the possibility of consensus in a particular issue or, in a more narrow perspective, mutual respect for reliably justified significance of competitive traditions. Discourse assumes that its participants show mutual respect for one another, being persuaded about the value and authenticity of another culture or a different lifestyle, even if they themselves do not share its self-understanding. A solution for respecting diversities and protecting

---

[122] Such organic community is based on an Aristotelian assumption that it is something natural, coming before individuals, more important than them and that the best interest of such a community is undoubtedly more significant than the interest of respective individuals. What is equally important is that individuals could not exist without such a community. Such a community is primarily of an exclusive character.

[123] J. Habermas, *Vom sinnlichen Eindruck zum symbolischen Ausdruck*, Frankfurt am Main: Suhrkamp Verlag, 1997, p. 39. Also G.H. Mead, *Mind, Self, and Society*, Chicago – London: The University of Chicago Press, 1967, p. 253.

the rights of ethnic, cultural, religious, and sexual minorities is not ethical neutrality of legal order but rather protection of every legal community and every democratic process of realizing human rights and the most fundamental rights.[124] It is also crucial to admit that in order for a discourse to take place it is necessary to ensure interpersonal solidarity, which is referred to by Habermas as "another side of justice," and which assumes the perceiving of another person not only as an equal but also as a unique individual.[125]

What functions here as institutional protection is discursively determined law based on the consensus of all cooperating citizens who believe in Habermas' "constitutional patriotism" manifesting solidarity of citizens.[126] The constitution has to guarantee equal coexistence of different ethnic groups and their cultural forms of life. Furthermore, the constitution has to take into account the structures of communication that account on the fact that the identity of every individual is combined with collective identities and can be established only in a certain cultural net.[127] "Constitutional patriotism," despite the fact

[124] J. Habermas, "Kampf um Anerkennung im demokratischen Rechtstaat," op. cit., p. 255.

[125] J. Habermas, "Justice and Solidarity: On the Discussion Concerning Stage 6," in: *The Moral Domain: Essays in the Ongoing Discussion between Philosophy and the Social Sciences*, ed. by Th.E. Wren, Cambridge: The MIT Press, 1990, pp. 224–251.

[126] Neil MacCormick expresses a similar view: "We need not overstress the requirements of culture or common ethnicity or language as essentially constitutive of a *demos* in the sense required for the concept of democratic government. I should like to suggest the possibility of our conceiving such a thing as a 'civic' *demos*, that is, one identified by the relationship of individuals to common institutions of a civic rather than an ethnic or ethnic-cultural kind. People can have a civic identity constituted perhaps by what Habermas has dubbed 'constitutional patriotism,' *Verfassungspatriotismus*. This is a common loyalty to a common constitutional order, regardless of differences of language, ethnic background, and the rest. People are sometimes willing to sink differences of culture, of language, of heritage, of history for the sake of their common participation in a lawfully constituted polity of commonwealth." N. MacCormick, *Questioning Sovereignty: Law, State, and Practical Reason*, Oxford: Oxford University Press, 2001, p. 144.

[127] In this aspect, Habermas considers the issue of "reversed discrimination." He points out that some threatened primeval cultures have a moral right to be supported. It does not mean, however, that every culture has "equal value" in the sense that its contribution in creating world civilisation is equal and that it has something important

that it supports the significance of liberal democracy, must promote the biggest kindliness towards diversity, it has to ensure the most tolerant and flexible political system. "Constitutional patriotism" constitutes a certain common minimum, which unifies groups and organic communities driven by diverse lifestyles, at the same time ensuring the protections of the rights of minorities and discriminated groups. In other words, the theory of discourse assumes that the agreement – which constitutes its goal – will be arrived at by means of ensuring a proper democratic procedure and communicative chain of political public spheres. Habermas notes in this context that human rights are the core of this agreement. These human rights are interwoven with the code of law, which institutionalizes them in the form of positive law. The system of law and the principle of democratic rule of law, in turn, have their sources in reasonable practice, which has led to the approval of the legal community in question in its primeval act of self-constitution.[128] This places Habermas' conception between legal positivism and the theories of natural law.

The agreement at issue which leads to a mutual respect is not feasible unless the representatives of diverse cultures, religions, lifestyles, or moral attitudes resign from imposing the professed beliefs by means of violence (military means, authority, or terror). They have to mutually regard one another as equal partners and participants of

---

for people. Ibidem, p. 258ff. A similar view was also expressed by Susan Wolf, "Comment," in: *Multiculturalism. Examining the Politics of Recognition*, ed. by A. Gutman, Princeton, NJ: Princeton University Press, 1994, p. 84. The task of the state – by means of law – is then only to enable cultural reproduction of lifeworlds. In other words, in multicultural societies, equal coexistence of different lifestyles gives an opportunity to every person, to every member of a given organic community, to preserve its traditions but it also enables its self-critical rejection. There is no room for fundamentalist standpoints which forbid the abandoning of one's own culture or for fanatically abiding by certain traditional dogmas. Habermas points out that such standpoints lack the awareness of fallibility of their claims and respect in case of "burdens of reason" – as described by Rawls. Fundamentalism does not allow for a reflective look at strange and diverse lifestyles that share the same universe of discourse. We should not confuse fundamentalism with dogmatism and orthodoxy.

[128] J. Habermas, "Zur Legitimation durch Menschenrechte," in: *Das Recht der Republik*, ed. by H. Brunkhorst, P. Niesen, Frankfurt am Main: Suhrkamp Verlag, 1999, pp. 386–403.

discourse irrespective of mutual respect for the significance of their traditions and preferred lifestyles. Habermas points out in this context that what is indispensable in such a situation is overcoming "fundamentalist self-understanding," which constitutes the disturbance of communication and, consequently, reflective overcoming of dogmatic claims to the truth. In multicultural society, a constitution can tolerate only lifestyles that are not based on fundamentalist premises, because equal coexistence of different lifestyles requires mutual recognition of culturally diverse lifeworlds.[129] What is then crucial is to create a political community of a constructivist character, which would symmetrically grant itself and its members freedom and the possibilities of changing perspectives, and ensure equality and mutual respect. Only such a community can be sensitive to the necessity of institutionalization of particular conditions of communication, namely institutionalization which guarantees compliance with human rights.

Jürgen Habermas accurately points out in this context that "in multicultural societies the basic rights and principles of the rule of law constitute crystallizing points of political culture which should unify all citizens of the state; this, in turn, lays the grounds for equal coexistence of groups and subcultures of specific origin and identity."[130] In other words, integration of citizens should ensure loyalty in relation to common political culture, deeply rooted in shared interpretation of constitutional principles. The basic aim for the members of such a community is not the maximisation of one's own interests, but discovering public (common) interest. Such common and shared interests are, among other things, safety and institutional protection against violence. We cannot belittle the role of organic communities, ethically integrated in such a constructivist community, but we should rather reinforce the diverse significance and integrity of dis-

---

[129] J. Habermas, "Kampf um Anerkennung im demokratischen Rechtstaat," op. cit., p. 262.

[130] J. Habermas, *Vom sinnlichen Eindruck zum symbolischen Ausdruck*, op. cit., pp. 94–95. He goes on to state that "Disconnecting these two levels of integration is indispensable if we want the culture of majority to stop exerting a pressure on a common political culture, to be rather subordinated to the latter and to be open to voluntary exchange with minority cultures."

tinct lifestyles, coexisting in multicultural society. It is worth noting once more that the element which binds such a political community of a constructivist character, which respects and includes multiplicity of various lifestyles, will be discursive procedure of law making and the process of executing power (deliberative politics or discursive democracy) as well as mutual recognition of members of a given community. In other words, universality and acceptability of legal principles is manifested in procedural consensus, which has to be suggested in the form of constitutional patriotism in the context of historically determined political culture.[131] Inclusive community, namely, one which comprises plurality of values and cultures, and different ethnicities and outlooks on life, functions due to a fundamental assumption of cooperation and due to its ability and readiness to go above the distinctions which result from the multiplicity of lifestyles, treating as its basis the idea of human dignity and discursive democracy. In this context, it can be stated that the society is not defined by a quasi-contractual definition of the scope of freedoms of particular individuals, but by mutual recognition of individuals as the members of this society and by respecting one another as human beings. R. Anthony Duff accurately points out that in a society constructed in this way (community), law is not only the imperative of the sovereign, but it constitutes the language of its members who express their own and presumably common political values.[132] As a consequence, the requirements made by law are treated as normative manifestations of values, where every member of the community or society should be involved in complying with these values. It has to be once more emphasised that being included in the society stands for being recognised and treated as an irreproachable member of a given community. This membership entails the entitlement to participate in the political sphere of the community by means of participating in law making and in exercising power, as well as in distribution of goods produced by this community (the state). Such an

---

131 J. Habermas, "Kampf um Anerkennung im demokratischen Rechtstaat," op. cit., p. 264.

132 R.A. Duff, *Punishment, Communication and Community*, Oxford: Oxford University Press, 2001, Chapter 2.3.1.

inclusive community should determine – by means of established law and state structure – a protection that ensures that members are treated as citizens who are worthy of respect and regard, and who deserve protection against violence.

Violence – which is referred to by Habermas as communicative pathology – constitutes the greatest threat for such a constructivist community. Habermas indicates that the spiral of violence is initiated as a disturbed communication, which transforms into the spiral of an uncontrolled lack of mutual trust and results in a collapse of communication.[133] We have to then think of how to protect our political community against violent attacks, and what should be done with the perpetrators. It is crucial to draw a distinction between violence characteristic for Western liberal democracy, which is manifested either in the form of social inequality, discrimination or marginalisation, or in committing crimes and intercultural violence, according to which "those who were firstly alienated due to methodically disturbed communication" do not recognize one another as participating members of a community. As I have already noted – referring to Nancy Fraser's and Axel Honneth's views – the best remedy for violence connected with unequal distribution is the reinstatement of recognition by means of improving the material situation of the oppressed group and ensuring their participation in public creation of will and opinion, whilst granting them social respect. In this context, it is crucial to recall Ronald Dworkin's words that:

> Government must treat those whom it governs with concern, that is, as human beings who are capable of suffering and frustration, and with respect, that is, as human beings who are capable of forming and acting on intelligent conceptions of how their lives should be lived. Government must not only treat people with concern and respect, but with equal concern and respect.[134]

The issue which still remains is the problem of violence consisting of committing a crime that in itself constitutes an infringement on the principle of mutual recognition. The subsequent chapters of this dis-

---

[133] J. Habermas in: G. Borradori, *Philosophy in a Time of Terror*, op. cit., p. 39.

[134] R. Dworkin, *Taking Rights Seriously*, London: Duckworth, 1977, pp. 272–273.

sertation will focus on different aspects of the abovementioned variations of violence, as well as on punishment as a form of reinstating undisturbed communication which constitutes the basis of a democratic and discursive constructivist community. Criminal punishment will be treated as a means of excluding a particular individual – who violates law and the basic social relations - from the society (constructivist community). Both the theory of discourse and the conception of mutual recognition constitute a theoretical and normative basis of criticism of reification, understood as a situation in which communication is systematically disturbed by violence, lack of recognition, and domination. It has to be noted that even radical discursive theories treat the state as the institution entitled to take collective decisions, including compulsion, in order to accomplish the state imperatives, like internal and external safety or increased welfare. In this context, a crime is understood as a wrong of a social rather than private character, and such an interpretation entitles a particular community to apply penalties. In other words, the existence of penalties – perceived as specific expression of factual states – becomes possible only in socialized human groups.

CHAPTER IV

Punishing as a negative reaction to illegal acts

1. The notion and justification of punishment in an inclusive constructivist community

On account of its social role, law, and, in particular, human rights, should constitute the core idea of life in a human community. One can agree with the view that law – as the element of practical philosophy in its fundamental perspective – serves the purpose of individual and collective self-reassurance, it specifies and systematizes "co-contributed" pre-understanding. From this perspective, it is critically oriented at the one who represents a *lack of moral sense*. It is crucial in every community and in every society for their members to have a moral feeling – a certain moral sensitivity. When this is taken into consideration, the most radical view was expressed by Protagoras, who stated that "the one who does not have the sense of justice, should be killed like sheep." John Rawls, on the other hand, perceived justice as a premise that enables deliberation over a well-ordered society and just institutions. John Finnis, in turn, proved that one should acknowledge certain pre-moral goods (life, health, friendship etc.) in order to be able to undertake a discourse on morality. In other words, a discourse concerning morality cannot be undertaken with a person who is morally insensitive. Such a discourse will never be constructive because such a subject is, indeed, disinterested in the latter. A lack of moral sense can be defeated only in the situation when we prove that being "good" is also an act that is good for me.[1] Human

[1] E. Tugendhat, *Vorlesungen über Ethik*, Frankfurt am Main: Suhrkamp Verlag, 2001, Chapter 5. Tugendhat writes here about moral scepticism. It has to be noted,

life is based on the question of what "I should do," namely why I want to assume "good" as a point of reference in my life. In assuming a certain conception of good, you will become or be a member of a particular community, a mostly moral one. In particular situations, such conceptions become a part of your identity. The representative of a *lack of moral sense*, on the other hand, will be - as a radical egoist - excluded from that in which the fundamental principle is the assumption of a certain conception of good, like a conviction about universality of human rights.

1.1. Constructivist community as an exponent of the openness of democratic society

The role of law is manifested here particularly as a bond of this community which, in the assumed understanding, constitutes an inclusive community of a constructivist character. Community, understood in this way, has become and - as I truly believe - it should become a paradigm among contemporary multicultural democratic societies.[2] Legal compulsion is treated here as procedural rationality, and an

however, that scepticism concerns a cognition of the basis of the undertaken moral judgements (a dispute between cognitivism and non-cognitivism; juxtaposing absolutism with objectivism on the grounds of moral reflection); controversies concerning particularism and universalism of judgments and moral norms; individual or cultural individualisation (relativization) of moral attitudes; and the problem of how norms or values exist. It can be, therefore, seen that moral scepticism does not always have to contradict moral sensitivity (e.g. emotivism).

[2] As it has been already noted in the previous chapter, I present the institution of a constructivist community by means of referring mainly to its conception presented by Rawls and Habermas. In an eclectic and critical manner, I assert the elements of both these conceptions which, in my opinion, are regarded as most crucial, and which should constitute the aim of social and legal transformations. I supplement this conception with the requirements resulting from the principle of mutual recognition, trying to combine in this conception the normative and sociological dimensions. I also point at its procedural character, which derives from the principle of a discourse and, at the same time, I attempt to prove that this community - by means of institutionalisation of human rights - has strong substantive (moral) roots. Broadly on the issue of "constructivism" in Rawls' understanding see: P. Roberts, *Political Constructivism*, London - New York: Routledge, 2007, Chapters 2 and 3.

appropriate communicative arrangement which should be used for the lawgiver's rational political will-formation and for the application of law.[3] Let us recall that such a community is comprised of various organic communities, however, it does not allow for the abovementioned lack of moral sense. At the same time, a normative model of such a community is based on the conception of an individual as a socialised advocate of the set of social roles, of the arrangement of roles internalised in the socialisation process, which is reproduced by the latter in undertaken interactions. In this perspective, an internalised, namely well-shaped social personality, ossifies quite autonomic symbols and normative models, which then leads to their externalisation. Such a community does not express a common morality, though it has as its basis the belief that a certain minimum of rules which protect human life, property, and compliance with obligations has to be accepted.[4] this means that in the spirit of communitaristic communication it demands particular values and forms of life, preserving the ability to judge others. It seems to be proved by the fact that discursively attained law - which constitutes its significant structuring element - manifests a certain universe in the form of requirements, of how people should perceive one another and what duties these perceptions entail.[5] What seems of the utmost importance here is the act of establishing these rights in human dignity and, what follows, the necessity of differentiating between a human being and a thing. Joseph Raz notes that respecting human dignity entails treating people as subjects who are able to plan their future. Law, on the other hand, assumes that people are rational and autonomous beings, and by means of respecting these features of human beings, law attempts to influence their activities.[6] To put it differently, the community at issue is, at the same time, of a liberal character, assuming as its fundamental values freedom, individual autonomy, and privacy.[7] It has

---

[3] J. Habermas, *Between Facts and Norms. Contributions to a Discourse Theory of Law and Democracy*, Cambridge, Mass.: The MIT Press, 1998, p. 453.

[4] H.L.A. Hart, *Law, Liberty and Morality*, London: Oxford University Press, 1964, p. 70.

[5] E.J. Weinrib, "Legal Formalism," *The Yale Law Journal* 1988, vol. 97, p. 965ff.

[6] J. Raz, *The Authority of Law. Essays on Law and Morality*, Oxford: Oxford University Press, 1983, Chapter 11.

[7] R.A. Duff, *Punishment, Communication and Community*, Oxford: Oxford University Press, 2001, p. 57.

to be noted as well that equity of citizens under law constitutes a sine qua non of moral cohesion of law and, as a result, a requirement of the admissibility of using a collective authority of the state.[8]

H.L.A. Hart points out in this context that law, and in particular criminal law, cannot treat people exclusively like things that undergo changes, and that can be predicted, mended, or manipulated.[9] It is just the opposite; the dynamic character of human dignity indicates that being a human means bearing responsibility for one's own and other people's dignity, namely he always has to be responsible and co-responsible.[10] We should postulate that the source of legitimization of punishment is the rules and principles governing a constructivist community that we are members of, namely, human rights, the principle of mutual recognition, and discursive procedures deeply rooted in our common, democratic identity.[11] As a consequence, human dignity is an institution that should encompass and interfere in all human activities in a community or society, reproducing, at the same time, group identity in the personal structure of every single individual. Human dignity, as a basic institution, is split; it transforms into different norm characteristics for particular situations or tasks.

Notably, humans have always attributed negative tendencies to unknown or excluded individuals or groups. We often apply the stereotype that "the strangers commit crimes." The consequence of this could be a conjecture that the elimination of delinquency could come down to collecting all strangers, isolating them, or sending them to the place where they came from and, in this way, the lost sense of

---

[8] R. Dworkin, *Law's Empire*, London: Fontana Press, 1986, p. 191ff.

[9] H.L.A. Hart, *Punishment and Responsibility. Essays in the Philosophy of Law*, Oxford: Clarendon Press, 1968, pp. 182–183.

[10] R. Ingarden, *Książeczka o człowieku* [A Book on Human Being], Kraków: Znak, 2003, p. 82; M. Środa, *Idea godności w kulturze i etyce* [The Idea of Dignity in Culture and Ethics], Warszawa: Multiprint, 1993, p. 89ff.; K. Wojtyła, *Osoba i czyn oraz inne studia antropologiczne* [A Person and an Act and Other Anthropological Studies], Lublin: Wydawnictwo Towarzystwa Naukowego Katolickiego Uniwersytetu Lubelskiego, 2000, p. 60ff.

[11] M. Pawlik, *Person, Subjekt, Bürger. Zur Legitimation von Strafe*, Berlin: Duncker und Humblot Verlag, 2004, p. 51. Some authors infer from the latter "the need of retribution." Cf. E. Morselli, "Vergeltung. Eine tiefenpsychologische Kategorie der Strafe?", *Archiv für Rechts- und Sozialphilosophie* 2001, vol. 87, p. 224ff.

safety would be regained. In other words, what has become a stereotype is the act of attributing responsibility for all ills and problems to others – the strangers and, in particular, to future strangers, especially immigrants.[12]

It has been already justified that at least the human rights that are grounded in inborn human dignity constitute a legal and axiological dimension, in which it is possible to order the living space of all people, irrespective of cultural, religious, or outlook differences that exist among them. Due to their institutionalised dimension, they are of a public character, which, in turn, guarantees that people who participate in social interactions know what limits of behaviour they can expect from one another and what activities are allowed. In other words, common rights constitute the basis of mutual justified claims and expectations.[13] In case of human rights, mutuality consists mostly of common resignation from admissibility of particular behaviour. Due to the latter, in the situations when human rights are approved and legitimized, everyone resigns from using violence towards others, for example, the right to life and health requires mutual resignation from killing, the right to property consists in common resignation from theft.[14]

The statement which can be perceived as being of particular importance in the context of obtaining and philosophically justifying

---

[12] See e.g.: D.G. McNeil Jr., "Politicians pander to fear of crime," *New York Times* 2002, May 5–6.

[13] Similarly: J. Rawls, *A Theory of Justice*, Oxford: Oxford University Press, 1999, p. 47f.

[14] O. Höffe, *Ethik und Politik. Grundmodelle und -probleme der praktischen Philosophie*, Frankfurt am Main: Suhrkamp Verlag, 1992, p. 111. Klaus Günther accurately points out that there are gaps between the significance and implementation of human rights. He writes as follows: "This gap must be contemporarily bridged by means of moral challenges. Morally legitimized challenges, however, can come as a threat on account of assuming fundamentalist approaches when they fail to aim at the implementation of legal regulations in favour of human rights. They require, on the other hand, making an order in the pattern of meanings which will include infringement of human rights when these infringements are the only source of implemented sanctions. Making a direct order can also result in the threat of taking the offender as a foe." K. Günther, "Kampf gegen das Böse? Zehn Thesen wider die ethische Aufrüstung der Kriminalpolitik," *Kritische Justiz* 1994, no. 27, p. 147.

legal-criminal norms is that the fact of having such a right as the right to live or the right to personal inviolability, namely the right to a certain "thing," means that such a duty is imposed on the state and on all people.[15] All people constitute a community of a constructivist character, which is based on the idea of communicative community and – what is connected with this – the principle of mutual recognition, which constitutes the basis of democratic society. From the above perspective, all people who could be potential addressees of the requirement of respecting particular rights would constitute not only "a rudimentary ethical" community, namely, one which is guided by the principle of discourse formulated in such an abstract way that it could encompass both the principle of democracy and morality, but also a community which can, by means of the norms of criminal law, force its members into obedience to moral norms that it is based on.[16]

In other words, the institution of constructivist community tends to treat each person as a member of a given political society understood as a just system of cooperation. People who belong to this community are endowed with at least two skills: a capacity for a sense of justice and for a conception of the good.[17] It merits pointing out that criminal law should constitute "the tool of policy," corresponding with the axiology of a democratic state of law, the basic task of which is the development and protection of human rights. In this context, criminal law deals with human dignity from the negative perspective, constituting the area that serves as its protection, defending it from the kind of behaviour that could pose a danger to its ideas.

It has to be noted that in order to create a communicative community, it is crucial that all of its members assume that mutual coexistence should be based on a procedural and rational paradigm of law,

---

[15] Cf. R. Alexy, *Theorie der Grundrechte*, Baden-Baden: Nomos Verlag, 1985, p. 172. One could even ponder over the question of whether we should not rather say that we are granted such a right that cannot be infringed by anybody. Joel Feinberg accurately points out that in this case, the addressee of such a requirement will be "the world at large." J. Feinberg, "Duties, Rights and Claims," *American Philosophical Quarterly* 1996, no. 3, p. 139.

[16] E. Tugendhat, *Vorlesungen über Ethik*, op. cit., Chapter 17.

[17] J. Rawls, *Political Liberalism*, New York: Columbia University Press, 1996, p. 93.

which has as its basis a universal principle of discourse and universal human rights that can be derived from the latter. It can be, therefore, observed that the act of recognizing and acknowledging all people - namely, respect for every human being, even the one who is considerably different from the point of view of culture or outlook on life - constitutes an indispensable element, which is fundamental for this community.

Such a community is - to the greatest extent possible - of an inclusive character, which constitutes a normative condition of the latter. It cannot be then driven by prejudices towards other communities (particularly religious, ethnic, or cultural ones), it is not created by means of hatred towards something which is strange and external, it is not secluded from different, strange subjects; just the opposite, this community induces the assumption that the principles that are binding within it and to become their members by means of opening to the expectations of modern world, which are connected with multicultural problems or plurality of values. This community does not negate a multiplicity of lifestyles, insofar as they are not against the principle of discourse, human rights, or the principle of mutual recognition. Such a community assumes the principle of mutuality and reliable, fair procedures, equality of its members, and cooperative participation in its activities. These principles result from the assumption that a constructivist community is a discursive community in which the power of the argumentation - namely, its significance and the extent to which it is accepted - is a "predominant factor," rather than the argument in the form of power. This community is, therefore, open to others, as long as they are willing to respect the principles of a discourse.

One of the targets of such a community is to give the sense of safety that enables life in unity with others. Life in a community constitutes a restriction on the exclusivist human drive for unhindered freedom and uniqueness, which often becomes the source of antisocial atomistic tendencies, driven by ambition and the power to win peculiar plaudits.[18] When focusing on social life, we deal with the

[18] A. Chmielewski, "Ekskluzywizm, jedność, interpasywność" [Exclusivity, unity, interpassivity], in: *Pytania współczesnej filozofii polityki* [The Questions of Modern Philosophy of Politics], ed. by D. Pietrzyk-Reeves, Kraków: Wydawnictwo Uniwersytetu Jagiellońskiego, 2007, p. 16ff.

dialectics of social unity and individual freedom, namely, on the one hand there is the drive for safety and, on the other hand, the drive for freedom. It is crucial to state at this point that every form of human community can be perceived as an infinite drive for a balance between decentralist tendencies to free oneself from the obligations towards others and the tendencies which coalesce it as a result of a uniform need for safety that can be warranted only by other people. Habermas perceives world-concepts as a formal scaffolding which allows people (who act communicatively) to order the world of life and deal with problems that arise in daily interactions.[19] Lifeworld, in this approach, is treated as the area of consent, developed by the community in which respective generations put much interpretive effort into, aiming at common significance in the area of a given society. Decentralisation of the lifeworld, on the other hand, changes the mode of referring to the contents included therein.

In *Theory and Practice,* Habermas at the same time acknowledges the need to open up to different lifestyles, satisfying at least the ideology of multiculturalism or cultural pluralism, because the need to come to an agreement is not satisfied in advance by a lifeworld interpreted in a criticism-resistant way. It is just the opposite – the agreement is reached by means of interpretive achievements of the participants themselves, and it allows the expectation of more rationally oriented activities. Habermas writes as follows:

> The more cultural traditions predecide which validity claims, when, where, for what, from whom, and to whom must be accepted, the less the participants themselves have the possibility of making explicit and examining the potential grounds on which their yes/no positions are based.[20]

The approach suggested by Habermas, in which respective stages of development are connected with overcoming egocentrism (or like in case of societies – sociocentrism or even ethnocentrism) accurately reflects the problems of modern multicultural societies, suspended between the irremovable pluralism of values and a drive for main-

[19] J. Habermas, *The Theory of Communicative Action,* vol. 1: *Reason and the Rationalization of Society,* Boston: Beacon Press 1984, p. 70.

[20] Ibidem, pp. 70–71.

taining permanent frames of reference in one's own "lifeworlds." It can be, therefore, stated that the solution of these dilemmas is a creation or institutional consolidation of inclusive community of a constructivist character. On the one hand, this solution encompasses organic communities driven mostly by culturally determined claims to significance. On the other hand, exclusive organic communities are enriched with this peculiar pluralistic and multicultural space, which includes new discourses and makes them feasible. These discourses touch upon and allow the discussion on the claims to significance that are often subject to criticism. What seems of the utmost importance at this point is the statement that every normative culture is sometimes the source of pain and suffering when it has to negate and eliminate illegal acts of causing such pain or suffering to the members of this culture by other participants who commit crimes. This principle is institutionally manifested in criminal law which, on the one hand, aims at preventing the situations of causing pain and suffering by a crime that has been committed and, on the other hand, it constitutes the source of this pain and suffering itself due to the implementation of a penalty as a means of punishment and prevention. In other words, this constructivist community, which is manifested in the state (whilst it is not a nation-state that is being presented here), treated as the institution of the citizens themselves, is created in order to protect its rights.[21] The state is then obliged to guarantee its citizens protection by means of the norms of criminal law and, by granting the latter, to monopolize violence. In this sense, criminal law is the "*consequence* of the process of differentiation in which a self-governing association of consociates under law becomes a legal community organized around a state."[22]

1.2. Punishment as a manifestation of standard social practice

It should be noted that, according to an anthropologically oriented philosophy of law, the notions of crime, punishment, offender, victim,

---

[21] R. Alexy, *Theorie der Grundrechte*, op. cit., p. 410ff.

[22] J. Habermas, *Between Facts and Norms…*, op. cit., p. 457.

human rights, and the dignity of a human being constitute the elements of legal rhetoric. From this perspective, the latter connects legal meaning with the meaning attributed to them by the addressees by means of a reference to the meanings that operate in a given culture. At the same time, they have a creative function because they co-create the legal community connected with a similar perception of the fundamental legal notions and common values.[23] It has to be pointed out that the understanding of punishment, and not only its justification, seems quite problematic. According to H.L.A. Hart, the institution of punishment should meet the following conditions:

"(i) It must involve pain or other consequences normally considered unpleasant.
(ii) It must be for an offence against legal rules.
(iii) It must be of an actual or supposed offender for his offence.
(iv) It must be intentionally administered by human beings other than the offender.
(v) It must be imposed and administered by an authority constituted by a legal system against which the offence is committed."[24]

In order to determine the character of a punishment, it is worth referring to Rawls' comments on the necessity of differentiating the justification of a certain permanent practice (in the understanding of a broader social institution) from the justification of a given activity undertaken as a part of such an institution. The institution is understood by Rawls as "a public system of rules which defines offices and positions ... These rules specify certain forms of action as permissible, others as forbidden; and they provide for certain penalties and defences, and so on, when violations occur."[25] In *Law of Peoples,* Rawls

---

[23] J.B. White, "Rhetoric and Law: The Arts of Cultural Communal Life," in: idem, *The Heracles' Bow: Essays on the Rhetoric and Poetics of the Law,* Madison: University of Wisconsin Press, 1985, p. 30.

[24] H.L.A. Hart, *Punishment and Responsibility...,* op. cit., pp. 4–5.

[25] J. Rawls, *A Theory of Justice,* op. cit., p. 48f. On the subject of interpreting punishment as social practice, see broadly: M. Davis, "How to make punishment fit the crime," in: *Criminal Justice,* ed. by J.R. Pennock, J.M. Chapman, New York: New York University Press, 1985, p. 121, who indicates that punishment as social practice should meet certain conditions. Firstly, the legal system should constitute the set of primeval

states that public character of the principles of a particular institution guarantees that the subjects who are engaged in its activity know what their mutual expectations are. Differentiation between the rules referring to the existence of a given institution and the rules regulating a certain practice of applying duties that result from this institution entails the necessity of a limited reference to utilitarian arguments when justifying the shape and principles according to which a particular institution functions.[26] It can be, therefore, noted that one should differentiate the justification of punishment[27] in general from the justification of inflicting the punishment in an individual case.

Punishment in the abovementioned context should be treated as a social institution, the characteristic feature of which is pluralism. As a part of this pluralistic social institution, it is necessary to strike a balance between partially different principles that constitute the basis of a society differentiated in terms of culture, outlook on life, religion, race, and sexuality. At the same time, punishment, as social

---

rules (which determine duties) as well as secondary ones, including, particularly, the principle of adjudication (which defines judicial systems in criminal cases, mostly criminal procedure: adjudicating principles and the rules of inflicting punishment). Secondly, the addressees of duties, namely citizens, should be able to act in accordance with primeval rules, able to make discretionary decisions and to take into account the risk of punishment in case of behaviour that is contrary to the proper one. This should be also rational and familiar with binding legal order (In my opinion, what is meant here is the possibility of its cognition). See also: D. Garland, *Punishment and Modern Society. A Study In Social Theory*, Oxford: Oxford University Press, 1990, pp. 293–304.

[26] J. Rawls, *A Theory of Justice*, op. cit., p. 77.

[27] It warrants noting at this point that it is postulated by some people that when referring to punishment, one should rather talk about "excusing" it. The latter is characteristic for non-descriptive statements, like the opinions that aim at assessment, whilst the term "justification" should be used exclusively in reference to descriptive statements. It is, therefore, the case why German literature, when referring to this matter, often applies the notion of "excusing" (*Rechtfertigung*) punishment. However, due to the well-established terminology of criminal law in this field, I will consistently apply the term of "justification" (*Begründung*) of punishment. It should be noted that, in case of the requirement of an excuse, a given activity can entail particular sanctions or it can be even admissible. The requirement of justification, on the other hand, forces legally binding activity. The relation between these two notions is sometimes of a contextual character.

institution, must find its justification in the values that are common for the whole democratically and constructively established community of free and rational people who mutually recognize and acknowledge one another. H.L.A. Hart perceives a multiplicity of moral conceptions, and approves the admissibility of preferring different lifestyles, at the same time, recognizing the possibility, or even necessity, of applying the distinct features of the world to criminal law. This is why this Hart emphasizes that the theory of punishment should take into account the multiplicity of different principles of punishing, and a complex character of the punishment and, in particular, it should not be limited to standard cases. The pluralistic character of punishment is also manifested in the trichotomic pattern of punishment as a stigma, compulsion, and loss.[28]

The most crucial aim of the theory of punishing is to provide the answer to the following questions: why are certain behaviours are forbidden by law? And why do they have the character of criminal and punishable acts[29]? An example of such a ban is "a general prohibition of killing," which is intersubjectively justified, that is to say, from the point of view of every human being. What is meant by the latter is a real primeval and fundamental interest – that is survival. It is obvious that every individual thinks primarily about his or her own survival, but in the long run it means that nobody can kill others with impunity, having been driven by egoistic instincts. Norbert Hoerster points out that sanctity of human life constitutes "a social institution which serves the interest of human beings," namely, it serves those who are particularly protected by this prohibition.[30] It can, therefore, be seen that this prohibition can be lifted only by particularly significant contrary interests.

I wish to discuss intercultural criminal law from the point of view of the ideology of soft multiculturalism, which is similar to cosmopolitan ideology and pluralism. The ideology of soft multiculturalism is based on a moderate cultural relativism that accepts only the exis-

---

[28] H. Jung, *Was ist Strafe? Ein Essay*, Baden-Baden: Nomos Verlag, 2002, p. 21. Such a pattern of punishment will be broadly discussed in the next chapter.

[29] H.L.A. Hart, *Punishment and Responsibility…*, op. cit., pp. 1–5, 171.

[30] N. Hoerster, *Abtreibung im säkularen Staat*, Frankfurt am Main: Suhrkamp Verlag, 1995, p. 20.

tence of different cultures and the necessity of making culturally relative judgements (that is to say, treating each other as an expression of some sort of particularist culture). This perspective is not flawless, but it gives us the possibility of preserving recognition and respect for foreign cultures. In order to be able to require recognition from others, foreign cultures must preserve this relation towards other cultures in accordance with the mutuality principle. This allows the possibility of avoiding extreme relativism or cultural universalism. The danger that exists behind these views is vividly described by Leszek Kołakowski in the following fragment:

> Whoever in Europe utters that all cultures are equal, would not normally be willing to have his hand cut off when he evades his taxes or in the situation of having a sexual intercourse with a person who is not his or her husband or wife he would not be willing to be publicly scourged or – in case of a woman – stoned to death. To say in such case "such are Koranic laws, one has to respect other traditions" it is like to say that as a matter of fact "we would consider it as hideous but it is proper for savages." We express no respect, but rather contempt for such other traditions, and the statement that "all cultures are equal" is the least proper to describe this attitude.[31]

This means that intercultural tolerance and the recognition of other cultures cannot be unlimited. In other words, the state cannot be neutral or indifferent to people's needs now and in the future. Therefore, this neutrality (indifference) must be limited. As a result, we need to have legal norms that will show that not every form of otherness can be tolerated and even accepted. In other words, not every other culture, or not every aspect of any other culture, and not every aspect of cultural differentiation is worth approving and respecting from the point of view of the European culture. I believe that it is not only the European perspective that will weigh in favour of negating certain behaviours, but it will be rather a reference to certain universal human values and principles of behaviour. These constitute the core of

---

[31] L. Kołakowski, "Szukanie barbarzyńcy. Złudzenia uniwersalizmu kulturowego" [Looking for a Barbarian. Illusions of Cultural Universalism], in: idem, *Czy diabeł może być zbawiony i 27 innych kazań* [Can the Devil be Saved and 27 other Sermons], London: Aneks, 1984, p. 17.

interhuman moral and legal discourse and, as a consequence, they are treated as the basis of existence for "intercultural criminal law." One cannot basically agree from the perspective of law for the application of double standards of assessment. What can be recalled as the example of such universality is the right to life, which constitutes the value without which human life is devoid of sense and humanity.

2. Double justification of punishment in Hegel's philosophy of law

Modern theories of punishment are deeply rooted in Kant's and Hegel's justification of punishment. The latter can be particularly seen in Hegel's philosophy of punishing,[32] in which a crucial role is played by the notion of intersubjectivity because it is inevitably connected with the notion of "recognition." In my opinion, this is the notion that constitutes the point of departure for current deliberations on intercultural justification of legal discourse and criminal law. Therefore, I would like to consider this conception more deeply. A criminal, when committing a crime, infringes not only the individuals' own rights, but also the fundamental relation, which connects real human community, which he himself participates in, in the form of mutual relation of recognition ("law as right"). The aim of punishment is to restore his recognition of other individuals and help him to once more become an irreproachable member of human community, and the means that allow this goal to be met is the loss of recognition (*Anerkennungsverlust*)[33] or, to be more precise, the loss of entitlement to claim one's recognition.

What can be noticed in Hegel's conception are two ways of punishment legitimization. Kurt Seelmann calls them "the argument of law" (*Gesetzesargument*) and "the argument of recognition" (*Anerken-*

[32] There are few reasons why I deal with Hegel's theory of punishment. Firstly, it constitutes a point of reference of justifying punishment as a means of depriving the offender of recognition. Secondly, it is not well-known to a Polish reader, whilst it is in full bloom in the academic world in general.

[33] G.W.F. Hegel, *Philosophy of Right*, Kitchener: Batoche Books, 2001 (hereinafter quoted as PR).

nungsargument).[34] Seelmann's conception is an attempt to overcome imperfections that were the flaws of the conception of the objectively-subjective[35] justification of punishment as the interpretation of Hegel's philosophy of punishing.

2.1. Argument from one's right

One of the ways of legitimizing the punishment is based on the assumption that the offender, by means of his act, establishes a "law" under which he himself wants to be subsumed.[36] This is based on the belief that the criminal implicitly maintains in his rationality the universalization of the maxim that constitutes the basis of his act.[37] This approach touches upon two issues. Firstly, a criminal act contains the rule recognized by the criminal, namely "you are entitled to treat me in the same way because it is a certain rule." Secondly, due to the fact that such is the rule, I do express my consent to the punishment.[38] In other words, a criminal has to be treated in accordance with his own

---

[34] K. Seelmann, *Anerkennugsverlust und Selbstsubsumtion: Hegels Straftheorien*, München: Karl Alber Verlag, 1995, passim.

[35] Such double argumentation for justification of the extent of punishment can be apparently noticed in O.K. Flechtheim, *Hegels Strafrechtstheorie*, Berlin: Duncker und Humblot Verlag, 1975, pp. 91–102 and in I. Primoratz, *Banquos Geist. Hegels Theorie der Strafe*, "Hegel-Studien" 1986, Beiheft 29. For more on this issue see also: J.-Ch. Merle, "Was ist Hegels Straftheorie?," *Jahrbuch für Recht und Ethik* 2003, Bd. 11, pp. 148–152.

[36] "The injury which the criminal experiences is inherently fair because it expresses his own inherent will; it is a visible proof of his freedom, and it is his right. But more than that, the injury is a right of the criminal himself, and is implied in his realized will or act. In his act, the act of a rational being, there is involved a universal element, which by the act is set up as a law. This law he has recognized in his act, and has consented to be placed under it as under his right." (PR § 100). This way of justifying punishment constitutes a variation of the so-called theory of consent (*Einwillungstheorie*), according to which the criminal actually gives his consent to be subjected to punishment because every human being (including the criminal) is aware of the fact that law provides punishment for a given act and, consequently, by committing such an act the criminal agrees to be punished. Ludwig Feuerbach was one of the initial supporters of this theory.

[37] K. Seelmann, "Wechselseitige Anerkennung und Unrecht. Strafe als Postulat der Gerechtigkeit," in: idem, *Anerkennugsverlust und Selbstsubsumtion...*, op. cit., p. 65.

[38] It should be noted at the same time that not all negative stimuli (pain, suffering) are understood as punishment.

will, according to his own maxim (which provides for punishment in case of a given crime) because the criminal, being a rational human being (which he is, despite committing a crime), would like to undergo the punishment. The latter can be presented in the form of the following formula: "This maxim [that is to say – punishment – B.W.] can be also applied in my case."[39] According to Hegel, therefore, the murderer says: "I can be killed," whilst he has already expressed his consent by means of his own act (PR, supplement to § 100 and 101). The criminal foresees not only the punishment in the form of a revenge, but also punishment as a deterrence – moral condemnation[40] in the form of general prevention on account of the fact that his punishable act entails the danger (being a negative example) that similar acts will be committed in the future by other members of the society, or that there is a fear that the criminal will return to his criminal activity.

Treating the criminal as a rational being can mean that an unreasonable act committed by him in an isolated case is something exceptional, far from his standard reasonableness. The latter constitutes a reference to Hegel's well-known comment: "What is rational is real; and what is real is rational" (PR, Preface, p. 18). Such an assumption, according to Hegel, constitutes a point of departure in determining both spiritual as well as natural *universum*. Such a legitimization of punishment can be treated as a development of Kant's thought about "the criminal's own judgement,"[41] according to which the offender conclusively agrees to punishment. This thought was earlier ex-

---

[39] K. Seelmann, "Versuche einer Legitimation von Strafe durch das Argument selbstwidersprüchlichen Verhaltens des Straftäters," in: idem, *Anerkennugsverlust und Selbstsubsumtion...*, op. cit., p. 91.

[40] For more on the issue of moral condemnation as an element of punishment see e.g. C. Roxin, *Strafrecht. Allgemeiner Teil. Grundlagen. Der Aufbau der Verbrechenslehre*, München: C.H. Beck, 1997, p. 740ff.; A. von Hirsch, *Dlaczego powinny istnieć sankcje karne?* [Why Should Criminal Sanctions Exist?], Warszawa: Ius et Lex, 2002, p. 11ff.

[41] I. Kant, *The Philosophy of Law: An Exposition of the Fundamental Principles of Jurisprudence as the Science of Right*, transl. by W. Hastie, Edinburgh: Clark, 1887, pp. 201–202: "If any one, then, enact a Penal Law against himself as a Criminal, it must be the pure juridically law-giving Reason (*homo noumenon*), which subjects him as one capable of crime, and consequently as another Person (*homo phenomenon*), along with all the others in the Civil Union, to this Penal Law." I fall under the latter, together with similar members of the same community.

pressed in "The Wisdom of Syrach" (**27**, 25–26) in the following adages: "Who tosses a stone, throws it on his head, and a blow deceitfully inflicted will also harm the one who strikes" and "The one who digs a ditch will fall into it and the one who lays snares for others will be caught in them himself."[42]

It can be a little perversely stated, using Herbert Schnädelbach's words, that such a conception of punishment, having as its basis the criminal's rationality, constitutes an attempt of the rehabilitation of the criminal, perceived, above all, as an *animal rationale*. Such an approach constitutes the manifestation of not only humanitarianism but also the expression of a belief that an inherently human feature is free will and reason, irrespective of individual cases of negative acts committed by a human being. Such a conception assumes the understanding of the notion of punishment, namely what can or what cannot be done. Hegel, therefore, writes that: "The criminal is honoured as reasonable, because the punishment is regarded as containing his own right" (PR, Note § 100). The transgressor who does not directly or conclusively foresee that he can be subject to punishment and, as a result, expresses his disapproval for inflicting the punishment, finds himself in a "performative contradiction." For example, a thief who knows that private property is the most fundamental economic right of a human being, something basic in contemporary interhuman relation, when committing a theft and not approving its punishment, establishes the following rule: "I know what private property means, and I am aware of the fact that private property is protected, but I can steal (I am not concerned with these principles)" or, in different way, "you have to come to terms with the fact that your assets will be diminished by me." Such criminal behaviour would be a self-denial of the offender and a peculiar "intellectual paralogism."[43]

2.2. Argument from the relation of mutual recognition

Another way of legitimizing the punishment was presented by Hegel in the following fragment: "An injury done to right as right is a posi-

[42] Quoted from *The Millennium Bible*, Poznań – Warszawa: Pallottinum, 1980.
[43] K. Seelmann, *Wechselseitige Anerkennung...*, op. cit., p. 69.

tive external fact; yet it is a nullity. This nullity is exposed in the actual negation of the injury and in the realization of right. Right necessarily brings itself to pass by cancelling the injury and assuming its place" (PR, § 97). This comment can be correctly understood only when law is comprehended as a multilateral relation of mutual recognition of free and equal people. Such understanding of law has the same function for Hegel as categorical imperative had for Kant.[44] The latter results from Hegel's belief that "the territory of right is in general the spiritual, and its more definite place and origin is the will, which is free. Thus freedom constitutes the substance and essential character of the will, and the system of right is the kingdom of actualised freedom" (PR, § 4). Law is something holy for Hegel "because it is the embodiment of the absolute conception and self-conscious freedom" (PR, § 30). Such significant role of law has its source in the fact that it constitutes the essence of spiritual, namely "human and social reason as such."[45]

On the other hand, universal recognition is possible only on the level of law. The basis of "legal recognition" is the attribution to every person "the abilities ... to reasonably determine moral issues in individual autonomy" whilst the latter concerns all individuals treated as the subjects of law. These subjects should be able to stipulate among one another the content of binding legal order in the form of social agreement.[46] Personal, political and social rights and freedoms were formulated in this way, by means of historical development of civic society (fight for recognition).

The offender, when committing a crime, harms not only another person as the subject of law but also infringes the fundamental relation which connects real human community of which the criminal is a member himself, in the form of mutual relation of recognition ("law as right") and, in a consequence, he harms himself as the party to this relation. Hegel therefore notes that:

---

[44] Similarly J.-Ch. Merle, *Was ist Hegels Straftheorie?*, op. cit., p. 163.

[45] M.J. Siemek, "Prawo etyczności i etyczność prawa" [The Law of Ethicality and the Ethicality of Law], in: idem, *Hegel i filozofia* [Hegel and Philosophy], Warszawa: Oficyna Naukowa, 1998, p. 89.

[46] Cf. A. Honneth, *Kampf um Anerkennung. Zur moralischen Grammatik sozialer Kämpfe*, Frankfurt am Main: Suhrkamp Verlag, 1994, p. 184ff.

> The fact that, when one member of a community suffers, all others suffer with him, alters the nature of crime, not indeed in its conception, but in its external existence. The injury now concerns the general thought and consciousness of the civic community, and not merely the existence of the person directly injured (PR § 218).

The significance of infringing on the interests of an individual subject of law for the whole community results from Hegel's understanding of the nature of the state.[47] I have already pointed out that, from this perspective, the act of punishing the offender constitutes the element of general prevention because its aim for the future is to reduce a particular victim and legal order merely to the means used by the offender to realize his own will. The punishment in the form of humiliation (reduction of the status) aims, on the other hand, at restoring the relation of equality.

It is, therefore, the case that one of the most crucial consequences of committing a crime is the loss of recognition (*Anerkennungsverlust*) or, more precisely, the loss of the entitlement to claim recognition. Hegel understands recognition as a mutual relation, according to which the one who recognizes must be recognized himself and, as such, he must be an inhabitant of the human world. The act of recognition is inseparable from the claim of being recognized. The principle of mutuality (*Gegenseitigkeit*) assumes that every individual being "knows itself recognized in the other free man, and is aware of this in so far as it recognizes the other and knows him to be free."[48] This claim constitutes one of the most fundamental elements of intersubjective communication because it is the relation of mutuality of dialogue and agreement that constitutes the basis of abstract law (PR, Remark § 71).

Hegel's abovementioned standpoint seems to be the outcome of the belief that intersubjective interhuman communication and the

[47] Broadly on this issue see: D. Klesczewski, *Die Rolle der Strafe in Hegels Theorie der bürgerlichen Gesellschaft. Eine systematische Analyse des Verbrechens- und des Strafbegriffs in Hegels Grundlinien der Philosophie des Rechts*, Berlin: Duncker und Humblot Verlag, 1991, p. 369ff.

[48] G.W.F. Hegel, *Encyclopaedia of the Philosophical Sciences* (1830), transl. by W. Wallace, § 436.

ethics of common social game have taken the place of primeval violence in the fight for obtaining a particular good. A communicative vision of modern society serves the purpose of realising such a state of things in which the unity of ideas is not something mechanically forced, but rather the state that corresponds with understanding and approval of presented arguments. Its participants have to be reasonable subjects, and if such is the case, then all their activities, irrespective of whether they are good or bad, cause foreseeable and acceptable results. The offender, at the same time, in his rationality foresees the punishment that is inflicted on him for a particular crime. Under such an understanding, the punishment is the consequence of a rational consensus agreed upon by means of intersubjective discourse – a fair exchange of mutual experiences. The compulsion of rationality and freedom contained in this cause every individual consciously and voluntarily to yield to common norms of human coexistence which derive from agreement arrived at in discursive way. In other words, it is a compulsion to understand and to recognise that "mine," for everyone, can only be accomplished through what everyone considers "ours."[49] The aim of punishment is to help the offender restore mutual recognition of other subjects of law, i.e. of the whole society.[50] Hegel directly writes that the fundamental aim of punishment is the restoration of the legal relation, which is based on equality.

In the context of Hegel's comments on recognition, the abovementioned remarks mean that discrediting the offender so deeply as it would be *prima facie* required by punishment for the crime committed (the denial of recognition) is not indispensable for preventive purposes. What is required is, rather, the exchange of the roles of the offender and the victim, taking mutual perspectives.[51] In other words, the change of perspective shows in an abstract (symbolic) way that if there is an individual infringement of law, then a compensation will be necessary in order to maintain future mutuality. An individual, in

---

[49] M.J. Siemek, "Wolność jako zasada świata nowoczesnego" [Freedom as a Rule of the Modern World], in: idem, *Hegel i filozofia* [Hegel and Philosophy], op. cit., p. 82.

[50] See e.g. K. Günther, "Möglichkeiten einer diskursethischen Begründung des Strafrechts," in: *Recht und Moral. Beiträge zu einer Standortbestimmung*, ed. by H. Jung, H. Müller-Dietz, U. Neumann, Baden-Baden: Nomos Verlag, 1991, p. 205ff.

[51] K. Seelmann, *Wechselseitige Anerkennung...*, op. cit., p. 75.

its particular process of thinking, assumes such an attitude, which is expressed in the attitudes assumed towards its behaviour by other subjects engaged with the latter in a particular social situation or in other social activities.[52]

Seelmann points out that one who wants to negate other people's rights comes into internal contradiction (contradicting oneself) because he negates something which is at the same time recognized by him by the mere act of negation.[53] It can be, therefore, seen that the one who poses arguments against recognition must assume that the latter is something argumentatively and interactively possible. The act of negating something assumes that the thing that is being negated exists. It cannot be stated, being "rationally argumentative," that by committing a crime (and the offender in his rationality is aware of his act) I do not infringe anybody's claim to be fully recognized, without assuming, at the same time, that mutual recognition exists. In other words, the binding nature of the claim of recognition cannot be questioned because the act of questioning itself is performed already in the frames of the assumed claim of recognition, because without this claim of recognition no process of argumentation, including the act of questioning, seems possible.

Due to an argument of recognition understood as such, Hegel anticipates what is today called "transcendentally-pragmatic ultimate justification (*transzendental-pragmatische Letztbegründung*)."[54] It can be, therefore, stated that the relation of mutual recognition is intransgressible.

---

[52] G.H. Mead, *Mind, Self, and Society*, Chicago – London: The University of Chicago Press 1967, pp. 155–156.

[53] K. Seelmann, *Versuche einer Legitimation...*, op. cit., p. 93ff.

[54] I do not refer here to the criticism of the conception of the ultimate justification as carried out by H. Albert in the form of the so-called Münchausen trilemma. Broadly on the issue of the possibility of ultimate justification as transcendental argument see: H. Albert, *Traktat über kritische Vernunft*, Tübingen: Siebeck, 1968, passim, in particular pp. 8–28; K.-O. Apel, "Das Problem der philosophischen Letztbegründung im Lichte einer transzendentalen Sprachpragmatik. Versuch einer Metakritik des ‚kritischen Rationalismus'," in: idem, *Auseinandersetzungen in Erprobung des transzendentalpragmatischen Ansatzes*, Frankfurt am Main: Suhrkamp Verlag, 1998, pp. 33–79. This issue has been already discussed in Chapter I.

3. Participation in communicative activities and responsibility

Intersubjectivity of interhuman relations constitutes the basic assumption both of the theories of discourse and in the ethics of discourse. On the other hand, discursive justification of criminal law constitutes, as I do believe, a certain variation of communicative theories of punishment,[55] although it uses a little different terminology, and the way of justifying formulated conclusions - in the light of the views at issue.

The discussion on punishment is based on the discursive and self-reflectional concept of man with inherent ethical space. From this perspective, man is treated as a self-interpreting individual. His main duties involve choice and the establishment of a hierarchy of values and behaviour. I assume that man is a rational being who is able to act in accordance with rational and moral principles. According to Kant, the rationality of human beings is a source of their moral subjectivity, since only a rational being can take actions. What allows us to attribute responsibility to humans is the fact that only human beings are able to enjoy freedom and make independent decisions. I assume that man is an individual who has his own identity and will. He is also subject to discursive relations. These relations give the opportunity to follow the procedures under which each participant of social interactions is equal, free from obligation, and accepted by others in the process of argumentation. It makes reference to Habermas' claims of importance, which in a legal discourse are supplemented with the requirements resulting from a binding legal system and universal conditions concerning discourse procedure. This concept is also based on the assertion that "the institution of language communication"[56] is the meta-institution of any other human institutions. This is where both the legitimization of moral and legal norms and the expression

---

[55] The notion of "communicative theories of punishment" is discussed in the next chapter of this dissertation.

[56] K.-O. Apel, "Sprechakttheorie und transzendentale Sprachpragmatik zur Frage ethischer Normen," in: *Sprachpragmatik und Philosophie*, ed. by K.-O. Apel, Frankfurt am Main: Suhrkamp Verlag, 1976, p. 102.

of acceptance for relevant institutions take place. The legitimization and expression of acceptance are achieved through rational dialogue. The departure point for the contemporary theory of punishment must be the assumption that each citizen is treated as a responsible and rational individual. This means that each individual is able to ponder over the notion of good and apply the result of his reflections to himself.[57]

It is crucial to treat each man as a free and autonomous individual who has the ability to practice self-control, think, or act independently. This individual should also bear responsibility for all his actions. Responsibility is significant in situations when a man carries out actions in a conscious and voluntary way. To judge these sorts of actions, we should consider the person's motives for a particular action, and also the context and circumstances of these actions being performed. The circumstances, however, are minor elements of moral action.[58] A sense of responsibility is possible if we take into consideration the objective existence of closely related and hierarchical values within the framework of which the positive values encourage us to take specific actions, whereas the negative ones forbid us to take the actions. From this perspective, it is important to assume that the autonomous individual has the ability to recognize, accept, and obey universal values expressed by law and typical of a particular community.

Lawyers in most cases equate responsibility with a failure to fulfil the imposed duties, namely, with infringing certain binding norms. Responsibility in a normative sense means that the society consciously regulates the behaviour of its members. This regulation aims at shaping proper social attitudes, and its goal is to arouse the awareness of its responsibility and to ensure its permanent realization, assuming that the latter constitutes the basis of a negative or positive behaviour of a member of a given community. It is worth noting that

[57] R.A. Duff, "Karanie obywateli" [Punishing Citizens], *Ius et Lex*, 2006, no. 1, p. 30.

[58] The circumstances contribute to the increase or decrease of moral good or moral wrong of the actions taken by people. Moreover, the circumstances can even decrease or increase the responsibility of the perpetrator (i.e. the action for fear of one's own life or the lives of family members). However, the circumstances cannot change the axiological quality of the act or, in other words, they cannot make actions evil.

the normative aspect of responsibility cannot be discussed *in abstracto*, but one has to relate it with particular conditions of a binding legal order and common social relations, which mostly concern perception and admissibility of infringing prescribed norms. It can, therefore, be seen that the justification of punishing is closely connected with the issue of responsibility, its feeling, and the possibility of attributing it to a particular subject.

A retrospective dimension of responsibility constitutes the effect of relating the individual with its behaviour, and a relative dimension is manifested in the answer of the subject of law to its behaviour, the addressee of which is not only the active subject itself but also other subjects who can be acquainted with this relation.[59] It should be noted in this context that

> ... harm caused in any social order has always required a sanction, as a guarantee of order, safety, and social bond, such a sanction which serves as a means of restoring trust and authority for the rules that were infringed by the criminal act. Goods ... and protected interests change over time, but the need of punishment for the wrong done (and the award for the good) are permanent.[60]

Presenting every human being as a rational, responsible individual, who is capable of self-reflection, places punishing – according to Kant – in the idea of practical reason, and the punishment itself means the loss of happiness.[61] In other words, responsibility, and as a result also

---

[59] R.A. Duff, "Who is Responsible, for What, to Whom," *Ohio State Journal of Criminal Law* 2005, no. 2, pp. 441–461.

[60] J. Kochanowski, *Subiektywne granice sprawstwa i odpowiedzialności karnej* [Subjective Borders of Perpetration and Criminal Responsibility], Warszawa: Wydawnictwo Prawnicze, 1985, p. 11.

[61] I. Kant, *The Critique of Practical Reason*, transl. by Thomas Kingsmill Abbott, 1788 (Gutenberg text), B. 1, Chapter 1, Par. 100: "Punishment, then, is a physical evil, which, though it be not connected with moral evil as a natural consequence, ought to be connected with it as a consequence by the principles of a moral legislation. Now, if every crime, even without regarding the physical consequence with respect to the actor, is in itself punishable, that is, forfeits happiness (at least partially), it is obviously absurd to say that the crime consisted just in this, that one has drawn punishment on himself, thereby injuring his private happiness (which, on the principle of self-love, must be the proper notion of all crime)."

the punishment, is closely connected with individual behaviour, intentional and driven by will. The application of criminal sanctions is possible only in respect of the offender who is capable of observing legal norms.

It should be noted at this point that the responsibility from the perspective of criminal law is of a peculiar character. R. Anthony Duff, for example, distinguishes different approaches to society. These approaches have as their basis single conceptions of responsibility. What Duff indicates in particular is liberal-individualistic, contractualistic, and communitarian models of society.[62]

4. The protection of interaction processes in the light of criminal law

When looking from a philosophical and sociological perspective, it can be stated that the punishment has, among others, the function of indicating what is negative or bad, that is based on the urge to harm the other person, the will to object a certain good, is a negligence, denial or betraying of something which is human and worthy of approval and, the punishment aims, as a result, at stigmatizing such behaviour. From a discursive point of view, punishment is not a response to evil, but it results from a compromise between the individual and society. Law should guarantee the freedom of particular individuals by strengthening the mutual interpersonal interactions between rational individuals. This means that we can punish a perpetrator only if he does morally and legally unacceptable things of his

---

[62] R.A. Duff, "Choice, Character, and Criminal Liability," *Law and Philosophy* 1993, no. 12, pp. 345–383. Konstantinos Papageorgiou, in turn, suggests differentiation of the three models of responsibility, namely deontological (Kantian – Hegelian), utilitarian (Bentham), and communitarian (Aristotelian – Hume's model). Broadly on this issue see: K. Papageorgiou, "Verantwortung, Gerechtigkeit, Sicherheit, Freiheit. Ein Plädoyer für die normative Autonomie und wider die ideale Theorie des Strafrechts," in: *Verantwortung in Recht und Moral*, ed. by U. Neumann and L. Schulz, Stuttgart: Steiner Verlag, 2000, p. 93ff. A characteristic feature of these typologies is their deep morally-philosophical grounding and justification.

own will.[63] The necessity of imposing punishment is closely related to this as punishment facilitates the restitution of the recognition of the social and legal relation between individuals and brings back the universal importance of law within a particular community through the cancellation of reprehensible infringement. The principal objective of punishment is to express discontent and outrage at particular criminal behaviours. Its major aim is also to express disapproval and condemnation on the part of society, whose rules and rights have been infringed. Joel Feinberg states then that punishment in the light of criminal law has a *symbolic meaning,* which is not usually the feature of other negative reactions.[64] In other words, punishment restores the feeling of justice, and enables the process of abiding by social and legal rules. In other words, it gives the meaning to acting responsibly and justifies responsible life in a human community. In this way, it presents a positive side of punishment, which is manifested in bringing the offender back to the society. It is a mistake to treat punishment merely as a means of causing violence to the offender.[65]

A human being, as a person, can enter into the relations of mutual recognition with other people. This results from the assumption that the transcendental relation of people's mutual recognition constitutes the condition of an empirical restoration of justice. The main task of criminal law is, then, the protection of elementary aspects of one's

---

[63] H.L.A. Hart, *Punishment and Responsibility. Essays in the Philosophy of Law,* Oxford: Clarendon Press, 1968, p. 231.

[64] J. Feinberg, "The Expressive Function of Punishment," in: idem, *Doing and Deserving,* Princeton: Princeton University Press, 1970, p. 98. Such an understanding of punishment alludes to a well-known Aristotelian comment that: "The Penal Law is a Categorical Imperative ... Even if a Civil Society resolved to dissolve itself with the consent of all its members – as might be supposed in the case of People inhabiting an island resolving to separate and scatter themselves throughout the whole world – the last Murderer lying in the prison ought to be executed before the resolution was carried out. This ought to be done in order that every one may realize the desert of his deeds, and that blood guiltiness may not remain upon the people; for otherwise they might all be regarded as participators in the murder as a public violation of Justice." I. Kant, *The Philosophy of Law: An Exposition of the Fundamental Principles of Jurisprudence as the Science of Right,* transl. by W. Hastie, Edinburgh: Clark, 1887, p. 195, 198.

[65] This issue will be discussed in details in the following part of this dissertation.

role as a participant of interaction, i.e. the protection of such rights without which the chain of mutual recognition and understanding could be freely and at any moment infringed by any given participant of interactions. A similar standpoint – expressed, however, from a utilitarian rather than transcendental perspective – was originally presented by John Stuart Mill, who stated that punishing is acceptable not only due to the fact that the society does not approve certain activities, but also because particular activities harm others.[66]

What needs to be analyzed here is the accusation concerning the protection of subjective laws.[67] We ought to look at subjective law from the perspective of Klaus Günther, who treats the matter in an "individualistic" and "intersubjective" way.[68] Subjective law is understood as a subject of the protection of penal law concerning the role of a participant in the interaction process. This interpretation of the notion of subjectivity does not mean involving the individual within the community. It means, however, that individual self-consciousness results from social interactions and allows each individual to overcome egoistic behaviour (self-attitude) by assuming the

[66] J.S. Mill, *On Liberty*, Harvard Classics 1909, vol. 25, Chapter 1: "... That principle is, that the sole end for which mankind are warranted, individually or collectively in interfering with the liberty of action of any of their number, is self-protection. That the only purpose for which power can be rightfully exercised over any member of a civilized community, against his will, is to prevent harm to others. His own good, either physical or moral, is not a sufficient warrant. He cannot rightfully be compelled to do or forbear because it will be better for him to do so, because it will make him happier, because, in the opinions of others, to do so would be wise, or even right. These are good reasons for remonstrating with him, or reasoning with him, or persuading him, or entreating him, but not for compelling him, or visiting him with any evil, in case he does otherwise. To justify that, the conduct from which it is desired to deter him must be calculated to produce evil to some one else. The only part of the conduct of any one, for which he is amenable to society, is that which concerns others. In the part which merely concerns himself, his independence is, of right, absolute. Over himself, over his own body and mind, the individual is sovereign."

[67] Subjective laws are referred to as the rights of the individual formulated by social interactions. In other words, volitional desires of the individual are discussed within the community, and are also approved in the form of intersubjective norms. Such discursively shaped law is finally liable to legal and penal protection.

[68] Cf. K. Günther, "Möglichkeiten einer diskursethischen Begründung des Strafrechts," op. cit., p. 210.

role of the Other. This sort of interpretation gives the possibility of mutual coexistence of individual autonomy and intersubjectivity. The course of interaction is determined by the system of cultural norms. Consequently, social activity is of significance only with reference to the cultural pattern regulating this activity. This pattern determines the values and norms that are put into practice through symbolic measures in the process of socialization. The values and norms are the indicators of social relations. The individuals reproduce the common minimum of norms and values by the means of clear and universal symbols. It is only through experience obtained during interactions with other individuals that preserving the contents and cultural demands becomes possible.

What is inspiring and significant for the further process of explaining the nature and justifying the infliction of punishment is a reference to the sociological thoughts of George H. Mead, Peter F. Strawson, or Jürgen Habermas. The idea of intercultural communication involves dividing two holistic systems of behaviour between at least two individuals, which means that each party acknowledges the discourse of his/her interlocutor as evidence of his/her own behaviour. What is especially worth noting is the conception of "exchangeability of perspectives," which, according to Alfred Schütz, is assumed by a natural approach.[69] If understood in the abovementioned way, the necessity of exchangeability of perspectives, together with the principle of mutual recognition, creates "a golden rule" manifested in the following maxims: "If you want people do something for you, you should act in the same way" (Lucas, 3: 31) or "Put yourself in the position of other beings (human and non-human)"

One person identifies the Other, or thimself through classification, which is based on a general thesis of the exchangeability of perspectives. This classification is socially legitimized, institutionalized, and consequently protected by measures concerning social control, including binding legal norms. P.F. Strawson treats resentment as the reverse side to freedom. Resentment is a reaction to ill will, or the

[69] A. Schütz, T. Luckmann, *The Structures of the Life-World*, London – New York – Paris: Gordon and Breach Science Publishers, 1974, p. 4ff. See also the previous chapter of this dissertation.

equilibrium of the Other towards us. While analyzing free will, Strawson notes that in the situation of interaction breakdowns, one may react in two different ways or take two different attitudes.[70] From the internal perspective of the participant of the communication process, we react when we find somebody responsible for some sort of behaviour. However, the external perspective of the observer allows us to judge this behaviour clearly, or even state an opinion as to the sanity or insanity of somebody who disrupts the interaction. We cannot make an absolute distinction between the participant and observer's behaviour. The merging of conduct in the interaction process is possible here. Strawson's concept is also based on the differentiation of some roles that can be adopted by the participant in the interaction process. Firstly, the participant adopts the personal-reactive attitude when he accuses another individual of violation or insult. Secondly, when the participant accuses himself of violation or insult to another individual and he feels guilty and remorseful on account of this, we can say that this participant adopts a self-reactive attitude.[71]

These two approaches are well grounded on the level of the dyadic relation between *ego* and *alter*. The difference between *ego* and *alter* consists in different placements in the world around us. Human being functions in a group, which formulates certain norms of behaviour, and specific requirements not necessarily fully accepted by egoistic and by nature narcissistic individuals. *Alter* needs, however, a certain identity, self-approval, which enables contacts with other individuals participating in this group. *Ego*, on the other hand, must consider in the motives of his activity that *alter* is grounded in a complex chain of interactions (communicative community of life), which are only partially available for *ego*.[72] Exchangeability of perspectives causes the personality of *alter* to be available for *ego*. In anticipating from *alter* a negative answer to his own speech act, and raising

[70] P.F. Strawson, "Freedom and Resentment," in: idem, *Freedom and Resentment and Other Essays*, London: Methuen & Co., 1974, p. 1ff.

[71] Ibidem, pp. 7ff., 15.

[72] Broadly on this issue see: N. Luhmann, "Soziologie der Moral," in: *Theorietechnik und Moral*, ed. by N. Luhmann, S. Pfürtner, Frankfurt am Main: Suhrkamp Verlag, 1978, p. 79ff.

against himself an objection that *alter* might raise, *ego* understands what it means to make a *criticizable* validity claim."[73] Consequently, *ego* can repeat the internalization of discursive relations once more.

What is characteristic, however, is that a human being relates his activity primarily to himself, and only then to what is outside, namely, to the effects of his activity in the world around him. From the philosophical perspective we relate activities to what is "outside us," and on this basis we understand ourselves. From a psychological perspective of cognitive processes, on the other hand, we remember most, firstly, that which has a reference to ourselves and, secondly, to people in general and, lastly, to things, events etc. It should be noted, at the same time, that *alter* will always be perceived by socially determined classifications of *ego*. In the light of this, what will be of the most fundamental importance for the way in which the community functions are values, principles, and rights. What is meant here, obviously, is the reflective process of confronting the assumed, permanent attitudes with an accidental event. This process has a significant role in case of intercultural communication. Richard Rorty writes in this context about "recontextualisation."[74] Rorty shows that the change of arrangement, resulting from assuming new attitudes, is gradable in relation to the tensions occurring between old and new arrangements. This can sometimes lead to correcting one's own attitudes in order to adjust them to a changing social context. From this point of view, it is, therefore, justified to state that assuming the attitudes consists in learning them by confronting old attitudes with the new ones, and the ability to preserve the holistic character of all beliefs, intentions, and

---

[73] J. Habermas, *The Theory of Communicative Action*, vol. 2: *Lifeworld and System: A Critique of Functionalist Reason*, Boston: Beacon Press, 1987, p. 74.

[74] Rorty states that: "as moving along a scale from habitual actions to the test – the instinctive adjustment of intention, by routine calculation to revolutionary science or politics – there is an increasing number of convictions added to or deducted from the system. There is a moment when the concept of 'recontextualisation' proves to be useful. The more widespread the changes are, the more we need the concept of a 'new context'. This new context may consist in a new explanatory theory, a new class of comparison, a new descriptive vocabulary, new personal or political goals, a recently read book, the person whom you last spoke with – the possibilities are endless." R. Rorty, *Objectivity, Relativity and Truth. Philosophical Paper*, vol. I, Cambridge: Cambridge University Press, 1991, p. 94.

urges present in mental space. Such communication allows us to enlarge and enrich the present lifeworld by means of opening it to new arrangements of propositional attitudes. It leads to a conclusion that the strangeness (otherness) of another human being is gradable because it depends, among other things, on the way in which I assume different attitudes to it. Hart, when polemicizing with lord Devlin, states in this aspect that the change of moral beliefs does not equal destruction of society. J.M. Kelly notes that such a "flexible principle" is something sufficient to restrict overzealous moral supervision, or materialization of laws when the primeval moral consensus which supported such undertakings diminishes."[75]

This does not, however, mean that all principles or laws will be subject to Rorty's recontextualisation – just the opposite – the confrontation with varied cultures, persons, beliefs, or lifestyles indicates what has been already emphasised, namely, that we have to talk about the existence of fundamental and universal values and principles, which are derived from every person's dignity, even if it is the strangest individual and, therefore, they deserve legal protection. Permanent fluctuation of holistic propositional attitudes does not encompass laws of a universal character. What is admissible, obviously, is their new interpretation, updating their content. Such updating, however, cannot infringe on the core of 'human dignity'. This issue was discussed earlier in when stating that Rawl's *overlapping consensus* is limited and "socially constructed." I maintain my standpoint that human dignity itself does not undergo renegotiation because it is unchangeable and it cannot be lost, but its notion is, rather, enlarged (reinterpreted), preventing a further relativization of the notion of "human being." The state of multiculturalism is then understood as the relation of interconnected ordering cultures – systems which influence one another and which even undergo destruction.[76]

---

[75] H.L.A. Hart, *Law, Liberty, and Morality*, op. cit., p. 153. J.M. Kelly, *A Short History of Western Legal Theory*, Oxford: Oxford University Press, 1992, p. 450.

[76] The multicultural world is then presented as a relation. On the one hand, we have the assessment (of the activities) of one human being in the context (activities) of another. On the other hand, one culture is perceived in relation to another. When we connect both these aspects, we end up with a two-dimensional picture of interhuman relations, where every human being represents (potentially) a different culture than

Coming back to P.F. Strawson's standpoint, it should be noted that it is also possible to assume the attitude from the "perspective of the third party," who negatively assesses the infringement of one participant's rights by another. We do not necessarily mean here a reference to a particular person whose rights were infringed, but a generalization of our expectations about certain behaviours, i.e. a criticism of a negatively assessed pattern of behaviour. We then assume "a *vicarious, impersonal,* or *disinterested* attitude."[77] An individual assumes in his particular line of thought such an attitude that is manifested in the attitudes of other subjects engaged together with the individual in a particular social situation or in a given social activity.

Tatjana Hörnle and Andrew von Hirsch point out in this context that "the core argument," which marks the change of the justification process in an internormative scope, consists in the fact that "the judgements which basically disapprove certain types of behaviour should inform the active participant, when there are not particular bases to announce the judgement."[78] It leads, further, to the significant conclusion that what constitutes the basis of such a statement is "recognition of the actor as a person with autonomic self-reference." J. Habermas alludes to this when stating that: "the intersubjective relation between participants in interaction, who adjust to one another and reciprocally take positions on one another's utterances, is reflected in the structure of the relation-to-self."[79] It allows the comprehension of everyone as a member of a community who, by his punishable act, infringed its requirements.

---

that of his partner's. Irrespective of whether (inter)cultural contact results in interhuman communication or not, it leads to the change of present holistic arrangements of propositional attitudes of both parties (or any of them), which (potentially) means that they form a common culture (when, for example, dominated culture undergoes atrophy under the influence of dominating culture, and its present representative assumes the role determined by the former culture).

[77] P.F. Strawson, "Freedom and Resentment," op. cit., p. 15ff.

[78] T. Hörnle, A. von Hirsch, "Positive Generalprävention und Tadel," in: *Positive Generalprävention. Kritische Analysen im deutsch- englischen Dialog*, ed. by B. Schünemann, A. von Hirsch, N. Jareborg, Heidelberg: C.F. Müller, 1998, p. 93.

[79] J. Habermas, *The Theory of Communicative Action*, vol. 2, op. cit., p. 10. Similarly: E. Tugendhat, *Selbstbewußtsein und Selbstbestimmung*, Frankfurt am Main: Suhrkamp Verlag, 1979, p. 245ff.

5. Changing roles between the victim and the offender, and the justification of punishment

The theory of the changes of perspectives, signaled already in the previous chapters of this dissertation, allows a different presentation of the problem of a loss of recognition as an element of punishment, particularly on the account that by means of the assumed reference to others, the whole structure of the interaction is changed. Communicative conditions of moral discourses assume that every participant of an argumentation process that takes place in all spheres of social life can assume the perspective common to all other participants.

G.H. Mead states that "the individual experiences himself as such, not directly, but only indirectly, from the particular standpoints of other individual members of the same social group, or from the generalized standpoint of the social group as a whole to which he belongs."[80] Briefly, Mead shows that it is only in the context of intersubjective change of perspectives (internalization of another person's behaviour) that cognition (feeling) of mutuality as reciprocal "I-identity (personality)" is possible. This means that the process of understanding other people is being carried out whilst taking the attitude of the other. This "I" has to enter into, that is, put itself in, the position of another subject to be able to recognize when the other person's rights are infringed. Mead understands the process of "assuming the other's attitude" as triggering off in oneself a reaction which is triggered in the other. The consequence of this is that we learn to communicate the roles of both the listener and the speaker. Mead writes that "the process of addressing another person is a process of addressing himself as well, and of calling out the response he calls out in another."[81] It is worthwhile to note at this point that Mead's conception is adequate to social communication and, to a lesser extent, to intercultural communication. In the context of multiculturality, globa-

---

[80] G.H. Mead, *Mind, Self, and Society*, op. cit., pp. 138ff., 153–164. "I-identity (personality)" is possible, according to Mead's school, only in the context of the change of perspectives. "I-identity" stands here for another relation of interaction rather than, in the case of contractual relation, where it is an establishing relation in reference to the relation of recognition as the potentiality to conclude contracts.

[81] Ibidem, p. 108.

lization, and cosmopolitism, assuming the attitude of the other is no longer so simple, until a given individual is not incorporated into a particular community that is driven by certain laws. We would deal here with a specific construction of the "meta-generalized" Other. The community that a given individual is a member of, such as a religious, ethnic, or cultural one, would stand for this "generalized Other," whilst the community that consists of all respective communities, i.e. the political community, would be the "meta-generalized Other." What is, then, obvious is the context of revealing these laws. This, however, is possible only with a complete participation in the political and social life of the whole society, and not merely one's own community.

Habermas notes, on the other hand, that exchangeability of perspectives serves the purpose of gradual sociocognitive, and moral assimilation of the objectively given structure of roles through which interpersonal relations are legitimately regulated.[82] The participant of interaction develops, then, the identity of a member of a particular community. The latter takes place in the course of symbolic reorganization of his orientations. Emphatic change of the perspective shows in an abstract (symbolic) way that in case of an individual infringement of law, compensation is necessary to maintain future mutuality. Habermas then writes that

> … patterns of behaviour … take on the external shape of social norms insofar as the sanctions connected with them are internalized through taking the attitude of the other, that is to say, to the degree that they are taken into the personality and thereby rendered independent of the sanctioning power … A pattern of behaviour that *A* internalizes in this sense takes on the authority of a suprapersonal will [*Willkür*]. Under this condition the pattern can be carried over to similar action situations, that is, it can be spatially and temporally generalized.[83]

People, being members of a particular community, expect from one another to follow certain behavioural patterns, and the importance of legal norm, allows them to overcome "the asymmetries built into so-

[82] J. Habermas, *The Theory of Communicative Action*, vol. 2, op. cit., p. 32.

[83] Ibidem, pp. 34–35.

cializing interaction."[84] Assuming the attitude of "a generalized other" has to be preceded by internalisation of roles and norms by the members of a particular social group. Habermas accurately notes, when analysing Mead, that the instance of a generalised Other determines the authority of the "common" will of the group. What can be inferred from this is that the identity of every "I" is based on the anticipation of symmetrical and unaffected relations of mutual recognition of one another's rights.

When making a reference to criminal law and punishment, it is indispensable to emphasise that the notion of "generalised other" is closely connected with the conception of constructivist community and, to a certain extent, with Durkheim's idea of the necessity of assuming the existence of group awareness. According to Durkheim, criminal law constitutes emanation of existing social bonds, and crime is perceived as the manifestation of a rebellion of individual awareness against group awareness. A crime, then, harms community or society, infringing its fundamental element, namely group awareness. In other words, particular behaviour is condemned by morality, not because it constitutes a crime or an evil, but because it is perceived in the latter way because it was condemned. What comes as a result is a punishment inflicted on the offender. The purpose of this punishment is to protect the bond of common morality. According to Durk-

[84] Ibidem, pp. 37–38. Habermas accurately refers to Mead's following comments: "If we assert our rights, we are calling for a definite response just because they are rights that are universal – a response which everyone should, and perhaps will, give. Now that response is present in our own nature; in some degree we are ready to take that same attitude toward somebody else if he makes the appeal. When we call out that response in others, we can take the attitude of the other, and then adjust our own conduct to it. There are, then, whole series of such common responses in the community in which we live, and such responses are what we term 'institutions.' The institution represents a common response on the part of all members of the community to a particular situation. ... One appeals to the policeman for assistance, one expects the state's attorney to act, expects the court and its various functionaries to carry out the process of the trial of the criminal. One does take the attitude of all of these different officials as involved in the very maintenance of property; all of them as an organized process are in some sense found in our own natures. When we arouse such attitudes, we are taking the attitude of what I have termed a 'generalized Other'." G. Mead, *Mind, Self, and Society*, op. cit., p. 261.

heim, punishment constitutes a manifestation of what is social (*sacrum*) against what is individual (*profanum*). If there was no punishment, social awareness infringed by a crime would have to lose its power, if emotional reaction of community [in the form of penalty] did not compensate this loss and if the result of this was a loosening of social solidarity.[85] The conception of "generalised Other" and Durkheim's sociological theory have at least one basic flaw, i.e. they do not necessarily justify the protection of legal interest, the protection of which depends on the will of the state.[86] We can face the situation in which social judgments will not overlap with the judgments expressed in criminal law, like penal-fiscal provisions concerning the application of penal sanctions in connection with tax or customs evasions. These theories should then be supplemented with conceptions that justify punishment from a different, more penal–legal perspective, the most adequate of which are those that allude to the understanding of punishment as a restoration of balance. Their description will, therefore, be necessary in the subsequent part of my dissertation.

Assuming the perspective of "a generalised Other" allows for a full participation in inclusive community of a constructivist character – which has been already described – because a characteristic feature of such a community is the universality of certain values, principles, and laws resulting from the fact that we assume the attitude of the whole community, of all rational beings.[87] It should also be added that what is meant by the latter is a democratically and discursively constituted will, based on human dignity, namely the one which can be understood, without any fears, as *overlapping consensus* in Rawls' understanding. In this context, I would like to make use of G.H. Mead's comment that the authority of norms that impose obligations is created in the process of internalising sanctions that constitute a real threat and which are actually enforced. What is characteristic is that he who infringes upon the law, harms not only the community or

---

[85] É. Durkheim, *The Division of Labor in Society*, New York: The Free Press, 1997, Chapter VI.

[86] D. Garland, *Punishment and Modern Society…*, op. cit., p. 48ff.

[87] G.H. Mead, *Mind, Self, and Society*, op. cit., pp. 379ff. Mead writes here about Kant's universality of judgments, but this argumentation can be also referred to universality of human rights.

society that he belongs to, but also himself. From this point of view, the sanction is inflicted on a group because it constitutes a reaction to an infringement of socially generalised, that is, internalised, patterns of behaviour. The institution of a "generalized Other" grounds the validity of norms.[88] Habermas states that:

> The authority of the "generalized Other" differs from authority based only on disposition over means of sanction, in that it rests on assent. When *A* regards the group sanctions *as his own*, as sanctions he directs at himself, he has to presuppose his assent to the norm whose violation he punishes in this way. Unlike socially generalized imperatives, institutions claim a validity that rests on intersubjective recognition, on the consent of those affected by it …[89]

In other words, following the norms that are binding in a particular community or society constitutes the manifestation of assuming the attitude of a "generalised Other," namely, abiding by the norms that constitute the manifestation of a consensus established among the members of this community. The process of abiding by these norms is, then, subject to social control, and in case of their infringement, the group is entitled, as a part of the authority internalised by the individuals, to inflict sanctions, including repressive penalties. Universal human rights merit legal protection due to the fact that their authority is based on common interests, and that the unity of this community and the possibility of its further cooperation depend on the protection of this interest. It is also worth noting Arthur Kaufmann's remark that criminal law should protect only the so-called simple elasticity (*einfache Sittlichkeit*), namely the rudimentary moral principles which are commonly accepted in society.[90]

One reservation, which seems crucial from the perspective of interculturality, is that "the members of a group dependent on cooperation – that is, on common efforts to attain collective goals – ask themselves whether the norms in question regulate the choices of members in such a way that every one of them can see his interests pro-

---

[88] J. Habermas, *The Theory of Communicative Action*, vol. 2, op. cit., p. 38.

[89] Ibidem, pp. 38–39.

[90] A. Kaufmann, "Strafrechtspraxis und sittliche Normen," *Juristiche Schulung* 1978, no. 6, pp. 361ff.

tected."[91] It is worth recalling the following principle of a discourse, quoted in Chapter II:

> Act only according to the maxim due to which you can assume – on the basis of a real agreement with the interested parties (*Betroffenen*), or – vicariously – with their plenipotentiaries, taking into consideration a relevant mental experiment – that the consequences and side effects which result from their common application in order to meet the interests of every potentially interested party, can be in some real discourse accepted, without any compulsion, by all of those which they concern.[92]

We could supplement the latter with the reservation which complies with the assumption of the attitude of "a generalised other" that exercised social control and inflicted penal sanctions are regarded as implemented in the best interest of all interested parties.

The authority of "a generalised Other" must then be based on the idea of human dignity and commonly accepted human rights, namely on the principle of mutual recognition and universal rules of a discourse, in particular on the authority of consensus, which constitutes the result of abiding by the rules of the discourse. These principles and laws make up the essence of the democratic legal order, which contemporarily constitutes the best system for enabling the internalization of the attitudes of others, even those considerably different from us. At the same time, the democratic state – in the most complete way of all – makes up the moral and legal authority of "a generalised Other." The unity of the collectivity can be established and maintained only as the unity of a communication community (and also an intercultural one), by means of a consensus arrived at communicatively in the public sphere.[93] Arriving at such a consensus is not feasible without granting a warranty of freedom, equality, and mutual recognition to all members of this community. Infringing this relation, on the other hand, must be connected with the necessity of restoring balance and law.

---

[91] J. Habermas, *The Theory of Communicative Action*, vol. 2, op. cit., p. 40.

[92] K.-O. Apel, *Diskurs und Verantwortung. Das Problem des Übergangs zur postkonventionellen Moral*, Frankfurt am Main: Suhrkamp Verlag, 1997, p. 123.

[93] J. Habermas, *The Theory of Communicative Action*, vol. 2, op. cit., p. 82.

In other words, the authority of "a generalised Other" is manifested in the fact that a crime invokes sanctions because the norms violated are valid. It should be noted that norms do not claim validity because they are connected with sanctions. If that were the case, they could not obligate the actors to obey, but only force them into submissiveness.[94] This is the result of a belief that both the authority of "a generalised Other" as well as the validity of norms (and their sanctions) imposed by the community, derive from an internalisation process. Consequently, the application of punishment is made possible by constituting a community which has a certain lifeworld, and by establishing the authority of "a generalised Other," which constitutes the basis of the latter. In other words, a community develops its awareness or group identity. Our identity, on the other hand, is formed as a result of a dialogue with others and, consequently, it is the outcome of the process of self-creation by means of interacting with the social and cultural world around us. It is, therefore, possible and necessary to internalise the attitudes of others in order to guarantee that the community functions properly. Internalisation of these attitudes in the form of norms is subject to the acknowledgement that "the relation between the rules of action and the consequences of action is conventional; on this basis, behaviour conforming to norms is rewarded, whilst behaviour deviating from norms is punished."[95]

It is, therefore, possible to assume the attitude referred to by Strawson as a *vicarious attitude*, understood as a "neutral Other," who will perceive individual violation of law as a simultaneous violation of all commonly recognised norms.[96] P.F. Strawson also emphasises that we correctly react to violation of law only when we do not treat the latter as an infringement of one's own right, but when we assume a generalising attitude, perceiving this violation as an infringement of the rights of all members of the society. He, therefore, refers to such an attitude as "moral reaction," indicating an internal relation between one's own feelings and the logic of interpersonal relations.

---

[94] G.H. Mead, *Mind, Self, and Society*, op. cit., p. 377; J. Habermas, *The Theory of Communicative Action*, vol. 2, op. cit., p. 45.

[95] Ibidem, p. 47.

[96] P.F. Strawson, "Freedom and Resentment," op. cit., p. 15ff.

6. Relation of criminal law to morality

In the situation when we react to violation of law with feelings of guilt, resentment, or offence from the perspective of a "generalised Other," we remain inside the relation of interaction, which connects us with others whilst the offender is still kept inside the "moral community."[97] There is no denying the fact that both law and morality serve the purpose of regulating interpersonal conflicts. Morality is understood here as the fundamental element of society that has a regulatory and, consequently, communicative function. From such a perspective, morality is to manifest human respect or contempt, whilst what is meant by the latter is a symmetrical and inclusive communication act, which is based on mutuality of partners.[98] It can obviously constitute only the source of the sanction system. Morality arises from the question "how do we live a good life?" In other words, it is an attempt to discern the way to make one's life meaningful: What life is a good life? What should one do to live a good life? What can I learn? What should I do to make my life good? The need for morality, on the other hand, arises from the fact that not every human being feels a natural tendency to take into consideration other people's interests when planning his own actions. Moral self-determination stands for obedience to norms recognised by a given individual in accordance with his unbiased judgment. Legal autonomy does not coincide with freedom in the moral sense. Freedom in the moral sense also comprises "the free choice of rationally deciding actors" and the free choice of ethically deciding persons."[99] As a consequence, private autonomy does not simply mean free choice within legally secure boundaries, but it also contains a protective cover for the individual's ethical freedom, in other words, every individual's freedom to pursue his own existential life project.

---

[97] K. Günther, "Möglichkeiten einer diskursethischen Begründung des Strafrechts," op. cit., p. 214; P.F. Strawson, "Freedom and Resentment," op. cit., p. 22.

[98] Cf. N. Luhmann, "Ethik als Reflexionstheorie der Moral," in: idem, *Gesellschaftsstruktur und Semantik. Studien zur Wissenssoziologie der modernen Gesellschaft*, Frankfurt am Main: Suhrkamp Verlag, 1981, p. 362ff.

[99] J. Habermas, *Between Facts and Norms…*, op. cit., pp. 450–451.

When referring to criminal law (and to law in general) there is a demand that it should not be morally involved, or an even more rigorous claim that it should be morally neutral.[100] In practice, it can come as a considerable difficulty to draw a strict distinction between legal and moral norms, because both moral values and laws remain in mutual relation, or even contingency, meeting and interchanging with each other on an abstract level. It is, therefore, difficult in the case of legal discourse to talk about the utter "moral neutrality of law," so strongly claimed by the believers of liberal conceptions of law.[101] We should agree with Wojciech Sadurski, who claims that the fact of assuming by the state the role of a guardian, or even a teacher, of morality, leads to a situation in which the state assumes a paternalistic attitude towards its own citizens.

In spite of this reservation, it seems that when referring to the protection provided by criminal law, Rawls' conception of "the veil of ignorance" does not prove useful because it concerns a different stage of goods distribution. From the perspective of criminal law, what is perceived as meaningful is the state in which we know what rights we are entitled to, what duties are imposed on us, and whether we put them to good use. This is also a flaw of impartial conceptions of justice, as well as the antinomic – in respect of justice – character of criminal law.[102] Fairness (impartiality) could be of importance for the aim of punishing under the absolute theory of penalty because the latter consists in restituting a certain profit, usurped by the offender. In a well-ordered society this profit would have to respectively increase the interests of every member of such a society and this, in turn, is contradicted by other aspects, which negate a crime as a source of this profit. Crime, on the other hand, constitutes a borderline as the usurpation of profit.[103]

---

[100] The frames of this dissertation are too modest for a thorough discussion of this significant, yet complex issue. I will, therefore, limit my comments to what is – in my opinion – the core of this subject.

[101] See: W. Sadurski, *Moral Pluralism and Legal Neutrality*, Dordrecht – Boston – London: Kluwer, 1990; D. Lyons, *Ethics and The Rule of Law*, Cambridge: Cambridge University Press, 1984, pp. 104–109; H.L.A. Hart, "Positivism and the Separation of Law and Morals," *Harvard Law Review* 1958, vol. 71, pp. 593–629.

[102] K. Papageorgiou, *Verantwortung, Gerechtigkeit, Sicherheit, Freiheit…*, op. cit., p. 95.

[103] H. Morris, "Persons and Punishment," *The Monist* 1968, no. 52, p. 477.

The institution of *fairness* itself, on the other hand, does not seem to constitute sufficient justification of punishment because the task of the latter is a proper division of burdens and goods instead of their peculiar redistribution by means of penal sanction.[104] The conception of justice as impartiality – due to its reference to a primeval situation – is of the utmost importance for creating proper principles and criteria of justice, fundamental for the most basic institutions of a society that consists of reasonable, rational, free, and equal citizens. Ethical ideals, however, such as non-contextual models of impartial morality, are not representative for criminal law. The aim of the institution of impartiality is, undoubtedly, to guarantee a reasonable and fair structure of society which enables the realisation of every lifestyle within the limits marked by the freedom of others, but this should be realised as a part of procedural justice. Proper understanding of penal law norms is based, on the other hand, on the knowledge of binding legal and moral order, namely in order to refer to a penal sanction we cannot find ourselves in a primeval situation in which we are not aware of our rights and duties or of our social position. A primeval situation behind the veil of ignorance is treated as a point of departure where, if we act at all, then it is only in a discursive way. This is such a point where nobody, as a rule, is able to commit a crime. One should only indicate what constitutes the most severe violation of fair social arrangements and then proceed with their hierarchization. In other words, only when establishing a fair social order do we get the answer to the question of what we should punish for. It is behind the veil of ignorance that we agree on what social balance is.[105]

It has to be expressly emphasised at this point that the main province of criminal law is neither "prosperity" nor "justice," though the latter is of significant importance, rather, "certainty" and "safety" are the principle characteristics for criminal law. Kant previously noted that the proper role of law comes down to ensuring the safety of community under its rule. When assuming this attitude, punishment

[104] On various problems of applying ethical ideals in case of criminal law, see: A. Kaufmann, *Strafrecht zwischen Gestern und Morgen*, Köln – Berlin – Bonn – München: Carl Heymanns Verlag, 1983, p. 179.

[105] This issue is discussed in more details in the subsequent chapter of this dissertation.

is not treated as an ethical consequence of guilt, but as a means of protection. The basic function of criminal law is not the protection of interpersonal relations against harmful attacks, that is, a preventive protection of legal interests.[106] As a part of its protective function, criminal law – by means of threat and, if necessary, by inflicting and enforcing punishment – aims at developing mechanisms that would deter the offender from committing the crime in the future (individual prevention), as well as all members of society from the possibility of committing crimes (general prevention). The guarantee function of criminal law, on the other hand, comes down to a determination of which acts are regarded by criminal law as crimes. This is manifested in a well-known principle of *nullum crimen, nulla poena sine lege anteriori,* which is commonly perceived as one of the most fundamental human rights. The justice function of criminal law aims at compensating the feeling of fairness, both for the victim as well as for the whole society by means of inflicting a fair penal punishment. The justice function mainly comes down to the necessity of restoring the balance upset by the punishable act. This issue will be broadly discussed in the subsequent part of the book.

Albin Eser puts forward a thesis that criminal law should guarantee and ensure certainty and peace among human beings, whilst simultaneously assuming their equal dignity and freedom. This is why the necessity of punishing is no longer justified by the need of realising justice as such, but its significant interpersonal and social goal is assumed by repression. This shows that the legislator, when establishing norms of criminal law, has to take into consideration binding moral norms. Dworkin points out that:

> ... our legislators must inevitably decide some moral issues. They must decide whether the institutions which seem threatened are sufficiently valuable to protect at the cost of human freedom. And they must decide whether the practices which threaten that institution are immoral, for if they are, then the freedom of an individual to pursue them counts for less.[107]

[106] In order to ensure compliance with certain norms that serve the purpose of protecting legal interests, criminal law inflicts punishment.

[107] R. Dworkin, *Taking Rights Seriously,* London: Duckworth, 1977, p. 246.

The latter allows perceiving criminal law not as "shaping the world" but rather as "interpreting the world."[108] Criminal law, by its expressive function, manifests disapproval for certain patterns of behaviour, at the same time enabling protection of particular values and fundamental principles which the society is driven by. Criminal law is then understood as the tool applied in the process of protecting certain legitimate interests and, as a result, guiding human behaviour.[109] In other words, a human being constitutes the element of a normative system, as a part of which he is obliged to refrain from committing acts forbidden by legal provisions; and if he breaches this duty, he bears liability. When assuming the latter perspective, we refer to certainty as inviolability of human dignity, universality and inalienability of human rights, or as democratic rule of law. Rawls accurately points out that a particular political conception is perceived as a stable and certain one "as long as the means of persuasion or enforcement can be found."[110] Even W. Sadurski indicates that criminal law, to a greater extent than other fields of law, expresses moral views of the society on permissible and impermissible behaviour.[111] It can be, therefore, seen that the dimension of axiological binding nature plays a crucial role in the area of criminal law when compared with other

---

108 K. Papageorgiou, *Verantwortung, Gerechtigkeit, Sicherheit, Freiheit…*, op. cit., p. 98; A. Zoll, "Prawo karne w systemie totalitarnym" [Criminal Law in Totalitarian System], *Znak* 1992, no. 450, pp. 111–122. The professor presents here a comment that criminal law as such, the aim of which is merely to protect social life, is "relatively close reflection of the political system that it itself should protect."

109 W. Hassemer, *Strafen im Rechtsstaat*, Baden-Baden: Nomos Verlag, 2000, p. 269ff.

110 J. Rawls, *Political Liberalism*, op. cit., p. 142. Rawls, a bit naively, proves that in order to provide a protection for such stability it is sufficient to assume the conception of justice as fairness (impartiality) because "… given certain assumptions, specifying a reasonable human psychology, and the normal conditions of human life, those who grow up under just basic institutions acquire a sense of justice and a reasoned allegiance to those institutions sufficient to render them stable. Expressed another way, citizens' sense of justice, given their traits of character and interests as formed by living under a just basic structure, is strong enough to resist the normal tendencies to injustice. Citizens act willingly so as to give one another justice over time."

111 W. Sadurski, *Teoria sprawiedliwości…*, op. cit., p. 257. The author writes, consequently, that empirical observation leads to a statement that a relation of criminal law with moral condemnation does not raise controversies.

branches of law (except church law). This does not mean that moral norms are contained in the system of norms of criminal law; not all moral norms are sanctioned by criminal law. According to Hart, such a conclusion would lead to the following assumption:

> ... if it were the case that whenever someone was about to break a rule of conduct, *only* threats of physical punishment or unpleasant consequences were used in argument to dissuade him, then it would be impossible to regard such a rule as a part of the morality of the society, though this would not be any objection to treating it as part of its law.[112]

The relation between criminal law and morality has neither a superior character to the system of moral norms over the norms of criminal law, nor an inferior character consisting in moral norms being included in the norms of criminal law. It can be, therefore, seen that the norms of criminal law and moral norms overlap.[113] This issue does not only concern the question of the extent to which criminal law overlaps with morality, and to which it regulates morally neutral behaviour. This issue also refers to an old division between *mala in se* and *mala prohibita*. In this meaning, law compensates for the functional imperfections of morality that frequently delivers cognitively indeterminate and motivationally unstable results.[114] The complementary feature of law and morality does not stand for a complete moral neutrality of law because moral arguments, as I have already noted, should be taken into consideration in the law making process.

The aim of criminal law is not to create new morality, but it manifests its basis of significance in a symbolic confirmation. In other words, punishment can be understood as interference of state authority into the offender's rights in order to maintain the authority of infringed, yet legally protected values. Consequently, perfectionist,

---

[112] H.L.A. Hart, *The Concept of Law*, op. cit., p. 175.

[113] Criminal law cannot be treated as "a minimum of morality." Such a statement does not obviously contradict his well-known thesis that a legal system, if its aspiration is to result in morally binding duties rather than to merely arouse compulsion, should respect certain rights, namely, that there is a peculiar minimum that is the right to life, freedom, property, and justice, which at least supports formal equity and the relation of mutual recognition. Ibidem, p. 189ff.

[114] J. Habermas, *Between Facts and Norms...*, op. cit., pp. 452–453.

paternalist, and moralistic tendencies oriented at criminal law should be negatively assessed. These tendencies do not render the spirit of multiculturality and pluralism of values and, consequently, they lead to serious conflicts and crises. The attempt to overcome these tendencies becomes possible, as it has been already noted, by means of discursive or deliberate policy. Contemporary discursive policy, which comprises criminal law, must be particularly sensitive to the variety of life in a multicultural society, multiplicity of lifestyles, and "the certainty of legal order," which constitutes the goal of the latter, must reflect complexity of such a society. What then becomes most crucial is to determine commonly accepted, namely, universal, laws, values, and principles.

Criminal law should, at the same time, reflect social reality rather than an ideal theory of morality that places criminal law in some primeval moral instinct. In other words, criminal law constitutes a manifestation of morality in which we are *ceteris paribus* present.[115] Punishment should then be based on such a conception as would be "morally acceptable."[116] In this context, Rawls accurately notes that:

---

[115] K. Papageorgiou, *Verantwortung, Gerechtigkeit, Sicherheit, Freiheit…*, op. cit., p. 100. This issue was already touched upon by Hart in his famous criticism of Devlin's views, which concerned criminal law. The following words are particularly significant to recall: Devlin goes on from an admissible assumption, according to which a certain common morality is necessary for the existence of every society, to the objectionable statement, according to which society is identical with its morality. H.L.A. Hart, *Law, Liberty, and Morality*, op. cit., pp. 51–52. It is not the case that every practice that the society perceives as immoral (like, for example, homosexuality – strongly stigmatised by Devlin) threatens its existence. The criticism of Devlin's views is also oriented to the context in which he defines "moral attitude." He uses this notion in its anthropological meaning, treating the assumption that every average, reasonable human being treats a given behaviour as moral or immoral as the basis of the accuracy of a given moral attitude. He also makes the assumption that no sane person can think differently, and, therefore, he cannot, for example, tolerate homosexuality! P. Devlin, *The Enforcement of Morals*, Oxford: Oxford University Press, 1965, p. 17ff.; 22ff. In my opinion, moral attitude of a particular community can be regarded as an indicator only in the situation when the consensus about this moral attitude was a result of a certain discourse, namely such a deliberative practice as took place in case of human rights. R. Dworkin, *Taking Rights Seriously*, op. cit., p. 248ff.; 254ff.

[116] H.L.A. Hart, *Punishment and Responsibility…*, op. cit., p. 1ff., 152.

> It is true that in a reasonably well-ordered society those who are punished for violating just laws have normally done something wrong. This is because the purpose of the criminal law is to uphold basic natural duties, those which forbid us to injure other persons in their life and limb, or to deprive them of their liberty and property, and punishments are to serve this end.[117]

Michał Królikowski, on the other hand, points out that a teleological theory of punishment, which so far dominates in the Polish doctrine of criminal law, is not sufficient to justify punishment. Justification of punishment must be supplemented with the arguments of moral character.[118] Consequently, we are forced to assume this morality, normatively bridle, and symbolically confirm the latter because its symbolic indomitability and interference constitute the fundamental basis of human undertakings. This morality at the same time constitutes the subject of our practical ability to interpret and (re)construct social reality.[119] Punishment that serves the purpose of maintaining and

---

[117] J. Rawls, *A Theory of Justice*, op. cit., p. 276.

[118] M. Królikowski, *Sprawiedliwość karania…*, op. cit., p. 70ff. The author takes a critical approach to views expressed by Lech Gardocki. L. Gardocki, *Zagadnienia teorii kryminalizacji* [The Issues of Criminalisation Theory], Warszawa: Wydawnictwo Prawnicze, 1990, p. 54ff. This recognised representative of the doctrine of criminal law does not entirely exclude arguments from morality from the discourse on the basis of punishing. He notes that only the assessment of whether a "moral norm itself is meaningful, whether it is supported by rational arguments" enables the protection of moral norms with the use of the tool applied in criminal law (ibidem, p. 173). Consequently, both these authors admit, and I strongly agree with them, that the discourse which justifies punishing must in its rational (and not merely emotional) argumentation refer to the most fundamental interests which are values themselves (like human dignity, the principle of mutual recognition, the right to life, etc.). We have to, at the same time, agree that punishment, which would be incapable of proving its own appropriateness, would be pointless from a practical point of view. This consideration does not mean that the appropriateness of modern punishment should be placed only within the limits of the so-called prevention. It does not even mean that the element of a revenge should be necessarily eliminated from the targets of punishment. It is worth pointing out that the theory of appropriateness of punishment is historically connected with the theory of binding force of the state, that is, its necessity is perceived in the duty of the state to provide justice, safety, and legal order. Such justification was indicated, inter alia, by Gustaw Radbruch. Cf. G. Radbruch, *Gesamtausgabe*, ed. by A. Kaufmann, Heidelberg: C.F. Müller, 1995, vol. VII.

[119] K. Papageorgiou, *Schaden und Strafe: auf dem Weg zu einer Theorie der strafrechtlichen Moralität*, Baden-Baden: Nomos Verlag, 1994, p. 33; idem, "Verantwortung,

preserving the certainty of legal and moral order by means of penalizing dangerous behaviour constitutes a symbolic protection for searching for individually diversified senses of life in society. Alternatively, we can state that the system of moral norms teaches the human being the ability to discern good bad, it recommends doing good and avoiding bad, and it serves the purpose of improving human beings. The system of legal norms, on the other hand, serves the purpose of ensuring internal and external safety, protecting the individual's freedoms and rights, and protecting its unencumbered development.

Some authors, like Scott Veitch, claim that the "neutral character of law," which is dominant in the liberal tradition, can be perceived only as a myth, at least in relation to moral disputes that take place in hard cases. As a result of this, Veitch builds his conception on liberal legalism, by which he understands such an ethical approach which people should assume in legal relations taking place among them as a part of a given community.[120] In my opinion, there is no doubt as to the fact that law supports morality, enabling and, at the same time, protecting independent and unencumbered choice of partners who we want to communicate with. There is, however, a certain caveat to be made: namely, as far as, on the one hand, law sometimes serves the purpose of protecting morality, in the situation where an individual is blackmailed by a particular religion or other group of reference, law should protect the individual's moral freedom. As Niklas Luhmann accurately points out:

> ... it can be seen that law has the property to neutralise – to some extent – dangerous tendencies of morality. In the situations of social malfunctions which lead to conflicts, law comes as a rescue. All that, however, requires "a considerable moral abatement of law".[121]

Gerechtigkeit, Sicherheit, Freiheit…," op. cit., p. 100; G. Jakobs, *Norm, Person, Gesellschaft. Vorüberlegungen zu einer Rechtsphilosophie*, Berlin: Duncker und Humblot, 1997, p. 63. Jakobs maintains that a norm, or alternatively, a system of norms, "constitute a pattern of meaning according to which the world is not sufficiently subordinate as a resultant of individual attempts, rather the opposite, namely, these attempts are subordinate to the pattern, that is the profits of the group."

[120] S. Veitch, *Moral Conflict and Legal Reasoning*, Oxford: Hart Publishing, 1999, p. 139ff.

[121] N. Luhmann, *Soziologie der Moral*, op. cit., p. 68.

In the context of pluralism of values, or even multiculturalism, it is significant that as far as in a given state there is only one legal system, its citizens can prefer various lifestyles and, consequently, different moral systems. It can be, therefore, seen that a complete coherency of legal system with moral systems is neither possible nor desirable. Criminal law and the assumed conception of punishment should not infringe well-established moral beliefs and, at the same time, the situation in which a legal system imposes one morality under the threat of penal sanction, constitutes a contradiction of democracy and pluralism. It is, therefore, not true, as stated by lord Devlin, that common morality is indispensable for the existence of every society.[122] My critical attitude to Devlin's views does not obviously mean, as I already emphasised, that there are no values and rights of a universal character, common to all lifestyles and all moral systems. The most vivid example is the norm "you shall not kill," which protects interests of utmost importance in every culture, namely human life. The latter constitutes one of the elements of the minimum content of natural law.[123] M. Delmas-Marty refers to such values as goods of absolute protection, which are protected by the provisions of constitutional or international law (he rates under this category human dignity, life, and territorial integrity of the state).[124] In order for human rights to be perceived as being of the utmost importance and enforced, people must be familiar with democratic ideals. In practice, people must be – more or less distinctly – connected with postconven-

---

[122] P. Devlin, *The Enforcement of Morals*, op. cit., pp. 13–14.

[123] See: A. Kaufmann, "Gesetz und Recht," in: *Rechtsphilosophie im Wandel*, ed. by A. Kaufmann, Frankfurt am Main: Vittorio Klostermann, 1972, p. 135ff.; H.L.A. Hart, *The Concept of Law*, op. cit., p. 189ff.

[124] Goods which are not absolutely protected, on the other hand, are also covered by the legal statutes of constitutional importance, but such which provide for some exceptions, namely, personal freedoms, property, personal or family life, natural environment. M. Delmas-Marty, "L'Harmonisation des sanctions et valeur communes: la recherché d' indicateurs de gravité et efficacité," in: *L'Harmonisation des sanction pénales en Europe*, ed. by M. Delmas-Marty et al., Paris: Société de Législation comparée, 2003, p. 585ff. Hart writes in this aspect – noting the multitude of moral conceptions – about "the moral convictions which most of us share." H.L.A. Hart, *Punishment and Responsibility...*, op. cit., p. 88.

tional morality or postmaterial values, namely "formal values," which enable intensification of material ones.

The observation that proves most crucial from the point of view of the deliberations at issue is that criminal law (and more precisely, penal sanctions imposed by certain norms) can be justified from the perspective of the participant of the interaction process.[125] Punishment constitutes social reaction taking place as a result of negative assessment of a certain behaviour as harmful for a particular community or social group. It is worth noting that the duty of the state to treat all its citizens as rational and responsible individuals gives rise to the assumption that the state should be the outcome of a discursively obtained consensus of citizens, particularly in the sphere of bans and orders justified by moral arguments.[126] As K. Günther notes, what constitutes the core issue is the notion of guilt,[127] this being understood as understanding and scrutinizing abandoned changes of perspectives. The act of understanding guilt becomes possible only in the situation when the culprit can take the perspective of the injured party and of a generalised Other and, at the same time, perceive the disturbance of the mutuality of the roles assumed by the participants of the interactions. This also proves that the charge that the offender encounters constitutes an essential justification of punishment. The offender who was not told what he was blamed for and what charges were put against him could have difficulties with understanding why the punishment was inflicted on him, and could perceive it as unjust.[128] Punishment, then, assumes guilt, in the sense of individually

[125] U. Neumann, "Neue Entwicklungen im Bereich der Argumentationsmuster zur Begründung oder zum Ausschluß strafrechtlicher Verantwortlichkeit," *Zeitschrift für Strafwissenschaft* 1987, no. 99, p. 590ff.; K. Günther, *Möglichkeiten...*, op. cit., p. 215.

[126] Broadly on this topic see e.g.: R. Alexy, "On Necessary Relations Between Law and Morality," *Ratio Juris* 1989, vol. 2, no. 2; J. Coleman, "On the Relationship Between Law and Morality," *Ratio Juris* 1989, vol. 2, no. 1, pp. 66–78; S. Grotefeld, "Wie wird Moral ins Recht gesetzt?," *ARSP* 2003, vol. 89, no. 3, pp. 299–317; R.A. Duff, *Punishment, Communication and Community*, op. cit., p. 80ff.

[127] See also: W. Grasnick, *Über Schuld, Strafe und Sprache. Systematische Studien zu den Grundlagen der Punktstrafen- und Spielraumtheorie*, Tübingen: Paul Siebeck, 1987.

[128] Cf. A. Kaufmann, *Über Gerechtigkeit*, Köln: Carl Heymanns Verlag, 1993, p. 59ff. It is worth noting that "the offender's guilt is assessed only in the case when he can be imputed of not abiding by a legal norm when committing an illegal, punishable, and

attributed infringement of a norm.[129] Understanding guilt allows the restoration of interrupted interaction and a communicative vision of common life, but it cannot fully (if at all) be forced by means of legal measures. Due to the feeling of guilt, the offender is able to accept the wrath of others, expressed towards his act and himself, and the feeling of shame makes it possible for him to internalise the values on account of which the society feels respect or resentment.

---

reprehensible act, although the compliance with the legal norm could have been required from the offender."

[129] Broadly on this issue see: U. Neumann, *Zurechnung und Vorverschulden. Vorstudien zu einem dialogischen Modell strafrechtlicher Zurechnung,* Berlin: Duncker und Humblot, 1985, p. 269ff.

CHAPTER V

Punishing as a condition of maintaining social balance

1. Punishment as the restoration of balance

It is hard to talk about justice, safety, and the feeling of one's own dignity if the rights of some members of society are ignored or even negated by others. It could even lead to a paralysis of social bonds and a breakdown of interpersonal communication. A legal system, when drawing a distinction between goods and burdens, requires compliance with law, even in the situation when a particular actor does not yearn for it. If such distributions and the legal system itself are to be justified, law should guarantee that those who do not abide by it do not gain unmerited profits as compared with those who obey the law.[1] This consideration, at the same time, draws attention to the function that penal law is supposed to have, namely, the protection of a proper (equitable and just) distribution of respective entitlements in society. What is meant by this is the distribution of profits consisting in negative freedom and burdens coming down to self-restriction of one's own behaviour. In light of this, the psychological-sociological concept of punishing, presented in the previous chapter, which is based on the exchange of perspectives and the theory of the "generalised Other," proves insufficient. It has to be, then, supplemented with a corresponding concept touching upon the distribution of goods and burdens, which constitutes one of the basic functions of law. Con-

[1] J.G. Murphy, "Three Mistakes about Retributivism," in: idem, *Retribution, Justice, and Therapy: Essays in the Philosophy of Law*, Dordrecht: Reidel, 1979, p. 78.

structivist community, as suggested in previous chapters, needs to be supplemented with a presumption of mutuality of narrowing. According to Robert Alexy, it is not only in the situation when other people hold a given person back, namely, in the situation when there is a compulsion of certain behaviour or deterrence,[2] that a man does not have unlimited negative freedom, but the members of community always find themselves in the situation of mutual limitation of their own goods; otherwise -without the determinant of "always" - there arises the question, about the character of this situation, of whether it is of a counterfactual character or whether it has a status resembling Rawls' theory of primeval situation. When aiming at the realisation of a common goal that requires limitation of one's own goods, and which can be clearly seen when there is the necessity of limiting freedom, the members of a community can demand similar restrictions in relation to those whose goods are not subject to such limitations and who would profit from reaching the assumed goal.[3]

Crime denotes a casting off of the burden of self-control by "allowing oneself extensive freedom in making choices" and "acting according to one's own will".[4] Thus, it lies in introducing injustice, in corruption, and sometimes even in the glorification of evil, in negating all that is good, whereas the necessity to limit one's freedom is the condition of realising individual autonomy - Even if this necessity is restricted to not interfering in the autonomy of another person, e.g., through refraining from assault and battery. To be more precise - crime causes the loss of something important on the victim's part, and targets the feeling of worth and dignity, which results in it becoming a source of inequality or injustice. For it is not justified for a criminal to have more freedom than other people, especially when acquiring

---

[2] R. Alexy, *Theorie der Grundrechte*, Baden-Baden: Nomos Verlag, 1985, p. 197ff. (idem, *A Theory of Constitutional Rights*, Oxford: Oxford University Press, 2002, p. 139ff.).

[3] H.L.A. Hart, "Are There Any Natural Rights?" in: *Theories of Rights*, ed. by J. Waldron, Oxford: Oxford University Press, 1984, p. 88; M. Smolak, *Uzasadnienie sądowe jako argumentacja z moralności politycznej. O legitymizacji władzy sędziowskiej* [Judicial Justification as Argumentation from Political Morality. On Legitimization of Judicial Authority], Kraków: Zakamycze, 2003, p. 101.

[4] J. Finnis, "The Restoration of Retribution," *Analysis* 1972, vol. 32, p. 131ff.; idem, *Natural Law and Natural Rights*, Oxford: Clarendon Press, 1992, pp. 262–263.

such a condition violates the freedom of others. In such situations, only punishment may serve to reinstate balance and maintain equilibrium, thus reinstating the perspective of participating in a moral and legal discourse for both the victim and the offender. This is only possible, however, through the preceding action of causing a psychological or physical complaint to an offender. Punishment reassures us and proves that doing harm does not bring any benefits. In other words, the duty of criminal law, and punishment applied on the basis of it, is "the distribution of benefits lying in the freedom from violating the autonomy of an individual."[5] In this meaning, the benefit of an extensive, hence unjustified freedom, determines the significant feature of each crime.

Aristotle understood injustice as "violation of proportionality," whilst proportionality was defined by means of the category of possession: "As far as injustice is concerned, having too little means experiencing the latter, having too much of it – causing harm."[6] The aim of punishment is to eliminate inequality by means of proportionally downgrading the profit gained by the criminal. It could be colloquially said that "who works hard, earns just money and who commits crime, earns punishment." The purpose of the punishment is supported by the idea of human dignity, which is external in relation to it, and by the principles of equality and mutual recognition of all men

---

[5] W. Sadurski, *Teoria sprawiedliwości. Podstawowe zagadnienia* [A Theory of Justice. Basic Arguments], Warszawa: PWN, 1988, p. 237.

[6] Aristotle, *Nicomachean Ethics*, transl. by W.D. Ross, Book V. In reference to restoring the balance, Aristotle's following words are of the utmost importance: Should a man suffer what he did, right justice would be done – for in many cases reciprocity and rectificatory justice are not in accord; e.g. (1) if an official has inflicted a wound, he should not be wounded in return, and if some one has wounded an official, he ought not to be only wounded, but punished in addition. Further (2) there is a great difference between a voluntary and an involuntary act. But in associations for exchange, this sort of justice does hold men together – reciprocity in accordance with a proportion and not on the basis of precisely equal return. For it is by proportionate requital that the city holds together. Men seek to return either evil for evil – and if they cannot do so, think their position mere slavery – or good for good – and if they cannot do so there is no exchange, but it is by exchange that they hold together. This is why they give a prominent place to the temple of the Graces – to promote the requital of services; for this is characteristic of grace – we should serve in return one who has shown grace to us, and should another time take the initiative in showing it."

– which derive from it – although there is, at the same time, an immanent and incontrovertible relation between the deed of the criminal and the punishment inflicted on him. Herbert Morris, in his classic text, *Persons and Punishment*, expresses the necessity of restoring balance using the following words: "it is right to punish those who violated laws and caused unfair allocation of benefits and burdens." A person who violates the rules has something that others have, namely he benefits from the system, but by the rejection of what others have accepted, that is, the burdens of self-restriction, he gained unfair advantage. Justice – that is punishing such individuals – restores balance between the benefits and burdens as a result of depriving such person of what they had taken, that is, by means of enforcing the debt.[7] It was Immanuel Kant who noted that the only justification for infringing the essential goods of every individual who is punished can be the fact that he himself infringed similar goods of another individual.[8] Punishment constitutes the tool that ensures that the criminal will not gain "unjust advantage" and that he will not gain "benefits from his activity, which illegally causes harm."[9] Punishment is justified because it serves to derivate or remove the criminal's false conviction of superiority above others, that is, above the victim and, secondly, above all members of the community to which he/she belongs. The aim of punishment is, first of all, to reinstate the weakened relation of balance and the concept of punishment, as such is a retributive theory. So, the affliction resulting from the punishment should be adequate and proportional to the size of freedom stolen by the offender. Punishment abolishes inequality through demonstrating that every member of a society has a duty to obey the law and to respect another person's dignity: a relation of mutual recognition without bias or discrimination for anyone.

---

[7] H. Morris, "Person and Punishment," *The Monist* 1968, vol. 52, p. 476.

[8] I. Kant, *The Philosophy of Law: An Exposition of the Fundamental Principles of Jurisprudence as the Science of Right*, transl. by W. Hastie, Edinburgh: Clark, 1887, p. 195: "Juridical Punishment can never be administered merely as a means for promoting another Good either with regard to the Criminal himself or to Civil Society, but must in all cases be imposed only because the individual on whom it is inflicted *has committed a Crime*. For one man ought never to be dealt with merely as a means subservient to the purpose of another, nor be mixed up with the subjects of Real Right."

[9] J.G. Murphy, *Retribution, Justice and Therapy...*, op. cit., p. 100.

John Finnis and Ernst J. Weinrib allude to Aristotle's concept of restoring balance and the notion of justice. Finnis accurately pointed out that crime constitutes and unjustified state of enrichment, a lack of balance, which results from the criminal's lack of respect for other individuals' entitlements. The aforementioned balance should be restored by means of inflicting punishment on the criminal.[10] Weinrib, on the other hand, by illegal behaviour understands infringement of equality by one individual at the expense of the other, assuming that at the beginning of every legal relation (closer to every transaction) the parties are regarded – like in a communication process – as equal and unhindered.[11] The institution of punishment is, at the same time, legitimized in compensatory justice, and its task is to compensate the harm. Punishment in this meaning is not understood as a goal in itself, but rather as compensation of injustice, restoration of a disturbed or even destroyed order of justice, and it is where the power of retributive theories can be contemporarily observed. It is the place where the role of the state is emphasised – the state that should ensure justice among its citizens.[12]

---

[10] Finnis notes as follows: "Sanctions are punishment because they are required in reason to avoid injustice, to maintain a rational order of proportionate equality, or fairness, as between all members of the society. For when someone, who really could have chosen otherwise, manifests in action a preference … for his own interests, his own freedom of choice and action, **as against the common interests and legally defined common way-of-action** [emphasis – B.W.], then in and by that very action he gains a certain sort of advantage over those who have restrained themselves, restricted their pursuit of their own interests, in order to abide by the law. … Punishment, then, characteristically seeks to restore the distributively just balance of advantages between the criminal and the law-abiding, so that, over the span of time which extends from before the crime until after the punishment, no one should actually have been disadvantaged – in respect of *this* special but very real sort of advantage – by choosing to remain within the confines of the law. This restoration of the order of fairness is accomplished be depriving the criminal of what he gained in his criminal act (in the presently relevant sense of 'gain'): viz. the exercise of self-will or free choice." J. Finnis, *Natural Law and Natural Rights*, op. cit., pp. 262–263.

[11] E.J. Weinrib, "Legal Formalism," *The Yale Law Journal* 1988, vol. 97, p. 980.

[12] G. Dux, "Gerechtigkeit: Die Genese einer Idee," in: *Jus humanum. Grundlagen des Rechts und Strafrecht. Festschrift für Ernst-Joachim Lampe zum 70. Geburtstag*, ed. by D. Dölling, Berlin: Verlag Walter de Gruyter, 2003, p. 82ff.

Ernest J. Weinrib points out that penal law also falls under the heading of compensatory justice because it assumes a particular importance of causing and experiencing harm. Corrective justice can be perceived as an ordering principle of all types of transactions: tort, restitution, or contract; in other words, it regulates the relations among equal subjects. The specific character of corrective justice in penal law derives from the fact that the criminal infringes the sole idea of formal equality of this justice, at the same time causing harm not only to a particular victim, but also offending the equality of all potential participants of such transactions (that is, potential offenders and injured parties) who would have regarded themselves as equal partners. Crime strikes at the principle of equality as the source of legitimization of particular regulations concerning transactions. It is, therefore, the case that the state, as the representative of this general equality, eliminates this offence by means of prosecuting crime and inflicting punishment.[13] Punishment, understood in the abovementioned terms, aims to strengthen the citizens' freedom by means of restoring the distribution of freedom, which is in accordance with law, i.e. it is supposed to serve the purpose of maintaining fair social order.

The same is claimed by W. Sadurski, who understands law as the imposition of the duty on every citizen to restrain his or her self in such way so as every other citizen could exercise the privileges given to him in the sphere protected by law.[14] As a result of this, the outcome of committing crimes is gaining excessive profits and simultaneous reduction of authorised encumbrances. Restoration of balance is possible by means of imposing additional burdens on a criminal,

---

[13] E.J. Weinrib, *Legal Formalism*, op. cit., p. 982ff. It is obviously not the case that the act of punishing can be justified only on the grounds of a justice-theoretical basis. It does not particularly mean that the state – as the authority entitled to punish – becomes the main defender of justice. Broadly on this topic see e.g. O. Höffe, *Kategorische Rechtsprinzipien. Ein Kontrapunkt der Moderne*, Frankfurt am Main: Suhrkamp Verlag, 1995, p. 318; idem, *Gibt es ein interkulturelles Strafrecht? Ein philosophischer Versuch*, Frankfurt am Main: Suhrkamp Verlag, 1999, p. 67ff.; U. Neumann, "Vom normativen zum funktionalen Strafverständnis," in: *Perspektiven der Strafrechtsentwicklung*, ed. by H. Jung, H. Müller-Dietz, U. Neumann, Baden-Baden: Nomos Verlag, 1996, p. 62.

[14] W. Sadurski, *Teoria sprawiedliwości...*, op. cit., p. 235ff.

like punishment, reducing, at the same time, excessive (unauthorised) profits. However, while Weinrib used for this purpose the notion of compensatory justice, Sadurski refers more to distributive justice. It is emphasised in contemporary discussion concerning the philosophy of punishing that the criminal owes compensation for damage, both to the victim of his punishable act as well as to the whole society, because by means of his act he infringed the legal order. What has derived as a result of this is the science of punishable acts as a certain "infringement of a binding nature of a norm" and on punishment as "confirmation of a binding nature of a norm."[15] It constitutes a reference to Hegelian ontologism, supplementing it, at the same time, with the communicative-theoretical perspective.

Certainly, a number of charges against seeing punishment as the reinstatement of balance are levelled.[16] Sadurski stresses out that the imperfection of using the theory of distributive and commutative symmetry of justice for the substantiation of punishment is due to its fragmentary nature, especially the detachment of liberal social justice from the whole. At this point, I would like to focus on one of the charges – particularly crucial from the perspective of my deliberations – consisting in the statement that balance can be reinstated irrespective of the victim. As has been noted by J.-C. Wolf, this charge is mainly based on a trivial *tu quoque* argument: "You deliberately committed the crime first, so now crime can be deliberately committed against you." The following counter arguments can be raised against such a mode of thinking and *ad personam* argumentation: "A) Infringement that was committed does not legitimize infringement against the offender. B) The situation of deliberate damage cannot neutralize illegality of the first act, but rather adds the second infringement to the first one."

---

[15] G. Jakobs, *Norm, Person, Gesellschaft. Vorüberlegungen zu einer Rechtsphilosophie*, Berlin: Duncker und Humblot, 1997, p. 98ff.; idem, "Erster Vortrag. Strafbegründung und positive Generalprävention," in: *Rechtsphilosophische Kontroversen der Gegenwart*, ed. by B. Keller, Baden-Baden: Nomos Verlag, 1999, p. 135ff.

[16] See e.g. J.-C. Wolf, "Strafe als Wiederherstellung eines Gleichgewichts," *Jahrbuch für Recht und Ethik* 2003, Bd. 11, p. 199–216. The author discusses in details charges against punishment understood in these terms, trying to present counter arguments in order to defend the conception that punishment constitutes reinstatement in the field of distribution of goods and burdens.

If we based our deliberations merely on a simple model of reinstatement, who punishes the criminal would be of no importance; it could be any avenger. Wolf accurately points out[17] that we would then find ourselves in a vicious circle of infringement, because in the situation when A hits B and B hits C, then C is entitled to hit A in order to reinstate balance. Such argumentation is obviously unacceptable. Punishment, therefore, can be given and inflicted either by the victim of the illegal act itself or on behalf of the victim. Wolf calls this "the model referring to dyadic interpretation of honesty." According to Wolf, it is only then that interaction between the victim and the perpetrator takes place. Punishment, at the same time, is always inflicted on behalf of the victim and not on behalf of a metaphysically and globally perceived balance, although, ultimately, it indirectly serves the purpose of reinstating it. One cannot contradict such argumentation because the act of reinstating the balance by means of punishment is to serve, apart from compensation of harm to the victim or the members of the victim's family, the function of strengthening social bonds and harmonizing the proper function of society, infringed by the perpetrator, particularly of democratic society, where equality and freedom of citizens are the most important qualities.

There arises the question of whether harm (Z_1) caused by A to B does not differ from harm (Z_2) caused by C (every X) to A. In both these cases, with the term "harm" - infringement is applied. There is a mistake of insufficient acknowledgement of the descriptive character of the notion of "harm," which can be perceived as physical suffering (K_1) but from the perspective of the concept of good, norms, or principles, "harm" is also recognized as moral wrong (K_2), which does not necessarily constitute this physical suffering. "Infringement," on the other hand, already from its definition constitutes something utterly different, since it is a description referring to a norm, from the perspective of which the latter is feasible. The idea of "a legitimate anger" appeared originally in Aristotle's *Nicomachean Ethics*. If something is of moral importance for me, it is crucial on account of the fact that I will not allow the situation of disrespecting it. In other words, I will not ignore the fact of opposing that which has

[17] Ibidem, pp. 213–214.

moral significance. It is, therefore, crucial to establish a certain legal order because a lack of any order amounts to the highest state of injustice, which has been acknowledged even by Hobbes. It has to be noted that "justice is a fixed and unchangeable will, granting to everyone the right which is due to him". A lack of such fixed, unchangeable will, or leaving the issue of punishment to subjective – that is, individually perceived – moral assessment of "any given avenger" constitutes illegality and injustice.

In Wolf's example, harm appears with a twofold meaning. It has to be kept in mind, however, that not every harm can be referred to as a "moral wrong" and not every instance of causing "moral wrong" is illegal. If this is taken into consideration, allowing harm of considerable moral significance (K_1), namely, causing harm to someone is wrong and should not be accepted and, consequently, should be prohibited under the threat of inflicting punishment. On the other hand, harm in the second meaning (K_2) is of significant moral importance because allowing considerable moral harm is unjust, but causing it does not necessarily have to be – though it can be – connected with imposing a sanction. It can be inferred, then, that those who carry out a normative description of a particular state of facts (K_1) should point at sanctions because they use the language of law that somehow constitutes normative metalanguage. On the account of the latter "any given avenger" is not able to reinstate the balance, because what is necessary is a prior legal – that is intersubjective – acknowledgement that a particular behaviour, normatively regulated in a form of order or prohibition, constitutes a considerable harm. The mere fact that people experience harm does not constitute any presumption. It is only in case of harm of considerable moral importance that there arises the necessity to legally condemn it by means of describing it as a punishable act with a given sanction. Assuming such perspective, A's harm constitutes harm to all members of a given community when causing harm to A is allowed. Punishment is treated as an affliction (harm) inflicted on the perpetrator, which should make him (and the whole society) aware of the extent of the wrong and, at the same time, in its retributive aspect, restore disturbed balance. The perpetrator's rehabilitation to full dignity (complete recognition) and his right to participate in the discourse are possible only after serving the sentence. In this context, punishment does not constitute moral harm par excellence.

Punishment treated as the restoration of balance is understood particularly well for the community which I named constructivist, but comprising of units remaining in the relation of mutual recognition, equal (at least formally), free, and responsible, connected by universally acceptable norms of conduct, i.e. based on the right to discourse, and the claim to recognize the good faith of subjects inflicting punishment. It seems accurate to state that in such a community even the retributive theory of punishment is just, because it is an acceptable consequence of the norms of conduct (including the rules of discourse and democracy) bringing benefit to everyone, including the criminal, who is treated as a citizen.[18] The objective of a normative constraint included in a repressive sanction is liberation on the one hand, and the provision of an outlet for the energy of the freedom of the arbitrary will, strategic operations, and self-realization that derive from subject laws on the other. What results from this is the fact that criminal law is concerned with getting the potential conflicts of "vivid" subject liberties under control. A naturally used normative constraint should result from an agreement reached in a democratic way. This is how it guarantees the protection of social integrity, which then takes a reflective shape: "by meeting its need for legitimation with the help of the productive force of communication, law takes advantage of a permanent risk of dissensus to spur on legally institutionalized public discourses."[19]

2. Public reaction to the evil in the form of condemning the offender

Punishment is a public reaction to the evil, and it manifests condemnation for the offender. It is surely necessary to remember that the person, their features of character, motives and intent, actions, the

[18] Similarly, J.G. Murphy, "Three Mistakes about Retributivism," op. cit., pp. 77–81.

[19] J. Habermas, *Between Facts and Norms. Contributions to a Discourse Theory of Law and Democracy*, Cambridge, Mass.: The MIT Press, 1998, p. 462.

intention or effects, are subjects to moral assessment according to various concepts. In other words, an offence is to be condemned:

- because of the effects;
- because of the effects and modus operandi [a permanent predisposition, e.g. a tendency toward cruel action];
- because of the effects, modus operandi, and the intention [a reflection controlling a permanent predisposition, e.g. a consciously executed cruel action]; or
- because of the effects, modus operandi, the intention, and the motive [a moral measure, an interpretation from the perspective of which the offender considered various reflections].

Consequently, in the form of punishment I turn communicatively to the offender who understands the enormousness of the evil caused by him/her, evil which he/she did not predict, and then I condemn his/her act. I may also turn to the offender, and he/she says: "Gold is all that counts in life." This precludes any discourse with such an offender, and in this case I need to condemn him/her. From this point of view John Finnis is right that there are premoral (basic) goods.[20] And only when these "goods" are goods for the other can I have a discourse on the moral good. Hence, it may be recognized as "a hermeneutic assumption of moral discourse." If they are not believed in, a discourse is impossible. It is worth mentioning that the goods singled out by Finnis are transcultural.

Criminal punishment is an expression of compulsion, complaint, and even suffering, forcibly inflicted by a country in the case of a conflict with criminal law. It is also worth noticing again that punishment here is presented as an element of rational communication within a society in which everyone is an equal, free, and mutually recognized partner in conversation. Criminal punishment includes the information that certain behaviour is punishable and that it needs to be refrained from. Significantly, representatives of so-called communicative theories of punishment are not in agreement as to whether punishment as a statement is an expression of social disapproval (in other words, a symbolic way of revenge), or whether it is, perhaps, an expression of sympathy for the offender. This statement as a reply

[20] J. Finnis, *Natural Law and Natural Rights*, op. cit., p. 83ff.

should enable the offender to answer: "I have improved, or I will not improve because I would have to change too much," assuming that he/she understands his/her actions.

Since morality is a means of communication, then also moral condemnation through punishment (*censure*)[21] is a variant of a moral communication process of the society with an offender, and a victim with an offender. Andrew von Hirsch proves that the theory of moral condemnation is based on the recognition of the unit's subjectivity in the society. It assumes that all members of the society, including the offender, are moral subjects, and as such they have the ability to distinguish good from evil, and predict negative consequences of their criminal behaviour.[22] As a consequence, what is meant by the latter is social indignation taking place when the values - constituting the basis of a particular community - were violated by the act that is commonly treated as a wrong. In other words, what is most crucial in punishment is the element of social condemnation of the act, which does not only constitute the border of a reasonable leniency of penal law but, at the same time, the border of the notion of punishment itself. There obviously arises the question, signaled already by Ronald Dworkin, of whether "We shall say that public condemnation is sufficient, in and of itself, to justify making an act a crime? This seems inconsistent with our traditions of individual liberty, and our knowledge that the morals of even the largest mob cannot come warranted for truth."[23] It does not mean, obviously, that the legislator - in the process of law making - should not take into consideration the fact of social indignation towards a particular type of behaviour. On the contrary, the legislator is obliged to take this into account, but only when

---

[21] See A. von Hirsch, *Censure and Sanctions*, Oxford: Oxford University Press, 1993, p. 12 ff. Similarly, R.A. Duff, "Law, Language and Community: Some Preconditions of Criminal Liability," *Oxford Journal of Legal Studies* 1998, no. 18, pp. 189–206.

[22] A. von Hirsch, "Proportionality in the Philosophy of Punishment: From 'Why Punish?' to 'How Much?'," in: *Crime and Justice: A Review of Research*, ed. by M. Tonry, Chicago: The University of Chicago Press, 1992, pp. 55–98; C. Roxin, *Strafrecht. Allgemeiner Teil*, Bd. I: *Grundlagen. Der Aufbau der Verbrechenslehre*, München: C.H. Beck, 1997, pp. 740–745.

[23] R. Dworkin, *Taking Rights Seriously*, London: Duckworth, 1977, p. 240. The author of *Law's Empire* makes a critical reference to Lord Devlin's views, pointed out in the previous chapter.

the consensus negating such behaviour is the outcome of deliberative procedure in which all members of a given community were allowed to participate. In the situation when social condemnation is the result of an open argumentative procedure, the legislator – taking into consideration all, even most, individualized standpoints – cannot afford to ignore the public's outrage.[24]

Andrew von Hirsh indicates that the theory of moral condemnation is based on the recognition of the individual's subjectivity in society. He assumes that all members of a given community, including the offender, are moral subjects, and as such they possess the ability to differentiate right from wrong and to predict negative consequences of their reprehensible behaviour. It was originally Hegel who noted that treating a criminal as a rational being constitutes a justification of inflicting a punishment on him. An offender has to be treated in accordance with his own will, according to his own maxim (which foresees punishment for a given crime) because – as a rational being, which he is, despite committing a crime – he would like to be subjected to this punishment. Such a way of legitimizing the punishment constitutes the development of Kant's thought about "the judgment of the Criminal himself,"[25] according to which the offender agrees – in a conclusive way – to be subjected to punishment. Condemnation aims at arousing the feeling of responsibility in the offender, forcing him to ponder over his deed. It is only then that any communication with the offender is possible. This communication – as von Hirsch writes – constitutes the essence of moral discourse among rational subjects.[26]

Condemnation seen as an element of punishment should be an inconvenience to the offender, because only an inconvenience can bring the intended result. It is, in particular, an inconvenience that is selected proportionally to the degree of blame for and social harmfulness of an act that may bring the intended utilitarian (preventive) result. It is not sufficient to understand symbolic condemnation as

---

[24] Ibidem, p. 255ff. Dworkin accurately points out that "we must not confuse strategy with justice, nor facts of political life with principles of political morality."

[25] I. Kant, *The Philosophy of Law…*, op. cit., p. 202.

[26] A. von Hirsch, *Dlaczego powinny istnieć sankcje karne* [Why Should Criminal Sanctions Exist?], transl. by A. Litwiniak, Warszawa: Ius et Lex, 2002, p. 16ff.

a method of condemning the crime. In such a case, punishment would exhaust itself in this formal condemnation, and this is not so. Also, passing a guilty verdict and executing the sentence in secret from the public would be internally contradictory, whilst in reality there is no such contradiction.[27] This is presented in the previous chapter through the pluralistic standard of punishment understood as a mark, constraint, and loss. Constraint and certain forms of loss do not raise major doubts, coming down to the necessity to compensate the victim and the society. In such a definition the function of punishment coincides with the civil law character of compensation for a prohibited act, particularly fines and criminal reparation: an obligation to repair the loss or compensatory damages are of such a character.

Stigmatization and moral condemnation, on the other hand, are of a different character. A stigma points at a peculiar nature of penal sanction, which can be observed in the case of corporal punishment and the kind of punishment that aims at restricting the offender's freedom. The function of stigmatization consists in communicating: "Be careful because this person was already punished." In contrast to a reprimand whose communicative and expressive elements emphasise an evaluative function of a punishment, stigmatization can consist in increasing public welfare by means of giving information that a potential participant of our integration is a convict. The latter allows the adoption of a proper protective attitude towards him.[28] Such a standpoint is criticised by Heike Jung, who perceives the so-called stigmatized punishment and the concept of "integrative shaming" as the danger of establishing disintegrating emotions.[29] Stigmatization is a form of punishment that obviously constitutes an additional grievance for an offender, apart from the punishment itself, like serving a sentence, but it constitutes an invaluable asset in the context of contemporary migration of people and anonymity of the neighbours who live around us. In some sense, stigmatization can

---

[27] W. Sadurski, *Teoria sprawiedliwości…*, op. cit., p. 257ff.

[28] This issue has been broadly discussed in Great Britain in the context of the so-called Sarah's Law, concerning the problem of warning neighbours about sexual crimes committed by an offender who has settled in a given neighbourhood.

[29] H. Jung, *Was ist Strafe? Ein Essay*, Baden-Baden: Nomos Verlag, 2002, p. 19.

be treated as a part of a reprimand, because without such information the warning expressed by punishment can be utterly useless. It does not mean, obviously, that the stigmatizing character of a punishment has to be unlimited – just the opposite – the stigmatizing expression of a punishment has to be well-planned, so that it does not get out of control since the stigma cannot be removed. In case of stigmatization it is me – as an offender – and not the act that I committed that is branded. To put it shortly, my act becomes impossible to expiate.

Coming back to the notion of a reprimand, it is worthwhile to recall R. Anthony Duff's words, to the effect that: "By causing harm, I deserved a reprimand both from the victims and from the members of society whose values I denied."[30] A. von Hirsch points out that punishment constitutes a socially understandable symbol that contains a message about moral disapproval for the act that has been committed. Punishment should have such influence as is required by "the needs in the scope of shaping legal awareness of the society." This points at the role of a positive general prevention, the function of which consists in formalizing social control of behaviour that infringes the system of sanctioned norms, in strengthening social-ethical values, they being the basis of sanctioned norms, in instilling the awareness of their binding nature, and, by means of the latter – arousing respect for the system of norms and strengthening trust in them. The state should effectively punish people for serious crimes so that others were not forced to do it ("any given avengers"), so that other people were not structurally forced to punish those who commit crimes of considerable social harmfulness (of considerable moral significance). It also allows the connection of the requirements and the aims of general and individual prevention with the assumption that individually inflicted punishment is socially accepted as proportional and just, so that it does not disturb the stable legal order.

The author of *Censure and Sanctions* claims that a reprimand as a punishment is characteristic of the theory of deserved punishment because "it gives the individual the possibility – in a way which is typical of his moral development – to acknowledge the harmful char-

---

[30] R.A. Duff, "Penal Communications: Recent Work in the Philosophy of Punishment," *Crime and Justice: A Review of Research* 1995, vol. 20, p. 23.

acter of his act, to feel pangs of conscience, to make effort in order to prevent a similar act in the future – or to provide reasons why such behaviour was not something utterly wrong."[31] The latter can also prove the thesis – formulated earlier in the study – that penal law and the punishment itself cannot be morally neutral. Punishment as a statement of moral disapproval must be understandable. What is, therefore, crucial is that recognizing which act is considered punishable and criminal is possible by means of standard abilities to distinguish good from evil, based on the values universally accepted in society, and on legal participation in a moral discourse, which fulfils Habermas' claim to correctness.

The theory of desert is mainly a development of this concept, treating punishment as the reinstatement of balance. In this meaning, gaining an unjust profit is the basis of the offender's desert, and the punishment is justified because it eliminates the ungrounded advantage that he/she gained by committing a crime. Of course, punishment will be accepted sooner in a certain society if it relates to coherent and relatively constant principles followed consistently, and not only on an *ad hoc* basis. Setting such principles means also setting the social policy of resentment. It is necessary to point out here that von Hirsch's concept is based mainly on the preventive theory of deterrent.[32] As a result, his concept gains a syncretic shape – a combination

---

[31] A. von Hirsch, "Punishment, Penance and the State," in: *Punishment and Political Theory*, ed. by M. Matravers, Oxford: Hart Publishing, 1999, p. 69. Quoted after S. Rex, "Proporcjonalność i resocjalizacja: Szanse na pojednanie" [Proportionality and Rehabilitation: The Prospects for Reconciliation], *Ius et Lex* 2006, no. 1 (IV), p. 91. The institution of a desert has become a fundamental category of the idea of retributive justice. See R.A. Duff, D. Garland, "Introduction," in: *A Reader on Punishment*, ed. by R.A. Duff, D. Garland, Oxford: Oxford University Press, 1994. W. Sadurski points out that the concept of "a desert" has three characteristic features: its property, which is personal, past, and subject to assessment. Idem, *Teoria sprawiedliwości...*, op. cit., Chapter V.

[32] A. von Hirsch, *Censure and Sanctions*, op. cit., p. 13; idem, "Tadel und Prävention: Die Übelzufügung als Element der Strafe," in: *Positive Generalprävention. Kritische Analysen im deutsch-englischen Dialog*, ed. by B. Schünemann, A. von Hirsch, N. Jareborg, Heidelberg: C.F. Müller Verlag, 1998, p. 105f.; idem, "Begründung und Bestimmung tatproportionaler Strafe," in: *Tatproportionalität. Normative und empirische Aspekte einer tatproportionalen Strafzumessung*, ed. by W. Frisch, A. von Hirsch, H.-J. Albrecht, Heidelberg: C.F. Müller Verlag, 2003, p. 54f.

of *censure and hard treatment* – because the patterns of punishment are set in various models of the legitimization of punishment. At the same time, von Hirsch stresses that the proportionality of punishment remains most important. It is noteworthy that the agreement that substantiating the punishment by means of "desert" is justified only when the law, which institutionalizes evil and sets the punishment, is right and correct. Thus, law should not only be legitimized through common values, such as universal human rights and democratic procedures, but also by properly distributing or redistributing certain goods. Lack of proper distribution (redistribution) can create a feeling of injustice and lack of admission, which has already been touched upon whilst discussing the claim of recognition and the dispute that takes place in this matter between Honneth and Fraser.[33] Social injustice can question the fact (belief) that the offender really "deserves" the punishment. A. von Hirsch, therefore, accurately points out that unless all members of a given society could enjoy a lifestyle that is free and which remains in accordance with law, the theory of punishment will arouse doubts and moral dilemmas.[34]

The above deliberations lead to an assumption, as noted by R.A. Duff, that the system of penal law should not be created for the society in an imperative way, but it should rather make use of the notions and norms that take into consideration values that are relevant for the whole community. Penal law, according to Duff, delineates the limits of the evil caused to the community. By means of placing sanctions on a particular behaviour and deeming it a crime, penal law manifests a negative assessment of such behaviour as a public wrong, at the same time giving a lesson to other members of the society about how to recognize wrong, and calling for not following a bad example in the future.[35] Condemnation, which is a part of punishment, is understood as a respect for the victim and for the values which were violated and which deserve institutionalised pro-

---

[33] See also D. Garland, *Punishment and Modern Society. A Study In Social Theory*, Oxford: Clarendon Press, 1990, p. 120ff.

[34] A. von Hirsch, *Doing Justice*, New York: Hill & Wang, 1976, p. 149.

[35] R.A. Duff, "Crime, Prohibition and Punishment," *Journal of Applied Philosophy* 2002, no. 19, p. 97.

tection. The condemnation also aims at restoration of the binding character of a norm by means of punishing the act of its infringement.[36]

3. Punishment as a means of restoring the relation of mutual recognition

An offender limits the freedom of other participants of the interaction process, placing above it his own unhindered freedom or even lawlessness. He/she violates social norms hammered out through agreement, as he/she does not limit his/her own actions despite an existing obligation. Crime means breaking with the law, thus questioning a binding legal order. As a result, Hegel's illegality of punishment and its consequence, namely punishment itself, can be understood as a "socially obvious sequence of the norm and the answer."[37] In other words, a criminal has to prove that reality does not contradict the norm, and the punishment has to uphold the norm. The task of punishment is to show that social reality has not changed as a result of the crime, hence to prove which actions need to be treated as being in conformity with, or contrary to the law. Lastly, punishment shows what is the inviolable foundation of interpersonal social relations, and what is the subject of legal protection, namely what rules, values, and principles the latter stand for. I have previously tried to prove that despite having assumed the standpoint of "soft" multiculturalism, or even cultural pluralism or cosmopolitism, it is feasible to establish that certain rights and principles are of a universal and common character. These rights and principles are primarily human rights, which are based on the idea of human dignity as well as the principle of mutual recognition and the rule of discourse, particularly in their procedural aspect. What is the issue here is a normative perspective of such needs and goals that are of a fundamental character for a "proper" picture of a human being, namely,

[36] C. Roxin, *Strafrecht. Allgemeiner Teil…*, op. cit., p. 38ff.
[37] G. Jakobs, *Erster Vortrag. Strafbegründung…*, op. cit., p. 136.

those that are common for all people, assuming different forms whose limits, however, are determined by the fundamental need of communicating with other similar beings.[38]

3.1. Penal consequences of infringing the principle of mutual recognition

The criminal goes beyond the universal rules of moral and legal discourse, imposing his/her position on others by force, but also not treating others as dialogue partners (adversaries), but as obstacles or a means of realising his/her intentions. In this process he/she acts against the fundamental principle of mutual recognition. In other words, a criminal treats the law instrumentally, as the medium of a discursive agreement, which implies the instrumental treatment of *people* who *in* this medium or *by* it have reached an agreement on relevant issues. Consequently, the offender instrumentalises, i.e. objectifies, people. In other words, he/she denies their recognition *as* people. Therefore, crime is the deepest expression of Hegel's concept of "negation." Therefore, if the offender deprives another individual (or group) of recognition, he/she has to be deprived of it within the society to restore a fair balance. This negative effect has its symbolic meaning in the word "mistake" (*mépris*). Granting the offender recognition again will mean that, according to social opinion, the served punishment, and especially its constraint, has been sufficient to restore the balance, whereas punishing the offender further would lead to disturbing the social balance if it were seen as unjust. We are dealing with dialectics of recognition, which expresses itself in the fact that "the criminal makes himself recognized in his rebellious singularity vis-à-vis the law that refuses to recognize [*méconnaît*] him,"[39] while depriving him/her of the recognition due to the fact that he/she violating this mutual reciprocity leads to his/her final negation of the committed mistake (crime), thus to regaining recognition.

---

[38] I. Berlin, *Four Essays on Liberty*, Oxford: Oxford University Press, 1990.

[39] P. Ricoeur, *The Course of Recognition*, Cambridge – London: Harvard University Press, 2005, p. 258.

Paul Ricoeur points out that this entanglement of misrecognition in recognition constitutes a background for a perpetual fight for recognition, a characteristic feature of which is a conflict itself.

Mutual recognition is the essence of human dignity and the foundation of a community of a constructivist character, which aims to protect each individual regardless of his/her cultural, social, national, racial, or gender membership. In accordance with the idea of mutual recognition, we must treat other people as equal subjects to law, subjects that are free and rational. In the case of crime, we deal with the inseparability of the concept of misrecognition in recognition. Contravening the principle of mutual recognition is an act of infringement, because it is a violation of another individual's rights and human dignity, and it simultaneously contravenes the foundation of a contemporary democratic legislative country. It deprives the citizen of what is most important and it destroys the feeling of safety and social balance. Of course, crime is a particularly serious violation of a mutual, legally constituted recognition.[40] Ernst Amadeus Wolff writes that "what can be considered as a crime is such infringement of recognition which the individual can be prepared for, which can be defeated by the individual's own power in some self-oriented life."[41] Using the terminology of a penal code, we could then state that the degree of social harm caused by an act is so significant that bringing back mutual recognition, i.e. legal order, is not possible through the independent actions of the victim and compensating the harm (e.g. through receiving a suitable indemnity and compensation based on civil law regulations). Rather, it is necessary to cause the offender a constraint in the form of criminal punishment.

In this meaning, punishment is a negative social reaction consisting of a certain constraint for the offender, hurting him/her in his/her goods. In criminal law, the constraint factor of punishment is associated with the "nature of punishment," or its function of retribution.

---

[40] Similarly: E.A. Wolff, "Die Abgrenzung von Kriminalunrecht zu anderen Unrechtsformen," in: *Strafrechtspolitik. Bedingungen der Strafrechtsreform*, ed. by W. Hassemer, R. Bergalli, Frankfurt am Main: Peter Lang Verlag, 1987, p. 140; M. Pawlik, *Person, Subjekt, Bürger. Zur Legitimation von Strafe*, Berlin: Duncker und Humblot Verlag, 2004, p. 69.

[41] E.A. Wolff, "Die Abgrenzung...," op. cit., p. 212.

The constraint of punishment must take into consideration human autonomy and dignity, both the victim's and the offender's, and the requirement to obey specific norms, which provides the protection of legal goods. This also means that the intensity of the punishment should be controlled by the importance of values protected by the punishment.

In the systems of retributive justice, constraint of a punishment constitutes the effect of balancing different principles, namely directives of inflicting the punishment – and in particular – the principles of humanitarianism and the directives of general prevention. It is claimed to apply punishment, which is less onerous in the first place (non-isolation punishment: a fine or a penalty of restricted freedom), and only if the punishment proved ineffective, can isolation penalties (like imprisonment) be applied. When taking into consideration such an assumption, the principle of humanitarianism of penal law is understood as a directive of minimising suffering, disadvantage, and inconvenience experienced by an individual when applying penal law, whereas the latter is construed as a directive of applying negative reactions only in such cases and to such extents in which it is indispensable for a proper realization of an applied norm of penal law. It has been often emphasised in the literature of the subject that it is unjust to abuse the offender and to inflict a more severe penalty only in order to deter others from committing similar acts. As a consequence of this consideration, abiding by the principles of justice when punishing the offender, constitutes a fundamental element of the theory of distribution of penalty, which is referred to as "a fair revenge."[42] This theory alludes to Kant's standpoint, expressed in the following words:

> This is the Right of Retaliation (*ius talionis*) and properly understood, it is the only Principle which in regulating a Public Court, as distinguished from mere private judgment, can definitely assign both the quality and the quantity of a just penalty. All other standards are wavering and uncertain; and on account of other considerations involved in them, they contain no principle conformable to the sentence of pure and strict Justice.[43]

---

[42] A. von Hirsch, *Censure and Sanctions*, op. cit., passim.

[43] I. Kant, *The Philosophy of Law…*, op. cit., pp. 196–197.

In *Critique of Pure Reason,* Kant believed, though, that the constraint caused by the punishment is identical with the constraint caused by the crime itself only in respect of its "intensity."

What is also significant in this context is the distinction made by Michael Köhler, who distinguishes between unaware infringement and crime. In the case of unaware infringement, there is a contravention of the victim's freedom, but it results from the lack of recognition of a specific category of norm or actual condition of its usage,[44] whilst at the moment of committing a crime the offender intentionally and consciously negates the autonomic law subjectivity of another, intersubjectively expressed freedom, and mutual reciprocity. Köhler sees crime as an intersubjective act. As a result, for him punishment means "a generalising equal situation of legal relation in the relation of externally expressed freedom (to another)," and it expresses the act of "bringing back legal intersubjectivity."[45] The term "intersubjectivity" is of key meaning, as it involves the reciprocity of dialogue (discourse) and reaching the agreement within this discourse. An intersubjective level of communicative actions allows for juxtapositions with strategic interactions because "*all* participants harmonize their individual plans of action with one another, and thus pursue their illocutionary aims *without reservation* 'communicative action'."[46]

It needs to be strongly stressed again that contravening mutual recognition has its negative consequences not only in the relation between the offender and the victim, but also in that it disrupts mutual recognition within the community. Therefore, if the disruption is "socially harmful to a serious degree" it is not enough to fix the damage and forgive the offender, because it is not sufficient atonement on the community's part. Punishment is also inflicted on behalf of the whole society (all citizens). Such punishment – accurately noticed by Otfried Höffe – is of the character of an additional negative value, which the victim does not deserve.[47] Punishment is an institution that restores

---

[44] M. Köhler, *Der Begriff der Strafe*, Heidelberg: Decker & Müller, 1986, p. 47.

[45] Ibidem, p. 51; 55ff.

[46] J. Habermas, *The Theory of Communicative Action*, vol. 1: *Reason and the Rationalization of Society*, Boston: Beacon Press, 1984, p. 294.

[47] O. Höffe, *Gibt es ein interkulturelles Strafrecht?*, op. cit., p. 109; idem, "Proto-Strafrecht: Programm und Anfragen eines Philosophen," in: *Die deutsche Strafrechtswis-*

order within a specific communicative and constructive society. It is important when we talk about a citizen of a democratic country who not only has certain rights but also duties. If we agree to neglect these duties, it can only set a dangerous precedent. Of course, each case needs to be treated individually, and maybe it will be possible to use the regulations that talk about refraining from imposing punishment, or conditional dismissal of proceedings, however, at the same time, these decisions should stress the negative (culpable) character of such a given act. A mere infringement of recognition is – both from the perspective of philosophy and penal law – a gradable and diversifiable notion. I have previously pointed out the philosophical nature of this notion in Chapter IV of this study. At this point, I aim at making a reservation that penal protection of "the relations of mutual recognition" does not have such a broad extent as the principle – discussed by Honneth – of a mutual recognition of an individual whose needs and wishes are of the utmost and only value for another individual, and whose abilities are of "a constitutive value for a particular community."[48] Such a broad perspective of "the principle of mutual recognition," the violation of which could bear penal liability, is undoubtedly impossible. What is meant by this principle is rather such violation of the relations of mutual recognition as would ruin the legal security and certainty, e.g. an attempt to kill or harm someone, rape, seizure of other people's property, or damaging other people's personal goods. There is no room here for the question of redistribution of goods, rather, certain forms of discrimination.

From the criminal law perspective, in cases of contravening mutual recognition, we can talk about: the unjustified downgrading of another person's potential in the sphere of free acting; the lack of respect for another subject's life plan; and finally, the violation of a citizen's duty to participate in maintaining a common public order. According to Hegel's terminology, these kinds of violations of mutual recognition may be defined as: infringement of a person, infringement

---

senschaft vor der Jahrtausendwende, ed. by A. Eser, W. Hassemer, B. Burkhardt, München: C.H. Beck, 2000, p. 329.

[48] A. Honneth, *Das Andere der Gerechtigkeit. Aufsätze zur praktischen Philosophie*, Frankfurt am Main: Suhrkamp Verlag, 2000, p. 187.

of a subject, and infringement of a citizen. This distinction results from the fact that everyone who has personality also has legal subjectivity, and is a member of a certain community and society as someone who has these attributes.

3.2. Is the act of committing a crime a condition to exclude an offender from the community?

Infringement towards a person targets Hegel's imperative "be a person and regard others as people."[49] Everyone has their own specific identity, and understanding of themselves and their range of freedom to act. If someone reduces my legally protected potential to act, they simultaneously target my value and the value of my legal goods. This involves violating the law to respect each subject as a person, and therefore human dignity. Treating someone like a person means letting them make choices and respecting the choices made by them. Violating the right to recognize me as a person also targets the legal community – which functions in an ordered way – that I belong to.[50] Violating me leads to the disruption of the organisation of the legal community, and the lack of respect for the specific life plan that I represent. Refusing the right to be treated as a person is – according to H. Morris – a denial of all rights and duties.[51] Breaking this law undermines the whole system based on the idea of human dignity. The infringement of a person shows itself as a subjectively attributed lack of respect for the victim's life plan, so it aims at his/her right to be a legitimate subject of a given community and society. Thus, it questions the subjective rights of a certain individual.

Rating under the category of a subject (*Zurechnung zum Subjekt*) is equally important for positive law in the light of proper norms and, in

---

[49] G.W.F. Hegel, *Philosophy of Right*, Kitchener: Batoche Books, 2001, § 36.

[50] G. Jakobs uses the term "organisation of a legal circle" to which a given person belongs. Idem, "Zum Begriff des Delikts gegen die Person," in: *Bochumer Beiträge zu aktuellen Strafrechtsthemen. Vorträge anlässlich des Symposiums zum 70. Geburtstag von Gerd Geilen*, ed. by K. Bernsmann, K. Ulsenheimer, Köln: Carl Heymanns Verlag, 2003, p. 65.

[51] H. Morris, "Persons and Punishment," *The Monist* 1968, vol. 52, pp. 475–501.

particular, from the point of view of provisions concerning legal capacity, capacity to act, court, and proceeding capacity. The subject of law, against whom some illegal act was committed, should be granted a legally guaranteed capacity to effectively seek his or her rights. He or she must be granted the right to court (under article 6 of the European Convention of Human Rights and article 45 of Polish Constitution), namely, the right to be given a conclusive judgment stating that somebody else's plan of life is less valuable (for example, due to the fact that it infringes the freedom of others, as is the case with terrorist attacks). It needs emphasising that rating under the category of a subject is not merely a supplement of rating under the category of a person (*Zurechnung zur Person*), but also "the truth" of the latter:

> It brings a liberation intention, which has already placed a complete and proper personal classification as the basis of the liberation intention. Who does not commit any subjectively classified illegal act does not perpetrate any criminally relevant infringement.[52]

I have pointed out the innate and indispensable character of human dignity. Is it, then, possible to take away dignity when a certain person violates other people's rights or duties regarding themselves? In Kant's opinion, in such a case the offender turns out to be unworthy of this "innate" humanity. This humanity may be returned if he/she recognises his/her culpability and compensates the victim in line with the law.[53] Such a conclusion does not seem to be justified from the perspective of the philosophy of human rights. According to its assumptions, it is understood that everyone's dignity remains something independent from the crime committed by them, just as it is independent from race, faith, or social class. Otherwise, no rehabilitation or expiatory function of punishment would make sense. Punishment would make the offender a tool in the hands of the country, which of course is contradictory to the idea of human dignity. Nor would it be possible to forgive the offender, because it is based on

[52] M. Pawlik, *Person, Subjekt, Bürger…*, op. cit., p. 79.

[53] I. Kant, *Die Metaphysik der Sitten*, Berlin: Akademie-Ausgabe der Königliche-Preussischen Akademie der Wissenschaften, 1902/1910.

understanding the finiteness of a guilty person, so owing to the inner belief that despite the committed crime, even a horrific one, he/she participates in the human condition.[54]

In this meaning, forgiveness does not determine reintroducing the offender to the world, but admitting that he/she has always been human, and recognizing his or her dignity over his or her guilt. Contemporary punishment is based on the change of attitude towards the offender as a responsible subject, the recognition of human dignity and equality as the chief principle of law, which does not let it be treated as a measure, but a purpose itself, demanding equal punishment for the same thing, and equal treatment of the offender and the victim. In other words, treating each individual as independent and as "a purpose itself" does not stand in contradiction to condemning him/her for the evil caused.[55] Certainly, from an average person's point of view, it may be seen as a "symbolic" seizure of dignity, but it is actually more about dignity as "a social regard" - respect, rather than the seizure of human dignity. From Kant's uncompromising imperative it appears that punishment may be inflicted only when a crime has been committed. Besides, the effect of such a conclusion is recognizing that specific punishment should be inflicted according to the rules determined by the principle of individual prevention.

The right to be a person, similarly, to the right to be a subject, emphasizes the meaning of legal relations and, in turn, the necessity for the legal adjudication of a specific legal conflict. It is obligatory to apply a specific sanction, particularly a repressive measure, especially when a given subject breaks the law, in this way showing their contempt not only for the binding legal norms, but also for other people, who deserve, as subjects, appropriate respect. Such a lack of respect is particularly clear and severe in multicultural societies, which are the topic of my dissertation. What I mean here is the lack of respect for foreign values, religions, or cultures, which turns to and reveals itself

---

[54] Ch. Delsol, *Éloge de la singularité. Essai sur la modernité tardive*, Paris: Table Ronde, 2000.

[55] R.A. Duff, *Punishment, Communication and Community*, Oxford: Oxford University Press, 2001, pp. 16–18. Duff claims even that ignoring the violation of law means betrayal of the universal values that deserve protection, and more importantly, lack of respect for an individual.

in various forms of discrimination, persecutions, or aggression. It will usually be actions of a criminal character, which must bring about criminal responsibility.

If the offender wants to avoid sanctions, he/she must prove that his/her own life plan is a priority, so in this case it has more significance than another subject's life plan. In other words, his/her life plan must be more worthy of maintaining than another subject's life plan. This issue is primarily connected with the notion of the so-called *cultural defence*,[56] which has its legal justification in article 27 of the International Covenant on Civil and Political Rights, which touches upon the right to an individual's own cultural life. The notion of *cultural defence* consists in using the argument of the offender's cultural membership as circumstances of mitigating or excluding his or her penal liability, or as the circumstances that influence a lesser penalty for a given crime.

As a part of the science of crime, punishable acts are typified as *culturally motivated crimes*: *cultural offences* and *cultural delicts*.[57] Generally speaking, *cultural defence* means that both when determining the offender's liability and when deciding the penalty, in a case when such liability has been determined, what is taken into consideration is diversity of cultural norms represented by an organic community, which the offender belongs to, from the perspective of commonly binding norms. It can be then seen that when determining the offender's penal liability, namely, whilst assessing his motives, awareness of illegality, and the character of the crime committed, the cultural context has to be taken into account. There arises an epistemic problem connected with a controversy of recognizing the distinct

---

[56] This issue is broadly discussed in an interesting study of A. Dundes Renteln, *The Cultural Defence*, New York: Oxford University Press, 2004; idem, "The Use and Abuse of the Cultural Defence," *Canadian Journal of Law and Society* 2005, vol. 20, no. 1, pp. 47–67.

[57] J. van Broeck, "Cultural Defence and Culturally Motivated Crimes (Cultural Offences)," *European Journal of Crime, Criminal Law and Criminal Justice* 2001, vol. 9, no. 1, pp. 1–32; M.C. Foblets, "Cultural Delicts: the Repercussion of Cultural Conflicts on Delinquent Behaviour, Reflections on the Contribution of Legal Anthropology to a Contemporary Debate," *European Journal of Crime, Criminal Law and Criminal Justice* 1998, vol. 6, no. 3, pp. 187–207.

character of the said cultural norms and determining their significance from an external position towards the environment (organic community) in which those norms function.[58] Referring to the argument of *cultural defence* undoubtedly leads to a restriction of a binding nature, or at least to relativization, of general norms which constitute the basis of inclusive constructivist community.

It can often be the case that the said cultural identities negatively influence the rest of the society and they are perceived by the society as not deserving a protection. Let us then return to our first issue, namely that it has to be proved that in a certain case my own life plan is relatively more significant than any other one (imposed on me). As long as we would be willing to accept such a solution in certain situations, for example in reference to lifting a ban on wearing safety helmets by Sikhs, in the situation when such cultural identities lead to infringement, or even only challenging, of the universality of human rights or the principles of a discourse – it arouses an objection (as in case of circumcising small girls). In fact, unfortunately, the argument of *cultural defence* very often infringes human rights, particularly on account of the fact that the victims of *cultural crimes* are primarily women and children who are subjected to such treatment which does not fit in commonly accepted frames. From this perspective, one has to be very careful and critical when using the *cultural defence* argument. It cannot be accepted that behind the façade of cultural pluralism or the ideology of multiculturalism, we will agree, or even legalise, such practices that infringe another individual's dignity, allowing the violation of the most fundamental human rights. It does not mean, obviously, that the argument of *cultural defence* should be rejected as a whole (just the opposite). A. Dundes Renteln is right when stating that this argument should be regarded as "official public policy in the situation when there are tools protecting against its abuse."[59]

---

[58] S. Sykuna, J. Zajadło, "Kontrowersje wokół tzw. 'obrony przez kulturę' – okoliczność wyłączająca winę, okoliczność łagodząca czy nadużycie prawa?" [Controversies around the issue of the so-called "cultural defence" – extenuating or mitigating circumstances or malpractice?], *Przegląd Sądowy* 2007, no. 6, pp. 27–28.

[59] A. Dundes Renteln, *The Use and Abuse of the Cultural Defence*, op. cit., p. 47.

With reference to the circumstances excluding or limiting the liability of certain behaviour, it is also worthwhile to consider the cases that stay within institutions: the state of special necessity or civil disobedience, cultural defence, or about the relative significance of specific goods (rules). In other words, inside the offender's individual value system his behaviour is not understood as a particular lack of respect for the victim, but as a belief that the existing law (incorrect of unjust) needs to be modified, or that it is necessary to break the law in order to save some other good that is more deserving of protection for obvious reasons. In such cases it is difficult to talk about the lack of respect for the Other's, diminished in this case, hence, subjectively shaken life plan, but it is more legitimate to talk about the relative significance of one plan over another. It is not about the state of lawlessness described by Hobbes. Quite the contrary, the third distinguished kind of infringement – the infringement of the citizen – shows that it is only within a country respecting civil rights that reaching an operationalising model of behaviour is possible.

Within a country, especially a democratic legislative country, a subject becomes a cooperating part of society, and its existence should not take a parasitic form of life. Rating among the category of a (*Zurechnung zum Bürger*) becomes a liberation-oriented, undeniable element of the process in which a free, equal, and mutually recognized individual is created as a part of particular community. A citizen is co-responsible for the adequate law order from which he/she draws specific claims regarding his/her own freedom too. In other words, the legal community protects the integrity of its members if they are the advocates of subjects' rights. He/she plays the double role of an entitled person and a co-advocate of law order.[60] A citizen is an entitled person when he/she understands the legal order as an institutional independence, and he/she exercises the individual activities resulting from it. From this point of view, every citizen should fulfil his/her responsibilities because of his/her co-citizens. As a co-advocate of the legal order, however, he/she recognizes the fact that law order serving freedom and equality cannot take place without the mutual cooperation of all co-citizens (members of a given

[60] M. Pawlik, *Person, Subjekt, Bürger…*, op. cit., p. 82.

community). Additionally, maintaining a state of safety and legal certainty has a fundamental meaning for freedom and appropriate cooperation. As a result, the duty to cooperate, thus also loyalty to the country and fellow citizens, derives from the duties of an individual to the community and society.[61] We are talking about multiplying *bonum communae* here. Such a statement is based on the belief that maintaining peace, freedom, and equality among the co-citizens requires the effort of all citizens.

Klaus Günther claims that an appropriate definition of a person, which legitimates attributing responsibility as a legal subject, is possible only when it concerns the criminal law idea of guilt, the idea of a democratic legitimization of legal norms, and a person as an advocate of law, taking part in the political processes of creating public will and judgment, thus, in the process of establishing law.[62] Each citizen of a democratic country is not only an addressee, but also an author of legal norms, which enables him/her as a human being and legal subject to participate in deliberative politics and social life. This is why the autonomy of a legal subject - a deliberative citizen - contains three different ingredients, i.e., apart from the commonly practiced autonomy of the citizens, also the capacities for rational choice, and for ethical self-realization.[63] This can be observed particularly in the ability to take a critical stance on judgments and activities, both alien and personal. A person who has the ability to take a critical stance can perform the cognitive act of adopting a justified position. In such circumstances, we can talk about his/her communicative freedom. At the same time, law is a normative expression of values, the realization of which every citizen should be engaged in.[64] It warrants pointing out at this point that the extent of guilt is determined by the following factors: recognizable character of the situation in the

---

[61] K. Günther, "Dritter Vortrag. Jenseits von idealistischer und rollenfunktionaler Strafbegründung, " in: *Rechtsphilosophische Kontroversen der Gegenwart*, ed. by P. Siller, & B. Keller, Baden-Baden: Nomos Verlag, 1999, p. 142ff.; idem, *Schuld und kommunikative Freiheit. Studien zur personalen Zurechnung strafbaren Unrechts im demokratischen Rechtsstaat*, Frankfurt am Main: Vittorio Klostermann, 2005, p. 250ff.

[62] K. Günther, *Schuld und kommunikative Freiheit…*, op. cit., p. 245ff.

[63] J. Habermas, *Between Facts and Norms…*, op. cit., p. 451.

[64] R.A. Duff, *Punishment, Communication…*, op. cit., Chapter 2, Section 3.1.

sphere of facts and on the level of its legal assessment (what is meant here are crucial facts for settling a particular case and a normative description of the state of facts); the possibility of assessing a proper motivational process and the process of taking a decision about the choice of law abiding behaviour; and the ability to manage one's own behaviour.[65]

Such a deliberative person should be able to participate in the processes of argumentations during which the claims of the importance of judgment will be raised. Not only in the causative sense is he/she the reason for judgment and action, but also because the course and result of a discourse depend on his/her critical stance, thus also on the way he/she speaks and acts.[66] Such a person may adopt the position of the Other, and when he/she looks at him/herself through the eyes of the defender, consider what his/her reaction to the critical opinion expressed by that person will be. In other words, he/she "acquires a *reflective attitude towards him/herself*."[67] So, a deliberative person internalizes the role of a participant in argumentation by becoming able to criticize him/herself. A socially shaped individual is – through learning his/her position in the community and making him/herself a point of reference for various social institutions – capable of a critical appraisal of him/herself. From this point of view we can formulate the following legal topic: "Nobody can be forced to obey the norms if it is not possible to learn their importance rationally."[68] At the same time, it is necessary to adopt an assumption that everyone is able to behave according to the norm.

An obvious conclusion results from this point that legal sanctions cannot be imposed if an offender (a deliberative citizen) has not been able to learn what the binding law is, and thus has not had the chance to take its imperatives into consideration. Moreover, guilt is a necessary condition of the criminality of an act, both in the form of a deli-

---

[65] J. Majewski, P. Kardas, "O dwóch znaczeniach winy w prawie karnym" [On Two Meanings of Guilt in Penal Law], *Państwo i Prawo* 1993, no. 10, p. 77.

[66] K. Günther, "Communicative Freedom, Communicative Power, and Jurisgenesis," *Cardozo Law Review* 1996, vol. 17, p. 801ff.

[67] J. Habermas, *Theorie des kommunikativen Handelns*, op. cit., p. 135.

[68] Ch. Larmore, "Die Wurzeln radikaler Demokratie," *Deutsche Zeitschrift für Philosophie* 1993, no. 41, p. 327.

berate accusation, and a non-deliberate one. Using the words of the retributivists, guilt relates to "desert." As a result, we should limit punishment to the subjects that have a normal ability and a suitable opportunity to be obedient.[69] Therefore, it can be seen that when defining the shape of the premises of fault (and at the same time guilt), the legislator should pay particular attention to the fact that they did not exceed the possible limits of abiding by a given norm (following law). When those limits are exceeded, namely in the situations of revising the sanctioned norm when the addressee did not have the opportunity to take such a decision which law requires from him, or he did not have the possibility to act in accordance with such a decision, the act of punishing is deprived of all ethical and moral grounds and justification; all humanistic sense of punishment is lost, becoming an unjustified act of oppression. The issue of *cultural defence* is also recalled in this context, i.e. the argument of *cultural defence* can consist in a mistake in unawareness of illegality of a particular act in the situation when the offender acted in accordance with his own cultural norms, being unaware that they are contrary to binding law.

Thus, everyone as a member of a constructive community is equipped in at least two aspects of practical rationality: willingness to propose and obey just conditions of social cooperation between subjects equal to themselves, and mutual recognition of this equality and freedom, as well as a willingness to accept the consequences of the burden of judgment.[70] The court sees it as correct and right because it is a result of a rational and judicious procedure, i.e. when it correctly reflects the principles of a practical reason (including the rule and principle of discourse). In other words, a deliberative person is capable of a volitional act which lies in following the socially accepted or demanded conduct, and, therefore, he/she is also able to guide him/herself by rational reasons in life. So, a deliberative person is able to take a critical stance toward his/her own or alien actions and

---

[69] H.L.A. Hart, *Punishment and Responsibility...*, op. cit., p. 201ff. Hart believes that we need to bear in mind *mens rea* as a necessary condition of responsibility. Thus, he writes that someone who could not have behaved in a different way should not be punished (ibidem, p. 207ff.)

[70] J. Rawls, *Political Liberalism*, op. cit.

judgment. A deliberative person is not only a citizen (of a country or the world), but also a member of a constructivist community, and as such he/she is reasonable and capable of self-determination. He/she may support his/her stance on the basis of the accepted rules, principles and forms, which are characteristic of a potential member of discourse. Democratic procedures join the processes of creating the binding norms with everyone's ability to take a critical stance toward judgments of other subjects (e.g. the legislative initiative). As long as a deliberative person supports his/her critical stance on the discursive forms and the rules of arguments, he/she is at least a virtual participant of the discourse. However, when a certain person does not maintain his/her critical stance on the rules of discourse, he/she contravenes commonly shared conduct, principles, and values, transgressing against the community constructed by democratic procedure. At the same time, he/she condemns him/herself to being expelled from the community, and exposes him/herself to the infliction of sanctions, including the imposition of criminal punishment if they commit a punishable act. Criminal punishment is a strong means of removing recognition from the offender, and may even lead to expulsion from society.[71] R. Antony Duff claims, however, that punishing the offender does not mean expelling him/her from society. He underlines the fact that if we exclude someone from participating in a political community, at the same time we negate his status as a citizen.[72]

It is hard to deny the statement that social exclusion is tantamount to removing civil rights, but it is still uncommon for the courts to de-

---

[71] Cf. L. Wacquant, "Deadly Symbiosis: When Ghetto and Prison Meet and Mesh," *Punishment and Society* 2001, no. 3, pp. 119–120. The author points out here that the expulsion will be stronger if it is connected with a so-called civil death, which is expressed in formally depriving the convict of the right to participate in public life. In our law system it is carried out by using a specific criminal measure (derivation of public rights) and not punishing. A similar effect – although less linked to citizenship – might be reached through a ruling on the prohibition to do a certain job, to have a certain activity, or to hold a certain position. It may lead to a stronger stigmatisation of the convict in his present professional environment, but also in the community in which they live, and that is even when the imposed punishment is not seclusion.

[72] R.A. Duff, "Karanie obywateli" [Punishing Citizens], *Ius et Lex* 2006, no. 1, p. 29.

prive people of their rights. I assume that Duff did not mean the death penalty when writing about punishment. Even if we exclude this principal punishment, it is worth asking the following question: What is the infliction of a prison sentence or life imprisonment upon the perpetrator? Saying that the perpetrator sentenced to life imprisonment is still treated as an estimable and commendable fellow citizen would be a sort of hypocrisy and naivety. The infliction of punishment upon him aims mainly at condemning his wrongdoing. Harsh punishment seems to contain the exclusive element that was introduced by this condemnation. Exclusion is referred to as removing the status of an equal participant in social interactions from the perpetrator and depriving him of recognition according to the Honnethian understanding of this relation. It should be added that it usually has a temporal character. The perpetrator will not deserve to be treated equally until he redresses his wrongdoings or restores the balance. Due to the fact that the perpetrator could not respect shared values in the past, it is hard to assume that he will be able to continue to cooperate with other members of the community in order to obtain and protect the values in the future. A lack of exclusion of criminals occurs in such penal systems that are based on corrective justice. Within the framework of corrective justice, it is assumed that public welfare, the restoration of peace, harmony, and appropriate relations between the communities are of overriding importance in the process of administering justice. To restore the values, the harmed party must accept the apologies given by the wrongdoer. Punishment is of lesser and marginal importance here. Corrective justice restores the image of humanity to criminals. In order to avoid vengeance against the perpetrators and their exclusion or alienation, punishment is replaced by reconciliation. Duff, however, looks at corrective justice from a different perspective. His viewpoint does not apply to the legal system which is based on the punishment of perpetrators.

Duff seems to be right, admitting that punishment is a measure aimed at including the perpetrator. Further, punishment could have a dual character. On the one hand, it could contain some excluding elements (based on removing recognition) until the moment when the balance was restored, but on the other hand its principal objective would be to resocialize, which is the major aim of punishment expressed by the institution of abolition of punishment. Without the possibility of bringing the offender back to normal life, it would not make any sense to discuss the issues concerning resocialization or the preventive character of punishment. As a consequence, the preventive character of punishment would come down to primordial vengeance and would deprive the perpetrator of a human's inherent dignity. The inclusion of the perpetrator would mean that punishment refers to the values which are protected by the law and the fact that the perpetrator who was punished for breaking the values is still treated as a member of the community that holds these values.[73] Therefore, it is difficult to agree with the opinion that social exclusion should be the major aim of dealing with criminals. It should also be emphasized that resocialization is only possible when the addressees of legal norms form the integrational social structure in which they live as isolated and anonymous individuals. The requirement concerning resocialization would be a very significant element for limiting punishment.[74] Punishment should not aim to destroy the perpetrators. This argument was obviously developed by those who objected to the death penalty, and those who make the topos of proportionality of claims and the suitability of punishment conditional on the degree of guilt or the social abhorrence of the act.

In cases where the abovementioned duties towards other members of the community or society have been neglected, it is not enough to pay a relevant amount of money in damages to the victim. From the perspective of the whole community, paying damages to the victim does not necessarily mean restoring the balance among those members of the community who were affected by offences and those whose sense of security, legal certainty, and solidarity was destroyed. Punishment here has more than an individual character.[75] Ernst-

---

[73] R.A. Duff, *Punishment, Communication…*, op. cit., p. 80ff.

[74] K. Rolinski, "Vom Strafen und von Strafe in indigenen und ‚modernen' Gesellschaften," in: *Muss Strafe sein? Kolloquium zum 60. Geburtstag von Herrn Professor Dr. Dr. h.c. Heike Jung*, ed. by H. Radtke, E. Müller, G. Britz, H. Koriath, H. Müller-Dietz, Baden-Baden: Nomos Verlag, 2004, p. 121.

[75] U. Ebert, "Das Vergeltungsprinzip im Strafrecht," in: *Geisteswissenschaften – wozu? Beispiele iherer Gegenstände und ihrer Fragen*, ed. by H.-H. Krummacher, Wiesbaden (Stuttgart): Steiner Verlag, 1988, p. 39; M. Pawlik, *Person, Subjekt, Bürger…*, op. cit., p. 89.

Joachim Lampe claims, however, that punishment "deprivatizes" the conflict between the perpetrator and their victim.[76] In other words, punishment perversely retains the interpersonal dimension of legal conflicts. It is also a reaction to the illegality of the citizen whose offence was against the rules governing the binding legal order. In this context, it is essential to find out how we should punish our fellow citizens, our neighbours, and finally, ourselves.[77] Punishment deprives the perpetrator of part of his own freedom. In order to achieve the appropriate effect, punishment must always teach a painful lesson. Multiculturalism, the pluralism of values, and diversity of lifestyles are very significant when imposing punishment and assessing its severity. Penalties should be arranged and meted out not only on the basis of the severity of particular behaviour, but also on the standards of the criminal's life. In other words, the court must take into account the fact that the painfulness of punishment will be different when considering a preferred way of life, or notably a glorified freedom of movement and privacy in some cultures.[78] In this context, fairness in punishment has a cultural dimension. In the context of the abovementioned concept of *cultural defence,* what can be perceived as an extenuating circumstance is the fact that the offender, when committing an illegal act, was determined by the feeling that he acts on the basis of cultural imperative, although he did realize that his behaviour was a criminal one.

The painfulness of sanctions should correspond with the degree of guilt, but the judgement ought to take into consideration the individual lifestyle of the perpetrator and the culture he was brought up in. It has to be kept in mind that administering justice, even within the lowest limits of statutory penalties can, in certain cases, lead to accumulation of constraint and, consequently, to increased level and extent of penal repression over rational need.[79]

---

[76] E.-J. Lampe, "Recht und Moral staatlichen Strafens," in: *Recht und Moral. Beiträge zu einer Standortbestimmung,* ed. by H. Jung, H. Müller-Dietz, U. Neumann, Baden-Baden: Nomos Verlag, 1991, p. 311.

[77] R.A. Duff, "Punishing Citizens," op. cit., p. 22.

[78] Broader on this issue see: A. von Hirsch, N. Jareborg, "Gauging Criminal Harm: A Living Standard Analysis," *Oxford Journal of Legal Studies* 1991, vol. 11, no. 1, pp. 1–38.

[79] K. Buchała in: K. Buchała, A. Zoll, *Kodeks karny. Część ogólna. Komentarz* [Penal Code. General Part. A Commentary], Kraków: Zakamycze, 1999, p. 302. As a conse-

The proportionality of guilt and penalty is one of the most basic elements of contemporary theories of punishment.[80] When meting out a penalty, we should also take into account the fact that the criminal is still a part of our society and should be treated as an individual who is governed by moral rules.[81] The abovementioned description of wrongdoers is a continuation of Hegel and Kant's thought, in which punishment is characterized by the institution which respects the autonomy of the rational individual and forbids the imposition of humiliating penalties. R.A. Duff claims that harsher penalties aim to force the perpetrator to understand the damage he did and make him express regret for what he did. This is extremely important in situations when someone has committed a heinous offence (crime).

Only the hard treatment of a perpetrator of a crime is normatively an appropriate response to the infringement of recognition, which was called wrongdoing.[82] It should be added that harsh treatment takes into account the mentality of the average citizen. Only punishment can be a solution for restoring social balance. It can also force all

---

quence, the author accurately points out that: "Just ... penalty [is such - B.W.] takes properly into account the kind of crime that has been committed as well as its consequences, circumstances in which it was committed (typical and extraordinary), the offender's personality, his properties and conditions, his family conditions and, mostly, the extent of guilt and negative content of his act, together with the contribution of the victim and the offender's behaviour after committing the crime, in particular his attempt to compensate the damage, and reconciliate with the victim by means of mediation. ... What has to be taken into consideration is the sum of negative consequences which the act has for the offender, and the consequences resulting from other provisions, like labour law, social and moral norms, e.g. divorce, being expelled from the university, social condemnation, etc." Ibidem, pp. 379–380.

[80] See: A. von Hirsch, "Tadel und Prävention: Die Übelzufügung als Element der Strafe," in: *Positive Generalprävention. Kritische Analysen im deutsch-englischen Dialog*, ed. by B. Schünemann, A. von Hirsch, N. Jareborg, Heidelberg: C.F. Müller Verlag, 1998; T. Hörnle, *Tatproportionale Strafzumessung*, Berlin: Duncker und Humblot Verlag, 1999; M. Królikowski, *Sprawiedliwość karania w społeczeństwach liberalnych* [Just Punishment in Liberal Democracies], Warszawa: C.H. Beck, 2005, passim.

[81] R.A. Duff, "Punishing Citizens", op. cit., p. 24; A. von Hirsch, *Censure and Sanctions*, op. cit., p. 11.

[82] M. Pawlik, *Person, Subjekt, Bürger...*, op. cit., p. 91. Cf. also N. Lacey, *State Punishment, Political Principles and Community Values*, London: Routledge, 1988.

fellow citizens to cooperate in an atmosphere of peace and treat each other as equal and free individuals, despite many social, cultural, religious, racial, and sexual differences, as well as different lifestyle preferences. Value pluralism and soft multiculturalism deserve protection. The actions which infringe human dignity will be liable to stigmatization through punishment.

This socio-psychological and communicative theoretical model of punishment legitimization is based on the assertion that most people can identify bad and punishable behaviour by means of a detailed and subtle assessment, which underlies the legal legitimation of the ability to punish particular behaviour.[83] G. Jakobs, however, successfully resolves the difficulties associated with justifying punishment. He notes that the meaning of the perpetrator's behaviour is not only objectified symbolically. In his view, the perpetrator also creates his own external world of people on the basis of his own assessment of his importance.[84] The basis of this statement is the recognition of the notional equivalence of the "perceptible" objectivisation moment and the expressive moment of punishment. It is true only when we assume that all citizens, including offenders, are members of a particular communicative community. Being part of the community, they can perform a thorough semantic and pragmatic analysis of each type of behaviour. Undoubtedly, the correct interpretation of a particular behaviour requires fulfilling certain language and pragmatic conditions that objectively allow us to decide the meaning and intention of a particular behaviour. Consequently, it is essential to react appropriately to the ignorance of discourse rules and the violation of mutual relations in a properly functioning society. Punishing the perpetrator is a way to give an appropriate reaction to disobeying the rules. R.A. Duff points out that punishment here could have the character of a conventional symbol.[85]

---

[83] E.-J. Lampe, *Strafphilosophie. Studien zur Strafgerechtigkeit*, Köln – Berlin – Bonn – München: Carl Heymanns, 1999, p. 75 ff.

[84] G. Jakobs, "Zur gegenwärtigen Straftheorie," in: *Strafe muß sein! Muß Strafe sein?*, ed. by K. Kodalle, Würzburg: Königshausen u. Neumann, 1998, p. 36.

[85] R.A. Duff, *Punishment, Communication…*, op. cit., pp. 79–80; idem, "Punishing Citizens," op. cit., p. 34ff.

4. Punishment as a message for society

The conceptions which allude to the so-called communicative theories of punishment have a special place in this dispute. Communicative theories of punishment treat it as a social symbol which resembles a *communicative act* or an *expressive act*. Punishment is perceived here as a means of rational communication. It can be, therefore, seen that the offender should be treated as a partner, and inflicting sanctions on him requires a prior consent expressed by the citizens, and should be motivated with proper moral arguments. By the act of punishing the offender we reprimand or condemn him for the wrong that he caused – which the society is informed about by means of the communication expressed by the punishment. Penal law and the punishment itself should point out to the society that certain behaviour is reprehensible, and they should aim at deferring unwanted behaviour.[86]

Due to the inflicting of the punishment, respective individuals get the message that the society treats harm that has been caused to someone as a wrong, and are familiarised with values that were recognized as being worth protecting at the expense of limiting our personal freedom (self-restriction in relation to others). In other words, it marks the extent of the so-called negative freedom.[87] Punishment formulates different messages depending on how severe it is, that is, on its type and extent.[88] R.A. Duff points out that the notions of a reprimand and condemnation have a key meaning for understanding the communicative act expressed by the punishment, namely, by means of punishment we either reprimand the offender or condemn him or her for the wrong that he or she caused. At the same

---

[86] H.L.A. Hart, *Punishment and Responsibility...*, op. cit., p. 6.

[87] What is meant in this context is, obviously, the autonomy of unhindered behaviour as a part of sphere that is defined by law. The protection of an individual's autonomy is linked with the duty of not infringing other people's autonomy, namely the duty of not interfering in legally the protected sphere.

[88] R.A. Duff, "Punishing Citizens," op. cit., p. 34. Duff states that "by inflicting more severe penalties as a deterrence, we give the following message to the convicts: We can no longer refer to you as to a fellow citizen, but from now on we will treat you as being immoral, someone who is able to understand and respond only to threats and to react simply in order to defend his own interests" (ibidem, p. 39).

time, punishment constitutes a significant message directed at the victim of a punishable act and the whole society in general, manifesting that the members of the community or society negatively perceive the act that was committed, treating it as wrong, and infringing crucial values that merit protection. In other words, condemnation stands for the respect for harm suffered by the victim and for the values that were violated, and respect for the whole society as cooperating individuals. Duff goes on to state that only the state is authorised to formulate the communicative act by means of punishment.[89]

This reservation is crucial on account of the fact that it additionally strengthens the position of state authority and, moreover, it expressly places the act of inflicting punishment in the public sphere despite the fact that its effects are equally significant in the private sphere. Duff once more accurately indicates that:

> Punishment – as a reprimand – appeals to the offender not as to a subject but as to a citizen, a member of political community. It addresses him not in coercion, but in the language of particular community, which the offender – being a citizen – should have recognized and respected. Harm caused by the perpetrator does not result in revenge, but it is presented as an evil inflicted on fellow citizens, whom the offender had to take care of, whose rules of life also apply to his life.[90]

Punishment constitutes then a kind of "secular atonement," namely a burden that the offender has to accept and bear in order to arouse, emphasise, or acknowledge the wrong that he or she caused and to express his or her regret.[91] What is also important is the fact that the offender is still treated as a rational member of a community who is able to bear liability, because it is only then that he or she can understand the message expressed by the punishment. Understanding is possible only when infringed values and sanctions which were inflicted were internalised by him or her in the process of exchanging perspectives, namely by means of the authority of the "generalised

[89] Ibidem, p. 36.

[90] Ibidem.

[91] R.A. Duff, *Punishment, Communication...*, op. cit., p. 106. It warrants emphasizing that Duff writes about recognizing common values and – in the effect – also an evil, rather than about a choice (ibidem, p. 53).

Other." The aim of punishment is also to provoke a real participation of an offender in a public discourse, in social interactions, according to their rules and norms, which are binding in his or her communicative community. Punishment, understood in such way, by means of its physical or mental discomfort, constitutes a key element of a communication between the society and the offender, which should force him or her to participate in a discourse, make him or her express regret for his or her act, and make him or her undertake to improve in the future. Punishment should, at the same time, constitute a kind of compensation for the wrong done, namely it should make up for the consequences of a punishable act. In this aspect, punishment is to reflect the extent of harm and show respect for the victim and, consequently, it should constitute an obligation "to perform something burdensome, something both for the benefit of the victim and widely understood society, which would assume the form of penitential suffering."[92] It has to, therefore, include a specific constraint, namely such that would have a proper effect of moral reaction. Duff truly believes that a far-reaching goal of punishment is a transformation of the offender by means of moral persuasion.

5. Intercultural and international penal law

The cosmopolitan perspective and the processes of globalisation showed that contemporary problems that other societies tackle, which were seemingly distant and foreign, often become our problems. Cosmopolitan critical theory – as I pointed out in the first chapter of this dissertation – blurs classic differences between internal and external politics. Global dangers connected with the threats for environment and massive infringement of human rights are no longer the problem of a particular sovereign state, but they should be discussed and dealt with in the international arena.[93] An example of such a danger could be terrorism, which – in horrifying way – has made an inte-

[92] R.A. Duff, "Punishing Citizens," op. cit., p. 41.

[93] U. Beck, *Macht und Gegenmacht im globalen Zeitalter. Neue weltpolitische Ökonomie*, Frankfurt am Main: Suhrkamp Verlag, 2002, p. 77.

grated community out of our world (in accordance with the Simmel-Coser law, namely that external conflict increases internal integrity and cohesion of a group). A fear of one's own life causes one to be interested in what is going on in distant Afghan mountains or in Pakistani villages. It also leads us to widen the scope in which penal law functions to such regions, and to devise tools that enable the administration of justice towards terrorists or the individuals committing homicide without the necessity of declaring war to the whole country, which would be, in a way, acceptable for the international community. It is, therefore, indispensable to devise such a global or cosmopolitan system of penal justice that would prevent treating justice in an extremely relativist way and making it conditional on national differences of standpoints.[94]

What is of the utmost importance in this context is the fact that the signatories of the Rome Statute expressed the connection of all people with the bonds of common cultural heritage as well as their fear about its further existence. It has also been stressed that this delicate structure can be at any time destroyed, which can be seen in the example of conflicts which took place in the 20th century and which - due to inconceivable cruelty - resulted in millions of victims. These events have deeply moved human conscience and provoked the world community to acknowledge the fact that the most serious crimes cannot be left unpunished.[95] In a broad, that is at least international - if not even world-wide - perspective, the following human rights have to undergo protection: freedom from slavery and serfdom and the protection of ethnic groups against mass crime and genocide. There is no doubt that violation of such rights merits condemnation both in western states and those that belong to other cultures.[96] The need to protect these rights is so strong that despite the fundamental

---

[94] P. Singer, *One Word. The Ethics of Globalization*, New Haven: Yale University Press, 2004, p. 29.

[95] M. Płachta, "Statut Międzynarodowego Trybunału Karnego: Podstawowe zasady kompetencyjne, organizacyjne i procesowe" [The Statute of International Criminal Court: Basic Competence, Organizational and Procedural Principles], *Państwo i Prawo* 1998, no. 12, p. 17ff.

[96] J. Rawls, *The Law of Peoples*, Cambridge: Harvard University Press, 1999, Chapter 10.

principle of tolerance towards other people – which is binding in liberal states and also in "well-ordered" non-liberal ones – humanitarian intervention in relation to the states which infringe human rights is allowed and acceptable. It remains disputable whether "well-ordered" liberal states have the right or a duty to apply such humanitarian intervention. This matter constitutes, to a large extent, a part of the so-called international penal law, or penal law of the states.

5.1. Notional relation of "intercultural" and "international" law

What seems of interest from a dogmatic perspective is the relation between the field of international penal law, or penal law of the states, and the notion of the intercultural character of penal law. This relation is of utmost importance on account of the fact that international penal law has recently been the subject of many discussions. To use the words of Michał Płachta – it has its "second youth." It seems, *prima facie*, that international and intercultural penal law are alike. This is not, however, the case, due to the fact of the positive origin of the former and social, cultural, or philosophical origin of the latter. It is, therefore, indispensable to make a proper division and arrangement of the terminology and an explanation of the relations between such differentiated spheres of penal law. It is also necessary to draw attention to the fact that the differentiation at issue and definition of the notions refer to "penal law" in its narrow meaning. Namely, they refer only to substantive penal law and, to be even more precise, to penal law dealing with crimes for which the offender stands trial in court, which also means that what will be traditionally rated under this category will not only be the provisions of procedural and executory character, but also norms of substantive law included in martial penal law, tax penal law, or law of offences. At this point, I would like to make some notional reservations and to explain what is understood by me under the notion of "intercultural penal law" and how this explanation matches a classic approach to penal law and, in particular, to the differentiation between international penal law and penal law of the states.

Differentiation between the abovementioned notions is indispensable also on account of the fact that already the notions of international penal law and penal law of the states arouse some notional doubts; they are used in different contexts and different authors or different native legal systems attribute diverse meaning to them. Regulations concerning international penal law are based on the assumption of four principles, namely, the personal principle (subjective nationality, citizenship); the protective principle (objective nationality); the principle of vicarious liability; and the principle of universally (commonly) expressed repression.[97] The last principle is closely connected with the issues of penal law of the states because it indicates the punishable nature of crimes that are in the sphere of interest for the international community from the perspective of prosecution and punishing. In other words, the offenders of such crimes should bear penal liability irrespective of the fact of which state they are the citizens of, in which place they committed a particular crime, and which provisions were binding in the place where the crime was committed. Such crimes are referred to as *delicta iuris gentium*.

The field of international penal law under discussion concerns, similarly to internal (state) penal law, individual penal liability of a person and not an established community as a legal person. In contrast to national penal law, international penal law assumes a relation of an offender to a community of international law, which results in

[97] Generally speaking, universal (common) jurisdiction stands for the right of any given state to judge the offender, irrespective of whether the country where he or she committed a crime is a signatory to a convention that guarantees international penal liability for such crime. Broadly on this topic see: *Universal Jurisdiction. National Courts and the Prosecution of Serious Crimes under International Law*, ed. by S. Macedo, Philadelphia: University of Pennsylvania Press, 2004. This study focuses on the so-called Prinston's principles of common jurisdiction. What has been accepted in them was the idea of universal jurisdiction, referring to the nature of a crime itself, without taking into consideration the place of committing a crime, nationality of an alleged or convicted offender, nationality of the victim, or any other bonds with the state of the proper jurisdiction in the case. The crimes that were counted among those that merit universal jurisdiction were as follows: piracy, enslavement, war crimes, crimes against peace, crimes against humanity, homicide, and tortures.

a proper qualification of a committed crime and its penal liability.[98] The necessity of differentiating such spheres of penal law results from the fact that single acts of murder should be differently treated to acts of genocide, which harm all other nations and the basis of international law as such. The latter leads to a conclusion that the punishable nature of an act and execution of the punishment will be irrespective of the offender's nationality. This does not obviously mean that the offender does not have any rights. Even bestiality, and enormity of his act could not outlaw him. It is, therefore, the basis of a requirement for establishing the principles and norms of international penal law that allows the administration of justice to an offender in the situation when his or her national law could prove powerless. International penal law will refer both to the infringement of human rights, which are of an interstate character, as well as to merely national violation of the same. From this perspective, the notion of international penal law turns out to be problematic on account of its complex character.[99] Lech Gardocki understands international penal law as:

> ... the branch of law which includes the norms of international public law, which shape, whether directly or indirectly, the scope of penalisation, the principles of penal liability and penal proceedings, as well as the norms of international and national law, which refer to the crimes with a foreign element or to the institutions of international cooperation in penal cases.[100]

Michał Królikowski points at the possibility of a dichotomy in approaching the definition of international penal law, differentiating

---

[98] M. Köhler, "Zum Begriff des Völkerstrafrechts," *Jahrbuch für Recht und Ethik* 2003, Bd. 11, p. 435.

[99] See broadly on this subject: L. Gardocki, *Zarys prawa karnego międzynarodowego* [An Outline of International Penal Law], Warszawa: PWN, 1985, pp. 7–21; M.Ch. Bassiouni, *Crimes Against Humanity in International Criminal Law*, London – Boston: Kluwer, 1999; K. Ambos, *Der Allgemeine Teil des Völkerstrafrechts. Ansätze einer Dogmatisierung*, Berlin: Duncker und Humblot, 2002, p. 40ff.; G. Manske, *Verbrechen gegen die Menschlichkeit als Verbrechen an der Menschheit*, Berlin: Duncker und Humblot, 2003, p. 266ff. Supranational penal law arouses controversies and doubts even in the situation when it is referred to as the European, union, or community penal law.

[100] L. Gardocki, *Zarys prawa karnego międzynarodowego*, op. cit., p. 19.

between its broad and narrow meaning.[101] When taking into consideration a broad understanding of international penal law, it will include all issues connected with internationalisation of penal law and, in particular, it will broadly define the catalogue of crimes, starting with those that are of a cross-border character to those which define the cases of the most severe infringement of human rights and most fundamental values. In a narrow meaning, on the other hand, international penal law is concentrated on a limited group of crimes described in respective international acts of law.

All comments made in this dissertation opt in favour of the thesis that international penal law is included in the scope of the notion of intercultural penal law. International penal law is justified, in other words, it constitutes a crystallisation of universally, commonly binding penal law.[102]

Prima facie, the thesis on the intercultural character of penal law should be rejected because penal law is such a field of law that is strongly based in culture. In other words, penal law is strongly conditioned by cultural reality and social norms of the area where it is binding, which is clearly seen in anthropological researches. Taking a traditional perspective, penal law of a given cultural area will only to a marginal extent take into consideration the system of penal law that is binding in other cultures.[103] When referring to this branch of law, we deal with its strong immunisation. This immunisation consists in the system becoming immune to changes and in protecting its balance and cohesion. It is, therefore, the case that people who settle in a given country in which there is a diverse legal culture are subject to law that is binding in this place, which can be seen as a contradiction to the thesis about the intercultural character of penal law.

This conflict can be observed when comparing the system of Islamic penal law and that of Christian culture. This conflict concerns

---

[101] M. Królikowski in: M. Królikowski, P. Wiliński, J. Izydorczyk, *Podstawy prawa karnego międzynarodowego* [The Basis of International Penal Law], Warszawa: Wolters Kluwers, 2008, p. 31.

[102] M. Köhler, *Zum Begriff des Völkerstrafrechts,* op. cit., p. 443.

[103] Cf. W. Hassemer, "Vielfalt und Wandel eines interkulturellen Strafrechts," in: O. Höffe, *Gibt es ein interkulturelles Strafrecht? Ein philosophischer Versuch,* Frankfurt am Main: Suhrkamp Verlag, 1999, p. 157.

primarily the sources of Islamic penal law, namely the Koran, the Prophet's sunna ("tradition") and the doctrine of Muslim law (*fikh*), unanimous opinions of learned people (*idżma*), and analogy (*kijas*). A distinguishing feature is also the principle of eternity and the unchangeable nature of law because it is the manifestation of God. The principle of divine origin of law does not, however, mean that a human being will not be liable for his or her own acts in respect of the community that he or she belongs to (especially the community of the faithful). It is emphasised in Islamic culture that a man who commits a crime, namely infringes law (divine order and social peace), transgresses not only against God and himself, but also against the whole community that he or she is a member of. A characteristic feature of Islamic penal law is *ius talionis* (*kisas*),[104] which does not constitute the standard in western legal culture. Strong emphasis is also placed on the right of revenge (*dijja*).

Moral relativists believe, then, that establishing intercultural law (human rights) and protecting them (for example, by means of humanitarian intervention) constitutes an expression of cultural imperialism. In this way, as they claim, they defend the right to preserve specific values attributable to everyone on account of being the members of different cultures. As has been pointed in Chapter I, such a way of thinking is not devoid of certain faults, which imply the legitimacy of rejecting moral relativism. It is undoubtedly true that the choices made by the individuals are deeply grounded in cultural contexts, which are invariably complex. It is the result of the fact that the duties and values discovered by the individual – in the conditions of cultural pluralism – are often in conflict. Pluralism, however, does not stand for relativism, but provides a multitude of choices or the existence of sometimes mutually contradictory duties. The conflict at issue exists and is experienced by the individuals because we can responsibly talk about significant aspects of particular goods or values, namely, about the fact that the significance of a choice is connected with Taylor's "horizons of meaning."[105] Rejection of rela-

[104] Such punishment was expressly predicted in Sura V 45 in the Koran.

[105] Ch. Taylor, *The Ethics of Authenticity*, Cambridge: Harvard University Press, 1991, Chapter IV.

tivism allows one to state that there exist values acknowledged by all cultures and recognized as significant and worth protecting, and that we can rationally discuss them irrespective of any particular culture. I truly believe that the principle of mutual recognition will be of the same universal character because in most cultures and religions it constitutes the basis of the so-called golden principle.

In the contemporary world, law constitutes the core of integration and coordination of a global system; it ensures cohesion of the whole social system. The key moment in the concept of intercultural penal law is perceiving punishment as a combination of a message denoting condemnation of the harm caused by the offender in the form of violating universal human rights, defined on the basis of the concept of interchanging perspectives and "a generalised Other" with the act of depriving the offender of the recognition, being the element of a constraint and constituting the part of social symbol manifested by means of punishment. Law can play the role of communicative medium, due to its abstract and general nature. Penal law aims at protecting common values, communicated by law, and in this approach, penal law – whilst protecting universal values – is of an objective and intercultural character.[106] The comments made in this dissertation show that certain values are of a common and universal character. It has to be emphasised that a constructivist community, which accepts pluralism and soft multiculturalism, and which is based on the principles of discourse and democracy, creates favourable conditions for different organic (exclusive) communities so that they could coexist on the condition that they abide by the principles of procedural justice. In particular, they have to accept the universality of human rights, freedom, and equality of all their members (citizens). What is meant by the latter is the necessity of respecting universal rights, which are indispensable, for a man to demand other rights and follow them. The moral point of view transcends, then, the borders of every particular legal community and establishes a barrier for ethnocentric aspirations of respective organic communities.

---

[106] Cf. D. Ivison, "Punishment In Intercultural Context: Whose Norms? Which Values?," in: *Punishment and Legal Theory*, ed. by M. Matravers, Oxford: Hart Publishing, 1999, pp. 98–100.

A constructivist community, based on democracy and mutual recognition of all individuals as free, cannot tolerate such practices that are harmful for other people, their communities, or even for the whole society. Penal law, by means of protecting universal values and beliefs, aims at reinforcing the feeling of solidarity among the members of a community; it enables them to take advantage of benefits of life in a free, democratic society. In order to fulfil this condition, it is necessary to prevent those who infringe a binding legal order, at the same time violating safety and peace, and who, in order to justify their behaviour, hide behind the façade of cultural diversity. One cannot, even in the name of protecting cultural identity, allow and accept harassment in a family, ritual murders, or mutilation of young girls. It has to be stated at this point that the best way to protect cultural minorities is to abide by human rights[107] instead of relativizing the binding nature of penal law norms to every single culture. When assuming such a perspective, Tariq Ramadan's comments prove to be of the utmost importance. He claims that "the use of violence is in a deep contrast with the basic principles of Islamic religion and with the most fundamental principles that democratic states are based on."[108] What is crucial in this reasoning is the juxtaposition of the principles of Islamic religion and democracy. This reasoning proves that the thesis about two contradictory poles and their irreconcilable basis is wrong. It is just to the contrary: the conclusions made by this eminent Muslim theologian and thinker clearly indicate that the abovementioned ideologies are similar, particularly when taking into consideration the peaceful coexistence of humanity. Terrorists, who often refer to Muslim ideology in order to justify their criminal activities, "contradict both western and Islamic culture." Ramadan is critical about the idea of "war of cultures," postulating the opposition against a dominant and, in his opinion, harmful and illusory polarisation of twofold elements that is

---

[107] J. Donnelly, *Universal Human Rights in Theory and Practice*, Ithaca – London: Cornell University Press, 2003, 156ff.

[108] T. Ramadan, "Przestańmy się bać terrorystów" [Let Us Stop Being Afraid of Terrorists], *Europa. Tygodnik Idei* 2007, no. 2, January 13. This thesis is also proved by the researches carried out as a part of the *World Values Survey* (available at: <http://www.worldvaluessurvey.org>).

"Islam which is radical and full of hatred towards western countries and the rest of the world."[109]

Consequently, this infringement of human rights should constitute the proof of penal liability. The orientation of penal law towards human rights assumes that people - cognitively and emotionally - take part in defining what a crime is as well as in the process of punishing it.[110] Winfried Hassemer notes that intercultural justification of the norms of penal law should be of a negative character. This means that the justification should be based on negative experience of violating law, namely, on defining what should not have taken place and how people should not act. Such *philosophia negative* allows the reaching and explanation of the consensus on what should be protected. What has become such starting point for reaching a consensus on universal human rights was a common shock connected with their violent infringement. In other words, one can avoid committing crimes only when possibly most numerous group of people believes in human rights and perceives themselves in moral terms.[111] We deal with the act of determining the objectivity of certain prohibitions or orders of a penal character in the sense that their content is connected, irrespective of cultural differentiations. The act of punishing exceeds, at the same time, culturally defined borders, and the system of human rights assumes globalisation of these rights.

We could even risk the statement that intercultural justification of penal law, oriented at human rights, assumes Rawls' requirement of justice as impartiality. It seems that each community that is hidden behind the veil of ignorance should minimise private and exclusive authority, aiming at fulfilling postulated intercultural requirements indispensable for such a system of penal law to be created and to

---

[109] T. Ramadan, "Przestańmy się bać terrorystów," op. cit.

[110] W. Hassemer, *Vielfalt und Wandel eines interkulturellen Strafrechts*, op. cit., p. 178; M.Ch. Bassiouni, "International Criminal Law and Human Rights," in: *International Criminal Law. Crimes*, ed. by M.Ch. Bassiouni, New York: Oxford University Press, 1986, pp. 15–32.

[111] P. Sieghart, *The Lawful Rights of Mankind: An Introduction to the International Legal Code of Human Rights*, Oxford: Oxford University Press, 1985, p. 40; E. Tugendhat, *Vorlesungen über Ethik*, Frankfurt am Main: Suhrkamp Verlag, 2001, Chapter 17.

function in a differentiated and diverse social life. Intercultural penal law constitutes the basic means of protection against infringement of human rights and solidarity with its victims. In this sense, we must treat violations of dignity and equality as "special moral crimes, beyond the reach of ordinary utilitarian justification."[112] To put it in other words, infringement of any human rights means treating someone as "less than a human being" or as "a human being worth less care than others." It is, therefore, indispensable to treat even the offender himself as a liable moral subject who is also entitled – despite the harm that he or she caused to others – to personal and political rights. In this sense, punishment should be just, namely, proportional and suitable in relation to the extent of guilt and social harmfulness of the punishable act. It is manifested by means of respecting the offender, who remains a human being that is a moral subject, able to recognize negative value of the act that he or she committed.

Law is effective, and as such it is perceived as just and equitable only when it is really applied in the whole area of its jurisdiction. In other words, an established culture of positive law is common for all members of a society. It, however, creates some difficulties, which can be seen in the example of French state, where it is difficult to judge the act of circumcising young girls – which is practised by Muslims – as mutilation. Undoubtedly, there exists natural law, which forbids crimes against humanity, although it is not certain whether we are appointed to its official application.[113] Chantal Delsol expresses his fear that "if there was only one tribunal – superior to all other tribunals – it would quickly turn into people's tribunal, an instance inspired by God's tribunal, with people being the substitutes of God."[114] There also appears a threat that this tribunal, being the last resort, would constitute divine power on the earth, which – as proved by history – could lead to unwanted consequences. As an alternative to such a world tribunal, Delsol points at the necessity of judging the crimes against humanity in one's own territory and, what is more, he

---

[112] R. Dworkin, *Taking Rights Seriously*, op. cit., p. 199.

[113] Ch. Delsol, *Éloge de la singularité*, op. cit., p. 179.

[114] Ibidem, p. 179.

encourages the acquirement of the skill of forgiving. He is not alone in such thinking, because it is a part of a recognized movement of the so-called transitive justice.[115]

5.2. The idea of the "end of impunity"

Zygmunt Bauman, in his article "Imiona cierpienia, imiona wstydu" [The Names of Suffering, the Names of Shame][116] claims that all evil deeds, similarly to in the theory of "the butterfly effect," which - due to the movement of their wings - provoke changes throughout the universe, have their significance. It is, therefore, important that in the context of global ethics they be stigmatised and punished. Bauman writes in this context that:

> Moral responsibility is indivisible - as self-creation of the nation or the authority that it demands. It requires the principle that the crimes against human beings be punished, and that those who prepare or plan the crime knew that they would not get away with it. Responsibility, however, requires also different factors, and without them it will not be fulfilled. If we bear liability for ensuring that in the world where we coexist there is no place for human harm, wrong, or suffering, we cannot rest until those who cause harm are caught and punished, but also until there is no injustice which leaves the feeling of harm, in which the evil is created and which evil people treat as the basis for their growth.[117]

The role of penal law is to protect human life. However, what is meant by this is multidimensional safety, whose most fundamental value is safe life. This drive for safety can be mostly seen in the prohibition "do not kill," but it also contains something of a higher significance, namely, an indication of the need to create optimal conditions for every human being, treated not only as an individual but also as a member of a certain community. It is, therefore, the case that differ-

---

[115] Broadly on this topic see e.g. R.G. Teitel, *Transitional Justice*, Oxford: Oxford University Press, 2000.

[116] *Tygodnik Powszechny* 2001, September.

[117] Ibidem.

ent forms of enfeebling or undermining the safety of the whole human species, like severe treatment of activities against humanity in the form of weapons of mass destruction or irrational policy towards natural environments, undergo negative moral and legal assessment. What are primarily criticised are the cases of "crimes against humanity," "genocide," or "crimes of aggression," which constitute an utter culmination of inhumane intentions and extermination practices. As Lech Gardocki writes:

> ... these crimes are considered to infringe common values of the international community as a whole and, at the same time, it is often difficult to attribute them to the authority of a particular state on the basis of other connections.[118]

Institutional protection of human life requires an assumption that the entitlements, the duties, and particular rights are created on the basis of fundamental needs, desires, and relations among human beings. The latter is of the utmost significance in reference to penal law, which aims at protecting proper human relations. It is, therefore, the case that tolerance, which constitutes a crucial element of our common, democratic identity, does not stand for indifference and axiological neutrality; it cannot be identified with moral indifference. It particularly refers to the cases of infringing human rights.

When assuming the above standpoint, it is necessary to create such legal systems as would make it impossible for offenders to avoid punishment by means of hiding behind the façade of a sovereignty of a particular state. The duty of punishing international crimes has, at the same time, the status of the universally accepted idea of the "end of impunity."[119] This idea was expressed in the preamble of the Rome Statute of the International Criminal Court:

---

[118] L. Gardocki, *Zarys prawa karnego międzynarodowego*, op. cit., p. 143.

[119] K. Ambos, *Straflosigkeit von Menschenrechtsverletzungen. Zur „impunidad" in südamerikanischen Ländern aus völkerstrafrechtlicher Sicht*, Freiburg im Breisgau: Max-Planck-Institut, 1997, p. 22. The belief about the legitimacy of such an idea and about the need for its implementation leads to a justification of a controversial conception of universal jurisdiction. Universal jurisdiction is, therefore, defined as "the entitlement of all subjects of international law to undertake activities aiming at judging and, if such will be the result of the proceedings, at punishing the offender of the most seri-

> The States Parties to this Statute. ... Affirming that the most serious crimes of concern to the international community as a whole must not go unpunished and that their effective prosecution must be ensured by taking measures at the national level and by enhancing international cooperation, determined to put an end to impunity for the perpetrators of these crimes, and thus to contribute to the prevention of such crimes, recalling that it is the duty of every State to exercise its criminal jurisdiction over those responsible for international crimes.

Such a requirement gives rise to the following question: if a crime against humanity is unquestionable, should every tyrant, even from Bora Bora, be judged in the same way as Eichmann? Can it be done by one positively appointed Tribunal? According to Singer, the process of creating international criminal tribunals (The International Criminal Tribunal for the former Yugoslavia, the International Criminal Tribunal for Rwanda, and the International Criminal Court) can be perceived as a success of the determination of all decent people who want to put an end to such tragedies as homicide or other crimes against humanity.

The creation of international criminal tribunals constitutes a proof of a certain change of a paradigm of the state on the international level and, in particular, about the fact that in the field of the so-called national crime, international penal law fights its way against classic state sovereignty.[120] We can conclude, in other words, that what has

---

ous crimes in the light of international law, irrespective of who the offender and his or her victims are and where the crime was committed." In other words, the conception of universal jurisdiction offers a utilitarian assumption that there is no escape from justice.

[120] J. Zajadło, "Filozofia prawa a prawo karne. Studium tzw. Mauerschützen" [Philosophy of Law and Penal Law. Mauerschützen Study], *Ius et Lex* 2003, no. 1, p. 194; idem, *Odpowiedzialność za mur. Procesy strzelców przy Murze Berlińskim* [Responsibility for the Wall. Murder Trials], Gdańsk: Arche, 2003, pp. 15–20, 135–138. See also Th. Meron, "International Criminalization of Internal Atrocities," *American Journal of International Law* 1995, vol. 89, no. 3, pp. 559–577. This last author notes that on the basis of art. 3, which is common for Geneva Conventions of 1949 on the protection of war victims, and on the basis of art. 4.1 and 2 II of an Additional Protocol of 1977 thereto, as well as under art. 4 of the Statute of the International Criminal Tribunal for Rwanda, that the norms of war are binding not only for the states but also for the

won is the need for international cooperation, manifested in the compromise between sovereignty and complementarism in the scope of mutual complementation of national and international jurisdiction. The institutions of international legal aid should be established in such way so that the offenders, when crossing the borders, could not escape their liability, but would bear it as a part of international structures of crime detection. The requirements of a democratic state of law impose a duty that in cases of mass violation of human rights or an infringement of international humanitarian law, one should aim at punishing the perpetrators of these crimes. The authority of the law itself is manifested by this duty, by means of acknowledging the harm caused to the victims and showing solidarity with them. Such behaviour is a manifestation of a respect for deliberative and civil institutions; it creates normative order, which is indispensable for a proper functioning of the society perceived as a cooperation of individuals.[121] In this context, it warrants reference to the standpoint of the International Criminal Tribunal for the former Yugoslavia, according to which, apart from the fact that punishment constitutes a necessary and natural consequence of infringing international humanitarian law –

> ... another crucial element of a punishment is universal manifestation of a lack of agreement for the impunity of offenders who committed crimes of international character. These activities are also undertaken in order to support everyone who acts for the benefit of fighting with international crime and to encourage trust and respect for a developing system of international criminal justice.[122]

Establishing international criminal tribunals, as initiated by Nuremberg, enables the punishing of crimes against humanity because they were treated as an act against the essence of human beings. Crucial arguments were provided by the American Military Tribunal in the *Einsatzgruppen* case:

---

individuals. He makes an accurate inference that international criminal liability of natural people takes place simultaneously with international state liability.

[121] M. Królikowski in: M. Królikowski, P. Wiliński, J. Izydorczyk, *Podstawy prawa karnego międzynarodowego*, op. cit., p. 100.

[122] Judgement of 14 January 2000 in the case of Kupreškić, the International Criminal Tribunal for the former Yugoslavia, Trial Chamber, IT-95-16-T (section 848).

> The existence of law assumes the existence of court … It would be treated as the evidence of helplessness if humanity turned out unable to establish a court which would guard human dignity and, at the same time, protect the human race.[123]

This justification can constitute the grounds of an inference that every human being has a fundamental and inborn right (as the right to live and to be healthy), irrespective of positive human rights. The latter can be proved by a famous formula expressed by Gustaw Radbruch:

> The conflict between justice and legal safety should be settled in such way as to grant priority to positive law, already granted by the legislation and state authority, even if it was unjust and pointless in its character, unless the contradiction between a positive statute with justice is of such an extent that the statute – as "unjust law" – should give way to justice.[124]

It is worthwhile to note that it was only modern democracy that made it possible to realize the idea of making people liable for the crimes committed during conflicts. It was the democracy that boasted itself as protecting pluralism of values and, on the other hand, it is such democracy that is the most faithful defender of universal human rights. The cosmopolitan perspective, quite common in modern times, also contributed to the creation of international criminal courts. What was characteristic for the cosmopolitan perspective was a natural state of international dialogue concerning not only world trade but also the principles of liability and, primarily, international liability for a universal system of protecting human rights in a political conception of liberal cosmopolitan justice. What merits mentioning is the fact that creating respective international criminal tribunals is mostly based on the ethics of discourse, which is manifested in an open procedure and public discussion on its functioning. This un-

---

[123] "U.S. vs. Ohlendorf," *IV Trials of War Crimes before the Nuremberg Military Tribunals under Control Council Law*, no. 10, pp. 499–500.

[124] G. Radbruch, "Ustawowe bezprawie i ponadustawowe prawo" [Statutory Illegality and Supra-statutory Law], in: M. Szyszkowska, *Zarys filozofii prawa* [An Outline of Philosophy of Law], Białystok: Temida 2, 2000, p. 262.

doubtedly proves helpful in the process of protecting the world against homicide.[125]

The establishment of the International Criminal Court is both the manifestation of the memory of the victims and the willingness to compensate their harm by means of punishing the offenders, but, at the same time, the aim of restoring trust to law and, in particular, universal human rights. According to Michał Płachta, such a tribunal will be "an effective tool in settling the conflicts and problems in the light of international policy, because it can permanently eliminate instigators of chaos from political life."[126] When assuming such meaning, penal law aims at preventing potential offenders acting by means of state repression from infringing human rights, as well as deterring the whole society from the temptation to cooperate in the violence supported by the state. In this aspect, the essential characteristic of the ideal of the rule of law is the possibility of creating a legal system that would be prepared to deal with serious cases of infringing human rights. In the field of criminal law, the latter means a proper use of the construction of *action libera in causa – action illica in causa,* which leads to the lack of a possibility to refer to the elements legalising the behaviour in the system of national law in case of the offenders who contributed to the latter or substantive approach of illegality, which is perceived as the source of the binding nature of a norm of a particular content and the requirement of recognizing a real meaning of one's own act by the offender and, consequently, inability of referring to extenuating circumstances in which guilt cannot be attributed. The requirement that the offenders who infringed human rights would be potentially punished results from the belief – grounded in the conception of general prevention – that penal punishment is the most effective means to deter the possibility of the crime being repeated, and to preserve peace in the world. Even international humanitarian law, which has as its subject determination of grave breaches committed in international military conflicts, emphasises the importance of penal sanctions. They are to constitute an

---

[125] K.-O. Apel, "On the Relationship between Ethics, International Law and Politico-military Strategy In our Time: a Philosophical Retrospective on the Kosovo Conflict," *European Journal of Social Theory* 2001, no. 1, pp. 29–40.

[126] The international tribunal constitutes the means of integration in internal affairs of a particular state, whilst having its legally and morally significant justification.

integral part of every system of justice, and the threat of implementing them is an element of deterrence from committing war crimes.[127]

It can be stated, on the grounds of the abovementioned conclusions, that a crime consisting in infringing universal human rights has the same meaning in all cultures, and it provokes opposition and justifies the act of punishing the offender. The words that could be recalled in this place are the ones expressed in the statute of the Nuremberg International Military Tribunal that the acts are crimes "irrespective of whether they infringe the law of the state in which they were committed."[128] The task of intercultural penal law is to negate and penalise such acts as would shock the moral conscience of every human being living in Rawls' "well-ordered society," namely democratic and respecting of human rights, irrespective of cultural identity, religion, nationality, race, religious beliefs, or outlook on life. What is rather meant by the latter is moral belief agreed in discursive process of reaching a settlement, foundation of humanity, and community. We assume, obviously, that people as citizens and entitled participants of a moral discourse (taking for granted, among other things, exchange of perspectives) possess the ability to judge their own behaviour in the category of good or bad. In this perspective, the aim of penal liability is not only punishing the harm caused by the offender but its determination. An example of such acts which penal law should deem reprehensible and punishable are those which, by causing harm consisting in infringing the most fundamental and universal human rights, bring death and suffering on people, such as murder or rape.

---

[127] M.T. Dutli, C. Pellandini, "The International Committee of the Red Cross and the Implementation of a System to Repress Breaches of International Humanitarian Law," *International Review of the Red Cross* 1994, no. 300, p. 241ff.

[128] Art. 6 Charter of the International Military Tribunal.

Conclusion

In contemporary communicative society, every real participant of the act of speech assumes that three fundamental conditions of communication are satisfied as closely as possible, namely that the speaker speaks sincerely, moreover, he communicates true sentences in such a way that the listener recognizes his statement as certain (correct), and that his statement is correct in the sense that the participants of communicative acts accept his statement in the assumed axiological system. Communication activities are also based on the assumption that discourse participants recognize one another and they are equal, free, and unfettered by the will of another equal individual. Crime violates these requirements and leads to distortion of free interaction, also affecting common values - developed by means of universal understanding - in particular, specific norms of ethical and legal behaviour, especially freedom. It is, therefore, necessary to remove the effects caused by crime in the communication process. Criminal penalty is treated here as a complex process operating in the communication structure of authority and condemnation. It belongs to a legal institution, which constitutes a part of social and cultural ritual, which uses the rhetoric of symbols of argumentative procedures and social ideas by means of which relationships between the state and participants of legal discourse, particularly those committing punishable acts, are built.[1]

Penalty has both the function of stabilization and of guarantee for the entire legal system, aiming to instil and enforce compliance with

[1] D. Garland, *Punishment and Modern Society*, Oxford: Oxford University Press, 1990, p. 17ff.; M. Foucault, *Discipline and Punishment: The Birth of the Prison*, New York: Vintage, 1977, p. 73ff.

legal norms by all members of the community or society. It is only in this way that goods, principles, and rights that are universal, and as such, deserve universal legal protection, may be established and guaranteed.

Criminal proceedings are of a non-liberal character and, as such, do not satisfy all Habermas' claims to validity, not least because of the dominating role played by the judge. At this point it is worth noting, following Hannah Arendt, that administering criminal justice entails specific actions of individual people, which results in the fact that verdicts are distorted by political agendas,[2] or by anthropologically justified moral attitudes of the community, as postulated by Lord Devlin.[3] Such distortions should not occur, and their elimination is possible only by awareness of their existence. Similarly, punishment is of an authoritative character, which, of course, does not mean that inflicting punishment is arbitrary, but only that it is of an imperious nature. Punishing the offender by the state is not preceded by a coercion- and domination-free discourse.[4] It does not mean that a discourse on the values that criminal law intends to protect also takes place without complying with the requirement of freedom from domination (*herrschaftsfrei Diskurs*). In Chapter III of my dissertation, I sought to demonstrate the opposite thesis, namely, that the requirements of discourse justify universal human rights and democracy. Only a breach of the procedural requirements of the discourse, human rights violations, and infringing discursive democracy may provide a basis for punishing the offender. My intention was to justify the thesis that human rights, based on human dignity, equality, and freedom of all people, and their mutual recognition, constitute common and universal values. The latter was proved by the thesis, assumed in my dissertation, of the soft version of multiculturalism and, connected with he latter, the approval of the pluralism of values (but not extreme moral relativism) as well as the approval of

---

[2] H. Arendt, *Eichmann w Jerozolimie: rzecz o banalności zła* [Eichmann in Jeruzalem: A Report on the Banality of Evil], London: Penguin, 2006, passim.

[3] P. Devlin, *The Enforcement of Morals*, Oxford: Oxford University Press, 1965, p. 17ff.; 22ff.

[4] Cf. W. Hassemer, *Einführung in die Grundlagen des Strafrechts*, München: C.H. Beck, 1981, p. 121.

a cosmopolitan vision of law. It should be noted that it is possible to specify only the basic values that law (especially criminal law) should protect. Human rights become an alternative to hard multiculturalism when their universality is recognized in deliberative democracy based on discourse ethics, which requires equal citizens to ensure that the reasons of individuals were not only recognized as formally submitted proposals, but as a manifestation of recognition of their individuality by the constructivist community. As far as the global dimension is concerned, all the people form a community of a constructivist character.

This consideration allows recognition that even in a multicultural world, namely, one which shares different ideological beliefs and lifestyles, including cultural, religious, ethnic, or sexual differences, there is a certain social and legal sphere, in the form of a constructivist community. This community is primarily of a procedural character, being tantamount to the acceptance of discourse rules that constitute the basis of discursive democracy, but also to the recognition of the universality of human rights, human dignity, and mutual recognition of all people as equal and deserving of protection and respect. Crime constitutes a violation of the foundation of such a community, which is non-organic and, consequently, it cannot be – in principle – excused by diversities of cultural nature. Acting against that community violates the fundamental principle of mutual recognition. and leads to an imbalance in the distribution of goods and burdens and, as such, requires the application of punishment that includes condemnation of a certain act as evil as well as affliction for the offender. This punishment has its social dimension, reflected mainly in depriving the offender of a claim to be recognized; a moral dimension, which constitutes a manifestation of disapproval for the action and, finally, a justice dimension, which is expressed in the need to restore distorted balance in a proper distribution of burdens and benefits.

The offender, by committing a prohibited act, not only harms another person as a legal entity, but also violates a fundamental relationship among real human community, which he belongs to, in the form of mutual relation of recognition and, consequently, harms himself as the party to that relationship. Therefore, one of the major consequences of committing a crime is – as suggested by Hegel, and what I pay particular attention to – the loss of recognition or, more precisely, the entitlement to demand being recognized. In such an understanding, punishment constitutes the consequence of a rational consensus concluded by means of intersubjective discourse, an equitable exchange of mutual benefits. Punishing should help the criminal to regain mutual recognition of other individuals, and thus of the whole society.

R.A. Duff rightly notes that restoring the offender to the community takes place through a process of communication between the perpetrator and the community, in which he learns about the consequences of his behaviour, about a violation of common values, and about the condemnation of his conduct.[5] By means of community communication, the offender is called upon to account for his negatively evaluated act. Depriving the offender of his claim to recognition is to mobilize him to reflect on his behaviour, express his remorse, and condemn his deed as well as to motivate potential (voluntary) remedy of damage or redress for the victim.

Punishment, as deprivation of recognition, aims not only at "getting even", restoring – to use Hegel's terminology – law as such, or deterring from committing crimes by other members of society, but its task is also to remove "distortions of social interactions." The latter aspect points to a fundamental social objective of punishment since it leads to a temporary or unlimited reduction of the offender's prestige in the society, because one of the reactions of a social group to a socially significant act is sometimes "social ostracism." In this context, it is worth recalling K.O. Apel's view that a man should not only take responsibility for the consequences of his behaviour but, in his rationality, he should also participate in collective responsibility organized in the form of practical discourses.[6]

In a liberal democracy, every individual chooses to participate in a certain intersubjective practice, namely, voluntary compliance with a normative system (including the sanctions regime), which creates

---

[5] R.A. Duff, *Punishment, Communication and Community*, Oxford: Oxford University Press, 2001, pp. 80–82.

[6] K.-O. Apel, *Diskurs und Verantwortung. Das Problem des Übergangs zur postkonventionellen Moral*, Frankfurt am Main: Suhrkamp Verlag, 1997, p. 206.

such a practice. No human community can do without punishment, which is a social phenomenon, sometimes treated as a fundamental concept of compensation for pain and suffering. Punishment, despite containing an element of coercion, is congruent with the requirements of modern deliberative democracy and rational legal discourse.

My intention was to show the punishment in its communication aspect. Punishment, like the law itself, is a phenomenon, which is realized in the communication process, being both the object and effect of that communication, which meets certain ethical requirements. The procedure of communicating and arguing takes place as a part of an inclusive constructivist community, providing – by means of legal sanctions – a variety of the ranges of freedom, characteristic of a pluralistic society. When referring to the conception of man, which became the basis for further reflection, the latter must be supplemented by a statement that it entails an individual for whom a community of communication is something primordial, that is creating it, particularly in terms of social convergence.[7]

The conception of punishment outlined in this dissertation is a part of mixed theories in which retributive elements seem to balance utilitarian ones, although the former, by emphasizing the loss of recognition as a part of a criminal punishment, gain the advantage. The latter also shows the pluralistic nature of punishment, combining, on the one hand, the sociological perspective of "the interchangeability of perspectives" between the perpetrator and victim, the need to take into account the institution of "a generalized Other" (representing the entire community), and depriving the offender of recognition as a consequence of a violation of the fundamental principle of mutual recognition as equal and free people and, on the other hand, a syncretic relationship of equitable request to restore the balance by means of punishing (severely treating) the offender, and the utilitarian deterrence against committing crimes in the future. This utilitarian approach justifies punishment as a means of repentance, reconciliation, and improvement in behaviour. Retributive perspective, on the other hand, is manifested by the need of severe treatment of criminals. I have the conviction that the theory of punishment pre-

[7] Cf. R. Dworkin, "Liberal Community," *California Law Review* 1989, vol. 77.

sented by me, meets the requirements set by H.L.A. Hart, and contains moral claims on the explanation of why punishment should, or can, be applied.[8]

This theory relates to contemporary philosophical trends based on the ethics of responsibility, social psychology, and philosophy of law, treating law as a linguistic act. Speech constitutes the main medium through which our social interactions take place, and by means of which we can also, using its performative power, punish individuals who violate intersubjectively accepted norms. Only partial fulfilment of ethical requirements of discourse, even coerced by the threat of criminal sanctions, allows one – in my opinion – to approach other individuals in a true and real way, to participate in social processes, necessarily identifying oneself with the group to which we belong, whilst respecting its individual members. It allows awareness of the desires or expectations placed on us by others and allows the signalling of the same the other way round. These results of inflicting punishment cannot be overestimated, and they constitute a strong argument for its justification. Punishment specifically appears to us as a culture-shaping institution, in which personality is treated as a structure rather than process.[9] The horizon of cultural meanings is internalized by the individual as the concept of oneself. In turn, a set of common meanings indispensable for communication is contained in a culture that determines individual interpretations through mutual sets of roles and social positions. In other words, we define our individual and collective identity in a way that is of great importance for the functioning of a community and society, and which also plays a fundamental role in justifying the institution of punishment. It is worth noting that both punishment, understood in the abovementioned way, and its justification are close to the concept of restorative justice. The theory of restorative justice also directly draws its justification from the requirements of discourse or social communication. The difference between the philosophy of punishment, even in the approach presented in this dissertation, and restorative justice, comes

[8] H.L.A. Hart, *Punishment and Responsibility. Essays in the Philosophy of Law*, Oxford: Clarendon Press, 1968, p. 72.

[9] Cf. D. Garland, *Punishment and Modern Society*, op. cit., pp. 249–276.

down to the postulate of replacing punishment with reconciliation, revenge on the perpetrators (visible also in depriving them of the claim to recognition) with help provided to victims, alienation or exclusion with inclusion to community and unification, and negativity and destruction with the remedy, forgiveness and grace.[10] Undoubtedly, the core of the approach presented by me as well as the philosophy of restorative justice is to treat the offender as an individual worthy of protection of his dignity and rights, despite harm done by him; but what differs in the two concepts is the manner of restoring him to society and redeeming his guilt.

In this respect, punishing is associated with determining what it means to be a person and how to understand the subjectivity of each individual. In other words, it shows specific assumptions regarding human beings and it gives them an institutional dimension. Punishment, therefore, creates symbols and positive patterns, which, as a part of cultural relations, can help to strengthen the subjectivity of individuals, and internalize social attitudes and various forms of authority. Pluralistic justification of punishment, as mentioned in this dissertation, demonstrates the dialectical nature of integrating the offender in social structures. The offender is indeed treated consistently with fellow citizens, as a responsible individual able to recognize the importance of his behaviour and capable of being guided by moral principles in his life.[11] This means that the punishment, primarily containing the elements that excluded the offender from the society, also constitutes a dialectical condition and means of re-integrating the offender into social structures. The obligation of re-integrating the offender should even be considered as an element that restricts punishment. This reduction of punishment by the requirements assumed within the conception of punishment can be clearly seen in topical requirement of proportionality and appropriateness of punishment. Proportionality of punishment is contemporarily understood as an ethical condition, which results from the adoption of a specific vision of man and society, characteristic for

---

[10] J. Consedine, *Restorative justice. Healing the effects of crime,* New Zealand: Ploughshares Publications, 1995, "Introduction."

[11] R. Duff, "Karanie obywateli" [Punisihing Citizens], *Ius et Lex* 2006, no. 1, p. 43.

multicultural democratic societies in which social and legal policy should combine the idea of homocentrism with sociocentrism, while meeting universal requirements of ethical and legal discourse.

An intercultural and legal-human point of departure for the criminalization of social patterns of behaviour defines the image of modern criminal law, at least in modern democracies.[12] In fact, its task is to protect the basic legal goods, which are contained in human rights: namely, life, health, freedom, individual autonomy, property, privacy, etc. Empirical studies of various legal systems allow specification of a common scope of criminal law protection. The classical scope of criminal law, contemporarily tantamount in multicultural democratic societies to universal human rights, allows one to speak about absolute intercultural applicability of criminal law.[13] In other words, the scope of criminal law protection concerning human rights is binding on every member of an inclusive constructivist community. This is due to the fact that criminal law does not celebrate cultural bias, but offers an unencumbered level for peaceful coexistence of different forms of life and culture. This perspective is formed by the experience acquired in interactions with the significant Others. Thus, criminal law creates a sphere, free for intercultural violence-free communication. Dieter Rössner aptly notes that "the more-cultural and pluralistic a society is, the more the criminal law border is stretched when resolving the conflicts - as much for the natives, and for strangers."[14]

Only when perceived in the abovementioned way, can criminal law act as a stabilization and a guarantee for the whole pluralistic and multicultural society. This is because it brings and cares for the good, the rules, and rights that are universal and, as such, deserve universal legal protection. Mere punishment shows that the offender's behaviour was contrary to the fundamental values and laws of the community, which he is a full member of. In such a context, criminal law

---

[12] O. Höffe, *Gibt es ein interkulturelles Strafrecht? Ein philosophischer Versuch*, Frankfurt am Main: Suhrkamp Verlag, 1999, p. 51ff.; 83ff., 104ff.; D. Rössner, "Kriminalrecht als Kontrollinstitution," in: O. Höffe, *Gibt es ein interkulturelles Strafrecht?...*, op. cit., p. 125.

[13] D. Rössner, "Kriminalrecht als Kontrollinstitution," op. cit., p. 125.

[14] bidem, p. 126.

does not seek the sense of punishment in the idea of retribution for its own sake, but presupposes the accomplishment of far-reaching social and interpersonal objectives because it seeks to safeguard or restore security and cooperation between people in the conditions of equal dignity and freedom. Only when construed in this way may law allow a relatively efficient identification of and compliance with binding legal order by all members of the community, who are yet diverse in terms of origin, religion, nationality, race, culture, gender, or preferred lifestyle. At the same time, it allows for making sanctions more discursive, thus allowing public discussion, even on such a traditional area of law as criminal law.

Literature

ACKERMAN BRUCE, *Social Justice in the Liberal State*, New Haven: Yale University Press, 1980

ACKERMAN BRUCE, "Why Dialogue," *Journal of Philosophy* 1989, vol. 86, no. 1

ALBERT HANS, *Traktat über kritische Vernunft*, Tübingen: Mohr Siebeck Verlag, 1968

ALEXY ROBERT, *Theorie der juristischen Argumentation*, Frankfurt am Main: Suhrkamp Verlag, 1978

ALEXY ROBERT, *Theorie der Grundrechte*, Baden-Baden: Nomos Verlag, 1985 (English edition: *A Theory of Constitutional Rights*, Oxford: Oxford University Press, 2002)

ALEXY ROBERT, "On Necessary Relations Between Law and Morality," *Ratio Juris* 1989, vol. 2, no. 2, pp. 167–183

ALEXY ROBERT, *Begriff und Geltung des Rechts*, Freiburg - München: Karl Alber Verlag, 1992

ALEXY ROBERT, "Discourse Theory and Human Rights," in: *Challenges to Law and the End of the 20th Century* (*17th IVR World Congress Bologna*, 17–21 June 1995, vol. II: *Plenary and Parallel Sessions*), Bologna: Cooperativa Libraria Universitaria Editrice Bologna, 1995

ALEXY ROBERT, *Recht, Vernunft, Diskurs. Studien zur Rechtsphilosophie*, Frankfurt am Main: Suhrkamp Verlag, 1995

AMBOS KAI, *Straflosigkeit von Menschenrechtsverletzungen. Zur „impunidad" in südamerikanischen Ländern aus völkerstrafrechtlicher Sicht*, Freiburg im Breisgau: Max-Planck-Institut, 1997

AMBOS KAI, *Der Allgemeine Teil des Völkerstrafrechts. Ansätze einer Dogmatisierung*, Berlin: Duncker und Humblot, 2002

APEL KARL-OTTO, *Transformation der Philosophie*, Band 2: *Das Apriori der Kommunikationsgemeinschaft*, Frankfurt am Main: Suhrkamp Verlag, 1973

APEL KARL-OTTO, "Sprechakttheorie und transzendentale Sprachpragmatik zur Frage ethischer Normen," in: *Sprachpragmatik und Philosophie*, ed. by K.-O. Apel, Frankfurt am Main: Suhrkamp Verlag, 1976

APEL KARL-OTTO, "Grenzen der Diskursethik? Versuch einer Zwischenbilanz," *Zeitschrift für philosophische Forschung* 1986, no. 40, pp. 3–31

APEL KARL-OTTO, "Diskursethik als Verantwortungsethik - eine postmetaphysische Transformation der Ethik Kants," in: *Ethik und Befreiung*, ed. by Raul Fornet-Betancourt, Aachen: Augustinus-Buchhandlung, 1990, pp. 10–40

APEL KARL-OTTO, "Diskursethik vor der Problematik von Recht und Politik: Können die Rationalitätsdifferenzen zwischen Moralität, Recht und Politik selbst noch durch die Diskursethik normativ-rational gerechtfertigt werden?," in: *Zur Anwendung der Diskursethik in Politik, Recht und Wissenschaft*, ed. by K.-O. Apel and Matthias Kettner, Frankfurt am Main: Suhrkamp Verlag, 1992

APEL KARL-OTTO, "Discourse Ethics as a Response to the Novel Challenges of Today's Reality to Coresponsibility," *The Journal of Religion* 1993, vol. 73, no. 4, pp. 496–513

APEL KARL-OTTO, "Diskursethik als Ethik der Mit-Verantwortung für kollektive Aktivitäten," in: *Rehabilitierung des Subjektiven. Festschrift für Hermann Schmitz*, ed. by Michael Grossheim, Hans-Joachim Waschkies, Bonn: Bouvier, 1993, pp. 191–207

APEL KARL-OTTO, "Die Vernunftfunktion der kommunikativen Rationalität. Zum Verhältnis von konsensualkommunikativer Rationalität, strategischer Rationalität und Systemrationalität," in: *Die eine Vernunft und die vielen Rationalitäten*, ed. by K.-O. Apel, Matthias Kettner, Frankfurt am Main: Suhrkamp Verlag, 1996

APEL KARL-OTTO, *Diskurs und Verantwortung. Das Problem des Übergangs zur postkonventionellen Moral*, Frankfurt am Main: Suhrkamp Verlag, 1997

APEL KARL-OTTO, "Zasada samoufundowania swoich podstaw w hermeneutycznej rekonstrukcji historii" [The Principle of Self-Founding One's Own Basis in Hermeneutic Reconstruction of History], in: *Rozumność i racjonalność* [Reason and Rationality], ed. by Tadeusz Buksiński, Poznań: Wydawnictwo Naukowe Instytutu Filozofii UAM, 1997

APEL KARL-OTTO, "Das Problem der philosophischen Letztbegründung im Lichte einer transzendentalen Sprachpragmatik. Versuch einer Metakritik des ‚kritischen Rationalismus'," in: idem, *Auseinandersetzungen in Erprobung des transzendentalpragmatischen Ansatzes*, Frankfurt am Main: Suhrkamp Verlag, 1998, pp. 33–80

APEL KARL-OTTO, "Diskursethik als Ethik der Mit-Verantwortung vor den Sachzwängen der Politik, des Rechts und der Marktwirtschaft," in: *Prinzip Mitverantwortung. Grundlage für Ethik und Pädagogik*, ed. by K.-O. Apel, Holger Burckhart, Würzburg: Königshausen & Neumann, 2001, pp. 69–96

APEL KARL-OTTO, "On the Relationship between Ethics, International Law and Politico-military Strategy In our Time: a Philosophical Retrospective on the Kosovo Conflict," *European Journal of Social Theory* 2001, no. 1, pp. 29–40

APEL KARL-OTTO, "Discourse Ethics, Democracy, and International Law. Toward a Globalization of Practical Reason," in: *The Challenges of Globalization. Rethinking Nature, Culture, and Freedom*, ed. by Steven V. Hicks, Daniel E. Shannon, Oxford: Blackwell Publishing, 2007, pp. 60–66

APPADURAI ARJUN, *Modernity at Large. Cultural Dimensions of Globalization*, Minneapolis: University of Minnesota Press, 1996

APPIAH KWAME ANTHONY, *Der Kosmopolit. Philosophie des Weltbürgertums*, München: C.H. Beck Verlag, 2007

ARENDT HANNAH, *The Origins of Totalitarianism*, Part 2, New York: Harvest Book, 1973

ARENDT HANNAH, *Elemente und Ursprünge totaler Herrschaft. Antisemitismus, Imperialismus, totale Herrschaft*, München – Zürich: Piper, 1986

ARENDT HANNAH, *Eichmann w Jerozolimie: rzecz o banalności zła* [Eichmann in Jerusalem: A Report on the Banality of Evil], London: Penguin, 2006

ARENS EDMUND, "Der Beitrag der Diskursethik zur universalen Begründung der Menschenrechte," in: *Begründung von Menschenrechten aus der Sicht unterschiedlicher Kulturen*, ed. by Johannes Hoffmann, Frankfurt am Main: Verlag für Interkulturelle Kommunikation, 1991

ARISTOTLE, *The Eudemian Ethics*, Oxford: Oxford University Press, 2005

ARISTOTLE, *Nicomachean Ethics*, translated by M. Ostwald (1962)

ARISTOTLE, *Rhetoric*, New York: The Modern Library, 1954

BAER SUSANNE, "Menschenwürde zwischen Recht, Prinzip und Referenz. Die Bedeutung von Enttabuisierungen," *Deutsche Zeitschrift für Philosophie* 2005, no. 4

BASSIOUNI M. CHERIF, "International Criminal Law and Human Rights," in: *International Criminal Law. Crimes*, ed. by M.Ch. Bassiouni, New York: Oxford University Press, 1986, pp. 15–32

BASSIOUNI M. CHERIF, *Crimes Against Humanity in International Criminal Law*, London – Boston: Kluwer, 1999

BAUMAN ZYGMUNT, *Postmodern Ethics*, Cambridge: Basil Blackwell, 1993 (Polish edition: *Etyka ponowoczesna*, Warszawa: Wydawnictwo Naukowe PWN, 1996)

BAUMAN ZYGMUNT, *Szanse etyki w zglobalizowanym świecie* [Chances of Ethics in a Global World], Kraków: Znak, 2007

BAYERTZ KURT, "Die Idee der Menschenwürde. Probleme und Paradoxien," *Archiv für Rechts- und Sozialphilosophie* 1995, vol. 81, no. 4

BAYNES KENNETH, "Discourse Ethics and Civil Society," in: *Universalism vs. Communitarianism: Contemporary Debates in Ethics*, ed. by D. Rasmussen, Cambridge, Mass.: The MIT Press, 1990

BECK ULRICH, *Macht und Gegenmacht im globalen Zeitalter. Neue weltpolitische Ökonomie*, Frankfurt am Main: Suhrkamp Verlag, 2002

BECK ULRICH, *Weltrisikogesellschaft. Die globalen Gefährdungen – vom Terror bis Klimawandel*, Frankfurt am Main: Suhrkamp Verlag, 2007

BECKA MICHELLE, *Anerkennung im Kontext interkultureller Philosophie*, Frankfurt am Main – London: Verlag für Interkulturelle Kommunikation, 2005

BECKER WERNER, *Das Dilemma der menschlichen Existenz. Die Evolution der Individualität und das Wissen um den Tod*, Stuttgart: W. Kohlhammer Verlag, 2000

BENHABIB SEYLA, *Selbst im Kontext*, Frankfurt am Main: Suhrkamp, 1995

BENHABIB SEYLA, "Toward a Deliberative Model of Democratic Legitimacy," in: *Democracy and Difference. Contesting the Boundaries of the Political*, ed. by S. Benhabib, Princeton: Princeton University Press, 1996

BENHABIB SEYLA, *Kulturelle Vielfalt und demokratische Gleichheit. Politische Partizipation im Zeitalter der Globalisierung*, Frankfurt am Main: Suhrkamp Verlag, 1999

BENHABIB SEYLA, "On the Philosophical Foundation of Cosmopolitan Norms," in: *Law and Legal Cultures in the 21st Century. Diversity and Unity*, ed. by Tomasz Gizbert-Studnicki, Jerzy Stelmach, Warszawa: Wolters Kluwer, 2007, pp. 61–80

BENTHAM JEREMY, *A Comment of the Commentaries; a Criticism of William Blackstone's on the Laws of England*, Oxford: Clarendon Press, 1928

BERLIN ISAIAH, *Four Essays on Liberty*, Oxford: Oxford University Press, 1990

BIELEFELDT HEINER, "Ideengeschichte(n) der Menschenrechte," in: *Menschenrechte – Globale Dimensionen eines universellen Anspruchs*, ed. by Nicole Janz, Thomas Risse, Baden-Baden: Nomos Verlag, 2007

BIELEFELDT HEINER, *Menschenrechte in der Einwanderungsgesellschaft. Plädoyer für einen aufgeklärten Multikulturalismus*, Bielefeld: Transcript, 2007

BLOOM ALLAN, *Closing of the American Mind*, New York: Simon & Schuster, 1987

BOHMAN JAMES, *Public Deliberation. Pluralism, Complexity, and Democracy*, Cambridge: The MIT Press, 1996

BOISTER NEIL, "Transnational Criminal Law," *European Journal of International Law* 2003, no. 5, pp. 953–976

BORRADORI GIOVANNA, *Philosophy in a Time of Terror. Dialogues with Jürgen Habermas and Jacques Derrida*, Chicago: The University of Chicago Press, 2003

BUCHAŁA KAZIMIERZ, ZOLL ANDRZEJ, *Kodeks karny. Część ogólna. Komentarz* [Penal Code. General Part. A Commentary], Kraków: Zakamycze, 1999

BUZAN BARRY, *From International to World Society?*, Cambridge: Cambridge University Press, 2004

CHMIELEWSKI ADAM, *Społeczeństwo otwarte czy wspólnota?* [An Open Society or a Community?], Wrocław: Wydawnictwo Uniwersytetu Wrocławskiego, 2001

CHMIELEWSKI ADAM, "Ekskluzywizm, jedność, interpasywność" [Exclusivity, unity, interpassivity], in: *Pytania współczesnej filozofii polityki* [The Questions of Modern Philosophy of Politics], ed. by Dorota Pietrzyk-Reeves, Kraków: Wydawnictwo Uniwersytetu Jagiellońskiego, 2007

COHEN JOSHUA, "Deliberation and Democratic Legitimacy," in: *The Good Polity. Normative Analysis of the State*, ed. by Alan Hamlin, Philip Pettit, Oxford: Polity Press, 1989

COLEMAN JULES L., "On the Relationship Between Law and Morality," *Ratio Juris* 1989, vol. 2, no. 1, pp. 66–78

COLES ROMAND, "Identity and Difference in the Ethical Positions of Adorno and Habermas," in: *The Cambridge Companion to Habermas*, ed. by Stephen K. White, Cambridge – New York: Cambridge University Press, 1995, pp. 19–45

CONSEDINE JIM, *Restorative justice. Healing the effects of crime*, New Zealand: Ploughshares Publications, 1995

COTTERRELL ROGER, *The Sociology of Law*, London: Butterworths, 1984

CROWDER GEORGE, *Liberalism and Value Pluralism*, London – New York: Continuum, 2002

DARWALL STEPHEN L., "Two Kinds of Respects," *Ethics* 1977/1978, no. 88

DAVIS MICHAEL, "How to make punishment fit the crime," in: *Criminal Justice*, ed. by J. Ronald Pennock, John W. Chapman, New York: New York University Press, 1985

DELMAS-MARTY MIREILLE, "L'Harmonisation des sanctions et valeur communes: la recherché d' indicateurs de gravité et efficacité," in: *L'Harmonisation des sanction pénales en Europe*, ed. by M. Delmas-Marty et al., Paris: Société de Législation comparée, 2003

DELSOL CHANTAL, *Éloge de la singularité. Essai sur la modernité tardive*, Paris: Table Ronde, 2000

DERRIDA JACQUES, *Politik der Freundschaft*, Frankfurt am Main: Suhrkamp Verlag, 2000

DEVLIN PATRICK, *The Enforcement of Morals*, Oxford: Oxford University Press, 1965

DEWEY JOHN, *Democracy and Education. An Introduction to the Philosophy of Education*, New York: Free Press, 1966

DEWEY JOHN, *Die Öffentlichkeit und ihre Probleme*, Bodenheim: Philo, 1996

DOHRMANN JONA A., "Ursprung und Entwicklung der Menschenrechte in Indien," in: *Menschenrechte – Globale Dimensionen eines universellen Anspruchs*, ed. by Nicole Janz, Thomas Risse, Baden-Baden: Nomos Verlag, 2007

DONNELLY JACK, *Universal Human Rights in Theory and Practice*, Ithaca – London: Cornell University Press, 2003

DROSTERIJ GERARD, HILDEBRANDT MIREILLE, HUPPES-CLUYSENAER ELISABETH A., "The Possibility of Intercultural Law," *Nederlands Tijdschrift voor Rechtsfilosofie & Rechtstheorie* 2006, vol. 35, no. 3

DRYZEK JOHN S., *Deliberative Democracy and Beyond: Liberals, Critics, Contestations*, Oxford: Oxford University Press, 2002

DUFF R. ANTHONY, "Choice, Character, and Criminal Liability," *Law and Philosophy* 1993, no. 12, pp. 345–383

DUFF R. ANTHONY, "Penal Communications: Recent Work in the Philosophy of Punishment," *Crime and Justice: A Review of Research* 1995, vol. 20

DUFF R. ANTHONY, "Law, Language and Community: Some Preconditions of Criminal Liability," *Oxford Journal of Legal Studies* 1998, no. 18, pp. 189–206

DUFF R. ANTHONY, *Punishment, Communication and Community*, Oxford: Oxford University Press, 2001

DUFF R. ANTHONY, "Crime, Prohibition and Punishment," *Journal of Applied Philosophy* 2002, no. 19

DUFF R. ANTHONY, "Who is Responsible, for What, to Whom," *Ohio State Journal of Criminal Law* 2005, no. 2, pp. 441–461

DUFF R. ANTHONY, "Karanie obywateli" [Punishing Citizens], *Ius et Lex*, 2006, no. 1

DUFF R. ANTHONY, GARLAND DAVID, "Introduction," in: *A Reader on Punishment*, ed. by R.A. Duff, D. Garland, Oxford: Oxford University Press, 1994

DUNDES RENTELN ALISON, *The Cultural Defence*, New York: Oxford University Press, 2004

DUNDES RENTELN ALISON, "The Use and Abuse of the Cultural Defence," *Canadian Journal of Law and Society* 2005, vol. 20, no. 1, pp. 47–67

DURKHEIM ÉMILE, *The Division of Labor in Society*, New York: The Free Press, 1997

DUTLI MARIA TERESA, PELLANDINI CRISTINA, "The International Committee of the Red Cross and the Implementation of a System to Repress Breaches of International Humanitarian Law," *International Review of the Red Cross* 1994, no. 300

DUX GÜNTER, "Gerechtigkeit: Die Genese einer Idee," in: *Jus humanum. Grundlagen des Rechts und Strafrecht. Festschrift für Ernst-Joachim Lampe zum 70. Geburtstag*, ed. by Dieter Dölling, Berlin: Verlag Walter de Gruyter, 2003

DWORKIN RONALD, *Taking Rights Seriously*, London: Duckworth, 1977
DWORKIN RONALD, *Law's Empire*, London: Fontana Press, 1986
DWORKIN RONALD, "Rights as Trumps," in: *Theories of Rights*, ed. by Jeremy Waldron, Cambridge: Harvard University Press, 1998
DWORKIN RONALD, *Sovereign Virtue: The Theory and Practice of Equality*, Cambridge, Mass.: Harvard University Press, 2000
DWORKIN RONALD, "Equality, Luck and Hierarchy," *Philosophy and Public Affairs* 2003, vol. 31, no. 2
DWORKIN RONALD, *Is Democracy Possible Here?: Principles for a New Political Debate*, Princeton: Princeton University Press, 2006
EBERT UDO, "Das Vergeltungsprinzip im Strafrecht," in: *Geisteswissenschaften – wozu? Beispiele ihrer Gegenstände und ihrer Fragen*, ed. by Hans-Henrik Krummacher, Wiesbaden (Stuttgart): Steiner Verlag, 1988
ELSTER JON, "The Market and the Forum," in: *Deliberative Democracy. Essays on Reason and Politics*, ed. by James Bohman, William Rehg, Cambridge: The MIT Press, 1997
Encyclopaedia of Public International Law, vol. 8: *Human Rights and the Individual In International Law: Internationals Economic Relations*, North-Holland, Amsterdam, New York, Oxford: North Holland Publishing Company, 1985
ENGLÄNDER ARMIN, *Diskurs als Rechtsquelle? Zur Kritik der Diskurstheorie des Rechts*, Tübingen: Mohr Siebeck Verlag, 2002
ESER ALBIN, "'Menschengerechte' Strafjustiz im Zeitalter von Europäisierung und Globalisierung," in: *Zasady procesu karnego wobec wyzwań współczesności. Księga ku czci profesora Stanisława Waltosia* [Criminal Procedure Rules in the Light of Modern Challenges. A Book in Honour of Professor Stanisław Waltoś], ed. by Janina Czapska, Andrzej Gaberle, Andrzej Światłowski, Andrzej Zoll, Warszawa: Wydawnictwo Prawnicze PWN, 2000
FEINBERG JOEL, "The Expressive Function of Punishment," in: idem, *Doing and Deserving*, Princeton: Princeton University Press, 1970
FEINBERG JOEL, "The Nature and Value of Rights," in: idem, *Rights, Justice, and the Bounds of Liberty. Essays in Social Philosophy*, Princeton, NJ: Princeton University Press, 1980
FEINBERG JOEL, "Duties, Rights and Claims," *American Philosophical Quarterly* 1996, no. 3
FERRY JEAN-MARC, *Les Puissances de l'expérience*, Paris: Editions du Cerf, 1991
FICHTE JOHANN GOTTLIEB, *Grundlage des Naturrechts nach Prinzipien der Wissenschaftslehre*, Hamburg: Felix Meiner Verlag, 1960
FICHTE JOHANN GOTTLIEB, "Einige Vorlesungen über die Bestimmung des Gelehrten," in: *Johann Gottlieb Fichte – Gesamtausgabe der Bayerischen Akademie der Wissenschaft*, ed. by Reinhard Lauth, Hans Jacob, Stuttgart – Bad Cannstatt: Frommann, 1964
FICHTE JOHANN GOTTLIEB, "Die Staatslehre, oder über das Verhältnis des Urstaates zum Vernunftreiche," in: *Fichtes Werke*, Bd. IV: *Zur Rechts- und Sittenlehre II*, Berlin: Walter de Gruyer & Co., 1971
FICHTE JOHANN GOTTLIEB, *Das System der Sittenlehre nach den Prinzipien der Wissenschaftslehre*, Hamburg: Felix Meiner Verlag, 1995

FINNIS JOHN, "The Restoration of Retribution," *Analysis* 1972, vol. 32
FINNIS JOHN, *Natural Law and Natural Rights*, Oxford: Clarendon Press, 1992
FINNIS JOHN, "The Priority of Persons," in: *Oxford Essays in Jurisprudence: Fourth Series*, ed. by Jeremy Horder, Oxford: Oxford University Press, 2001
FLECHTHEIM OSSIP K., *Hegels Strafrechtstheorie*, Berlin: Duncker und Humblot Verlag, 1975
FOBLETS MARIE-CLAIRE, "Cultural Delicts: the Repercussion of Cultural Conflicts on Delinquent Behaviour, Reflections on the Contribution of Legal Anthropology to a Contemporary Debate," *European Journal of Crime, Criminal Law and Criminal Justice* 1998, vol. 6, no. 3, pp. 187–207
FOUCAULT MICHEL, *Discipline and Punishment: The Birth of the Prison*, New York: Vintage, 1977
FRASER NANCY, HONNETH AXEL, *Umverteilung oder Anerkennung? Eine politisch-philosophische Kontroverse*, Frankfurt am Main: Suhrkamp Verlag, 2003
FREEMAN MICHAEL, *Human Rights. An Interdisciplinary Approach*, Cambridge: Polity Press, 2004
FREUD SIGMUND, *Civilization and Its Discontents*, New York: W.W. Norton & Company, 1989
FUKUYAMA FRANCIS, *Our Posthuman Future: Consequences of the Biotechnology Revolution*, New York: Picador, 2003
GADAMER HANS-GEORG, *Wahrheit und Methode, Grundzüge einer philosophischen. Hermeneutik*, Tübingen: J.C.B. Mohr (Paul Siebeck), 1960
GALSTON WILLIAM A., *Liberal Pluralism: The Implications of Value Pluralism for Political Theory and Practice*, Cambridge: Cambridge University Press, 2002
GARDOCKI LECH, *Zarys prawa karnego międzynarodowego* [An Outline of International Penal Law], Warszawa: PWN, 1985
GARDOCKI LECH, *Zagadnienia teorii kryminalizacji* [The Issues of Criminalisation Theory], Warszawa: Wydawnictwo Prawnicze, 1990
GARLAND DAVID, *Punishment and Modern Society. A Study In Social Theory*, Oxford: Oxford University Press, 1990
GARLAND DAVID, *The Culture of Control. Crime and Social Order in Contemporary Society*, Chicago: The University of Chicago Press, 2001
GLENNY MISHA, *McMafia: Crime without Frontiers*, London: Bodley Head, 2008
GOULD CAROL C., *Globalizing Democracy and Human Rights*, Cambridge: Cambridge University Press, 2004
GRASNICK WALTER, *Über Schuld, Strafe und Sprache. Systematische Studien zu den Grundlagen der Punktstrafen- und Spielraumtheorie*, Tübingen: Paul Siebeck, 1987
GRAY JOHN, *Two Faces of Liberalism*, Cambridge: Polity Press, 2000
GRILL PETER, "Alexys Version einer transzendental-pragmatischen Begründung der Diskursregeln im Unterschied zu Habermas," *Archiv für Rechts- und Sozialphilosophie* 1997, vol. 83
GROTEFELD STEFAN, "Wie wird Moral ins Recht gesetzt?," *ARSP* 2003, vol. 89, no. 3, pp. 299–317

GÜNTHER KLAUS, "Möglichkeiten einer diskursethischen Begründung des Strafrechts," in: *Recht und Moral. Beiträge zu einer Standortbestimmung*, ed. by Heike Jung, Heinz Müller-Dietz, Ulfrid Neumann, Baden-Baden: Nomos Verlag, 1991

GÜNTHER KLAUS, "Kampf gegen das Böse? Zehn Thesen wider die ethische Aufrüstung der Kriminalpolitik," *Kritische Justiz* 1994, no. 27

GÜNTHER KLAUS, "Communicative Freedom, Communicative Power, and Jurisgenesis," *Cardozo Law Review* 1996, vol. 17

GÜNTHER KLAUS, "Dritter Vortrag. Jenseits von idealistischer und rollenfunktionaler Strafbegründung, " in: *Rechtsphilosophische Kontroversen der Gegenwart*, ed. by Peter Siller, & Bertram Keller, Baden-Baden: Nomos Verlag, 1999

GÜNTHER KLAUS, *Schuld und kommunikative Freiheit. Studien zur personalen Zurechnung strafbaren Unrechts im demokratischen Rechtsstaat*, Frankfurt am Main: Vittorio Klostermann, 2005

GUTMANN AMY, "Introduction," in: *Multiculturalism: Examining the Politics of Recognition*, ed. by A. Gutmann, Princeton, NJ: Princeton University Press, 1994

GUTMANN AMY, *Identity in Democracy*, Princeton: Princeton University Press, 2004

HABERMAS JÜRGEN, *The Theory of Communicative Action*, vol. 1: *Reason and the Rationalization of Society*, Boston: Beacon Press, 1984

HABERMAS JÜRGEN, "Über Moralität und Sittlichkeit – Was macht eine Lebensform 'rational'?" in: *Rationalität. Philosophische Beiträge*, ed. by Herbert Schnädelbach, Frankfurt am Main: Suhrkamp Verlag, 1984

HABERMAS JÜRGEN, *Vorstudien und Ergänzungen zur Theorie des kommunikativen Handelns*, Frankfurt am Main: Suhrkamp Verlag, 1984

HABERMAS JÜRGEN, "Moralität und Sittlichkeit. Treffen Hegels Einwände gegen Kant auch auf die Diskursethik zu?" in: *Moralität und Sittlichkeit. Das Problem Hegels und die Diskursethik*, ed. by Wolfgang Kuhlmann, Frankfurt am Main: Suhrkamp Verlag, 1986

HABERMAS JÜRGEN, *The Theory of Communicative Action*, vol. 2: *Lifeworld and System: A Critique of Functionalist Reason*, Boston: Beacon Press, 1987

HABERMAS JÜRGEN, "Towards a Communication-Concept of Rational Collective Will-Formation. A Thought-Experiment," *Ratio Juris* 1989, vol. 2, no. 2

HABERMAS JÜRGEN, "Justice and Solidarity: On the Discussion Concerning Stage 6," in: *The Moral Domain: Essays in the Ongoing Discussion between Philosophy and the Social Sciences*, ed. by Thomas E. Wren, Cambridge: The MIT Press, 1990, pp. 224–251

HABERMAS JÜRGEN, "Yet Again: German Identity – A Unified Nation of Angry DM – Burghers," in: *When the Wall Came Down: Reactions to German Unification*, ed. by Howard James and Marla Stone, London: Routledge, 1992, pp. 86–102

HABERMAS JÜRGEN, "Human Rights and Popular Sovereignty: The Liberal and Republican Versions," *Ratio Juris* 1994, vol. 7, no. 1

HABERMAS JÜRGEN, *Vom sinnlichen Eindruck zum symbolischen Ausdruck*, Frankfurt am Main: Suhrkamp Verlag, 1997

HABERMAS JÜRGEN, *Between Facts and Norms. Contributions to a Discourse Theory of Law and Democracy*, Cambridge, Mass.: The MIT Press, 1998

HABERMAS JÜRGEN, "Jürgen Habermas und Gerhard Schröder über die *Einbeziehung des Anderen*. Reihe; Kultur in der Diskussion. Band 5," in: *Philosophie und Politik III*, ed. by Julian Nida-Rümelin, Wolfgang Thierse, Essen: Klartext Verlag, 1998

HABERMAS JÜRGEN, *Die Einbeziehung des Anderen. Studien zur politischen Theorie*, Frankfurt am Main: Suhrkamp Verlag, 1999

HABERMAS JÜRGEN, "Zur Legitimation durch Menschenrechte," in: *Das Recht der Republik*, ed. by Hauke Brunkhorst, Peter Niesen, Frankfurt am Main: Suhrkamp Verlag, 1999, pp. 386–403

HABERMAS JÜRGEN, "Richtigkeit versus Wahrheit. Zum Sinn der Sollgeltung moralischer Urteile und Normen," in: idem, *Wahrheit und Rechtfertigung. Philosophische Aufsätze*, Frankfurt am Main: Suhrkamp Verlag, 2004

HART HERBERT L.A., "Positivism and the Separation of Law and Morals," *Harvard Law Review* 1958, vol. 71, pp. 593–629

HART HERBERT L.A., *Law, Liberty and Morality*, London: Oxford University Press, 1964

HART HERBERT L.A., *Punishment and Responsibility. Essays in the Philosophy of Law*, Oxford: Clarendon Press, 1968

HART HERBERT L.A., "Social Solidarity and the Enforcement of Morality," in: idem, *Essays in Jurisprudence and Philosophy of Law*, Oxford: Oxford University Press, 1968

HART HERBERT L.A., "Are There Any Natural Rights?" in: *Theories of Rights*, ed. by Jeremy Waldron, Oxford: Oxford University Press, 1984

HASSEMER WINFRIED, *Einführung in die Grundlagen des Strafrechts*, München: C.H. Beck, 1981

HASSEMER WINFRIED, "Vielfalt und Wandel eines interkulturellen Strafrechts," in: Otfried Höffe, *Gibt es ein interkulturelles Strafrecht? Ein philosophischer Versuch*, Frankfurt am Main: Suhrkamp Verlag, 1999

HASSEMER WINFRIED, *Strafen im Rechtsstaat*, Baden-Baden: Nomos Verlag, 2000

HEGEL GEORG W.F., *Encyclopaedia of the Philosophical Sciences* (1830), translated by William Wallace

HEGEL GEORG W.F., *Phenomenology of Mind*, translated by J.B. Baillie (1910)

HEGEL GEORG W.F., *Philosophy of Right*, Kitchener: Batoche Books, 2001

HELD DAVID, "Die Rückkehr der Politik," in: *Was wird aus der Demokratie?*, ed. by Thomas Assheuer, Werner A. Perger, Opladen: Westdeutscher Verlag, 2000

HERSKOVITS MELVILLE J., *Man and his Works. The Science of Cultural Anthropology*, New York: Alfred A. Knopf, 1948

HIRSCH ANDREW VON, *Doing Justice*, New York: Hill & Wang, 1976

HIRSCH ANDREW VON, JAREBORG NILS, "Gauging Criminal Harm: A Living Standard Analysis," *Oxford Journal of Legal Studies* 1991, vol. 11, no. 1, pp. 1–38

HIRSCH ANDREW VON, "Proportionality in the Philosophy of Punishment: From 'Why Punish?' to 'How Much?'," in: *Crime and Justice: A Review of Research*, ed. by M. Tonry, Chicago: The University of Chicago Press, 1992, pp. 55–98

HIRSCH ANDREW VON, *Censure and Sanctions*, Oxford: Oxford University Press, 1993

HIRSCH ANDREW VON, "Tadel und Prävention: Die Übelzufügung als Element der Strafe," in: *Positive Generalprävention. Kritische Analysen im deutsch-englischen*

Dialog, ed. by Bernd Schünemann, A. von Hirsch, Nils Jareborg, Heidelberg: C.F. Müller Verlag, 1998

HIRSCH ANDREW VON, "Punishment, Penance and the State," in: *Punishment and Political Theory*, ed. by Matt Matravers, Oxford: Hart Publishing, 1999

HIRSCH ANDREW VON, *Dlaczego powinny istnieć sankcje karne?* [Why Should Criminal Sanctions Exist?], transl. by Adam Litwiniak, Warszawa: Ius et Lex, 2002

HIRSCH ANDREW VON, "Begründung und Bestimmung tatproportionaler Strafe," in: *Tatproportionalität. Normative und empirische Aspekte einer tatproportionalen Strafzumessung*, ed. by Wolfgang Frisch, A. von Hirsch, Hans-Jörg Albrecht, Heidelberg: C.F. Müller Verlag, 2003

HOERSTER NORBERT, *Abtreibung im säkularen Staat*, Frankfurt am Main: Suhrkamp Verlag, 1995

HÖFFE OTFRIED, *Ethik und Politik. Grundmodelle und -probleme der praktischen Philosophie*, Frankfurt am Main: Suhrkamp Verlag, 1992

HÖFFE OTFRIED, *Kategorische Rechtsprinzipien. Ein Kontrapunkt der Moderne*, Frankfurt am Main: Suhrkamp Verlag, 1995

HÖFFE OTFRIED, *Vernunft und Recht. Bausteine zu einem interkulturellen Rechtsdiskurs*, Frankfurt am Main: Suhrkamp Verlag, 1996

HÖFFE OTFRIED, *Vernunft und Diskurs. Bausteine zu einem interkulturellen Rechtsdiskurs*, Frankfurt am Main: Suhrkamp Verlag, 1998

HÖFFE OTFRIED, *Gibt es ein interkulturelles Strafrecht? Ein philosophischer Versuch*, Frankfurt am Main: Suhrkamp Verlag, 1999

HÖFFE OTFRIED, "Proto-Strafrecht: Programm und Anfragen eines Philosophen," in: *Die deutsche Strafrechtswissenschaft vor der Jahrtausendwende*, ed. by Albin Eser, Winfried Hassemer, Björn Burkhardt, München: C.H. Beck, 2000

HOLLINGER DAVID A., *Postethnic America*, New York: Basic Books, 2000

HONNETH AXEL, "Moralischer Entwicklung und sozialer Kampf. Sozialphilosophische Lehren aus dem Frühwerk Hegels," in: *Zwischenbetrachtungen. Im Prozeß der Aufklärung*, ed. by A. Honneth, Thomas McCarthy, Claus Offe, Frankfurt am Main: Suhrkamp Verlag, 1989

HONNETH AXEL, *Kampf um Anerkennung. Zur moralischen Grammatik sozialer Kämpfe*, Frankfurt am Main: Suhrkamp Verlag, 1994

HONNETH AXEL, *Das Andere der Gerechtigkeit. Aufsätze zur praktischen Philosophie*, Frankfurt am Main: Suhrkamp Verlag, 2000

HONNETH AXEL, *Leiden an Unbestimmtheit. Eine Reaktualisierung der Hegelschen Rechtsphilosophie*, Stuttgart: Reclam, 2001

HONNETH AXEL, "Diskursethik und implizites Gerechtigkeitskonzept. Eine Diskussionsbemerkung," in: *Moralität und Sittlichkeit. Das Problem Hegels und die Diskursethik*, ed. by Wolfgang Kuhlmann, Frankfurt am Main: Suhrkamp Verlag, 1986, pp. 268–274

HÖRNLE TATJANA, *Tatproportionale Strafzumessung*, Berlin: Duncker und Humblot Verlag, 1999

HÖRNLE TATJANA, HIRSCH ANDREW VON, "Positive Generalprävention und Tadel," in: *Positive Generalprävention. Kritische Analysen im deutsch-englischen Dialog*, ed. by Bernd Schünemann, A. von Hirsch, Nils Jareborg, Heidelberg: C.F. Müller, 1998

HUNTINGTON SAMUEL P., *Clash of Civilizations and the Remaking of World Order*, New York: Simon and Schuster, 1996

IHERING RUDOLF VON, *Der Zweck im Recht*, Leipzig 1905

INGARDEN ROMAN, *Książeczka o człowieku* [A Book on Human Being], Kraków: Znak, 2003

INGLEHART RONALD F., "Culture and Democracy," in: *Culture Matters. How Values Shape Human Progress*, ed. by Lawrence E. Harrison, Samuel P. Huntington, New York: Basic Books, 2000

ISIN ENGIN F., "Metropolis Unbound: Legislators and Interpreters of Urban Form," in: *City Lives and City Forms: Critical Urban Research and Canadian Urbanism*, ed. by John Caufield, Linda Peake, Toronto: University of Toronto Press, 1996

IVISON DUNCAN, "Punishment in Intercultural Context: Whose Norms? Which Values?" in: *Punishment and Legal Theory*, ed. by Matt Matravers, Oxford: Hart Publishing, 1999

JAKOBS GÜNTHER, *Norm, Person, Gesellschaft. Vorüberlegungen zu einer Rechtsphilosophie*, Berlin: Duncker und Humblot, 1997

JAKOBS GÜNTHER, "Zur gegenwärtigen Straftheorie," in: *Strafe muß sein! Muß Strafe sein?*, ed. by Klaus Kodalle, Würzburg: Königshausen u. Neumann, 1998

JAKOBS GÜNTHER, "Erster Vortrag. Strafbegründung und positive Generalprävention," in: *Rechtsphilosophische Kontroversen der Gegenwart*, ed. by Bertram Keller, Peter Siller Baden-Baden: Nomos Verlag, 1999

JAKOBS GÜNTHER, "Zum Begriff des Delikts gegen die Person," in: *Bochumer Beiträge zu aktuellen Strafrechtsthemen. Vorträge anlässlich des Symposiums zum 70. Geburtstag von Gerd Geilen*, ed. by Klaus Bernsmann, Klaus Ulsenheimer, Köln: Carl Heymanns Verlag, 2003

JASPERS KARL, *Die philosophische Glaube angesichts der Offenbarung*, München: R. Piper, 1984

JASPERS KARL, *Von der Wahrheit*, München: Piper, 1991

JUCHACZ PIOTR W., *Demokracja – deliberacja – partycypacja. Szkice z teorii demokracji ateńskiej i współczesnej* [Democracy – Deliberation – Participation. Essays on the Theory of Athenian and Contemporary Democracy], Poznań: Wydawnictwo Naukowe Instytutu Filozofii UAM, 2006

JUNG HEIKE, *Was ist Strafe? Ein Essay*, Baden-Baden: Nomos Verlag, 2002

KALDOR MARY, *Global Civil Society: An Answer to War*, London: Sage, 2004

KANIOWSKI ANDRZEJ M., *Supererogacja. Zagubiony wymiar etyki* [Supererogation. Lost Dimension of Ethics], Warszawa: Oficyna Naukowa, 1999

KANT IMMANUEL, *The Critique of Practical Reason*, 1788, translated by Thomas Kingsmill Abbott

KANT IMMANUEL, *Grundlegung zur Metaphysik der Sitten*, Leipzig: Ph. Reclain, 1797

KANT IMMANUEL, *The Philosophy of Law: An Exposition of the Fundamental Principles of Jurisprudence as the Science of Right*, translated by William Hastie, Edinburgh: Clark, 1887

KANT IMMANUEL, *Die Metaphysik der Sitten*, Berlin: Akademie-Ausgabe der Königliche-Preussischen Akademie der Wissenschaften, 1902/1910

KANT IMMANUEL, *The Critique of Pure Reason*, Cambridge: Cambridge University Press, 1999

KANT IMMANUEL, *The Metaphysics of Morals*, Cambridge: Cambridge University Press, 1996

KAUFMANN ARTHUR, "Gesetz und Recht," in: *Rechtsphilosophie im Wandel*, ed. by A. Kaufmann, Frankfurt am Main: Vittorio Klostermann, 1972

KAUFMANN ARTHUR, "Strafrechtspraxis und sittliche Normen," *Juristiche Schulung* 1978, no. 6

KAUFMANN ARTHUR, *Strafrecht zwischen Gestern und Morgen*, Köln – Berlin – Bonn – München: Carl Heymanns Verlag, 1983

KAUFMANN ARTHUR, *Über Gerechtigkeit*, Köln: Carl Heymanns Verlag, 1993

KELSEN HANS, *Reine Rechtslehre*, Wien: Franz Deuticke Verlag, 1960

KELSEN HANS, *Was ist Gerechtigkeit?*, Wien: Franz Deuticke Verlag, 1975

KESSLER CLIVE, "Globalization: Another False Universalism?," *Third World Quarterly* 2000, no. 21, pp. 931–942

KLESCZEWSKI DIETHELM, *Die Rolle der Strafe in Hegels Theorie der bürgerlichen Gesellschaft. Eine systematische Analyse des Verbrechens- und des Strafbegriffs in Hegels Grundlinien der Philosophie des Rechts*, Berlin: Duncker und Humblot Verlag, 1991

KMITA JERZY, *Wymykanie się uniwersaliom* [Escaping Universalities], Warszawa: Oficyna Naukowa, 2000

KOCHANOWSKI JANUSZ, *Subiektywne granice sprawstwa i odpowiedzialności karnej* [Subjective Borders of Perpetration and Criminal Responsibility], Warszawa: Wydawnictwo Prawnicze, 1985

KÖHLER MICHAEL, *Der Begriff der Strafe*, Heidelberg: Decker & Müller, 1986

KÖHLER MICHAEL, "Zum Begriff des Völkerstrafrechts," *Jahrbuch für Recht und Ethik* 2003, Bd. 11

KOŁAKOWSKI LESZEK, "Szukanie barbarzyńcy. Złudzenia uniwersalizmu kulturowego" [Looking for a Barbarian. Illusions of Cultural Universalism], in: idem, *Czy diabeł może być zbawiony i 27 innych kazań* [Can the Devil be Saved and 27 other Sermons], London: Aneks, 1984

KOŁAKOWSKI LESZEK, *Mini-wykłady o maxi-sprawach* [Mini-Lectures on Maxi-Issues], Kraków: Znak, 2004

KRÄMER GUDRUN, "Islam, Menschenrechte und Demokratie: Anmerkungen zu einem schwierigen Verhältnis," in: *Menschenrechte – Globale Dimensionen eines universellen Anspruchs*, ed. by Nicole Janz, Thomas Risse, Baden-Baden: Nomos Verlag, 2007

KRÄMER HANS, *Integrative Ethik*, Frankfurt am Main: Suhrkamp Verlag, 1995

KRÓLIKOWSKI MICHAŁ, *Sprawiedliwość karania w społeczeństwach liberalnych* [Just Punishment in Liberal Democracies], Warszawa: C.H. Beck, 2005

KRÓLIKOWSKI MICHAŁ, Wiliński Paweł, Izydorczyk Jacek, *Podstawy prawa karnego międzynarodowego* [The Basis of International Penal Law], Warszawa: Wolters Kluwers, 2008

KRYGIER MARTIN, "Legal Traditions and Their Virtue," in: *Prawo w zmieniającym się społeczeństwie* [Law in Changing Society], ed. by Grażyna Skąpska et al., Kraków: Uniwersytet Jagielloński – Wydawnictwo Adam Marszałek, 1992

KYMLICKA WILL, *Multicultural Citizenship: a Liberal Theory of Minority Rights*, Oxford: Oxford University Press, 1995

KYMLICKA WILL, *Finding our Way. Rethinking Ethnocultural Relations in Canada*, Oxford: Oxford University Press, 1998

LACEY NICOLA, *State Punishment, Political Principles and Community Values*, London: Routledge, 1988

LAMPE ERNST-JOACHIM, "Recht und Moral staatlichen Strafens," in: *Recht und Moral. Beiträge zu einer Standortbestimmung*, ed. by Heike Jung, Heinz Müller-Dietz, Ulfrid Neumann, Baden-Baden: Nomos Verlag, 1991

LAMPE ERNST-JOACHIM, *Strafphilosophie. Studien zur Strafgerechtigkeit*, Köln – Berlin – Bonn – München: Carl Heymanns, 1999

LARMORE CHARLES, *Patterns of Moral Complexity*, Cambridge: Cambridge University Press, 1986

LARMORE CHARLES, "Die Wurzeln radikaler Demokratie," *Deutsche Zeitschrift für Philosophie* 1993, no. 41

LAZARI-PAWŁOWSKA IJA, *Etyka. Pisma wybrane* [Ethics. Selected Works], Wrocław – Warszawa – Kraków: Ossolineum, 1992

LESZCZYŃSKI LESZEK, "Importance and Topicality of the Problems of Human Rights," in: *Protection of Human Rights in Poland and European Communities*, ed. L. Leszczyński, Lublin: Wydawnictwo UMCS, 1995

LESZCZYŃSKI LESZEK, "Prawo japońskie" [Japan Law], in: *Główne kultury prawne współczesnego świata* [Main Legal Cultures of Contemporary World], ed. by Henryk Rot, Warszawa: Wydawnictwo Naukowe PWN, 1995

LEVY JACOB T., *The Multiculturalism of Fear*, Oxford: Oxford University Press, 2000

LUHMANN NIKLAS, "Soziologie der Moral," in: *Theorietechnik und Moral*, ed. by N. Luhmann, Stephan H. Pfürtner, Frankfurt am Main: Suhrkamp Verlag, 1978

LUHMANN NIKLAS, "Ethik als Reflexionstheorie der Moral," in: idem, *Gesellschaftsstruktur und Semantik. Studien zur Wissenssoziologie der modernen Gesellschaft*, Frankfurt am Main: Suhrkamp Verlag, 1981

LYONS DAVID, *Ethics and The Rule of Law*, Cambridge: Cambridge University Press, 1984

MACCORMICK NEIL, WEINBERGER OTA, *An Institutional Theory of Law. New Approaches to Legal Positivism*, Dordrecht – Boston – Lancaster – Tokyo: Kluwer, 1986

MACCORMICK NEIL, *Questioning Sovereignty: Law, State, and Practical Reason*, Oxford: Oxford University Press, 2001

MACINTYRE ALASDAIR, *After Virtue: A Study in Moral Theory*, Notre Dame, Indiana: University of Notre Dame Press, 2007

MAJEWSKI JAROSŁAW, KARDAS PIOTR, "O dwóch znaczeniach winy w prawie karnym" [On Two Meanings of Guilt in Penal Law], *Państwo i Prawo* 1993, no. 10
MANSKE GISELA, *Verbrechen gegen die Menschlichkeit als Verbrechen an der Menschheit*, Berlin: Duncker und Humblot, 2003
MCCARTHY THOMAS, "Dialogical Freedom and Democratic Deliberation," in: *Multiculturalism and Law: a Critical Debate*, ed. by Omid A. Payrow Shabani, Cardiff: University of Wales Press, 2007
MCNEIL DONALD G. JR., "Politicians pander to fear of crime," *New York Times* 2002, 5–6 May
MEAD GEORGE HERBERT, *Mind, Self, and Society*, Chicago – London: The University of Chicago Press, 1967
MERLE JEAN-CHRISTOPHE, "Was ist Hegels Straftheorie?," *Jahrbuch für Recht und Ethik* 2003, Bd. 11, pp. 148–152
MERON THEODOR, "International Criminalization of Internal Atrocities," *American Journal of International Law* 1995, vol. 89, no. 3, pp. 559–577
MERRYMAN JOHN HENRY, *The Civil Law Tradition*, Stanford: Stanford University Press, 1985
MILL JOHN STUART, *On Liberty*, Harvard Classics 1909, vol. 25
MORAWSKI LECH, *Główne problemy współczesnej filozofii prawa. Prawo w toku przemian* [Main Problems of Modern Philosophy of Law. Law in the Course of Transformations], Warszawa: LexisNexis, 2003
MORRIS HERBERT, "Persons and Punishment," *The Monist* 1968, vol. 52, pp. 475–501
MORSELLI ELIO, "Vergeltung. Eine tiefenpsychologische Kategorie der Strafe?", *Archiv für Rechts- und Sozialphilosophie* 2001, vol. 87
MURPHY JEFFRIE G., *Retribution, Justice and Therapy: Essays in the Philosophy of Law*, Dordrecht: Reidel, 1979
NEUMANN ULFRID, *Zurechnung und Vorverschulden. Vorstudien zu einem dialogischen Modell strafrechtlicher Zurechnung*, Berlin: Duncker und Humblot, 1985
NEUMANN ULFRID, "Vom normativen zum funktionalen Strafverständnis," in: *Perspektiven der Strafrechtsentwicklung*, ed. by Heike Jung, Heinz Müller-Dietz, U. Neumann, Baden-Baden: Nomos Verlag, 1996
PAPAGEORGIOU KONSTANTINOS, *Schaden und Strafe: auf dem Weg zu einer Theorie der strafrechtlichen Moralität*, Baden-Baden: Nomos Verlag, 1994
PAPAGEORGIOU KONSTANTINOS, "Verantwortung, Gerechtigkeit, Sicherheit, Freiheit. Ein Plädoyer für die normative Autonomie und wider die ideale Theorie des Strafrechts," in: *Verantwortung in Recht und Moral*, ed. by Ulfrid Neumann and Lorenz Schulz, Stuttgart: Steiner Verlag, 2000
PAWLIK MICHAEL, *Person, Subjekt, Bürger. Zur Legitimation von Strafe*, Berlin: Duncker und Humblot Verlag, 2004
PICKER EDUARD, *Menschenwürde und Menschenleben. Das Auseinanderdriften zweier fundamentaler Werte als Ausdruck der wachsenden Relativierung des Menschen*, Stuttgart: Klett-Gotta, 2002
PIECHOWIAK MAREK, *Filozofia praw człowieka. Prawa człowieka w świetle ich międzynarodowej ochrony* [Philosophy of Human Rights. Human Rights in the Light of their International Protection], Lublin: Towarzystwo Naukowe KUL, 1999

PŁACHTA MICHAŁ, "Statut Międzynarodowego Trybunału Karnego: Podstawowe zasady kompetencyjne, organizacyjne i procesowe" [The Statute of International Criminal Court: Basic Competence, Organizational and Procedural Principles], *Państwo i Prawo* 1998, no. 12

PLESSNER HELMUTH, "Die Grenzen der Gemeinschaft," in: idem, *Gesammelte Schriften*, Bd. V, Frankfurt am Main: Suhrkamp Verlag, 1981

POGGE THOMAS, *World Poverty and Human Rights. Cosmopolitan Responsibilities and Reforms*, Cambridge: Polity Press, 2005

PRIMORATZ IGOR, "Banquos Geist. Hegels Theorie der Strafe," *Hegel-Studien* 1986, Beiheft 29

PUTNAM ROBERT, *Making Democracy Work: Civic Traditions in Modern Italy*, Princeton: Princeton University Press, 1993

RADBRUCH GUSTAW, *Gesamtausgabe*, vol. VII, ed. by Arthur Kaufmann, Heidelberg: C.F. Müller, 1995

RADBRUCH GUSTAW, "Ustawowe bezprawie i ponadustawowe prawo" [Statutory Illegality and Supra-statutory Law], in: Maria Szyszkowska, *Zarys filozofii prawa* [An Outline of Philosophy of Law], Białystok: Temida 2, 2000

RAMADAN TARIQ, "Przestańmy się bać terrorystów" [Let Us Stop Being Afraid of Terrorists], *Europa. Tygodnik Idei* 2007, no. 2, January 13

RAWLS JOHN, *Political Liberalism*, New York: Columbia University Press, 1996

RAWLS JOHN, *The Law of Peoples*, Cambridge: Harvard University Press, 1999

RAWLS JOHN, *A Theory of Justice*, Oxford: Oxford University Press, 1999

RAZ JOSEPH, *The Authority of Law. Essays on Law and Morality*, Oxford: Oxford University Press, 1983

RAZ JOSEPH, *The Morality of Freedom*, Oxford: Clarendon Press, 1986

Das Recht der Republik, ed. by Hauke Brunkhorst, Peter Niesen, Frankfurt am Main: Suhrkamp Verlag, 1999

REDFIELD ROBERT, "The Universally Human and The Culturally Variable," in: *Ethical Relativism*, ed. by John Ladd, Belmont: Wadsworth Publishing Company, 1973

REX SUE, "Proporcjonalność i resocjalizacja: Szanse na pojednanie" [Proportionality and Rehabilitation: The Prospects for Reconciliation], *Ius et Lex* 2006, no. 1 (IV), pp. 85–105

RICOEUR PAUL, *The Course of Recognition*, Cambridge: Harvard University Press, 2005

RIPSTEIN ARTHUR, *Equality, Responsibility, and the Law*, Cambridge: Cambridge University Press, 2001

RISSE THOMAS, "Menschenrechte als Grundlage der Weltvergemeinschaftung? Die Diskrepanz zwischen Normanerkennung und Normeinhaltung," in: *Menschenrechte – Globale Dimensionen eines universellen Anspruchs*, ed. by Nicole Janz, Th. Risse, Baden-Baden: Nomos Verlag, 2007

ROBERTS PERI, *Political Constructivism*, London – New York: Routledge, 2007

ROBERTSON ROLAND, *Globalization: Social Theory and Global Culture*, London: Sage, 1992

ROLINSKI KLAUS, "Vom Strafen und von Strafe in indigenen und ‚modernen' Gesellschaften," in: *Muss Strafe sein? Kolloquium zum 60. Geburtstag von Herrn Professor*

Dr. Dr. h.c. Heike Jung, ed. by Henning Radtke, Egon Müller, Guido Britz, Heinz Koriath, Heinz Müller-Dietz, Baden-Baden: Nomos Verlag, 2004

RORTY RICHARD, *Objectivity, Relativity and Truth. Philosophical Paper*, vol. I, Cambridge: Cambridge University Press, 1991

ROSENFELD MICHEL, "Law as Discourse: Bridging the Gap between Democracy and Rights," *Harvard Law Review* 1995, vol. 108, pp. 1163–1189

ROUSSEAU JEAN JACQUES, *Discourse on the Origin of Inequality*, Indianapolis: Hackett Publishing Company, 1992

ROXIN CLAUS, *Strafrecht. Allgemeiner Teil. Grundlagen. Der Aufbau der Verbrechenslehre*, München: C.H. Beck, 1997

SADURSKI WOJCIECH, *Teoria sprawiedliwości. Podstawowe zagadnienia* [A Theory of Justice. Basic Arguments], Warszawa: PWN, 1988

SADURSKI WOJCIECH, *Moral Pluralism and Legal Neutrality*, Dordrecht – Boston – London: Kluwer, 1990

SCHELER MAX, "Der Formalismus in der Ethik und die materiale Wertethik," in: idem, *Gesammelte Werke*, Bd. 2, Bern: Francke Verlag, 1966

SCHNÄDELBACH HERBERT, "Kultura" [Culture], in: *Filozofia. Podstawowe pytania* [Philosophy. Fundamental Questions], ed. by Ekkehard Martens, H. Schnädelbach, transl. by Krystyna Krzemieniowa, Warszawa: Wiedza Powszechna, 1995

SCHÜTZ ALFRED, LUCKMANN THOMAS, *The Structures of the Life-World*, London – New York – Paris: Gordon and Breach Science Publishers, 1974

SEELMANN KURT, *Anerkennugsverlust und Selbstsubsumtion: Hegels Straftheorien*, München: Karl Alber Verlag, 1995

SEN AMARTYA, *Development as Freedom*, Oxford: Oxford University Press, 2001

SENECA, *Myśli* [Thoughts], Kraków: Wydawnictwo Literackie, 1989

SENGHAAS DIETER, "Internationale Gerechtigkeit. Überlegungen im Lichte des zivilisatorischen Hexagons," in: *Probleme der Internationalen Gerechtigkeit*, ed. by Karl Graf Ballestrem, Bernhard Sutor, München: Otto-von-Freising Vorlesungen der Katholischen Universität Eichstätt, 1993

SHAW MARTIN, *Global Society and International Relations*, Cambridge: Polity Press, 1994

SIEGHART PAUL, *The Lawful Rights of Mankind: An Introduction to the International Legal Code of Human Rights*, Oxford: Oxford University Press, 1985

SIEMEK MAREK J., *Hegel i filozofia* [Hegel and Philosophy], Warszawa: Oficyna Naukowa, 1998

SIEP LUDWIG, *Anerkennung als Prinzip der praktischen Philosophie*, Freiburg – München: Karl Alber, 1979

SINGER BETH J., *Pragmatism, Rights and Democracy*, New York: Fordham University Press, 1999

SINGER PETER, *One Word. The Ethics of Globalization*, New Haven: Yale University Press, 2004

SMOLAK MAREK, *Uzasadnienie sądowe jako argumentacja z moralności politycznej. O legitymizacji władzy sędziowskiej* [Judicial Justification as Argumentation from Political Morality. On Legitimization of Judicial Authority], Kraków: Zakamycze, 2003

STRAWSON PETER F., "Freedom and Resentment," in: idem, *Freedom and Resentment and Other Essays*, London: Methuen & Co., 1974

SYKUNA SEBASTIAN, ZAJADŁO JERZY, "Kontrowersje wokół tzw. 'obrony przez kulturę' - okoliczność wyłączająca winę, okoliczność łagodząca czy nadużycie prawa?" [Controversies around the issue of the so-called "cultural defence" - extenuating or mitigating circumstances or malpractice?], *Przegląd Sądowy* 2007, no. 6, pp. 27–28

SZAHAJ ANDRZEJ, *Jednostka czy wspólnota? Spór liberałów z komunitarystami a „sprawa polska"* [An Individual or Community? Dispute between Communitarians and 'Polish Issue'], Warszawa: Aletheia, 2000

SZAHAJ ANDRZEJ, "Kilka uwag o idei wspólnotowości oraz ideologii wielokulturowości" [Few Comments on the Idea of Community and the Idea of Multiculturalism], in: *Pytania współczesnej filozofii polityki* [Questions of Contemporary Philosophy of Politics], ed. by Dorota Pietrzyk-Reeves, Kraków: Wydawnictwo Uniwersytetu Jagiellońskiego, 2007

ŚRODA MAGDALENA, *Idea godności w kulturze i etyce* [The Idea of Dignity in Culture and Ethics], Warszawa: Multiprint, 1993

TAYLOR CHARLES, *The Ethics of Authenticity*, Cambridge: Harvard University Press, 1991

TAYLOR CHARLES, "The Politics of Recognition," in: *Multiculturalism: Examining the Politics of Recognition*, ed. by Amy Gutmann, Princeton, NJ: Princeton University Press, 1994

TEITEL RUTI G., *Transitional Justice*, Oxford: Oxford University Press, 2000

THOMPSON SIMON, "Is Redistribution a Form of Recognition? Comments on the Fraser - Honneth Debate," *Critical Review of International Social and Political Philosophy* 2005, vol. 8, no. 1, pp. 85–102

TSCHENTSCHER AXEL, *Prozedurale Theorien der Gerechtigkeit. Rationales Entscheiden, Diskursethik und prozedurales Recht*, Baden-Baden: Nomos Verlag, 2000

TUGENDHAT ERNST, *Selbstbewußtsein und Selbstbestimmung*, Frankfurt am Main: Suhrkamp Verlag, 1979

TUGENDHAT ERNST, *Vorlesungen über Ethik*, Frankfurt am Main: Suhrkamp Verlag, 2001

TULLY JAMES, "The Practice of Law-Making and the Problem of Difference: An Introduction to the Field," in: *Multiculturalism and Law: a Critical Debate*, ed. by Omid A. Payrow Shabani, Cardiff: University of Wales Press, 2007

TUORI KAARLO, "Discourse Ethics and the Legitimacy of Law," *Ratio Juris* 1989, vol. 2, no. 2, pp. 125–142

Universal Jurisdiction. National Courts and the Prosecution of Serious Crimes under International Law, ed. by Stephen Macedo, Philadelphia: University of Pennsylvania Press, 2004

"U.S. vs. Ohlendorf," *IV Trials of War Crimes before the Nuremberg Military Tribunals under Control Council Law* [rok?] no. 10, pp. 499–500

VAN BROECK JEROEN, "Cultural Defence and Culturally Motivated Crimes (Cultural Offences)," *European Journal of Crime, Criminal Law and Criminal Justice* 2001, vol. 9, no. 1, pp. 1–32

VEITCH SCOTT, *Moral Conflict and Legal Reasoning*, Oxford: Hart Publishing, 1999

WACQUANT LOÏC, "Deadly Symbiosis: When Ghetto and Prison Meet and Mesh," *Punishment and Society* 2001, no. 3, pp. 119–120

WALZER MICHAEL, *Spheres of Justice. A Defense of Pluralism and Equality*, New York: Basic Books, 1983

WARREN MARK E., "The self in discursive democracy," in: *The Cambridge Companion to Habermas*, ed. by Stephen K. White, Cambridge – New York: Cambridge University Press, 1995

WEINRIB ERNEST J., "Legal Formalism," *The Yale Law Journal* 1988, vol. 97

WESCHE STEFFEN, "Robert Alexys diskurstheoretische Menschenrechtsbegründung," *Rechtstheorie* 1999, no. 30

WHITE JAMES B., "Rhetoric and Law: The Arts of Cultural Communal Life," in: idem, *The Heracles' Bow: Essays on the Rhetoric and Poetics of the Law*, Madison: University of Wisconsin Press, 1985

WOJTYŁA KAROL, *Osoba i czyn oraz inne studia antropologiczne* [A Person and an Act and Other Anthropological Studies], Lublin: Wydawnictwo Towarzystwa Naukowego Katolickiego Uniwersytetu Lubelskiego, 2000

WOLF JEAN-CLAUDE, "Strafe als Wiederherstellung eines Gleichgewichts," *Jahrbuch für Recht und Ethik* 2003, Bd. 11

WOLF SUSAN, "Comment," in: *Multiculturalism. Examining the Politics of Recognition*, ed. by Amy Gutman, Princeton, NJ: Princeton University Press, 1994

WOLFF ERNST AMADEUS, "Die Abgrenzung von Kriminalunrecht zu anderen Unrechtsformen," in: *Strafrechtspolitik. Bedingungen der Strafrechtsreform*, ed. by Winfried Hassemer, Roberto Bergalli, Frankfurt am Main: Peter Lang Verlag, 1987

YOUNG IRIS MARION, *Justice and the Politics of Difference*, Princeton: Princeton University Press, 1990

ZAJADŁO JERZY, "Filozofia prawa a prawo karne. Studium tzw. Mauerschützen" [Philosophy of Law and Penal Law. Mauerschützen Study], *Ius et Lex* 2003, no. 1

ZAJADŁO JERZY, *Odpowiedzialność za mur. Procesy strzelców przy Murze Berlińskim* [Responsibility for the Wall. Murder Trials], Gdańsk: Arche, 2003

ZAJADŁO JERZY, "Uniwersalizm praw człowieka w konstytucji – bezpieczne i niebezpieczne relatywizacje" [Universalism of Human Rights in Constitution – Safe and Dangerous Relativization], *Przegląd Sejmowy* 2007, no. 4, p. 93

ZHANG JUNHUA, "Ist das Menschenrechtsbild in China konfuzianisch oder universal? Fortschritte und Probleme in Theorie und Praxis der Menschenrechte," in: *Menschenrechte – Globale Dimensionen eines universellen Anspruchs*, ed. by Nicole Janz, Thomas Risse, Baden-Baden: Nomos Verlag, 2007

ZIRK-SADOWSKI MAREK, "Pozytywizm prawniczy a filozoficzna opozycja podmiotu i przedmiotu poznania" [Legal Positivism and Philosophical Opposition of the Subject and the Object of Cognition], in: *Studia z filozofii prawa* [Studies in the Philosophy of Law], vol. 1, ed. by Jerzy Stelmach, Kraków: Wydawnictwo Uniwersytetu Jagiellońskiego, 2001

ZOLL ANDRZEJ, "Prawo karne w systemie totalitarnym" [Criminal Law in Totalitarian System], *Znak* 1992, no. 450, pp. 111–122
ZURN CHRISTOPHER F., "Anerkennung, Umverteilung und Demokratie. Dilemmata in Honneths Kritischer Theorie der Gesellschaft," *Deutsche Zeitschrift für Philosophie* 2005, vol. 53, no. 3
ZURN CHRISTOPHER F., "Schwerpunkt: Anerkennung," *Deutsche Zeitschrift für Philosophie* 2005, vol. 53, no. 3

DIA-LOGOS
Schriften zu Philosophie und Sozialwissenschaften
Studies in Philosophy and Social Sciences

Herausgegeben von
Edited by
Tadeusz Buksiński & Piotr W. Juchacz

"*Dia-Logos. Studies in Philosophy and Social Sciences* is a peer-reviewed book series publishing valuable monographs and edited volumes on various aspects of philosophy and social sciences. The series is intended to be an interdisciplinary forum of deliberation according to our firm belief that challenges of the contemporary world require common and multilevel research. The *Dia-Logos* series does not represent a single ideology or school of thought, but it is open to different trends and various styles of reflection, trying to understand better the contemporary world. We invite the submission of manuscripts of monographs and edited volumes from academic philosophers and social scientists."

Bd./Vol. 1 Piotr W. Juchacz / Roman Kozłowski (Hrsg.): Freiheit und Verantwortung. Moral, Recht und Politik. 2002.

Bd./Vol. 2 Norbert Leśniewski / Ewa Nowak-Juchacz (Hrsg.): Die Zeit Heideggers. 2002.

Bd./Vol. 3 Marek Kwiek (ed.): The University, Globalization, Central Europe. 2003.

Bd./Vol. 4 Ewa Czerwińska-Schupp (Hrsg.): Philosophie an der Schwelle des 21. Jahrhunderts. Geschichte der Philosophie, Philosophische Anthropologie, Ethik, Wissenschaftstheorie, Politische Philosophie. 2003.

Bd./Vol. 5 Danuta Sobczyńska / Pawel Zeidler / Ewa Zielonacka-Lis (eds.): Chemistry in the Philosophical Melting Pot. 2004.

Bd./Vol. 6 Marek Kwiek: Intellectuals, Power, and Knowledge. Studies in the Philosophy of Culture and Education. 2004.

Bd./Vol. 7 Marek Kwiek: The University and the State. A Study into Global Transformations. 2006.

Bd./Vol. 8 Andrzej Przylebski (Hrsg.): Das Erbe Gadamers. 2006.

Bd./Vol. 9 Ewa Czerwińska-Schupp (ed.): Values and Norms in the Age of Globalization. 2007.

Bd./Vol. 10 Tadeusz Buksiński (ed.): Democracy in Western and Post-Communist Countries. Twenty Years after the Fall of Communism. 2009.

Bd./Vol. 11 Marek Zirk-Sadowski / Mariusz Golecki / Bartosz Wojciechowski (eds.): Multicentrism as an Emerging Paradigm in Legal Theory. 2009.

Bd./Vol. 12 Bartosz Wojciechowski: Philosophical Approach to the Interculturality of Criminal Law. 2010.

www.peterlang.de